SELECTED READINGS IN

MARRIAGE

AND FAMILY

SELECTED READINGS IN

MARRIAGE AND FAMILY

Lorene H. Stone, Professor of Sociology,
Lamar University, *Book Editor*

David L. Bender, *Publisher*
Bruno Leone, *Executive Editor*
Bonnie Szumski, *Editorial Director*
Stephen E. Schonebaum, *Series Editor*
Editorial Advisory Board
Susan S. Coady, The Ohio State University
Mary Riege Laner, Arizona State University
Katherine McDade, Pacific Lutheran University
Patricia Searles, University of Wisconsin,
Whitewater
Peter J. Stein, William Paterson University

Contemporary Perspectives

GREENHAVEN PRESS, INC., SAN DIEGO, CA

5/99

39495625

Library of Congress Cataloging-in-Publication Data

Selected readings in marriage and family / Lorene H. Stone, book editor.
p.   cm. — (Contemporary perspectives)
Includes bibliographical references (p.   ) and index.
ISBN 1-56510-903-1 (alk. paper). — ISBN 1-56510-902-3 (pbk. : alk. paper)
1. Family. 2. Marriage. 3. Interpersonal relations. I. Stone, Lorene H. II. Series: Contemporary perspectives (San Diego, Calif.)
HQ518.S435   1999
306.8—dc21   98-33930
                                                                              CIP

Copyright ©1999 by Greenhaven Press, Inc.
P.O. Box 289009
San Diego, CA 92198-9009

Printed in the USA

CONTENTS

FOREWORD   10

EDITOR'S PREFACE   11

PART I: CHANGING FAMILIES IN A CHANGING WORLD

CHAPTER 1: EXPLORING TODAY'S FAMILIES

Introduction   15

Reading 1: Relatively Speaking   16
by Jan Borst
An upcoming wedding leads the author to rethink the concept of family.

Reading 2: The Way We Weren't: The Myth and Reality of the "Traditional" Family 18
by Stephanie Coontz
Coontz reviews family forms throughout American history.

Reading 3: What's Ahead for Families   23
by Joseph F. Coates
*Five key societal trends are dramatically altering the future prospects for
families.*

CHAPTER 2: DIVERSITY IN FAMILY LIFE

Introduction   31

Reading 4: Racially and Ethnically Mixed Families   32
by Bruno Oriti, Amy Bibb, and Jayne Mahboubi
*In the past twenty-five years, "mixed" relationships across racial/ethnic lines
have become increasingly prevalent.*

Reading 5: Homeless Policy: The Need to Speak to Families   42
by Elaine A. Anderson and Sally A. Koblinsky
*The authors summarize current research on the characteristics of homeless
families and provide an overview of government homeless policy.*

PART II: ESTABLISHING INTIMATE RELATIONSHIPS

CHAPTER 3: GENDER ROLES

Introduction   54

Reading 6: Parents, Children, and Gender Roles   55
 by Susan D. Witt
 As children move through childhood and into adolescence, the strongest
 influence on their gender role development seems to occur within the family
 setting.

Reading 7: Families and Gender Equity   59
 by Scott Coltrane
 Coltrane explores the barriers to gender equity in the family and in the larger
 society.

CHAPTER 4: LOVE, DATING, AND MATE SELECTION

Introduction   64

Reading 8: The Origin of Romantic Love and Human Family Life   65
 by Helen Fisher
 Fisher looks at the psychological, physiological, and social components of
 love, monogamy, and divorce.

Reading 9: Love Lessons   69
 by Hara Estroff Marano
 Couples can learn how to manage conflict without reciprocating, retaliating,
 or invalidating their partner.

Reading 10: Mate Selection Preferences Among African American College Students   75
 by Louie E. Ross
 Ross looks at how skin color, social status, and other factors affect the
 attitudes and preferences of African American college students in dating and
 future mate selection.

CHAPTER 5: HUMAN SEXUALITY/SEXUAL EXPRESSION

Introduction   85

Reading 11: Teens and Sex   86
 by Jeannie I. Rosoff
 In a culture abundant in sexual stimuli, how can American teens be taught to
 resist the normal biological urges of adolescence?

Reading 12: How Men View Sex, Contraception, and Child Rearing   91
 by William R. Grady et al.
 The authors examine men's perceptions about their roles when couples make
 decisions about sex, contraception, and the rearing of children.

PART III: THE MARRIAGE EXPERIENCE

CHAPTER 6: MARRIAGE AND PARTNERSHIPS

Introduction   102

Reading 13: The Future of Marriage   103
 by Frank F. Furstenberg Jr.
 Women's increased economic independence, modern contraception, and other
 shifts have led Americans to evaluate marriage outside of traditional
 constraints.

Reading 14: The Case for Gay (and Straight) Marriage 108
by Jonathan Rauch
Rauch reviews the arguments for and against gay marriage.

Reading 15: Does Your Marriage Pass the Test? 114
by Florence Isaacs
*A test developed by a marriage therapist gives couples the opportunity to
identify potential trouble spots in their marriage.*

CHAPTER 7: MARRIAGE: COMMUNICATION AND POWER
Introduction 118
Reading 16: Women, Men, and Money 119
by Kim Clark
*Many upper-income women outearn their husbands, which can create some
problems.*

Reading 17: But What Do You Mean? 122
by Deborah Tannen
*Seven common conversation traps can keep men and women apart at work
and at home.*

CHAPTER 8: FAMILIES AND WORK: FACING THE ECONOMIC SQUEEZE
Introduction 127
Reading 18: Mothers in the Labor Force 128
by Shannon Dortch
The percentage of women in the labor force continues to increase.

Reading 19: Is Your Family Wrecking Your Career? 130
by Betsy Morris
*Ambitious two-income couples are discovering that the demands of corporate
America are taking a toll on their family lives.*

Reading 20: Moonlight and Child Care 137
by Shelly Reese
*The availability of nighttime child care is not keeping up with the number of
employees who work nonstandard hours.*

PART IV: PARENTS AND CHILDREN

CHAPTER 9: TO PARENT OR NOT TO PARENT
Introduction 141
Reading 21: Feminism and the Family 142
by Mary Ann Glendon
*The feminism of the 1970s is insufficient in addressing the issues that face
marriage, motherhood, and family life in the 1990s.*

Reading 22: Balancing Act 148
by Marlene Lozada
*Traditional one-income families are no longer the norm, and American
businesses are making changes to accommodate the swelling number of
parents they employ.*

Reading 23: The Mother Market   155
    by Patricia Braus
    The twenty-first century will bring new challenges to organizations that
    market prenatal and maternity services.
Reading 24: New Mothers, Not Married   162
    by George A. Akerlof and Janet L. Yellen
    The authors look at the reasons for the dramatic rise in out-of-wedlock births.

CHAPTER 10: RAISING CHILDREN
Introduction   168
Reading 25: Normal Families: Research on Gay and Lesbian Parenting 169
    by Gary Sanders
    Sanders addresses four common myths that argue against gay and lesbian
    parenting.
Reading 26: The Lost Art of Fatherhood   174
    by Dan Fost
    As the United States faces a crisis of fatherlessness, some groups are
    campaigning for ways to make fathers more involved and responsible.
Reading 27: The Changing Meanings of Spanking   176
    by Phillip W. Davis
    Traditional arguments about spanking have been supplemented by new
    criticisms that reflect cultural concerns about abuse.

CHAPTER 11: OTHER FAMILY RELATIONSHIPS
Introduction   189
Reading 28: Grandparents Raising Grandchildren   190
    by Nancy M. Pinson-Millburn et al.
    Children and youths are being raised by grandparents in greater numbers
    than would be expected by choice or by chance.
Reading 29: Caring for Aging Parents   197
    by Virginia Morris
    Morris discusses five common mistakes not to make in caring for aging
    parents.
Reading 30: The Sibling Syndrome   200
    by Diane Crispell
    American siblings take extraordinary steps to share assistance and emotional
    support and, in the process, boost the economy.

PART V: CHALLENGES CONFRONTING FAMILIES IN THE 21ST CENTURY

CHAPTER 12: FAMILY VIOLENCE AND ABUSE
Introduction   209

Reading 31: Behind Closed Doors   **210**
    by Kristen Golden
    A mother and daughter relate their battle with domestic violence.
Reading 32: A Day in the Life   **217**
    by Bill Hewitt
    Over a twenty-four hour period, the author exposes the grim reality of child
    abuse and the efforts of those who work to protect them.

CHAPTER 13: DIVORCE: THE PROCESS OF UNCOUPLING
Introduction   **225**
Reading 33: Divorcing Reality   **226**
    by Stephanie Coontz
    Coontz argues that new laws that delay divorce could be harmful to children.
Reading 34: Family Law at Century's End   **230**
    by Milton C. Regan Jr.
    Regan demonstrates how our society's complicated human connections are
    reflected in the area of family law.

CHAPTER 14: REMARRIAGE AND STEPFAMILIES
Introduction   **234**
Reading 35: Combining Grown Families   **235**
    by Susan Littwin
    Joining two families can lead to problems involving jealousy, money, and
    discipline, but it can also be an enriching experience.
Reading 36: Parenting Stepchildren and Biological Children   **239**
    by William L. MacDonald and Alfred DeMaris
    The authors study the effect of adding biological children to a stepfamily.

INDEX   **249**

FOREWORD

The purpose of the Contemporary Perspectives series is to provide college students with a convenient collection of readings with various points of view from a variety of sources. The readings are chosen with care for depth and breadth and presented in a low-cost format to introduce students to the subject discipline. Each anthology is organized to reflect the standard course, and each book is indexed.

The information explosion of recent years has made special demands of instructors. It has become difficult to remain informed about one's own specialty, let alone wade through the enormous amounts of material (in journals, magazines, books, and on-line) not directly related to one's research but relevant to students and teaching. Searching for useful readings in all forms of media (including the Internet—a tremendous resource, but often of suspect quality) and preparing a cohesive collection is a time-consuming exercise.

Each Contemporary Perspectives reading is selected to emphasize representative points of view in the discipline and expand on high-interest areas often slighted in texts. The editor of each volume is an expert in the subject area and has taught the course for many years. The advice and guidance of an editorial board ensures the usefulness of these high-quality selections. An instructor's manual with test bank, written by the editors, is available for busy instructors.

Each Contemporary Perspectives editor believes that exposure to diverse opinions effectively leads students to read critically and generates class discussion. To encourage students to become more discerning readers, the editor has prepared helpful pedagogy, including insightful introductions to each chapter's readings, discussion questions, and descriptions of pertinent websites to encourage further exploration.

Thoughtful examination of these readings can help students bridge the gap between theory and application and broaden their understanding of key issues in the discipline. Contemporary Perspectives anthologies also serve as an introduction to the range of material that students can expect to navigate in the course of their school career.

The editors of this series hope that it will serve the needs of instructors by instilling in students a desire for investigation. We value your opinions and experience and welcome your comments.

EDITOR'S PREFACE

As we approach the twenty-first century, marriage and family issues continue to dominate society's attention. Turn on the television, listen to the radio, or open a newspaper or magazine, and you will be exposed to explosive debates over the family. Lack of "family values," the "dysfunctional family," and the "breakdown of the traditional family" are not only blamed for most contemporary social ills, but play a central role in current political, religious, and social agendas.

Over the past several decades, family scholars have pointed out that the American family has been changing. The imperatives to marry, to stay married, to have children, to restrict sexual activity to marriage, and to maintain separate and distinctive roles for males and females all have weakened. Marriage is no longer a prerequisite to childbearing, and as a result, the structure of families is changing.

On one side of the family debate, conservatives keep the public attention on the "problems" of divorce, out-of-wedlock births, homosexuality, teenage pregnancy, and latchkey kids. They characterize many of today's families as troubled and unstable, and they propose a return to "family values," that is, the traditional two-parent family. On the other side, liberals view this proposal as biased and based on inaccurate, nostalgic views of the stereotypical traditional family rather than on what family life was really like in the past. Focusing more on how today's families must cope with the society in which they live, liberals emphasize the adaptive strengths of diverse family forms.

Persons on both sides of this highly charged debate are concerned about the welfare of children and our society, and they all consider themselves to be "pro-family." Thus, the debate is really about preferences for a particular pattern of family and gender arrangements. The intent of this reader is not to take the value stance that family change means decline but rather to recognize the diversity in family relationships and to show how differing options produce different life experiences.

To the student of marriage and the family, an introductory textbook often does not directly link theory and application or reflect the wide range of opinions in the discipline. Some of the selections in *Selected Readings in Marriage and Family* represent extreme positions and views of family-related topics, and they are intended as a thought-provoking basis for class discussion. Virtually all of us grow up in a family setting, and as adults, most of us will form some type of family. Yet we also have more choice today than ever before. We are freer to postpone marriage and childbearing, we have the option to cohabit, and we can raise children as single parents. Thus it is hoped that this reader will help students critically examine their thinking about various family choices.

The readings in this book have been selected to met two criteria. First, they provide specific examples of family-related topics to supplement the general content of survey courses or introductory textbooks on marriage and family. Standard textbooks must survey so much information that in-depth coverage of some topics is not possible. My years of teaching experience have given me a good understanding of issues that are both of interest to students and valuable pedagogically. This collection provides students with important supplemental information on key topics that will help instructors initiate stimulating discussion and debate.

Second, the readings reflect the various opinions that exist in our society concerning marriage and family diversity. Over the past forty years, interest in and concern over the family has intensified on the part of academics, theologians, politicians, family practitioners, and the general public. Families have been placed under a microscope. Consequently, a host of professional journals, books, magazines, television shows, and official reports now cover nearly every imaginable aspect of family living. Selections for this reader have been taken from mass-distribution periodicals like *Newsweek* and *Psychology Today*, specialized professional journals (e.g., *Family Relations* and *Journal of Black Studies*), writings of family therapists and other notable experts in the field, and publications that lean toward the right as well as the left. The readings were selected to provide information relevant to today's marriages and families.

The reader's structure and organization were designed to follow the organization and content of standard introductory marriage and family textbooks. Two to four readings are used in each chapter, and although the readings may be of different lengths, the total words per part are equivalent, allowing instructors to make part assignments with the confidence that each part will require a similar amount of reading time by the student.

Several pedagogical tools have been incorporated to help the student learn. Introductory comments precede each chapter, tie the readings together, and focus the student on essential issues. Chapter conclude with discussion questions and World Wide Web addresses that allow students to gather more information from the Internet.

Teacher's Guide

Peter J. Stein at William Paterson University has prepared a teacher's guide with suggested exercises and a test bank with multiple-choice, true-false, and essay questions. Please contact Greenhaven Press or your Greenhaven Press sales representative for more information.

Acknowledgments

I owe a debt of gratitude to reviewers whose fine suggestions improved the book immeasurably. I am also grateful to Dan Leone and Greenhaven Press for the opportunity to participate in this project. Finally, my thanks to Steve Schonebaum, the managing editor of Greenhaven's college division, for his help and guidance.

Lorene H. Stone
Department of Sociology
Lamar University
Beaumont, TX 77705

CHANGING FAMILIES IN A CHANGING WORLD

CONTENTS

PART I: CHANGING FAMILIES IN A CHANGING WORLD

CHAPTER 1: EXPLORING TODAY'S FAMILIES
    READING 1: RELATIVELY SPEAKING   16
    READING 2: THE WAY WE WEREN'T: THE MYTH AND REALITY
      OF THE "TRADITIONAL" FAMILY   18
    READING 3: WHAT'S AHEAD FOR FAMILIES   23

CHAPTER 2: DIVERSITY IN FAMILY LIFE
    READING 4: RACIALLY AND ETHNICALLY MIXED FAMILIES   32
    READING 5: HOMELESS POLICY: THE NEED TO SPEAK TO FAMILIES   42

CHAPTER 1: EXPLORING TODAY'S FAMILIES

An important and increasingly complex question facing us today is, What is a family? Over the years, the meaning of family—who makes up the family unit, what functions the family fulfills—has changed. A number of recent trends in American family life have contributed to our difficulty in defining family such as: 1) people are postponing marriage and childbearing and are having fewer children; 2) high divorce rates are leading to a growing number of single-parent families; 3) there is an increase in cohabitation and out-of-wedlock births; and 4) the majority of mothers today are employed outside the home. The readings in this chapter explore the present-day meaning of family in our society.

Less than 10 percent of U.S. families fit the stereotypical form of an employed father and a homemaking mother who takes care of the children on a full-time basis; thus the word *family* may be confusing to many people. The first reading, "Relatively Speaking" by Jan Borst, illustrates how the definition of family has broadened as a result of divorce and remarriage and how relationships among people defined as "family" have become more complicated.

In "The Way We Weren't," family historian Stephanie Coontz points out the realities of family life from colonial days through the 1990s. She challenges many popular notions about the so-called traditional family of the past and documents how there have been many forms of families throughout American history. The author emphasizes how families have had to adapt to and cope with their social environment and she challenges the assumption that restoring "family values" and the breadwinner-homemaker dynamic will solve our society's social problems.

Joseph Coates's article, "What's Ahead for Families: Five Major Forces of Change," examines several societal trends that will impact families in the future. He discusses, for example, how families change as a result of economic conditions, how divorce will continue to affect many Americans' lives, how nontraditional family forms will become more common, and how increased longevity will reshape family living. While the family institution continues to change, Coates asserts that most Americans remain committed to families and that valuing families remains an important theme in people's lives, no matter what form the family takes.

RELATIVELY SPEAKING

Jan Borst

As a wedding approaches, Jan Borst, an instructor in family sociology at Emporia State University in Kansas, rethinks the concept of family.

Our daughter will be getting married soon.

My husband and I recently met our future son-in-law, Ed, who seems to be a great guy. He has a good job providing a comfortable income. He's a spiritual man, with many talents, well thought of in the community, and, more important, he's head over heels in love with our daughter—as she is with him.

We especially pray for their happiness because they're not your average twentysomething couple starting their marital journey with all the idealism of youth. They're in their late 30s, each bringing to this union the baggage of failed prior marriages. They wish to recommit—to try again, in Samuel Johnson's words, "the triumph of hope over experience." As all parents do, we want this marriage not only to succeed but to flourish.

Like many other couples starting over, they have children—his daughter, her two girls. Their honeymoon will be brief. Then it's instant family. Mothering and fathering children they've known a short time. Two last names on the mailbox. Two girls in the house, a third there every other weekend. Child-support payments going out and coming in. One child's mother across town, a father a state away. Children confused over loyalties to the parents they live with and those they visit. The couple pulled in opposite directions by the wants and needs of their kids and their own need to form a successful, intimate marital relationship.

Their situation is pretty complex, but, these days, quite common. Some "step" families are more complicated than the word implies. Ours is one such family. I began by saying that our daughter will be getting married. Technically this is not true. My husband and I are in a second marriage ourselves, and the bride is my husband's child.

Fragile Bonds

He was a widowed father of nine and I the divorced mother of four when we met at Parents Without Partners 16 years ago. Of the 13 children between us, only his four oldest were out of the house and on their own. The other nine children ranged in age from 4 to 19. Even though he and I were crazy about each other, we knew that combining our two households was not a good idea. Too many kids reared with different parenting styles. Two religions. Two income levels. Too much age difference (he is nearly a generation older than I). Yet we loved each other, so we became a weekend family of sorts, courting one another while surrounded by kids. Eventually the kids grew up, and six years ago we married. Our long courtship helped solidify the mutual affection all of us now enjoy. We are a family. But still the bonds are fragile.

Questions arise as to who is family. Will our daughter's new family be a family of four, made up of those who live in the house? Or a family of five—the four plus the child who visits on weekends? In their home, who is the real parent? Who sets the rules? When does the mother relinquish some of her parenting role to her husband? When does the stepparent step in; when does he or she back off? How much time should the visiting child spend alone with her father and how much time with her new family?

Then there's the question of what they call one another. If a child calls her stepfather "Dad," does this take something away from her real father? When children speak about their parents, whom are they referring to? When parents say "our children," should they explain the relationship?

In divorce, some words have taken on new meaning in our vernacular. Most states don't call it "divorce," but rather "dissolution of marriage," as if the process were some chemical reaction. A former spouse is an "ex"—it implies a prior position that no longer exists, but also suggests the unknown in math. Do our former in-laws become "ex-laws"? Or "out-laws"?

When "joint," "shared," "residential," "sole" or "split," parents either have, lose or give up "custody" of their offspring—custody being a term applied to criminals. "Visitation" used to mean making a call to someone hospitalized or going to a funeral home; now it means seeing your own children via some prearranged schedule, possibly devised with the assistance of a family mediator, perhaps by court order.

Our language is even more heavily laden with family terms beginning with "step." Ed will be my stepson-in-law, but there's no simple way to state the relationship between his daughter, Amy, and me. She and I will be related only by the slender threads of two remarriages: her father's to my husband's daughter and mine to my husband. Amy becomes my husband's stepgranddaughter, his daughter's stepdaughter, his granddaughters' stepsister or his son-in-law's daughter. But to me, the linguistic link is truly unwieldy: my husband's stepgranddaughter, my stepdaughter's stepdaughter, my stepgrandchildren's stepsister!

Part of the Family

Yet whatever we choose to call this relationship created through two remarriages, Amy will be part of our family. She will likely spend some Christmases at our home. She may join our granddaughters when they come to Kansas for their vacation. We've already begun sending her birthday cards and the same holiday treats and trinkets grandmothers (even stepgrandmothers) send grandchildren throughout the year. We will remember her in our thoughts and prayers as we do the other kids in the family.

All this has not escaped Amy, 11 years old going on 35. At our last meeting she asked me, "What shall I call you? You're like a grandmother, but not really my grandmother. I have two grandmothers already, you know." (What she didn't say was that should her mother remarry, she will have one more.)

"I know," I said with a sigh, "it is pretty complicated." We talked a bit, trying to make sense of this convoluted, many-branched, pruned and grafted family tree. We discussed some of the choices, tried out some of the step-this, step-that options, even suggested a step/step or double-step something or other. Each sounded more ridiculous than the last. Finally we decided it would be "Amy and Jan, Jan and Amy." That would have to do.

READING 2

THE WAY WE WEREN'T: THE MYTH AND REALITY OF THE "TRADITIONAL" FAMILY

Stephanie Coontz

Stephanie Coontz reviews family forms throughout American history and concludes that romanticizing "traditional" families is misguided and not a solution for present problems. Coontz teaches history and family studies at Evergreen State College in Olympia, Washington. Her publications include The Way We Never Were: American Families and the Nostalgia Trap *and* The Way We Really Are.

Families face serious problems today, but proposals to solve them by reviving "traditional" family forms and values miss two points. First, no single traditional family existed to which we could return, and none of the many varieties of families in our past has had any magic formula for protecting its members from the vicissitudes of socioeconomic change, the inequities of class, race, and gender, or the consequences of interpersonal conflict. Violence, child abuse, poverty, and the unequal distribution of resources to women and children have occurred in every period and every type of family.

Reprinted from Stephanie Coontz, "The Way We Weren't: The Myth and Reality of the 'Traditional' Family," *National Forum: The Phi Kappa Phi Journal*, vol. 75, no. 3 (Summer 1995), ©1995 by Stephanie Coontz, by permission of the publishers.

Second, the strengths that we also find in many families of the past were rooted in different social, cultural, and economic circumstances from those that prevail today. Attempts to reproduce any type of family outside of its original socioeconomic context are doomed to fail.

Colonial Families

American families always have been diverse, and the male breadwinner–female homemaker, nuclear ideal that most people associate with "the" traditional family has predominated for only a small portion of our history. In colonial America, several types of families coexisted or competed. Native American kinship systems subordinated the nuclear family to a much larger network of marital alliances and kin obligations, ensuring that no single family was forced to go it alone. Wealthy settler families from Europe, by contrast, formed independent households that pulled in labor from poorer neighbors and relatives, building their extended family solidarities on the backs of truncated families among indentured servants, slaves, and the poor. Even wealthy families, though, often were disrupted by death; a majority of colonial Americans probably spent some time in a stepfamily. Meanwhile, African Americans, denied the legal protection of marriage and parenthood, built extensive kinship networks and obligations through fictive kin ties, ritual co-parenting or godparenting, adoption of orphans, and complex naming patterns designed to preserve family links across space and time.

The dominant family values of colonial days left no room for sentimentalizing childhood. Colonial mothers, for example, spent far less time doing child care than do modern working women, typically delegating this task to servants or older siblings. Among white families, patriarchal authority was so absolute that disobedience by a wife or child was seen as a small form of treason, theoretically punishable by death, and family relations were based on power, not love.

The Nineteenth-Century Family

With the emergence of a wage-labor system and a national market in the first third of the nineteenth century, white middle-class families became less patriarchal and more child-centered. The ideal of the male breadwinner and the nurturing mother now appeared. But the emergence of domesticity for middle-class women and children depended on its absence among the immigrant, working class, and African American women or children who worked as servants, grew the cotton, or toiled in the textile mills to free middle-class wives from the chores that had occupied their time previously.

Even in the minority of nineteenth-century families who could afford domesticity, though, emotional arrangements were quite different from nostalgic images of "traditional" families. Rigid insistence on separate spheres for men and women made male-female relations extremely stilted, so that women commonly turned to other women, not their husbands, for their most intimate relations. The idea that all of one's passionate feelings should go toward a member of the opposite sex was a twentieth-century invention—closely associated with the emergence of a mass consumer society and promulgated by the very film industry that "traditionalists" now blame for undermining such values.

Early Twentieth-Century Families

Throughout the nineteenth century, at least as much divergence and disruption in the experience of family life existed as does today, even though divorce and unwed motherhood were less common. Indeed, couples who marry today have a better chance of celebrating a fortieth wedding anniversary than at any previous time in history. The life cycles of nineteenth-century youth (in job entry, completion of schooling, age at marriage, and establishment of separate residence) were far more diverse than they became in the early twentieth-century. At the turn of the century a higher proportion of people remained single for their entire lives than at any period since. Not until the 1920s did a bare majority of children come to live in a male breadwinner–female homemaker family, and even at the height of this family form in the 1950s, only 60 percent of American children spent their entire childhoods in such a family.

From about 1900 to the 1920s, the growth of mass production and emergence of a public policy aimed at establishing a family wage led to new ideas about family self-sufficiency, especially in the white middle class and a privileged sector of the working class. The resulting families lost their organic connection to intermediary units in society such as local shops, neighborhood work cultures and churches, ethnic associations, and mutual-aid organizations.

As families related more directly to the state, the market, and the mass media, they also developed a new cult of privacy, along with heightened expectations about the family's role in fostering individual fulfillment. New family values stressed the early independence of children and the romantic coupling of husband and wife, repudiating the intense same-sex ties and mother-infant bonding of earlier years as unhealthy. From this family we get the idea that women are sexual, that youth is attractive, and that marriage should be the center of our emotional fulfillment.

Even aside from its lack of relevance to the lives of most immigrants, Mexican Americans, African Americans, rural families, and the urban poor, big contradictions existed between image and reality in the middle-class family ideal of the early twentieth century. This is the period when many Americans first accepted the idea that the family should be sacred from outside intervention; yet the development of the private, self-sufficient family depended on state intervention in the economy, government regulation of parent-child relations, and state-directed destruction of class and community institutions that hindered the development of family privacy. Acceptance of a youth and leisure culture sanctioned early marriage and raised expectations about the quality of married life, but also introduced new tensions between the generations and new conflicts between husband and wife over what were adequate levels of financial and emotional support.

The nineteenth-century middle-class ideal of the family as a refuge from the world of work was surprisingly modest compared with emerging twentieth-century demands that the family provide a whole alternative world of satisfaction and intimacy to that of work and neighborhood. Where a family succeeded in doing so, people might find pleasures in the home never before imagined. But the new ideals also increased the possibilities for failure: America has had the highest divorce rate in the world since the turn of the century.

In the 1920s, these contradictions created a sense of foreboding about "the future of the family" that was every bit as widespread and intense as today's. Social scientists and popular commentators of the time hearkened back to the "good old days," bemoaning the sexual revolution, the fragility of nuclear family ties, the cult of youthful romance, the decline of respect for grandparents, and the threat of the "New Woman." But such criticism was sidetracked by the stock-market crash, the Great Depression of the 1930s, and the advent of World War II.

Domestic violence escalated during the Depression, while murder rates were as high in the 1930s as in the 1990s. Divorce rates fell, but desertion increased and fertility plummeted. The war stimulated a marriage boom, but by the late 1940s one in every three marriages was ending in divorce.

The 1950s Family

At the end of the 1940s, after the hardships of the Depression and war, many Americans revived the nuclear family ideals that had so disturbed commentators during the 1920s. The unprecedented postwar prosperity allowed young families to achieve consumer satisfactions and socioeconomic mobility that would have been inconceivable in earlier days. The 1950s family that resulted from these economic and cultural trends, however, was hardly "traditional." Indeed, it is best seen as a historical aberration. For the first time in 100 years, divorce rates dropped, fertility soared, the gap between men's and women's job and educational prospects widened (making middle-class women more dependent on marriage), and the age of marriage fell—to the point that teenage birth rates were almost double what they are today.

Admirers of these very *nontraditional* 1950s family forms and values point out that household arrangements and gender roles were less diverse in the 1950s than today, and marriages more stable. But this was partly because diversity was ruthlessly suppressed and partly because economic and political support systems for socially-sanctioned families were far more generous than they are today. Real wages rose more in any single year of the 1950s than they did in the entire decade of the 1980s; the average thirty-year-old man could buy a median-priced home on 15 to 18 percent of his income. The government funded public investment, home ownership, and job creation at a rate more than triple that of the past two decades, while 40 percent of young men were eligible for veteran's benefits. Forming and maintaining families was far easier than it is today.

Yet the stability of these 1950s families did not guarantee good outcomes for their members. Even though most births occurred within wedlock, almost a third of American children lived in poverty during the 1950s, a higher figure than today. More than 50 percent of black married-couple families were poor. Women were often refused the right to serve on juries, sign contracts, take out credit cards in their own names, or establish legal residence. Wife-battering arrests were low, but that was because wife-beating was seldom counted as a crime. Most victims of incest, such as Miss America of 1958, kept the secret of their fathers' abuse until the 1970s or 1980s, when the women's movement became powerful enough to offer them the support denied them in the 1950s.

The Post-1950s Family

In the 1960s, the civil rights, antiwar, and women's liberation movements exposed the racial, economic, and sexual injustices that had been papered over by the Ozzie and Harriet images on television. Their activism made older kinds of public and private oppression unacceptable and helped create the incomplete, flawed, but much-needed reforms of the Great Society. Contrary to the big lie of the past decade that such programs caused our current family dilemmas, those antipoverty and social justice reforms helped overcome many of the family problems that prevailed in the 1950s.

In 1964, after fourteen years of unrivaled family stability and economic prosperity, the poverty rate was still 19 percent; in 1969, after five years of civil rights activism, the rebirth of feminism, and the institution of nontraditional if relatively modest government welfare programs, it was down to 12 percent, a low that has not been seen again since the social welfare cutbacks began in the late 1970s. In 1965, 20 percent of American children still lived in poverty; within five years, that had fallen to 15 percent. Infant mortality was cut in half between 1965 and 1980. The gap in nutrition between low-income Americans and other Americans narrowed significantly, as a direct result of food stamp and school lunch programs. In 1963, 20 percent of Americans living below the poverty line had *never* been examined by a physician; by 1970 this was true of only 8 percent of the poor.

Since 1973, however, real wages have been falling for most Americans. Attempts to counter this through tax revolts and spending freezes have led to drastic cutbacks in government investment programs. Corporations also spend far less on research and job creation than they did in the 1950s and 1960s, though the average compensation to executives has soared. The gap between rich and poor, according to the April 17, 1995, *New York Times*, is higher in the United States than in any other industrial nation.

Family Stress

These inequities are *not* driven by changes in family forms, contrary to ideologues who persist in confusing correlations with causes; but they certainly exacerbate such changes, and they tend to bring out the worst in *all* families. The result has been an accumulation of stresses on families, alongside some important expansions of personal options. Working couples with children try to balance three full-time jobs, as employers and schools cling to policies that assume every employee has a "wife" at home to take care of family matters. Divorce and remarriage have allowed many adults and children to escape from toxic family environments, yet our lack of social support networks and failure to forge new values for sustaining intergenerational obligations have let many children fall through the cracks in the process.

Meanwhile, young people find it harder and harder to form or sustain families. According to an Associated Press report of April 25, 1995, the median income of men aged twenty-five to thirty-four fell by 26 percent between 1972 and 1994, while the proportion of such men with earnings below the poverty level for a family of four more than doubled to 32 percent. The figures are even worse for African American and Latino men. Poor individuals are twice as likely to divorce as more affluent ones, three to four times less likely to marry in the first place, and five to seven times more likely to have a child out of wedlock.

As conservatives insist, there is a moral crisis as well as an economic one in modem America: a pervasive sense of social alienation, new levels of violence, and a decreasing willingness to make sacrifices for others. But romanticizing "traditional" families and gender roles will not produce the changes in job structures, work policies, child care, medical practice, educational preparation, political discourse, and gender inequities that would permit families to develop moral and ethical systems relevant to 1990s realities.

America needs more than a revival of the narrow family obligations of the 1950s, whose (greatly exaggerated) protection for white, middle-class children was achieved only at tremendous cost to the women in those families and to all those who could not or would not aspire to the Ozzie and Harriet ideal. We need a concern for children that goes beyond the question of whether a mother is waiting with cookies when her kids come home from school. We need a moral language that allows us to address something besides people's sexual habits. We need to build values and social institutions that can reconcile people's needs for independence with their equally important rights to dependence, and surely we must reject older solutions that involved balancing these needs on the backs of women. We will not find our answers in nostalgia for a mythical "traditional family."

READING 3

WHAT'S AHEAD FOR FAMILIES

Joseph F. Coates

Joseph F. Coates examines five key societal trends that are dramatically altering the future prospects for families. Coates is president of Coates and Jarratt, a social research firm.

No adequate theory in the social sciences explains how values change, so it is very difficult to anticipate changing social values. On the other hand, the social sciences are outstanding in reporting and exploring historic patterns of social change and in reporting contemporary social values through surveys, opinion polls, and observational research.

Identifying long-term shifts in values is complicated by the great deal of attention given to fads—that is, transient enthusiasms. A good example is "family values," a topic of great interest in recent political seasons. Both the family and values are undergoing shifts, and the challenge for futurists and other observers of social change is to identify the long-term trends and implications in both of these important areas. Social values are slowly evolving trends.

To help . . . understand the myriad of evolving patterns in families, this article describes several major trends and forecasts in families and values and suggests what they may imply for the future.

From Joseph F. Coates, "What's Ahead for Families: Five Major Forces of Change." This article originally appeared in the September/October 1995 issue of *The Futurist* and is used by permission of the World Future Society, 7910 Woodmont Ave., Suite 450, Bethesda, MD 20814; 301-656-8274; http://www.sfs.org.

Trend 1: Stresses on Family Functions

The family in the United States is in transition. While the forces at play are clear and numerous, the outcomes over the next decades remain uncertain.

Anthropologists agree that the family is a central, positive institution in every society. It performs two functions: the nurturing and socialization of children and the regulation of the expression of sexuality. In European and North American society, the family serves another basic function: companionship. Also important are the economic functions of families, such as providing care for the elderly and sick and social support for unemployed members.

All of these family functions are being stressed by structural changes in society. Among the patterns that have long-term implications are:

• Increased life-spans mean that adults live well past the period in which nurturing and socialization of children is central to their lives. In many cases, longevity leads to the death of one spouse substantially before the other, creating a companionship crisis.

• Sexual behavior is increasingly being separated from its procreative function, thanks to reproductive technologies such as artificial insemination and *in vitro* fertilization, as well as contraceptives.

• New patterns of work and leisure mean that people are developing interests and activities that are different from other members of their family. In many cases, this leads to conflicting interests and expectations rather than convergence and mutual support. As a result, the companionship function of families comes under increasing stress.

• Television and magazines create images of lifestyles, which may influence people's expectations of each other and the roles of families.

• The anonymity of metropolitan life eliminates many of the social and community pressures on families. There are no watchful and all-knowing eyes in the big city that compare with those in smaller and more cohesive communities, where "What will the neighbors think?" is a critical socializing factor.

These forces will not wipe out the family or the commitment to family, but they will continue to reshape it.

Implications of Stress on Family Functions

• Substitutes for family functions will develop. As family members seek other sources of companionship, and nurturing children becomes less important in matured families, institutions will have a challenge and opportunity to meet human needs. Already, people are finding companionship and even forming committed relationships on the Internet. Schools, businesses, and governments are all under more demand for meeting human services once provided in families, such as health and medical care, child care, retirement care, unemployment compensation, etc.

• Interest groups will proliferate. Support groups have burgeoned in recent years to help people with special health or emotional problems. Similarly, special-interest groups such as book-discussion salons, travel and adventure societies, or gourmet dinner circles could see a renaissance as individuals seek others with similar interests outside their own families.

• "Recreational sex" may become more acceptable as the connection between sexual activity and childbearing diminishes. Greater access to information on health and "safe sex" will allow people—including the very young and the very old—to engage in sexual activity more safely, both physically and emotionally.

Trend 2: Economics Drives Family Changes

The greatest changes in families have to do less with the family structure and more with economics. The change richest in implications is the rise of the two-income household. The United States has a way to go. Sweden and Denmark are the standards for mothers participating in the labor force. Sixty-five percent of U.S. mothers with children under age 18 are in the work force, compared with 86% in Denmark and 89% in Sweden. For children under 3, the figures are 53% in the United States, 84% in Denmark, and 86% in Sweden. Among the significant patterns emerging are:

• By 2000, women will make up just under half of the work force.

• Women are older when they marry and have their first child, deferring family formation until after they finish their education and get their first

---

Enduring Family Values
(Percentage of adults saying
these values are important)

Respecting your parents	.70%
Providing emotional support for your family	.69%
Respecting people for who they are	.68%
Being responsible for your actions	.68%
Communicating your feelings to your family	.65%
Respecting your children	.65%
Having a happy marriage	.64%
Having faith in God	.59%
Respecting authority	.57%
Living up to your potential	.54%
Being married to the same person for life	.54%
Leaving the world in a better shape	.51%

Source: *American Demographics* (June 1992), from the Massachusetts Mutual American Family Values Study, 1989.

job. In 1988, the median age of mothers of first-born children was 26, the oldest at any time in U.S. history.

• Although the average income of the family household has stayed relatively flat over the last 15 years, the growth of the two-income household is allowing couples to make a higher average income.

Implications of Changes in Family and Economics

• Two incomes, two decision makers. Both breadwinning members of two-income households will have broader opportunities to start a new career or business initiative. Any change of job or relocation offer will thus affect two incomes rather than just one, making life/career planning doubly complicated.

• Women disappear from the community. Women's greater commitment to work means a long-term change in their commitment to home and the community. Like male breadwinners of the past, women may be rarely seen in stores, in their neighborhood, at home, and so on. In the shopping mall of the future, for instance, the only daytime customers may be the very old, the very young with their mothers or minders, and after-school teenagers.

• A masculinization of the home will spread to the community. Telecommuting allows one or both breadwinners of the dual-income household to work at home. Many men are choosing this option in order to be more available for domestic responsibilities such as cooking, cleaning, and chauffeuring children to various activities. Men may also increasingly become involved in volunteer activities, especially those that directly benefit their own families, such as neighborhood crime-watch groups and the PTA.

• An economy of convenience will emerge. A working lifestyle for most families will also continue to shape their preferences in eating, at home, for entertainment, and in shopping. Many families will be willing to pay a premium for convenience in all goods and services they purchase.

Families in the U.S. Labor Force, 1940–1993

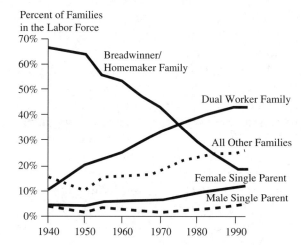

Source: U.S. Department of Labor, Bureau of Labor Statistics

Trend 3: Divorce Continues

Divorce may be viewed as a way to correct social mistakes and incompatibility. In the 1940s, for example, there was a surge of marriage in the early 1940s as young Americans went off to war, and at the end of the war there was a surge of divorces in 1945–1947, apparently correcting impetuous mistakes. There was an even greater surge in post-war marriages.

Divorce is seen by many as the death knell of family values. On the other hand, a high divorce rate could be seen as a positive social indicator. It represents an unequivocal rejection of a bad marriage. For the first time anywhere in a mass society, the United States has had the income, the wealth and prosperity, and the broad knowledge base to allow people previously trapped in life-long misery to reject that state and search for a better marriage. The evidence is clear, since the majority of divorced people either remarry or would remarry were the opportunity available.

Among the patterns emerging in divorce are:

• Divorce rates fell below 10 per 1,000 married women between 1953 and 1964, then surged to a high of almost 23 per 1,000 married women in 1978. Divorces have continued at about 20 to 21 per 1,000 for the last decade.

• Commitment to marriage continues, as

demonstrated in the fact that the majority of divorced people remarry. One-third of all marriages in 1988 were remarriages for one or both partners. The average time until remarriage is about two and a half years.

• The shorter life-spans of many families has led to serial marriages. Almost surely there will continue to be people who have three, four, or five spouses, without any intervening widowhood. In the long term, it is much more likely that society will settle down into a pattern of later marriage, earlier sexual engagement, and much more careful and effective selection of life mates.

Implications of Divorce Trends

• Marriages and families will be businesses. Families may increasingly be treated as business units, which form legal partnerships and plan and evolve their own lifecycles as an integrated activity. Families may even incorporate to obtain tax and other benefits. Divorces will be handled as simple business or partnership dissolution.

• Teenage sex—but not pregnancy—will increase. Teenagers will observe and emulate their parents' distinct separation of sexuality and commitment.

• Companies will share and care. Businesses will offer their employees training in household economics and management, as well as family and divorce counseling. These courses could also be marketed as a service to the community.

• Opportunities for marketing to new families will emerge. Many of the families in the top income segments will include remarriages and second and third families, in which the parents will have a strong incentive to tie together the new relationships. Aiming at this concern could offer opportunities. For example, a new blended family may want financial planning and related services to reallocate its resources. Club memberships for the new family, new homes, etc., all could be important among this group.

• A "pro-family" movement will take new directions. One of the most important underlying causes of divorce is that no institution in

U.S. Divorce Rate, 1940–1992

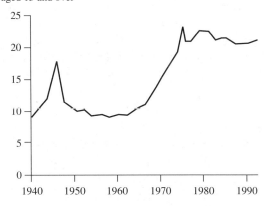

Rate per 1,000 married women, aged 15 and over

Source: National Center for Health Statistics

the United States—school, church, Boy Scouts, or other—teaches and trains people about what it is like to be married, to live in a two-income household, or to share and be involved in a new division of domestic labor. The search for a good marriage is not supported by the right tools to aid that search. Over the next decade, society will focus more on creating more-effective families. A new "pro-family" movement will encourage better and more effective matchmaking, as well as better teaching and training on marriage lifestyles and on economic and household management.

Trend 4: Nontraditional Families Proliferate

A variety of nontraditional family forms are evolving in the United States, shaped by economic and social changes. For example, higher expectations for education mean young people spend more years in the educational system and marry later. The greater tolerance of divorce and remarriage affects how often people dissolve and re-form families. Many people enter long-term cohabiting relationships before marriage. And many single-parent families are being formed among low- and middle-income communities, as a result of divorce, widowhood, or out-of-wedlock childbearing.

The emerging patterns include:

- More couples are cohabiting. In 1988, one-third of all women aged 15–44 had been living in a cohabiting relationship at some point.
- The number of "boomerang" families is increasing. Young people—post-high school or post-college children who would otherwise be on their own—are returning home to live with Mom and Dad. To a large extent, this is a money-saving move more commonly practiced by men than by women.
- Blended families are becoming the norm. Blended families result from divorced parents who remarry, either linking stepfamilies together or linking the children of one partner to the subsequent children of both. It is estimated that, for nearly 16% of children living with two parents in 1990, one of those parents is a stepparent.
- Technology is creating new families. These may involve adopted children matched for similar genetic inheritance, children from surrogate parents, and eventually children from cloned embryos.
- Gay families are surfacing as a result of the new openness in society. Aside from the social approval so valuable to many in the gay community, acknowledgment offers substantial economic benefits in corporate or business health and recreation benefits packages. Time will make family resources available to members of nontraditional families.
- Group living, with or without sexual intimacy, is likely to remain a transitional life stage for an increasing number of people, often as an alternative to living alone.
- Single-parent families are increasingly common across all socioeconomic groups. The unmarried woman who bears a child is one of these family styles. It is unclear what the consequences are for middle- and professional-class mothers and children in these voluntary single-parent households. Evidence is strong that teenage childbearing, particularly by unmarried mothers, is socially destructive of the future well-being of both the mother and the child. Some single-parent families are single by divorce or separation.

Implications of the Proliferation of Nontraditional Families

- Rearranged families will rearrange the workplace. The work force will continue to be profoundly affected by new family structures. The proliferation of family arrangements will create new pressures on employers to be flexible and responsive in relation to working hours.
- Businesses will make attitude adjustments. Employers will be hard-pressed to justify accepting one type of family arrangement among their employees and not another. One company decided to offer benefits to gay couples because they could *not* get married and deny them to male-female couples living together because they *could*. Workers did not accept this justification.
- "Nonfamily" families will gain in status. Many groups of people consider themselves families, even though they do not fit traditional definitions (e.g., gay couples, unmarried couples with or without children, foster parents, long-term housemates, etc.). This has implications for business and nonbusiness issues, for example in marketing, housing codes and covenants, loans, billing, leasing, and so on.
- Family-oriented organizations will reinvent themselves. For example, Parent-Teacher Associations may broaden into Family-Teacher or Community-Teacher Associations. Schools may provide more counseling for students in nontraditional families.
- Flexible architecture will be mandatory. Housing will become more flexible, with walls that can be easily taken down and rearranged to form new rooms depending on the needs of new family members.

Trend 5: An Aging Society

The traditional family in past decades was the nuclear family: a working father, a homemaker mother, and children. As the children aged and left home, the traditional family was two adults with no children living at home; then one or the other died, leaving an elderly single person alone.

Aging creates a crisis in traditional families' lifecycles. The patterns to watch now include:

- Death rates of men are relatively high compared with women. Men also tend to marry women younger than themselves. As a result, at age 75 and older, 66% of men but only 24% of women are living with a spouse. At age 65, for every 100 men there are 150 women. At age 85, for every 100 men there are 260 women.
- The savings rate among working adults is now just 4.1% of personal income, compared with 7.9% in 1980; this low rate bodes ill for Americans' economic status in retirement.
- Voting rates among seniors are traditionally higher than for younger people (60.7% of those 65 years and older voted in 1994, compared with 16.5% for 18- to 20-year olds and 22.3% for 25- to 34-year olds). It is likely that the baby boomers' influence on public policy will gain strength as they approach retirement years.

Implications of Age and Family

- The end of retirement? A combination of several factors may lead to the end of retirement: the emotional need of seniors to feel useful when their families no longer demand their daily attention, the financial needs of seniors who didn't save enough during their working years, the improved mental and physical health of older people, and the need in businesses for skilled, experienced workers.
- Economic priorities shift away from children. There is already concern among the elderly about balancing their economic assets against commitments to their children. Personal savings during their working years for their kids' college education may have left them ill-prepared for retirement.
- Parents will "boomerang" back to their kids. Just as adult children of the 1980s and 1990s moved back into their parents' home for economic security, elderly parents in the twenty-first century may increasingly move into the homes of their grown children. "Granny flats" and mother-in-law apartments will be common additions to houses.
- No retirement from sex. The sexual experimentation characteristic of baby boomers' youth may be brought to their old age. New drugs and therapies, such as penile implants, will help.
- Elders will have roommates or form other shared-living arrangements. A substantial increase in cohabitation offers the benefits of companionship without compromising the individual's financial survival or reducing the children's inheritance. We may see some college campuses convert into retirement communities, with dorm-style living.

The Effects of Population Changes on Values

Changes in values in the United States will depend to some extent on demographic change. Social institutions will continue to be stressed when population groups such as the aging baby boomers pass through society.

The baby boomers' children, the echo generation, now number more than 80 million people; they will be an even larger generation and a bigger social force than the baby boom was. They may be expected to stress and reshape education, justice, and work in turn, beginning now and accelerating through 2005, when they reach 20 and are ready to go to work.

Through the 1990s, the young echo boomers will increase school enrollment, then college enrollment. As they reach their late teens and move into their violence-prone years, the United States could experience an increase in violent crimes after the turn of the century. At around the same time there may be some risk of social unrest either in universities or in cities, as the echo boom goes through its years of youthful idealism and discontent.

The aging of the baby boom in the 1990s and 2000s may push the dominant values of U.S. society to be more conservative, more security conscious, and more mature and less driven by youthful expectations. In 2010, the first of the baby boomers turn 65. If the conservatism of their elders becomes repressive, the echo boomers could have more to rebel against.

As the U.S. population grows, if the economy affords only shrinking opportunities, this may promote more conservative views. At the same time, there may be an emerging social activism around worker rights, employment stability, and related issues.

Effects of Shifting Family Patterns

As a flexible institution, the family will continue to accommodate itself to the economy and the values of the Information Age. In many societies, this means an ongoing shift to dual-income partnerships.

It has also meant a shift in what work is available for the family to earn its income—away from agriculture and manufacturing and to information and services. This shift has brought millions of women into the work force because the work now requires education rather than raw physical might—mind, not muscle.

In many societies, men are finding it more difficult to find work unless they, too, can shift to information-based work. It is possible that women will become the higher wage earners in millions of families. It is also possible that as a result child care and family responsibilities will be more equally distributed between men and women.

People will continue to want to be part of families, but for some the economic necessity to do so will be less. For example, young people will need to spend more time in acquiring their education, and they will form their families later.

Women with substantial careers will have less economic need to remarry after divorce.

Education, prosperity, and a decline in regard for authority will continue to secularize U.S. society, but concern for the family and community will tend to promote ties with religion. The church will continue to be a source of support for those who feel in some way disadvantaged by current values and attitudes. The other attractions of religion are its rituals, its shared experiences, its mysteries, and its social events. These will continue to bring in and keep people in religious groups, unless urban society develops some alternatives.

Conclusion: Belief in the Family Remains High

Anticipations of family life have not diminished to a significant degree in the last decades. In general, Americans are committed to the family as the core of a successful life. It is particularly gratifying to see this view widely maintained by young people. The percentage of college freshmen saying that raising a family is "essential" or "very important" has been fairly constant in the past quarter century: 67.5% in 1970 and 69.5% in 1990.

Adults' commitment to the family has become somewhat tempered by the higher likelihood of divorce. But most people still agree that being happily married and having a happy family is an important goal.

DISCUSSION QUESTIONS

1. The U.S. Bureau of the Census defines *family* as: two or more people related by blood, marriage, or adoption who share a common residence. Do you consider this definition to be too broad, too narrow, or acceptable? According to this definition, who would be included in the family? Who would be left out?

2. What does *family* mean to you?

3. How has U.S. family life changed to keep pace with changing societal conditions?

4. Do we as a society value families less today than in the past? Why or why not?

5. What will be the realities of family life in the twenty-first century?

WEBSITES

www.hec.ohio-state.edu/famlife/technol/guide/guide98.htm
This introduction to the Internet and the World Wide Web is maintained at the Ohio State University Department of Human Development and Family Science.

www.census.gov/population/www/socdemo/hh-fam.html
The U.S. Census Bureau posts a wealth of statistics on the family, including Current Population Surveys (CPS).

www.census.gov/main/www/subjects.html#M
An especially useful way to navigate all of the information that can be found at the Census Bureau is through their subject index. You may want to bookmark this site because it has data on all aspects of the family.

CHAPTER 2: DIVERSITY IN FAMILY LIFE

The "traditional" nuclear family, comprising a married couple and their biological children, is no longer an accurate conception of family in our society. Today in the United States we find a growing diversity and complexity of family forms, including dual-earner families, single-parent families, child-free families, stepfamilies, extended families, and racially mixed families. In addition, we find a high rate of "domestic partnerships" involving heterosexual and gay and lesbian cohabiting couples, many of whom have children living in the home.

Family scholars contend that the trend toward family diversity is increasing, not diminishing, and that because the family is a responsive system that operates within the larger societal context, this trend simply reflects broad social change. As societal attitudes and behaviors change, a growing number of nontraditional family structures emerge and are accepted. Widespread divorce and remarriage, maternal employment, the decisions of unmarried mothers to keep their babies, effective contraception, and increased tolerance of homosexual partnerships are a few of the factors that affect the family institution.

Since the 1967 U.S. Supreme Court ruling that state laws prohibiting interracial marriage were unconstitutional, attitudes and behaviors regarding "mixed" marriage and multiracial individuals have changed. An increasing number of Americans are crossing racial and ethnic boundaries to marry and form families, and Americans are more accepting of this practice. The first selection, "Racially and Ethnically Mixed Families," provides contemporary perspectives and guidelines that reflect current thinking on interracial families.

As the second reading of this chapter points out, the fastest growing segment of the homeless population is homeless families. Elaine Anderson and Sally Koblinsky address the characteristics and concerns of this diverse group and provide an overview of policies and programs that affect homeless families.

READING 4
RACIALLY AND ETHNICALLY MIXED FAMILIES

Bruno Oriti, Amy Bibb, and Jayne Mahboubi

Over the past twenty-five years, racially and ethnically mixed relationships have become increasingly prevalent. The authors provide perspectives on mixed-race and -ethnic families and offer guidelines to help clarify the role that therapists play in helping these diverse and complex families. Bruno Oriti is a psychologist and associate faculty member at the Family Institute of New Jersey in Metuchen, where Amy Bibb is an associate. Jayne Mahboubi is a psychotherapist in private practice in Smyrna, Georgia.

Being mixed is like that tingling feeling you have in your nose just before you sneeze— you're waiting for it to happen but it never does.

James McBride, *The Color of Water* (1995)

Interracial/ethnic families and multiracial individuals are literally changing the face of America and challenging the validity and utility of the way race and ethnicity traditionally have characterized the social and psychic fabric of the United States. Since the U.S. Supreme Court decision to strike down state laws preventing interracial marriage 25 years ago (Simpson & Yinger, 1985), attitudes and practices regarding interracial mar-

riage in America appear to be moving toward greater acceptance (Root, 1992, 1996). Root (1996) reports on Gallup Poll results indicating that since 1967 Black-White intermarriage has gained in approval among both racial groups, with both groups sharing an approval rating of approximately 48% and a disapproval rating of approximately 42%. Of the 50 million marriages in the United States, 246,000 are reported to be Black-White unions (Rosenblatt, Karis, & Powell, 1995). Crohn (1995) notes that currently almost 60% of children born to Japanese Americans have a White parent. The number of Hispanic-non-Hispanic marriages in the United States has doubled to more than a million since 1970, and 50% of all Jewish marriages today are intermarriages, compared with 6% in 1956 (Crohn, 1995). Children with an American Indian lineage have a greater incidence of having a White parent than another American Indian parent; Asian and Pacific Islander immigrants coparent with White Americans approximately 40% of the time (Crohn, 1995).

These data coincide with the breakdown of racial and ethnic barriers in Europe and with dramatic changes in United States immigration patterns, which have shifted from 80% European immigrants in 1960 to 80% originating from Latin American, Caribbean, and Asian nations (Crohn, 1995).

Against this backdrop of sweeping and global "mixing," family practitioners must inform their

From Bruno Oriti, Amy Bibb, and Jayne Mahboubi, "Family-Centered Practice with Racially/Ethnically Mixed Families," *Families in Society: The Journal of Contemporary Human Services*, November 1996, pp. 573–82; © Families International, Inc. Reprinted by permission of Manticore Publishers.

profession and join with families whose members may become segregated by the divisive forces of oppression. As family practitioners, we must reformulate our definitions of race and ethnicity as well as how we understand our own racial/ethnic identities.

A New Perspective on Ethnic Families

In family-centered practice with mixed-race and -ethnic families, theory has begun to respond to these broad cultural changes (Root, 1992). In moving beyond prejudiced notions of race and ethnicity, we are learning to honor the contributions of groups of peoples and to challenge the pseudoscientific taxonomies, exclusivity, and hierarchy that have historically been the mechanisms for preserving stereotypes. Modern genetics and anthropological studies inform us that no universal fragmentation of human genetic lineage subdivides our species, neither historically nor geographically, despite the fact that culturally we are divided into racial or ethnic groups (Alland, 1971; Marks, 1995). Further, defining racial and ethnic categories has varied greatly across cultures and time and within cultures (Alland, 1971; Fish, 1995; Marks, 1995).

Alland (1971), in considering the issue of race, concludes,

> I am completely in accord with those . . . who feel that the concept of race is of absolutely no value in the study of human variation and adaptation. I also lean towards those whose position is that the concept of race is a fuzzy one even when it is "carefully" defined and related only to historical questions. The use of the term "race" leads to infinite confusion (pp. 61–62).

Clinical implications can be drawn from anthropological consensus regarding race and ethnic groupings arrived at in the past 30 years:

• From a standpoint of anthropology and genetics, racial and ethnic distinctions are interchangeable (Alland, 1971; Marks, 1995; Plous & Williams, 1995).

• Racial and ethnic classifications are inherently intertwined with social hierarchies that appear stable from a vantage point within a given culture at a given time but vary among cultures and across time.

• Although certain physical characteristics, patterns of behavior, and styles of perception can be considered typical of localized ethnic groups, culturally determined variations within these patterns exist. Further, genetic and phenotypic commonalities are subject to modification over time and are most accurately applied to regionalized populations and not to universal and temporally stable racial/ethnic groups (Alland, 1971; Marks, 1995).

Those labeled with the prefix "multi-" and/or "inter-" allow us to see with the wider lens of anthropology that racial and ethnic boundaries are genetically and culturally fluid. However, on one hand, racial/ethnic mixing and multiplicity are antithetical to societal practices that strive to maintain a racially based and oppressive hierarchy among peoples. Similarly, on the other hand, highlighting the facts of racial "mixing" can contradict political practices based on racial solidarity that seek to preserve, both in the literal and cultural sense, oppressed peoples from the annihilating forces of racism. Given these highly emotional and politically driven dynamics, how do we understand the sociopolitical niche held by racially mixed families? How do we understand what constitutes healthy adaptation in a racist and otherwise oppressive context?

Historical Context

Understanding the political space occupied by multiracial individuals can serve as a starting point to answering these questions. To understand how multiracial families were constructed historically in the United States, we can draw from early definitions of *mulatto*, a term for children of Black-White ancestry. Among the definitions of mulatto in the 1962 edition of *Webster's New World Dictionary* was "a young mule." This linking of multiracial people to a subhuman category supports the notion that multiracial children are frequently seen as the embodiment of racial taboos that their parents have violated (Holt, 1995). This view persists together with racist assumptions and stereotypes despite the larger culture's publicly touted opinions regarding misce-genation (Davidson, 1992). For many, the existence of multiethnic/racial people is evidence of "forbidden" emotionally and physically intimate encounters. Presumptions about the intelligence, judgment, sexuality, and phenotype of multiracial people abound (Comas-Diaz, 1994). Such presumptions influence practitioners' ideas about treatment directions and psychological health.

The literature is replete with descriptions of the multiple problems faced by interracial/ethnic families and individuals. Identity confusion, acting out, rebellion, and overcompensation for poor self-esteem are a few behaviors and motivations assigned to members of multiracial/ethnic unions (Aldridge, 1978; Berry & Blassingame, 1982; Brown, 1990; Davidson, 1992; Gibbs & Moskowitz-Sweet, 1991; Spaights & Dixon, 1984).

Ethnicity from a Strengths Perspective

Recently Root (1992, 1996) examined the multiracial person's experience from a strengths rather than pathological perspective. This view emphasizes the adaptability rather than the maladjustment of multiracial persons. Some experts believe that a mixed heritage implies a unique ability to embrace multiple identities, perhaps transcending the tribalism of an antimiscegenist or even monoracial/ethnic experience (Reynolds & Pope, 1991; Root, 1996).

A growing body of literature documents that a large proportion of interracial/ethnic unions are characterized by both partners sharing a desire to overcome oppressive forces operating in their culture, valuing independent thinking, and hungering for diversity (Rosenblatt et al., 1995). Other persons couple across racial/ethnic lines in sympathetic response to oppressive forces such as racism and colonialism (Janiewski, 1995). Here, cross-racial/ethnic union occurs because one partner from a subjugated culture becomes further oppressed within the marriage and host culture. Examples of these unions include "war brides" (Kim, 1995), whereby one partner is from a culture that is colonizing or occupying another. Some cross-racial/ethnic adoptions occur as a result of

parents relinquishing their children because of poverty, state-imposed limitations on family size, or ethnic and gender-based infanticide.

The strengths perspective is essential for clinicians who wish to avoid perpetuating racist beliefs regarding the unnatural character of interracial/ethnic unions. However, some professionals, in reaction to tribalism and separatism, may overemphasize the adaptive aspects of multiracial unions and deny or minimize the complex cultural issues surrounding racial/ethnic differences. Taken in isolation, such views tend to minimize racial inequities and obscure the impact of social stratification, privilege, oppression, and tribalism on individuals and families.

Speaking to both the sociopolitical and developmental contexts, Root (1992, 1996) discusses the effects of oppression and privilege on the multiracial family's racial identity across the life cycle. Root notes that the dominant culture's discomfort with and profit from racism encourage families to remain silent on the issue of racism despite the fact that racial thinking saturates the fabric of our communities (Terkel, 1992). As a result of this silence discussion of racism is often limited to issues of racial conflict. Root (1992) adds that acknowledging oppression and social inequities based on race/ethnicity is not equivalent to either condoning separatism or passively accepting elitist practices. Ideally, acknowledging the oppressive stratifications in our society is the starting point at which multiracial/ethnic families begin to establish a context of safety and to expand their efforts to manage their racial and ethnic identity. Practitioners need to be well versed in the dynamics of privilege and oppression as well as the cultural practices and history of the group with whom they work (Hines, Garcia-Preto, McGoldrick, Almeida, & Weltman, 1992) to help families address the complex issues surrounding multiracial identity.

Case Example

The following case example illustrates how a therapist can balance a strengths perspective with sociopolitical understanding to guide a multiracial/ethnic family in crisis.

The Ks were a multiracial couple with three children. Mrs. K was African American and Mr. K Polish American. They entered treatment because they were concerned about their adolescent son, M, who had had a recent altercation with the police. Neither Mr. nor Mrs. K cited racial conflicts or identity concerns as part of their presenting problem. When racial difference in the context of their relationship and family life was initially explored, both maintained that it was of little consequence. However, as the therapist posed questions in the context of constructing a multigenerational genogram, both members of the dyad articulated that at the point of their coupling, family members, as a result of intense emotional reactions, withdrew contact because of the couple's decision to marry outside their race.

M, the middle of three brothers, spoke more freely about race than did his parents and indicated that he was struggling with racial-identity issues. Although light skinned, he had Black features, including kinky hair. M viewed race as an important factor in his life, explaining that the police mistreated him because of his race. This contrasted with his parents' view that color was not an issue. The therapist pushed forward, asking the parents to consider whether their gender and racial differences may have led to differing assumptions, roles, and anxieties regarding race in their mutual love and caring for their children. Both Mr. and Mrs. K then articulated their individual and shared reactions to racism in the outside world and how each adapted to racism by not emphasizing race in their marriage and in raising their children. Moreover the couple also did not associate with persons who emphasize racial difference, including those whose views of differences were not based on racist beliefs. This practice resulted in a narrow social network with little contact with extended family and friends. The couple communicated to their children that others might dislike them because of their mixed ancestry, stating that this was wrong and that people should value human rather than racial characteristics.

The therapist focused the family so that each member could address his or her fears of being alienated in the family and the community. M articulated his anger and shame at being biracial, which was generalized toward his parents and the culture. He felt angry and anxious that race was an issue in his life and because the culture attributed differences in status to each family member on the basis of their racial markings. Mr. and Mrs. K were afraid that the rejection visited upon them by their extended family for "mixing" would play out with their children, who would blame them for the pain and confusion of their isolation. In fact, each parent's family had predicted that this would happen as the children got older. Thus, Mr. and Mrs. K had internalized racist beliefs that mixing either genetically or socially was bad and punishable by rejection. As a result, they had not fully prepared their children for the conflicts they might experience. Rather than questioning and challenging the cultural taboo of racial mixing, they internalized it.

Both parents stated that they feared that M would be forced to choose a race if the issue was acknowledged. They further concluded that his appearance and experience of racism might cause him to reject his father because he was White. This fear stymied their ability to buffer their sons and guide them through a racist culture as well as prevented them from passing on their beliefs about inclusion and transcendence. As a result, the sons were not prepared to deal with racism. In addition, they did not see themselves as the embodiment of an inclusive and adaptable family structure, but instead had internalized assumptions that as multiracial persons they were born out of conflict and into an unnatural order. As these beliefs and assumptions were spoken and challenged, the parents and children began to understand the strength and value of their diversity. This enabled them to join together in efforts to cope with racism and racist authority in their extended family and community.

This case example highlights multiracial persons' struggle to adapt to oppression and remain fluid in their perspectives. The strengths model teaches us that the multiracial/ethnic person can instruct and challenge all of us to recognize oppression and to adopt an inclusive and fluid perspective in our understanding of human experience. In the K family, the parents and thus M found it difficult to acknowledge the White aspect of the family identity because of their fear that M would either reject the oppressive status of being White or identify with the oppressor. The notion that multiracial persons must choose between two bad options is born of the racism that pits oppressors against the oppressed in our society.

James McBride, son of an African American father and Polish/Jewish mother, articulates political conflict as it applies to his biracial experience:

> Given my black face and upbringing it was easy for me to flee into the anonymity of blackness, yet I felt frustrated to live in a world that considers the color of your face an immediate political statement whether you like it or not. It took years before I began to accept the fact that the nebulous "white man's world" wasn't as free as it looked; that class, luck, religion, all factored in as well; that all Jews are not like my grandfather and that part of me is Jewish too. Yet the color boundary in my mind was and is the greatest hurdle. In order to clear it, my solution was to stay away from it and fly solo (McBride, 1995, p. 215).

For McBride and other heterosexual men of color, "the greatest hurdle" is often race, although gender, sexual orientation, and class identity can make prioritizing the hurdles (i.e., sexism, racism, homophobia, elitism) even more complicated for multiracial/ethnic families (Almeida, Woods, Messineo, Font, & Heer, 1994; Comas-Diaz, 1994; Hooks, 1984; Pinderhughes, 1986; Root, 1992). Multicultural individuals and families are too often saddled with the burden of carrying the mantle of inclusion and solving the ills of the racial/ethnic reasoning of the dominant culture. As the following case example illustrates, this perceived responsibility to combat racism can prevent multiracial/ethnic families from addressing divisive issues, especially if family members have a shared history of racial/ethnic oppression.

Case Example

In the case of R, an adopted biracial woman who was raised in a monoracial African Ameri-

can family, and L, a Guam-American, two persons from oppressed but different cultures united but were unable to share their respective experiences of oppression, including their internalized racism and elitism. Problems in their relationship revolved around class differences as well as ignorance of each other's cultural traditions.

R was adopted and raised in an affluent intact southern family. She attended a historically Black college and received a master's degree in the performing arts. L was raised in the North by his mother, who had immigrated to the United States after her husband's death when L was very young.

The birth of their children raised issues of class, race, and tradition that were first voiced through their respective in-laws. These issues resurfaced later in ways that sabotaged the couple's relationship. Although R and L remained silent on racial issues out of fear of hurting each other, issues of race and class prejudice emerged under the pressure of life-cycle challenges related to child rearing. The couple initially enjoyed a sense of protection around their mutual identification as being racially oppressed in the larger White society. This in turn shut down open discussion of the racism and class prejudice in their ethnic communities and families. Thus, the couple eventually internalized the prejudices of their own families. Their multiracial children were at the center of society's and their families' conflicts regarding multiethnic identity.

From outside the ranks of family therapy (McIntosh, 1990; West, 1993), as well as from within (Almeida et al., 1994; Falicov, 1988; Lappin & Hardy, in press; McGoldrick, 1994), professionals have called us to hold ourselves to ethical standards that recognize that we are composed of multiple racial, ethnic, gender, class, and sexual-orientation identities and that we must not rest until oppressive sociopolitical stratification is illuminated and dismantled through empowerment and accountability. To embrace such an ethic, we must hold ourselves accountable in dealing with the complex struggles of the human systems we encounter.

In navigating the multiple oppressions prevalent in the United States, political historian Cornel West (1993) speaks of the need to combat racism along with the dangers associated with "the pitfalls of racial reasoning" (p. 35). Borrowing in part from Hooks (1990) and other feminists of color who stress the need to recognize multiple oppressed voices in the struggle for equality, West notes that in responding to the Clarence Thomas–Anita Hill media event,

> most black leaders got lost in the thicket of reasoning and hence got caught in a vulgar form of racial reasoning; black authenticity [leading to] black closing ranks mentality [leading to] black male subordination of black women in the interests of the black community in a hostile white racist country (p. 38).

West adds that this racial reasoning was not called into question, perpetuating an infighting along gender lines "as Bush and other conservatives sit back, watch and prosper" (p. 38). Closing ranks in order to preserve a sense of group identity, be it racial, ethnic, gender, or otherwise, is always risky because, as Hooks (1990) and others (Almeida et al., 1994; McGoldrick, 1994) observe, it tends to silence the multiple voices within a given group that can illuminate a range of issues surrounding oppression. Feminist theorists (Almeida & Bograd, 1990; Hooks, 1984, 1990) note that exclusive focus on racial subordination/oppression over other kinds of oppression obscures and perpetuates male heterosexual dominance.

West (1993) calls for a "prophetic" framework so that "instead of cathartic appeals to Black authenticity, a prophetic viewpoint bases mature Black self-love and self-respect on the moral quality of Black responses to undeniable racist degradation in the American past and present" (p. 43). Encouraging an antiracist stance without privileging a monolithic racial/ethnic essence, this framework "encourages a moral assessment of the variety of perspectives held by Black people and selects those views based on Black dignity and decency that eschew putting any group on a pedestal or in the gutter" (p. 43). Such an ethical framework is relevant to conflicts around any

racial/ethnic or other "in-group" reasoning.

Similarly, Reynolds and Pope's (1991) Multidimensional Identity Model pertains to individuals/families whose identity is affected by multiple oppressions. Drawing from an African epistemology of "optimal conceptualization," which posits that an individual's inner life is an extension of multiple influences, Reynolds and Pope encourage therapists to reflect upon these influences as they affect families across time and circumstance. In other words, individuals may promote one aspect of their identity, for example, as a member of a racially oppressed community (e.g., I am Latino), or proclaim various identities within a community (e.g., I am a gay woman of color).

Reynolds and Pope (1991), like Root (1992, 1996), encourage therapists to understand that multiply oppressed persons may adopt various political orientations to counter oppression. We concur that therapists should be wary of adopting a view that privileges one political stance (e.g., I am multiethnic) over another (e.g., I am monoethnic). In fact, multiracial/ethnic individuals and families may assert their monoracial identity during a particular circumstance or life phase, then assert their multiracial/ethnic identity when circumstances or their life issues change. Or they may even assert both these identities simultaneously. Multiracial/ethnic families may experience fragmentation as a result of the influence of a framework that imposes one identity over another in rigid ways. Therapists must be ready to help family members articulate the deeply personal experiences that go along with the political pros and cons of privileging particular racial or other oppressions. Individuals choose their politics according to their circumstances. This is most adaptive when it is done in full awareness of the multiple political perspectives embodied in their family system and the consequences of their political stances.

Thus, family adaptation and conflict are embedded in the sociopolitical struggles and oppressions of the larger society. Understanding and healing occur to the extent that individuals' and families' multiple perspectives are articulated. This broad view involves movement away from

Eurocentric/patriarchal frameworks that emphasize vertical stratification and competition toward a framework that views identity and cultural history as multiple realities (McIntosh, 1990). Like West's prophetic framework, these feminist models embrace multiplicity and hold that if one participates in or condones oppression or marginalization of any group, one fragments and marginalizes him- or herself. Multiracial persons often feel they cannot promote one aspect of their racial identity without marginalizing another.

In embracing multiplicity, family practitioners create disequilibrium in the sociopolitical structure of families organized around racial/ethnic dichotomies. In this way, family therapists join with multiracial persons whose very existence is a source of disequilibrium in that they embody the taboos and biological truths that threaten an oppressive order (Stasiulis & Yuval-Davis, 1995). Helping families illuminate and manage this disequilibrium is a critical task for family therapists. Such help takes the form of linking racial/ethnic identity with other value-laden aspects of cultural identity (gender, sexual orientation, religious preference) (Falicov, 1988). In this way, families can focus their struggles on multiracial/ethnic-identity issues within a sociopolitical context and thus avoid internalizing and personalizing conflicts.

Case Example

The following case example illustrates the impact of multiple oppressions on an interracial/ethnic system.

H, an American citizen who immigrated to the United States from Lebanon as an infant, entered treatment with concerns about his relationships with women, which were fraught with ambivalence and difficulties. H maintained several ongoing and intense relationships simultaneously. His physical appearance and self-identification was nonwhite/Middle Eastern. The women with whom he developed relationships were White and came from families that were several generations postimmigration in the United States. A relationship with a woman with Northern European ancestry had produced several children.

As treatment began, H spoke about inner psychological processes in himself and others as key to explaining his relationship difficulties. He also described the relationships in his family of origin as highly problematic. He had little knowledge of his family's immigration history and apparently troubled life in Lebanon. He said he was always reluctant to ask about these matters partly because information was not freely offered.

The therapist helped H "story" his life in racial/ethnic and gender terms. Initially, the therapist wondered with him about the impact of race and the family's immigration and earlier life in Lebanon on his presenting problems. H began describing his relationship problems in terms of a larger story of his family's attempts to assimilate into a society structured according to the ideals of White masculinity. He said that he was chosen from among his siblings to "make it" according to the standards of White American culture. In ways that were shameful to himself and unacknowledged within his family, H renounced his native culture by attempting to move upward socially and occupationally, choosing women from the dominant culture with whom to establish relationships, maintaining friendships with white men primarily, and identifying with White men's focus on individualism. He tended to deny the impact of racism, patriarchy, and other sociopolitical factors in people's lives.

As these narratives unfolded, H began to view his relationships with women in the context of the patriarchy and racial conflict in both the United States and his country of origin. Growing up, H developed a behavior pattern of acting White and hating himself and his family for being Lebanese. He said his peers would often make fun of him or others who were "foreign." He was caught in the double bind of achieving in White culture, which meant adopting an identity that subordinated women and Lebanese ethnicity, or not achieving and facing racism and oppression. H managed this no-win situation by taking a harsh and rejecting stance toward Lebanese women, whom he described as difficult temperamentally and holding to traditions and ways of relating that he found intrusive and "smothering."

The family's immigration story also figures importantly into H's emerging narratives. Lebanon has been marked by a long history of racial/ethnic warfare. His family had survived the brutalities of invasion and threats of occupation. Women of the oppressed group had been subjected to rape and torture and were often considered spoils of war. These stories of the old country were woven into the family history and H's experience with American racism reawoke these traumas. H adapted by attempting to assimilate and resist assimilation simultaneously and to subjugate and honor women simultaneously. Such behaviors reflected positions that he and other men he knew adopted.

The multiple oppressions in this mixed race/ethnic family required the therapist and client to question their accountability as men in positions of status compared with the women and less Americanized members of H's family. At the same time, H's history of victimization as a racial/ethnic minority was linked to his further oppressing those who had less status than he (women and less Americanized family members). This had far reaching implications for his biracial/ethnic children who were at risk of internalizing the prejudice and cross-racial conflicts. To counter this, H was coached to find out the stories of women his children knew, both from Lebanon and the United States. In addition, he was encouraged to detail the preimmigration history of both men and women in his family. He then explored how these people's stories were complicated by the White male privilege in the United States and the male privilege in his native culture. H was challenged to adopt his own ethical and moral stance toward diversity in his family and community.

Guidelines for Working with Racially/Ethnically Mixed Families

Incorporating political processes into family-based interventions is a complex task. In this article we have tried to avoid promoting a particular school or technique of systems intervention. We feel the ideas and guidelines offered can be woven into most conventional models of casework and family therapy. However, the practitioner needs to be able to consider political fac-

tors (i.e., race, ethnicity, gender, class, sexual orientation, oppression) as central to work with clients rather than at the margins.

The following guidelines can facilitate work with racially/ethnically mixed persons and their families.

• *Examine your knowledge and beliefs about what race and ethnicity mean to you.* Track how race and ethnicity have shaped how you engage with others and with whom you interact. How have they affected the way you are treated in different contexts? Examine how you manage diversity issues. For example, what do you privilege and what do you tend to keep private regarding matters of race, ethnicity, class, and sexual orientation in your family?

• *Be open to people with different political positions regarding racial/ethnic issues.* Encourage people to articulate the benefits and difficulties of supporting a monoracial/ethnic or multiracial/ethnic identity in a given context. Keep in mind that Americans tend to see things in monoracial/ethnic terms and to display intolerance for "bi-" or "multi-" labels in general.

• *Remember, "invisibility" is a central component of oppressive practices.* When persons promote a particular aspect of their identity, they make other dimensions of themselves and their community less visible.

• *Help people see that racially/ethnically mixed people's conflict around identity is a reaction to the political hierarchy and oppression of our culture.* This can help counter the internalization of prejudiced thinking that frames identity conflicts as inevitable when mixing distinct races or ethnic groups.

• *In many ways, racially/ethnically mixed people are the least visible minority.* Experiences with people like themselves can help bolster a sense of political power and visibility. Communing with others in similar situations can help these families become more visible in the face of political forces. Organizations uniting "mixed" people and families can be very helpful. See Crohn (1995) for a comprehensive listing of such groups.

• *Help multiracial/ethnic families give voice to*

the traditions, rituals, political aspirations, and aesthetics that make up their legacy. Often, the more privileged persons (White, male, heterosexual) in a family need the most help embracing the mixed status of the family. Because of their relative sense of privilege, majority members often get caught in ethnocentric ways of thinking and become paralyzed by fear and anger, emotions associated with loss of power. For minority, monoracial family members, close identification with mixed status people may raise fears about losing ground in the struggle for political equality. A "mixed" identity can undermine the sense of solidarity and political power resulting from identity with larger monoracial group identities. If one or both parents are monoracial and at a loss in understanding the experiences of a biracial/ethnic child, the fear and anger can become intensified for the children. They may feel that no one shares their "mixed" status and can be a source of support and model in their struggles with being "mixed."

• *Question the system not the individual.* Does the family, school, workplace, and community respect and understand all groups equally? If they do not, why? Can the family use education about diversity, coalition building in their community, planned public confrontation/protest, tolerance, avoidance, and the like to manage the inequities of the social system?

• *Be patient and persistent with yourself and your clients.* It can often take a while to see how oppression based on race/ethnicity and other cultural dimensions can literally determine our patterns of thought and behavior. "Not getting it" can be a symptom, not the cause, of racial/ethnic prejudice.

These guidelines are by no means exhaustive. Families can be ingenious in their ability to adapt and survive. Family members in mixed situations are the ultimate source of guidance on these matters, particularly those who have suffered.

Attending to multiple oppression requires an ethic that values strengths and multiple perspectives. Therapists must allow the ongoing mixing of cultures to inform their therapeutic practices. Our life experience has been indelibly marked by the various multicultural contexts in which we live—racial/ethnic, gender, class, generation, and so forth. The way forward involves appreciation of the context of our lives and the linking of perspectives with others who are both different and similar. Therapists must appreciate the limitations of their own cultural perspectives and appreciate the knowledge and wisdom inherent in multiple perspectives in order to guide multicultural clients through the complex issues of their lives.

REFERENCES

Aldridge, D. (1978). Interracial marriages: Empirical and theoretical considerations. *Journal of Black Studies, 8,* 355–368.

Alland, A. (1971). *Human diversity.* New York: Columbia University Press.

Almeida, R., & Bograd, M. (1990). Sponsorship: Men holding men accountable for domestic violence. *Journal of Feminist Family Therapy, 2,* 243–256.

Almeida, R., Woods, R., Messinie, T., Font, R., & Heer, C. (1994). Violence in the lives of the racially and sexually different. *Journal of Feminist Family Therapy, 5,* 99–126.

Berry, M.F., & Blassingame, J.W. (1982). *Long memory: The black experience in America.* New York: Oxford University Press.

Brown, P.M. (1990). Biracial and social marginality. *Child and Adolescent Social Work, 7,* 319–337.

Comas-Diaz, L. (1994). Latinegra: Mental health issues of African Latinas. *Journal of Feminist Family Therapy, 5,* 35–74.

Crohn, J. (1995). *Mixed matches.* New York: Fawcett Columbine.

Davidson, J. (1992). Theories about black-white interracial marriage: A clinical perspective. *Journal of Multicultural Counseling and Development, 20,* 150–157.

Falicov, C. (1988). Learning to think culturally. In H.A. Liddle, D.C. Breulin, & R. Schwartz (Eds.), *Handbook of family therapy training and supervision* (pp. 335–357). New York: Guilford.

Fish, J.M. (1995). Why psychologists should learn some anthropology. *American Psychologist, 50,* 46–47.

Gibbs, J.T., & Moskowitz-Sweet, G. (1991). Clinical and cultural issues in the treatment of biracial and bicultural adolescents. *Families in Society, 72,* 579–592.

Hines, P.M., Garcia-Preto, N., McGoldrick, M., Almeida, R., & Weltman, S. (1992). Intergenerational relationships across cultures. *Families in Society, 73,* 323–338.

Holt, T.C. (1995). Marking: Race, race-making, and the writing of history. *American Historical Review, 100,* 1–20.

Hooks, B. (1984). *Feminist theory from margin to center.* Boston: South End Press.

Hooks, B. (1990). *Yearning: Race, gender, and cultural*

politics. Boston: South End Press.

Janiewski, D. (1995). Gendering, racializing and classifying: Colonization in the United States, 1590–1990. In D. Stasiulis & N. Yuval-Davis (Eds.), *Unsettling settler societies* (pp. 132–160). Thousand Oaks, CA: Sage Publications.

Kim, C. (1995). *The church and transcultural experience: Women in shadow.* Unpublished doctoral diss., Princeton Theological Seminary, Princeton, NJ.

Lappin, J., Hardy, K.V. (in press). Keeping context in view: The heart of supervision. In T. Todd & C. Storm (Eds.), *The complete systemic supervisor: Context, philosophy, and pragmatics.* Eastham, MA: Allyn & Bacon.

Marks, J. (1995). *Human biodiversity: Genes, race, and history.* New York: Aldine de Gruyter.

McBride, J. (1995). *The color of water.* New York: Riverhead Books.

McGoldrick, M. (1994). Family therapy: Having a place called home. *Journal of Feminist Family Therapy, 5,* 127–156.

McIntosh, P. (1990). *Interactive phases of curricular and personal re-vision with regard to race.* Center for Research on Women, Wellesley College.

Pinderhughes, E.R. (1986). Minority women: A nodal position in the functioning of the social system. In M. Ault-Riche (Ed.), *Women and family therapy* (pp. 51–64). Rockville, MD: Aspen Systems.

Plous, S., & Williams, T. (1995). Racial stereotypes from the days of American slavery: A continuing legacy. *Journal of Applied Social Psychology, 25,* 795–817.

Reynolds, A.L, & Pope, R.L. (1991). The complexities of diversity: Exploring multiple oppressions. *Journal of Counseling and Development, 70,* 174–180.

Root, M.M.P. (1992). *Racially mixed people in America.* Newbury Park, CA: Sage Publications.

Root, M.M.P. (Ed.). (1996). *The multicultural experience.* Thousand Oaks, CA: Sage Publications.

Rosenblatt, P.C., Karis, T.A., & Powell, R.D. (1995). *Multiracial couples.* Thousand Oaks, CA: Sage Publications.

Simpson, G., & Yinger, G. (1985). *Racial and cultural minorities: An analysis of prejudice and discrimination* (5th ed.). New York: Plenum.

Spaights, E., & Dixon, H.E. (1984). Sociopsychological dynamics in pathological Black-White romantic alliances. *Journal of Instructional Psychology, 11,* 132–138.

Stasiulis, D., & Yuval-Davis, N. (Eds.). (1995). *Unsettling settler societies.* Thousand Oaks, CA: Sage Publications.

Terkel, S. (1992). *Race: How blacks and whites think and feel about the American obsession.* New York: New Press.

West, C. (1993). *Race matters.* New York: Vintage Books.

HOMELESS POLICY: THE NEED TO SPEAK TO FAMILIES

Elaine A. Anderson and Sally A. Koblinsky

During the 1980s, Americans saw the rise of a new homeless group—homeless families. Elaine A. Anderson and Sally A. Koblinsky, both in the family studies department at the University of Maryland, College Park, discuss current research on homeless family characteristics and summarize the government's homeless policy.

For years the most popular stereotype of the homeless in the United States was the bum on skid row, drinking wine from a brown paper bag or seeking handouts from passersby. However, during the last decade, the scarcity of affordable housing—coupled with other social and economic changes—thrust many new faces into the homeless population. Unemployed workers, able-bodied veterans, farmers, and runaway youth joined the ranks of the homeless in growing numbers (Rossi, 1990). Perhaps the most distressing change in the composition of the homeless was the increasing number of homeless families. Families with children now represent the fastest growing segment of the homeless, accounting for

From Elaine A. Anderson and Sally A. Koblinsky, "Homeless Policy: The Need to Speak to Families," *Family Relations*, vol. 44, no. 1 (January 1995), pp. 13–18. Copyright 1995 by the National Council on Family Relations, 3989 Central Ave. NE, Suite 550, Minneapolis, MN 55421. Reprinted by permission.

approximately 43% of the homeless population (U.S. Conference of Mayors, 1993). The Institute of Medicine (1988) estimates that as many as 100,000 American children are homeless on any given night. In addition to the "official" homeless, there are countless thousands of families precariously doubled-up with relatives or friends, just one crisis away from becoming homeless.

The present article focuses on homeless families, the "new" group among the homeless. The article summarizes current research on the characteristics of these families, presents a brief history of government homeless policy, and makes suggestions for formulating future homeless policies that incorporate family principles.

Characteristics of Homeless Families

Recognizing that families now constitute a sizeable percentage of the homeless, researchers and policy makers have begun to examine their characteristics. Nine out of 10 homeless families with children are female-headed households with a mean of two children per family (Kondratas, 1991). Three quarters of these families are members of racial and ethnic minority groups. The median age of homeless mothers is in the late 20s, approximately half have never been married, and approximately half have never finished high school (Milburn & Booth, 1990). Most homeless families receive public assistance, including Aid to Families with Dependent Children (AFDC).

Research suggests that many homeless families enter shelters because of a crisis event, such as the loss of a job, illness, change in a personal relationship (e.g., divorce, desertion), or loss of housing due to fire or flood. Homeless mothers have been found to experience a relatively high prevalence of disruptive family events, including divorce, illness, physical abuse, and sexual abuse (Goodman, 1991). Some studies have found that homeless mothers are more likely than housed mothers to experience social isolation and to lack supportive relationships with family, friends, and neighbors (e.g., Bassuk & Rosenberg, 1988). In contrast to single homeless adults only, about 10% of homeless parents report that they have been hospitalized for mental illness or treated for substance abuse (Kondratas, 1991).

The vast majority of families are homeless for economic reasons. As McChesney (1987) reports, most homeless families were poor before they became homeless, frequently living from month to month and struggling to pay their bills. Such families often live in neighborhoods characterized by rampant violence, persistent unemployment, poor schools, and limited access to medical and social services. Although eviction or relationship problems precipitate homelessness for many single-parent households, the reality is that neither welfare payments nor the minimum wage earnings of these low-skilled women are sufficient to pay the rent, cover child care, and meet health care and other living expenses. Such economic problems may increase parental feelings of hopelessness, dependency, and depression, contributing to family dysfunction.

In 1993, the U.S. Conference of Mayors (1993) reported a 13% increase in shelter requests from homeless families over the previous year. However, due to minimal housing resources, the 26 cities surveyed were unable to satisfy almost 30% of family requests for temporary shelter. Homeless families, unlike members of the larger homeless population, generally do not live on the streets. Large numbers of homeless families re-

side in emergency shelters or welfare hotels characterized by crowding, little privacy, high noise levels, and often limited stays. In recent years, some cities have developed transitional housing programs that offer families reduced-rent apartments for one to two years while the parents complete school or job training programs (Bassuk, 1991). Such programs may provide homeless families with supportive services such as day care, employment counseling, GED classes, health care, and substance abuse counseling.

History of Homeless Policy for Families

Many (e.g., Gulati, 1990; McChesney, 1990) argue that changes in federal social policies have played a significant role in the rise in homelessness, and particularly in the increase in the number of homeless families. The Omnibus Reconciliation Act of 1982 removed many of the working poor from AFDC, resulting in sharp reductions in family income. Those who continued to receive aid were also affected because the value of AFDC benefits declined by one-third in constant dollars between 1970 and 1980 (Katz, 1989). The recession between 1980 and 1982 almost doubled the unemployment rate of 1979, and millions of families faced adverse economic events over which they had no control (McChesney, 1989).

As income dropped for many individuals, housing costs rose and the supply of low income housing decreased. New starts for federal low-income housing dropped from 183,000 in 1980 to 28,000 in 1985 (Dolbeare, 1988). Gentrification, urban renewal, and the conversion of hotels and apartments to condominiums further diminished the availability of affordable housing.

Income and housing-related factors continue to play a significant role in the growth of homeless families. In a recent study, it was reported that in 19 of 26 cities surveyed (U.S. Conference on Mayors, 1993) unemployment and underemployment were principal causes of homelessness. Employment alone may not erase the problem of homelessness; indeed, five of the cities in the above study reported that at least 30% of homeless adults were employed in full- or part-time jobs. Families headed by women are particularly vulnerable to high-priced housing markets; rising rents or unexpected expenses may force them into homelessness.

Despite growing public awareness of the homeless during the early 1980s, it was not until June 1987 that Congress passed the first federal comprehensive homeless legislation, the Stewart B. McKinney Homeless Assistance Act (P.L. 100-77). The bill authorized spending for homeless aid, including temporary shelter and housing, job training, health and mental health services, alcohol and other drug abuse services, and education for children and adults. Three years later, the Stewart B. McKinney Homeless Assistance Amendments Act of 1990 expanded the concept of shelter beyond emergency facilities to the provision of "supportive services" for those in shelters and more permanent living facilities (Federal Task Force on Homelessness and Severe Mental Illness, 1992). Supportive services included longer-term transitional housing, child care, job counseling, literacy education, and related activities. In fiscal year (FY) 1994, McKinney Act programs were appropriated almost $1.2 billion, an amount more than double the original FY 1987 appropriation.

The continuing debate over homeless program funding centers around which programs should receive increased financial resources. Emergency shelter providers argue that there remains a need for temporary food and shelter, largely because state budget cuts and continued unemployment have maintained the need for emergency services. Others argue that such emergency assistance merely enables the problem of homelessness to persist, and that investment in more transitional housing with comprehensive services or permanent low-income housing would better help the homeless move toward self-sufficiency.

Both the Clinton Administration and Congress have recognized that homelessness is a growing problem that demands a priority response. The Department of Housing and Urban Development has proposed replacing the current fragmented system of homeless services with a comprehensive "continuum of care" approach (U.S. Department of Housing and Urban Development, 1994).

This strategy would help communities design and implement a system of transition from the streets to emergency shelter; from emergency shelter to transitional housing (if necessary); and ultimately to permanent housing, jobs, and independent living. The plan, to be coordinated by the Federal Interagency Council on the Homeless, would link local governments, federal agencies, nonprofit organizations, and shelters to bring a coordinated effort to the problem. Proposals to build stronger linkages between local housing, employment offices, school districts, social service providers, and homeless advocates are aimed at breaking the cycle of homelessness and preventing future episodes of homelessness.

Incorporating Family Principles in Homeless Policy

Recent policy initiatives that focus on access to housing and social services can play an important role in improving the well-being of homeless families. However, policy makers should also consider family principles when designing homeless family policy (Family Impact Seminar, 1988). Such principles recognize the diversity of family life, and reinforce marital, parental, and family commitment and stability. The principles further acknowledge the interdependence of family relationships, as well as the contribution of social support to optimal family functioning. Finally, family principles encourage professionals to collaborate with family members as partners in human service delivery.

Many of the current policies devised to combat family homelessness assess outcomes for individuals, rather than focus on the family unit (Shinn & Weitzman, 1990). Moreover, the majority of these policies are short term and crisis oriented (Bassuk, 1991). In homeless policy making, the absence of a family perspective that addresses prevention as well as short- and long-term intervention may result in policies and programs that have negative effects on family life.

Professionals involved in developing public or private homeless policies must critically assess how their policies, programs, or services affect family functions, family relationships, and family cohesion. Specifically, policy makers should examine how policies influence the family's ability to remain a unit and to provide economic support, health care, education, and physical protection to its members. Local policy, particularly that related to human service delivery, should also assess the extent to which policies enable homeless parents to develop family identity and autonomy, provide intimacy and caring, establish social control, and transmit values and traditions to their children.

The importance of the family should be recognized in the process of homeless policy making and policy analysis, whether it be at the federal, state, or local levels. The following seven recommendations provide a foundation for developing homeless policies that are sensitive to family needs.

Recognize Diversity Among Families

Policy makers and service providers often treat homeless families as a homogeneous group. Drawing on research that summarizes the characteristics of homeless individuals, social service professionals often focus on what is "wrong" with the homeless, including the prevalence of mental illness, substance abuse, and other problems (Shinn & Weitzman, 1990). Appropriate services are developed to address these deficiencies. This victim blaming approach may reinforce stereotypes about the entire population of homeless families, and distract attention from the causes and consequences of homelessness for individual families.

In fact, homeless families have diverse backgrounds and needs. Examples of this diversity, compiled from the authors' study of homeless families in Baltimore and Washington, DC, are presented below:

The Sawyers, a white family from Alabama with four children, moved to Baltimore when Mr. Sawyer lost his job at a poultry plant. For five months, the family lived with friends in Baltimore City and Mr. Sawyer worked occasionally as a janitor. Their friends asked them to leave the apartment when the landlord threatened to evict both families. After staying in a motel for a week, the family ran out of funds and sought emergency shelter. Mrs. Sawyer and her three younger children were housed in one city shelter, but the shelter did not permit her 14-year-old son, Robbie, to stay with his mother and siblings. Robbie was temporarily placed in foster care and Mr. Sawyer moved into a men's shelter. After being robbed in the shelter, Mr. Sawyer began sleeping in the bus station and seeking odd jobs during the day in an effort to earn enough money to reunite his family.

Ms. Rodriguez, a Hispanic single mother with a 4-year-old daughter, became homeless when her boyfriend became addicted to crack cocaine. Ms. Rodriguez and her daughter entered a church-sponsored shelter for women and families. The family was grateful for a place to stay, but were unhappy with the mealtimes (6:30 a.m. breakfast, 7 p.m. dinner), the restricted playroom hours, and the rules that required children and parents to be in bed by 8 p.m. Ms. Rodriguez quickly developed a close relationship with another homeless mother in the shelter. She enrolled in the AFDC program, but after two months, expressed interest in obtaining a secretarial job. However, the shelter had no child care facility and shelter policies prevented Ms. Rodriguez from leaving her daughter in the care of her new friend.

Ms. Ward is an African American single mother of two sons, an infant and a preschool child. A lifetime resident of Washington, DC, Ms. Ward became homeless when her mother died, because her AFDC check was not sufficient to pay the rent on her mother's apartment. After spending six months in three emergency shelters, she was admitted to a transitional housing program where she could live for up to 18 months. The housing facility was located on the other side of the city from where Ms. Ward had grown up. Ms. Ward wanted to continue taking her son, Dante, to his old Head Start program, but her caseworker told her the busfare was too expensive and moved Dante to a closer Head Start center. The caseworker arranged for Ms. Ward to attend a computer training program and she was pleased about the possibility of obtaining a future job. However, she desperately missed her old friends and couldn't attend the Baptist church in her old neighborhood because the shelter required her to take "front desk duty" on Sundays.

As these cases illustrate, homeless families differ along many dimensions, including family structure, family size, racial/cultural background, housing history, and pathways to homelessness (e.g., job loss, substance abuse problems, death of a family member). Other family variables further differentiate homeless families: extent of parental education, intergenerational interaction, family cohesion, family conflict, life stress, and amount of social support. Homeless families also differ in their need for community resources, such as food, housing, education, or protection from abusive family members.

Homeless policies and programs must be sensitive and responsive to the diversity of homeless family life. In addition to identifying individual family problems (e.g., health/mental health status of members), family professionals must investigate other factors that may have contributed to the family's homelessness, such as poverty, unemployment, illiteracy, and destruction of low-income housing. Research on both the underlying causes of homelessness and the characteristics of homeless families is essential when analyzing and selecting policy options for sheltering and assisting needy families.

Service providers who work with homeless families must have extensive resource networks to address the diverse needs of their clients. Providers must be able to respond quickly to specific requests for help with food, shelter, a sick child, or transportation to a job interview. Because some homeless families receive assistance from multiple providers, efforts must often be made to coordinate or consolidate fragmented social and health care services. Policies must further recognize that the emergencies of homeless families occur at odd hours and in varied settings;

flexibility is essential in addressing each family's unique needs.

Foster Family Stability

Families generally serve their functions best when the individuals in the family have access to other members, including contact between generations. Public policies on homeless issues such as housing, psychosocial support services, education, and day care can foster, limit, or completely cut off contact among family members. For example, in the U.S. Conference of Mayors (1993) report, it was acknowledged that in 64% of the cities surveyed, homeless families may have to separate in order to obtain accommodation in emergency shelters. As in the case of the Sawyer family described above, emergency shelter policies often prevent fathers and boys over 10 or 12 years of age from residing with mothers and younger children (Mihaly, 1989). Sometimes older boys are separated from their families and placed in foster care.

Homeless policy initiatives must consider how policy alternatives foster or discourage family contact. Efforts should be made to shelter family members in the same facility, and to preserve and increase the stability of the family. Policies should strengthen marital, parental, and other relationship commitments, except when these relationships threaten to harm family members. For example, service providers should develop strategies and design shelter environments that support family intimacy, encourage family routines, provide opportunities for parent/child interaction (e.g., scheduled family hours in the children's playroom), and enable families to maintain religious and ethnic traditions.

Family professionals who work with homeless families must also recognize that family stability is threatened by change. When families make the transition from homeless shelters to transitional or permanent housing, providers must help family members establish new support networks, make certain that children are receiving appropriate school services, and insure that parents are able to pursue their vocational and family goals in their new housing arrangements.

Empower Families to Become Self-Sufficient

In an effort to assist homeless families and particularly homeless mothers, service providers may assume a paternalistic attitude toward their clients. Homeless mothers are perceived as dependent caregivers, who receive benefits (e.g., AFDC, shelter) because of their helplessness (Coontz, 1992). This perspective justifies interventions that demand certain behaviors of the homeless families in order for them to continue receiving assistance. Such paternalism may deprive homeless parents of a sense of power and control over their lives, and prevent the development of a collaborative relationship between service providers and homeless shelter residents.

Overwhelmed by the urgent needs of their clients, family professionals charged with case management may assume full responsibility for obtaining an array of services for homeless families, including health care, mental health counseling, food, substance abuse treatment, education, job training, and child care. Although their efforts are well intentioned, it must be recognized that a major goal of homeless programs is to empower families and help them become self-sufficient. Homeless programs should not take ownership of the problems of homeless families; rather, they should prepare family members to work more effectively with agencies and institutions to obtain the services their families need.

Service providers with predetermined notions of client needs and priorities cannot adequately help family members develop a sense of self-efficacy. Such providers must learn to respect the views and goals of members of homeless families, and to work as partners with homeless parents to promote family well-being (Bassuk, 1990). Family professionals can help to empower homeless clients by including them in the development and implementation of their case management plans. Efforts can be made to teach homeless parents how to access needed services and acquire skills that promote economic and emotional security. Policies should empower homeless adults to make and carry out the decisions that affect their lives.

Sheltered families suffer from a lack of privacy. In some facilities, an entire family resides in a single room; in other barracks-style shelters, sheets hung between the beds may be the only barriers separating families. Dining and bathroom facilities are often shared by all shelter residents. This lack of privacy forces homeless parents to conduct almost every aspect of parenting in full public view (Boxill & Beaty, 1990). Parents are forced to express the joys and frustrations of parenting in the presence of strangers, where their behavior is often judged and criticized by others. Such scrutiny may create substantial stress and contribute to an "unraveling of the parent role," with parents giving up some of their traditional duties and responsibilities (Boxill & Beaty, 1990).

Either as a consequence of parental abdication or efforts to help their clients, shelter providers and volunteers who work with homeless families often assume the parenting functions of the homeless adults. In one observational study of public night shelters, researchers discovered that shelter staff made the decisions about children's meals, children's play schedules, family rest times, bath times, and when the lights were to be turned on and off (Boxill & Beaty, 1990). In the case of Ms. Rodriguez described above, the Baltimore shelter personnel determined mealtimes, playroom hours, bed times, and who could serve as a child-care provider. The shelter caseworker of another homeless parent, Ms. Ward, determined that her son should be moved to a new Head Start center, rather than help his mother develop a plan to keep him in his original program. When homeless parents are deprived of opportunities to serve as the primary decision makers, nurturers, and teachers of their children, they may lose confidence in their parenting abilities and begin to withdraw from their children (Boxill & Beaty, 1990).

Homeless service providers should respect the autonomy of homeless families and encourage parents to make choices and decisions for their children. In some shelters, policies should be modified to enable parents to become involved in choosing and preparing meals; determining play, bed, and meal times; and setting rules for children's behavior. Opportunities should be provided for parents to participate in selecting child care and educational placements for their children. When possible, shelter space should be allocated for rooms where parents can spend private time teaching and playing with their children.

In some cases, the homeless parents' history of family dysfunction may result in their use of parenting practices that fail to nurture children adequately or manage their behavior appropriately (e.g., harsh physical punishment for misbehavior). Shelter staff can provide educational programs and individual counseling to teach homeless parents about child development, effective discipline, child health, and ways to facilitate children's cognitive, motor, and social development (Walsh, 1990). Family professionals can work with homeless parents to establish support groups that will enable parents to discuss the effects of homelessness on their children, and to share strategies for strengthening parent/child relationships.

While encouraging homeless parents' active involvement in childrearing, family professionals must continue to be sensitive to the many burdens that tax homeless caregivers. Homeless parents, the majority of whom are single, must often deal with the competing demands of locating housing, job training, employment, health care, child care, and other services. Homeless parents may also experience additional personal problems, such as domestic violence, the illness of a family member, substance abuse, depression, or low self-esteem. Expecting these homeless families to handle it all alone is just as unrealistic as expecting middle class families to be able to function successfully without supports such as child care, carpooling, or flexible work hours (Glazer, 1993). Efforts to provide homeless families with occasional respite care, transportation assistance, and related support services may play an important role in helping them to cope with their basic survival, social, and emotional needs.

Because families are systems, anything that affects one family member will have an impact on others within the family, including those in older and future generations. A homeless mother's needs cannot be addressed in isolation from those of her children, nor can a child's needs be met without considering the mother. For example, when policies require homeless mothers to work, attend job training, participate in drug treatment, or search for housing, provision must be made for child care. Unstable, inadequate child care may contribute to children's development of health problems, developmental delays, or behavioral disturbances. Likewise, maternal concerns about poor quality child care can undermine a homeless mother's motivation to continue with education or employment and impede her transition to self-sufficiency.

Homeless policies must recognize that families are multigenerational units. Service providers need to work with two, if not three, generations. Efforts to support homeless parents and other adult family members will better equip these individuals to nurture and educate their own children. Shelter activities (e.g., special dinners, children's programs, Al-Anon) that unite homeless families with important family members who live outside the shelter may help to maintain family communication and strengthen family bonds. Permanently housed family members may have the opportunity to observe changes in homeless adults' parenting practices, life skills (e.g., money management, cooking) and job preparation, as well as their potential resolution of substance abuse problems. Regular family contact may reduce some of the embarrassment and shame that some families experience about their homeless family members, and encourage their involvement in helping the homeless family to return to the community.

Build Social Support Networks

For many homeless families, housing alone is not sufficient to meet the family's support needs. Becoming homeless not only means losing physical shelter, but may also result in loss of connection to family members, friends, and other sources of support. Before becoming homeless, many families double-up with family and friends in overcrowded living situations, straining relationships, depleting resources, and even destroying social support networks (Shinn, Knickman, & Weitzman, 1991). When they become homeless, these families are faced with having to rebuild a community of caring individuals who can help them meet their economic and psychosocial needs.

Some homeless families develop a new concept of family that includes not only one's family of origin or procreation, but also one's present "family of function" (Anderson, 1989). Although members of the latter family are not biologically or legally related, they perform the affectional and instrumental functions of traditional families. In the case of single-parent homeless families, the functional family may include one's non-marital partner and other close friends. For homeless families in doubled-up living arrangements, the family may include non-related individuals who provide emotional and material support.

Service providers who work with homeless families must recognize that families have varying structures and compositions. The middle-class nuclear family is certainly not the sole model of family stability. As a result of economic necessity and cultural traditions, many different household arrangements have developed into strong and adaptive families. When working with homeless clients, service providers should recognize that many homeless parents receive considerable support from their families of function. For example, homeless families living in shelters may rely on other sheltered parents to carry out traditional family roles, such as provision of child care, or assistance with food, clothing, and transportation. Equally important, these families of function may provide homeless parents with information, guidance, companionship, and reassurance of personal worth.

Strengthen Neighborhoods and Communities

Homeless individuals, like those who are housed, come from communities with strengths and weaknesses. Many urban homeless families grew up in neighborhoods that are now plagued with violence, crime, and substance abuse that threaten family safety and security. Rural home-

less families may be residents of communities that have become depleted of resources due to obsolete industries, downsizing of business, or limited educational and training opportunities.

Family professionals must recognize that solutions to homelessness require the strengthening of both the family and community environments. Strong communities provide adequate housing and economic opportunities, address the family's educational and public safety needs, and promote self-sufficiency and family pride. Although the revitalization of threatened communities will require a massive investment of public and private funds and energy, family professionals must continue to pursue comprehensive strategies for healing communities at the same time they work to empower individual families.

In evaluating the neighborhoods and communities of homeless families, policy makers and service providers should focus on strengths as well as weaknesses. A large percentage of homeless parents seek shelter in the same towns and cities where they grew up, and have deep roots in the community. As in the case of the homeless mother, Ms. Ward, many homeless parents have strong ties to churches, Head Start centers, public schools, and social groups.

Homeless programs should address local needs and build on community strengths. Homeless families should be helped to maintain their ties to formal and informal institutions that can offer social support networks. There are many ways in which service providers can help to integrate homeless families into the larger community, for example: including shelter residents as part of neighborhood community organizations that address issues of housing, child care, outdoor recreation, or crime prevention; transporting homeless families to churches, school meetings, and libraries; enrolling homeless children in neighborhood sports or scouting groups; or helping homeless parents join clubs and recreational activities in areas of personal interest. Building community ties may help to reduce the depression and loneliness experienced by many homeless parents and children (Bassuk, Rubin, & Lauriat, 1986), and may assist the family's transition to permanent housing. Moreover, the maintenance of such linkages may increase non-homeless citizens' awareness of the family values, needs, and goals they share with their homeless neighbors.

Conclusions

Homeless policy makers must recognize that good public policy strengthens and supports families. Interventions designed to assist homeless families should be based on an understanding of the dynamics and diverse characteristics of the families to be served. Homeless policies and programs should aim to increase the stability, integrity, and dignity of the homeless family. Homeless families will benefit from efforts to increase their sense of power and self-esteem, enhance their parenting and self-sufficiency skills, and strengthen their support systems within families and communities

Comprehensive homeless policies should not only seek to improve the welfare of individual families, but should also advocate change in social structures, policies, and values that contribute to the causes of homelessness. Policies must address such issues as wage levels, unemployment, illiteracy, welfare assistance, mental health care, fair market rentals, and the availability of low-income housing. Policy makers who use family principles to formulate homeless policy may not only improve the immediate quality of homeless family life, but may also save tax dollars and protect future generations from the tragedy of homelessness.

REFERENCES

Anderson, E.A. (1989). Implications for Public Policy: Towards a pro-family AIDS social policy. In E. Macklin (Ed.), *AIDS and families* (pp. 187–228). Binghamton, NY: Harrington Park Press, Inc.

Bassuk, E.L. (1990). General principles of family-oriented care: Working effectively with clients. In E.L. Bassuk, R. Carman, L. Weinred, & M. Herzig (Eds.), *Community care for homeless families: A program design manual* (pp. 25–31). Newton, MA: Better Homes Foundation.

Bassuk, E.L. (1991). Homeless families. *Scientific American, 265*(6), 66–74.

Bassuk, E.L., & Rosenberg, L. (1988). Why does family homelessness occur? A case-control study. *American Journal of Public Health, 78*, 783–787.

Bassuk, E.L., Rubin, L., & Lauriat, A.S. (1986). Characteristics of sheltered homeless families. *American Journal of Public Health, 76*, 1097–1101.

Boxill, N.A., & Beaty, A.L. (1990). Mother/child interaction among homeless women and their children in a public night shelter in Atlanta, Georgia. *Child and Youth Services, 14*, 49–64.

Coontz, S. (1992). *The way we never were: American families and the nostalgia trap.* New York: Basic Books.

Dolbeare, C. (1988, November). *The low-income housing crisis and its impact on homelessness.* Paper presented at the Advisory Committee on Intergovernmental Relations Policy Conference, "Assisting the Homeless in an Era of Retrenchment," Washington, DC.

Family Impact Seminar. (1988). *Incorporating family criteria in policymaking and program evaluation.* Washington, DC: Author.

Federal Task Force on Homelessness and Severe Mental Illness. (1992). *Outcasts on Main Street.* Washington, DC: Interagency Task Force on Homelessness.

Glazer, N.Y. (1993). *Women's paid and unpaid work.* Philadelphia: Temple University Press.

Goodman, L.A. (1991). The prevalence of abuse among homeless and housed poor mothers: A comparison study. *American Journal of Orthopsychiatry, 61*, 489–500.

Gulati, P. (1990). Ideology, public policy and homeless families. *Journal of Sociology and Social Welfare, 45*(8), 113–128.

Institute of Medicine. (1988). *Homelessness, health and human needs.* Washington, DC: National Academy Press.

Katz, B. (1989). *The undeserving poor.* New York: Pantheon.

Kondratas, S.A. (1991). Ending homelessness: Policy challenges. *American Psychologist, 46,* 1226–1231.

McChesney, K.Y. (1987). *Characteristics of the residents of two inner-city emergency shelters for the homeless.* Los Angeles: University of Southern California, Social Sciences Research Institute.

McChesney, K.Y. (1989, April). *Macroeconomic issues in poverty: Implications for child and youth homelessness.* Paper presented at the Conference of the Institute for Policy Studies, Johns Hopkins University, "Homeless Children and Youth: Coping with a National Tragedy," Baltimore, MD.

McChesney, K.Y. (1990). Family homelessness: A systemic problem. *Journal of Social Issues, 46*, 191–205.

Mihaly, L. (1989, April). *Beyond the numbers: Homeless families with children.* Paper presented at Conference of the Institute for Policy Studies, Johns Hopkins University, "Homeless Children and Youth: Coping with a National Tragedy," Baltimore, MD.

Milburn, N.G., & Booth, J. (1990). Sociodemographic, homeless state, and mental health characteristics of women in shelters: Preliminary findings. *Urban Research Review, 12*(2) 1–4.

Rossi, P.H. (1990). The old homeless and the new

homeless in historical perspective. *American Psychologist, 45*, 954–959.

Shinn, M., Knickman, J.R., & Weitzman, B.C. (1991). Social relationships and vulnerability to becoming homeless among poor families. *American Psychologist, 46*, 1180–1187.

Shinn, M., & Weitzman, B.C. (1990). Research on homelessness: An introduction. *Journal of Social Issues, 46*, 1–11.

U.S. Conference of Mayors. (1993). *A status report on hunger and homelessness in America's cities: A 26-city survey.* Washington, DC: Author.

U.S. Department of Housing and Urban Development. (1994). *FY 1995 Budget: Executive Summary.* Washington, DC: Author.

Walsh, M.E. (1990). Development and socio-emotional needs of homeless infants and preschoolers. In E.L. Bassuk, R. Carman, L. Weinred, & M. Herzig (Eds.), *Community care for homeless families: A program design manual* (pp. 91–100). Newton, MA: Better Homes Foundation.

DISCUSSION QUESTIONS

1. Do you think that American families, in general, are in a state of decline? Or are American families simply changing and becoming more diverse? Why?

2. Americans have become more tolerant of a variety of family forms in recent decades. What accounts for the diversity of present-day families?

3. Are the many different family forms a threat to the traditional family? Why or why not?

WEBSITES

nch.ari.net/

The National Coalition to End Homelessness is an advocacy network whose website offers a comprehensive list of resources concerning homelessness.

www.nethelp.no/cindy/biling-fam.html

The Bilingual Families Web Page provides bilingual parents with information and resources to help them raise their children bilingually.

PART II

ESTABLISHING INTIMATE RELATIONSHIPS

CONTENTS

PART II: ESTABLISHING INTIMATE RELATIONSHIPS

CHAPTER 3: GENDER ROLES
    READING 6: PARENTS, CHILDREN, AND GENDER ROLES   55
    READING 7: FAMILIES AND GENDER EQUITY   59

CHAPTER 4: LOVE, DATING, AND MATE SELECTION
    READING 8: THE ORIGIN OF ROMANTIC LOVE AND HUMAN FAMILY LIFE   65
    READING 9: LOVE LESSONS   69
    READING 10: MATE SELECTION PREFERENCES AMONG AFRICAN
    AMERICAN COLLEGE STUDENTS   75

CHAPTER 5: HUMAN SEXUALITY/SEXUAL EXPRESSION
    READING 11: TEENS AND SEX   86
    READING 12: HOW MEN VIEW SEX, CONTRACEPTION, AND
    CHILD REARING   91

CHAPTER 3: GENDER ROLES

All societies assign specific traits, behaviors, and patterns of social interaction to their members on the basis of sex. Across cultures, the male-female distinction is given meanings and rankings of importance that have a wide range of implications for individuals, families, and the larger society.

Individuals, especially children, assemble ideas through the socialization process about appearance, personality, and behaviors that are identified as female or male. In other words, we learn our appropriate gender role. Gender roles give us information on how to dress and behave, how to walk and talk, what activities we like to engage in, and what skills we develop. Traditional gender traits of femaleness/femininity stress passivity, dependence, emotionality, weakness, and nurturance. In contrast, maleness/masculinity in our society has been defined in terms of being tough, aggressive, independent, strong, and competitive. The two readings in this chapter emphasize how the traditional differentiation of male and female roles has come into serious question in the United States and how gender roles directly affect the family.

Gender role socialization usually begins in the home; learned gender messages then are reinforced in schools, the mass media, and peer interactions. As pointed out in Susan Witt's article, the primary influence on a child's gender role development occurs within the family setting, with parents teaching gendered behavior and attitudes. Witt suggests that an androgynous gender role orientation in the home is more beneficial to children than rigid and stereotyped gender roles. She encourages parents to raise girls and boys alike in order to produce men and women equal in capabilities and social status.

However, the second reading, "Families and Gender Equity" by Scott Coltrane, documents how gender inequality still exists and affects patterns of family life. He notes, for example, that though employment opportunities have been expanded for females, resulting in a growing number of women now working outside the home, women still are paid less than men. And while husbands now are more likely to share in housework and child rearing, wives still must shoulder most of this responsibility. Coltrane advocates additional gender equity in the family and in society.

PARENTS, CHILDREN, AND GENDER ROLES

Susan D. Witt

As children move through childhood and into adolescence, they are exposed to many factors which influence their attitudes and behaviors regarding gender roles. These attitudes and behaviors are generally learned first in the home and are then reinforced by the child's peers, school experience, and television viewing. However, the strongest influence on gender role development seems to occur within the family setting, with parents passing on, both overtly and covertly, their own beliefs about gender. Susan D. Witt, who teaches in the School of Home Economics and Family Ecology at the University of Akron, reviews the impact of parental influence on gender role development and suggests that an androgynous gender role orientation may be beneficial to children.

Children learn at a very early age what it means to be a boy or a girl in our society. Through myriad activities, opportunities, encouragements, discouragements, overt behaviors, covert suggestions, and various forms of guidance, children experience the process of gender role socialization. It is difficult for a child to grow to adulthood without experiencing some form of gender bias or stereotyping, whether it be the ex-

pectation that boys are better than girls at math or the idea that only females can nurture children. As children grow and develop, the gender stereotypes they are exposed to at home are reinforced by other elements in their environment and are thus perpetuated throughout childhood and on into adolescence (Martin, Wood, & Little, 1990).

A child's burgeoning sense of self, or self-concept, is a result of the multitude of ideas, attitudes, behaviors, and beliefs to which he or she is exposed. The information that surrounds the child and which is internalized comes to the child within the family arena through parent-child interactions, role modeling, reinforcement for desired behaviors, and parental approval or disapproval (Santrock, 1994). As children move into the larger world of friends and school, many of their ideas and beliefs are reinforced by those around them. A further reinforcement of acceptable and appropriate behavior is shown to children through the media, in particular, television. Through all these socialization agents, children learn gender stereotyped behavior. As children develop, these stereotypes become firmly entrenched beliefs and thus, are a part of the child's self-concept. Figure 1 illustrates some of the factors involved in parental influence on a child's self concept.

Parental Influence

A child's earliest exposure to what it means to be male or female comes from parents (Lauer &

From Susan D. Witt, "Parental Influence on Children's Socialization to Gender Roles," *Adolescence*, vol. 32, no. 126 (Summer 1997), pp. 253–58. Reprinted by permission of Libra Publishers.

Lauer, 1994; Santrock, 1994; Kaplan, 1991). From the time their children are babies, parents treat sons and daughters differently, dressing infants in gender-specific colors, giving gender-differentiated toys, and expecting different behavior from boys and girls (Thorne, 1993). One study indicates that parents have differential expectations of sons and daughters as early as 24 hours after birth (Rubin, Provenzano, & Luria, 1974).

Children internalize parental messages regarding gender at an early age, with awareness of adult sex role differences being found in two-year-old children (Weinraub et al., 1984). One study found that children at two and a half years of age use gender stereotypes in negotiating their world and are likely to generalize gender stereotypes to a variety of activities, objects, and occupations (Fagot, Leinbach, & O'Boyle, 1992; Cowan & Hoffman, 1986). Children even deny the reality of what they are seeing when it does not conform to their gender expectations (i.e., a child whose mother is a doctor stating that only men are doctors) (Sheldon, 1990).

Sons have a definite edge as far as parental preference for children is concerned. Most parents prefer male children throughout the world (Steinbacher & Holmes in Basow, 1992, p. 129). Also, people who prefer sons are more likely to use technology for selecting the sex of their child (Steinbacher & Gilroy, 1990). This preference for male children is further emphasized by the finding that parents are more likely to continue having children if they have only girls than if they have only boys (Hoffman, 1977).

Reasons given by women for their preference for sons are to please their husbands, to carry on the family name, and to be a companion to the husband. Reasons for wanting daughters include having a companion for themselves and to have fun dressing a girl and doing her hair (Hoffman, 1977).

Parents encourage their sons and daughters to participate in sex-typed activities, including doll playing and engaging in housekeeping activities for girls and playing with trucks and engaging in sports activities for boys (Eccles, Jacobs, & Harold, 1990). Children's toy preferences have

Figure 1. Parents' Influence on Child's Self-Concept

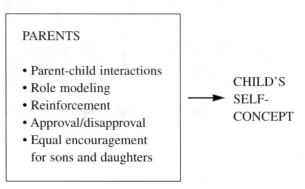

been found to be significantly related to parental sex-typing (Etaugh & Liss, 1992; Henshaw, Kelly, & Gratton, 1992; Paretti & Sydney, 1984), with parents providing gender-differentiated toys and rewarding play behavior that is gender stereotyped (Carter, 1987). While both mothers and fathers contribute to the gender stereotyping of their children, fathers have been found to reinforce gender stereotypes more often than do mothers (Ruble, 1988).

A study of children's rooms has shown that girls' rooms have more pink, dolls, and manipulative toys; boys' rooms have more blue, sports equipment, tools, and vehicles (Pomerleau, Bolduc, Malcuit, & Cossette, 1990). Boys are more likely to have maintenance chores around the house, such as painting and mowing the lawn, while girls are likely to have domestic chores such as cooking and doing the laundry (Basow, 1992). This assignment of household tasks by gender leads children to link certain types of work with gender.

Some studies have suggested that parent shaping as a socializing factor has little impact on a child's sex role development (Lytton & Romney, 1991; Maccoby & Jacklin, 1980). Other research, however, suggests that parents are the primary influence on gender role development during the early years of life (Santrock, 1994; Miller & Lane in Berryman-Fink, Ballard-Reisch, & Newman, 1993; Kaplan, 1991). Because socialization is a two-way interaction, each person in the interaction influences the other (Lewis & Rosenblum, 1974); thus, parents and children engage in reciprocal interaction, with children both responding to and eliciting behaviors (Kaplan, 1991). Also, development is influenced by many social factors, and children may best be understood in terms of their environment (Bronfenbrenner, Alvarez, & Henderson, 1984).

Many studies have shown that parents treat sons and daughters differently (Jacklin, DiPietro, & Maccoby; Woolett, White, & Lyon; Parke & O'Leary, in Hargreaves & Colley, 1986; Snow, Jacklin, & Maccoby, 1983; Power, 1981). The parent-child relationship has effects on development that last well into adulthood. Because of these long-lasting effects, the parent-child relationship is one of the most important developmental factors for the child (Miller & Lane in Berryman-Fink et al., 1993).

Parental attitudes toward their children have a strong impact on their developing sense of self and self-esteem, with parental warmth and support being key factors (Richards, Gitelson, Petersen, & Hartig, 1991). Often, parents send subtle messages regarding gender and what is acceptable for each gender—messages which are internalized by the developing child (Arliss, 1991). Sex role stereotypes are well established in early childhood. Messages about what is appropriate based on gender are so strong, that even when children are exposed to different attitudes and experiences, they will revert to stereotyped choices (Haslett, Geis, & Carter, 1992).

Gender Roles

While there may be some benefit to adhering to strict gender role stereotypes (i.e., providing a sense of security, facilitating decision making), there are also costs involved in the maintenance of gender role stereotypes. These costs include limiting opportunities for both boys and girls, ignoring talent, and perpetuating unfairness in our society (Beal, 1994). Parents who espouse an egalitarian attitude regarding gender roles are more likely to foster this attitude in their children. Androgynous individuals have been found to have higher self-esteem (Lundy & Rosenberg, 1987; Shaw, 1983; Heilbrun, 1981), higher levels of identity achievement (Orlofsky, 1977), and

more flexibility in dating and love relationships (DeLucia, 1987).

Children whose parents have strong egalitarian values tend to be more knowledgeable about non-sex-typed objects and occupations than are other children (Weisner & Wilson-Mitchell, 1990). Children whose mothers work outside the home are not as traditional in sex role orientation as those whose mothers stay home (Weinraub, Jaeger, & Hoffman, 1988). In fact, preschool children whose mothers work outside the home experience the world with a sense that everyone in the family gets to become a member of the outside world, and their sense of self includes the knowledge that they have the ability to make choices which are not hindered by gender (Davies & Banks, 1992).

Families with one or more androgynous parents (i.e., a mother who repairs the family car or a father who bakes cookies for the PTA meeting) have been found to score highest in parental warmth and support. These androgynous parents are found to be highly encouraging regarding achievement and developing a sense of self-worth in sons and daughters (Sedney, 1987; Spence & Helmreich, 1980). Because of the strong influence of parents on gender role socialization, those parents who wish to be gender fair and encourage the best in both their sons and daughters would do well to adopt an androgynous gender role orientation and encourage the same in their children.

REFERENCES

Arliss, L.P. (1991). *Gender communication*. Englewood Cliffs, NJ: Prentice-Hall.

Basow, S.A. (1992). *Gender stereotypes and roles, 3rd ed.* Pacific Grove, CA: Brooks/Cole.

Beal, C. (1994). *Boys and girls: The development of gender roles.* New York: McGraw-Hill.

Berryman-Fink, C., Ballard-Reisch, D., & Newman, L. H. (1993). *Communication and sex role socialization.* New York: Garland Publishing.

Bronfenbrenner, U., Alvarez, W., & Henderson, C. (1984). Working and watching: Maternal employment in parents' perceptions of their three-year-old children. *Child Development, 55,* 1362–1378.

Carter, D.C. (1987). *Current conceptions of sex roles and sex typing: Theory and research.* New York: Praeger.

Cowan, G., & Hoffman, C.D. (1986). Gender stereotyping in young children: Evidence to support a concept-learning approach. *Sex Roles, 14,* 211–224.

Davies, B., & Banks, C. (1992). The gender trap: A feminist poststructuralist analysis of primary school children's talk about gender. *Journal of Curriculum Studies, 24,* 1–25.

DeLucia, J.L. (1987). Gender role identity and dating behavior: What is the relationship? *Sex Roles, 17,* 153–161.

Eccles, J.S., Jacobs, J.E., & Harold, R.D. (1990). Gender role stereotypes, expectancy effects, and parents' socialization of gender differences. *Journal of Social Issues, 46,* 186–201.

Etaugh, C., & Liss, M.B. (1992). Home, school, and playroom: Training grounds for adult gender roles. *Sex Roles, 26,* 129–147.

Fagot, B.I., Leinbach, M.D., & O'Boyle, C. (1992). Gender labeling, gender stereotyping, and parenting behaviors. *Developmental Psychology, 28,* 225–230.

Hargreaves, D., & Colley, A. (1986). *The psychology of sex roles.* London: Harper & Row.

Haslett, B., Geis, F.L., & Carter, M.R. (1992). *The organizational woman: Power and paradox.* Norwood, NJ: Ablex.

Heilbrun, A.B. (1981). Gender differences in the functional linkage between androgyny, social cognition, and competence. *Journal of Personality and Social Psychology, 41,* 1106–1114.

Henshaw, A., Kelly, J., & Gratton, C. (1992). Skipping's for girls: Children's perceptions of gender roles and gender preferences. *Educational Research, 34,* 229–235.

Hoffman, L.W. (1977). Changes in family roles, socialization, and sex differences. *American Psychologist, 42,* 644–657.

Kaplan, P. (1991). *A child's odyssey.* St. Paul: West Publishing Company.

Lauer, R.H., & Lauer, J.C. (1994). *Marriage and family: The quest for intimacy.* Madison: Brown & Benchmark.

Lewis, M., & Rosenblum, L.A. (1974). The effect of the infant on its caregiver. New York: Wiley.

Lundy, A., & Rosenberg, J.A. (1987). Androgyny, masculinity, and self-esteem. *Social Behavior and Personality, 15,* 91–95.

Lytton, H., & Romney, D.M. (1991). Parents' differential socialization of boys and girls: A meta-analysis. *Psychological Bulletin, 109,* 267–296.

Maccoby, E.E., & Jacklin, C.N. (1980). Psychological sex differences. In M. Rutter (Ed.), *Scientific foundations of child psychiatry.* London: Heineman Medical.

Martin, C.L., Wood, C.H., & Little, J.K. (1990). The development of gender stereotype components. *Child Development, 61,* 1891–1904.

Orlofsky, J.L. (1977). Sex role orientation, identity formation, and self-esteem in college men and women. *Sex Roles, 3,* 561–574.

Paretti, P.O., & Sydney, T.M. (1984). Parental toy choice stereotyping and its effect on child toy preference and sex role typing. *Social Behavior and Personality, 12,* 213–216.

Pomerleau, A., Bolduc, D., Malcuit, G., & Cossette, L. (1990). Pink or blue: Environmental gender stereotypes in the first two years of life. *Sex Roles, 22,* 359–367.

Power, T. (1981). Sex typing in infancy: The role of the father. *Infant Mental Health Journal, 2,* 226–240.

Richards, M.H., Gitelson, I.B., Peterson, A.C., & Hartig, A.L. (1991). Adolescent personality in girls and boys: The role of mothers and fathers. *Psychology of Women Quarterly, 15,* 65–81.

Rubin, J., Provenzano, F., & Luria, Z. (1974). The eye of the beholder: Parents' views on sex of newborns. *American Journal of Orthopsychiatry, 44,* 512–519.

Ruble, D.N. (1988). Sex role development. In M.H. Barnstein, & M.E. Lamb (Eds.), *Developmental psychology: An advanced textbook, 2nd ed.* Hillsdale, NJ: Erlbaum.

Santrock, J. (1994). *Child development, 6th ed.* Madison: Brown & Benchmark.

Sedney, M.A. (1987). Development of androgyny: Parental influences. *Psychology of Women Quarterly, 11,* 311–326.

Shaw, J.S. (1983). Psychological androgyny and stressful life events. *Journal of Personality and Social Psychology, 43,* 145–153.

Sheldon, A. (1990). "Kings are royaler than queens": Language and socialization. *Young Children, 45,* 4–9.

Snow, M.E., Jacklin, C.N., & Maccoby, E.E. (1983). Sex of child differences in father-child interaction at one year of age. *Child Development, 54,* 227–232.

Spence, J.T., & Helmreich, R.L. (1980). Masculine instrumentality and feminine expressiveness: Their relationship with sex role attitudes and behaviors. *Psychology of Women Quarterly, 5,* 147–163.

Steinbacher, R., & Gilroy, F. (1990). Sex selection technology: A prediction of its use and effect. *Journal of Psychology, 124,* 283–288.

Thorne, B. (1993). *Gender play: Girls and boys in school.* New Brunswick, NJ: Rutgers University Press.

Weinraub, M., Clemens, L.P., Sachloff, A., Ethridge, T., Gracely, E., & Myers, B. (1984). The development of sex role stereotypes in the third year: Relationships to gender labeling, gender identity, sex-typed toy preferences, and family characteristics. *Child Development, 55,* 1493–1504.

Weinraub, M., Jaeger, E., & Hoffman, L.W. (1988). Predicting infant outcomes in families of employed and nonemployed mothers. *Early Childhood Research Quarterly, 3,* 361–378.

Weisner, T.S., & Wilson-Mitchell, J.E. (1990). Nonconventional family life-styles and sex typing in six-year-olds. *Child Development, 61,* 1915–1933.

FAMILIES AND GENDER EQUITY

Scott Coltrane

Scott Coltrane explores the barriers to gender equity in the family and in the larger society. Coltrane is a professor of sociology at the University of California, Riverside, and the author of numerous journal articles and book chapters.

As we approach the millennium, Americans are faced with a perplexing paradox about gender equity. Although most people think men and women should be equal, gender remains one of the most important determinants of a person's life chances. Compared with men, women are more likely to earn low wages, take orders from others, perform domestic labor, live in poverty, and be raped or abused. Men, in contrast, are more likely to kill someone, be a victim of homicide, be involved in a lethal accident, commit suicide, and die soon after retirement. Contrary to popular opinion, these gender differences are neither natural nor inevitable. Subservient women and macho men are the product of historically specific social, political, and economic arrangements and are both cause and consequence of identifiable patterns of family life.

Women can now attend military academies, start businesses, play professional sports, run for public office, and in principle rise to the top in almost any personal or professional endeavor. In practice however, it is rare for women to accomplish these things. Although most Americans say that they would vote for a woman for president, no woman has ever been nominated for that office by a major party. More women have been elected to public office than ever before, but most of them sit on local school boards and city councils, and only one in ten members of Congress is a woman. Women now outnumber men in college, but they are rarely as successful as men once they enter the labor market. Women are almost as likely as men to be employed, but they still earn only three-fourths of what men do and typically occupy gender-segregated jobs with fewer benefits and with limited opportunities for advancement. Now, as in the past, it pays to be a man. To understand why men enjoy special privileges, we need to look beyond politics and economics to consider gender equity in the family.

The primary justification for excluding women from positions of authority is a holdover from the nineteenth century. According to the Victorian ideal of separate spheres, frail but morally pure women found true fulfillment in their domestic roles as wives and mothers, and rugged manly men left home to earn a family wage. The ideal middle-class woman was supposed to tend children and humanize husbands, providing them respite from the cruel and competitive world beyond the home. The actual boundary between

Reprinted from Scott Coltrane, "Families and Gender Equity," *National Forum: The Phi Kappa Phi Journal*, vol. 77, no. 2 (Spring 1997), ©1997 by Scott Coltrane, by permission of the publishers.

home and work was never as distinct as the ideal implied, especially for poor families, but the romantic image of separate spheres enjoyed unprecedented popularity.

As recent "family values" rhetoric attests, the idealized separation of work and family continues to carry strong messages about gender. Women are seen as naturally self-sacrificing and emotionally sensitive, rendering them perfectly suited to care for children, serve husbands, and keep house. Fathers, in contrast, are seen as competitive protectors and providers, enabling them to assume their "rightful" position as head and master of the family. Modern versions of the separate-spheres ideal suggest that women can be happy only if they marry and devote themselves to raising families. Men, in contrast, are admonished to be breadwinners first and to avoid sissy stuff like cleaning house or playing peek-a-boo.

Emotionally laden images of separate spheres belie the reality of life in most American households, since both men and women are now called on to hold jobs and do family work. Holding on to mythical ideals about rigid gender roles and inalterable sex differences makes it difficult for today's couples to negotiate equitable living arrangements and for parents to meet the needs of their children. Social-science research conducted over the last few decades demonstrates unequivocally that gender ideals are transformed as societies change and that family practices reflect and reproduce economic and political arrangements. Historical and cross-cultural studies show that when men share in routine child care, women enjoy higher public status and share political authority with men. When fathers are intimately involved in the lives of young children, men are unlikely to celebrate their manhood through combative contests, vociferous oratory, and violent rituals. These findings suggest that if we want to move toward gender equity in the society, we should abandon the Victorian ideal of separate spheres. If women are to be equal participants in the economy and the polity, men must become equal partners in maintaining homes and raising children.

The Rise of Working Mothers

In 1950, U.S. families with breadwinner fathers and stay-at-home mothers were twice as numerous as any other family type. Today, there are twice as many two-earner families as families where only the man works. The rapid increase in the number of mothers holding jobs is arguably the most important social trend of the past half-century. Today, three of four mothers with school-aged children and two of three mothers with preschool children are in the paid labor force, most working full-time. In a dramatic departure from the 1950s, most mothers return to work before their first child turns one year old.

Why have mothers entered the labor market in record numbers? Some take jobs for reasons of personal fulfillment or to be able to afford luxury items, but most women work for wages to meet basic living expenses. More than 80 percent of Americans now agree that it takes two paychecks to support a family, and one of three children is lifted out of poverty by a mother's earnings. In spite of these recent trends, many Americans continue to assume that men are the "real" breadwinners and that women should be responsible for child care and housework. Even though enacting the separate-spheres ideal is increasingly difficult, its romantic imagery continues to influence our thoughts and feelings.

How have family practices changed since the 1950s? One big change is that men are more involved in the birth process. Gone are popular images of anxious and isolated expectant fathers pacing hospital waiting rooms and passing out cigars. As late as the early 1970s, only one in four men attended the birth of their children, but now over eight of ten fathers are present in the delivery room. Men are also doing more child care after the baby comes home, though studies suggest that popular depictions of involved fathers may overstate their actual contributions.

Scholars argue over whether the image of the involved "New Father" originated in this century or the last, but most agree that cultural ideals promoting father involvement have increased recently. Contrary to images of aloof breadwinner fathers from the 1950s, opinion polls show that two of three American men say that they value families over jobs, and two of three wives say that they want husbands to spend more time with the children. Whether these attitudes will motivate men to share in the full range of family tasks remains to be seen, but fathers appear to be doing more than they formerly did.

Census surveys show that when mothers of preschoolers are on the job, fathers watch the children as often as grandparents (though still less than day-care providers). And when children reach school age, fathers become their most common substitute caregivers. If mothers hold part-time jobs, or work a nonday shift, fathers are especially likely to look after children regularly. When married couples are sampled nationwide about their parenting, they typically report that fathers are now doing about a third of the child care.

In the 1960s, researchers asked whether fathers were capable of taking care of infants. Not surprisingly, they discovered that men learn baby care in much the same way that women do—through on-the-job training. In addition to discovering that men could feed and care for infants when pressed into service, psychologists discovered that fathers preferred playing with their children, especially sons. Compared with mothers, men spend more of their child-care time in games or rough-and-tumble play. We now know that children learn important skills in this kind of interaction, such as how to regulate their emotions. Some studies also show that children with involved fathers do better socially and academically. Questions remain about whether benefits stem from having the income and attention of two parents or whether there is something unique that fathers contribute to children's development. Because men are also more likely than women to sexually and physically abuse children, we need to focus on what fathers do for children and not just assume (as some family-values advocates do) that the simple presence of a father is beneficial.

Most fatherhood research has studied men who are primary breadwinners and secondary parents, so we are just beginning to discover how more involved styles of fathering might influence both adults and children. We do know that the number of fathers who are sharing everyday parenting with their wives is increasing, as is the number of single fathers. Such men are intimately involved in the details of their children's lives, and while they do not act exactly like mothers, they adopt some similar styles of parenting, including treating sons and daughters alike. As everyday parents, men are more in touch with their child's developing needs and abilities and participate in setting realistic goals for them. They learn to anticipate what children need and to provide subtle encouragement that helps them develop competence. Everyday fathers (and mothers) tend to do less directing and more listening and comforting—styles of interaction that allow a special type of intimacy to develop. Predictably, men who assume responsibility for routine parenting report that it is profoundly enriching. They usually develop the kinder and gentler sides of themselves that are rarely displayed on the job or in all-male social groups. The experience of caring for children also generalizes to other relationships: men who do more parenting report they are more in touch with their emotions, are more compassionate, and can relate better to their wives.

Though men are doing more parenting than their own fathers did, changes have been slower than anticipated. Some of the major barriers to father involvement stem from job demands and the structure of the workplace. Work-family programs (like flextime and parental leave) are almost always designed with women in mind, though "daddy tracks" emerged in the 1990s, giving some men more schedule flexibility and shorter hours. Nevertheless, as women have discovered, there are costs associated with making children a priority, including slower promotions, lower earnings, and a general perception that one is not "serious" about work.

Men's family involvement also has been limited because women and men resist it. Because mothering can be gratifying, many women are reluctant to relinquish responsibility over home or children. Conversely, because many men worry about their masculinity, they refuse to perform activities they consider "women's work." But perhaps most importantly, men do little family work because they can get away with doing so. On the basis of being men, they expect to benefit from the domestic services of women. This outdated sense of masculine entitlement, coupled with women feeling obligated, leads to divisions of family work that are markedly unbalanced.

It used to be that American women said they did not want men's help with housework, but things are changing. Since the 1970s, men have roughly doubled their contributions to the inside household chores of cooking, cleaning, and washing (from about two to three hours per week to about five to eight hours per week). Nevertheless, men still do only about a third as much as their wives, who have cut down the number of hours they spend in these tasks (to about twenty hours per week). Which tasks are men doing? Although the division of household chores varies widely among families, as a group, men are assuming more responsibility for grocery shopping, cooking, and meal clean-up. Men's share of housecleaning, laundry, and other repetitive indoor tasks has increased only modestly, but even here, studies show that men are doing more, especially when asked to "help" their wives rather than becoming equal participants.

When do men do more? In general, men perform more housework and child care when they are employed fewer hours, when their wives work longer hours or earn more money, and when both spouses believe in gender equity. Although men who do more child care also do more housework, the two do not always go together. Shared housework is usually a practical response to outside demands and occurs when wives bargain for it. Shared child care, in contrast, often results from the man's initiative. If couples deliberately divide tasks early in the relationship, a pattern of sharing becomes self-perpetuating. If couples assume that sharing will happen on its own, women end up doing virtually everything.

Conflict often increases when men become involved in what was previously the wife's domain. As men take on responsibility for parenting and housework, frequent discussions take place about what should be done and whose standards should be followed. One of the most effective strategies for sharing is to have definite "on-duty" times and for men to assume full responsibility for specific tasks. This strategy minimizes conflict and enables men to move out of a "helper" role. Parents who share child care and housework invariably report that it is difficult, but that the rewards outweigh the costs.

There will be more involved fathers in the future but also more absent ones. This situation comes about because both patterns of fatherhood result from similar social forces: marriage and parenting are becoming more optional and individualized. The biggest change in marriage has been that men's jobs no longer guarantee them spouses, and women no longer select husbands based primarily on earning potential. People are freed from older constraints, but marriage now depends on individual initiative. As more men and women are forced to negotiate new divisions of labor, many marriages will end in divorce, but many others will be strengthened by the new partnership arrangements.

The social and economic conditions promoting the breakdown of separate spheres will only increase. Economic restructuring will produce more low-paying jobs, more women will be employed, and limited governmental assistance will encourage family self-reliance. Women will remain primary parents in most families, but more fathers will get involved in the details of running homes and raising children.

As fathers become more active parents, social processes will be initiated that could have far-reaching effects. If more men care for children, daughters' and sons' emotional dispositions and cognitive frameworks will become more similar. This similarity will prepare future generations for a world that is less polarized by gender than the one we know. Because sharing family work is linked to cooperation in other realms, men's involvement could increase women's public status and reduce men's propensity for violence. By instituting gender equity in the family, we will move closer to achieving gender equity in the larger society.

DISCUSSION QUESTIONS

1. Jessie Bernard, a well-known feminist sociologist, has suggested that females and males are born into two different worlds—the "pink world" of girls and the "blue world" of boys. How are boys and girls socialized into sex-typed traits and behavior in our society?

2. What are the advantages and disadvantages of being raised in a more egalitarian (or androgynous) home environment?

3. An increasing proportion of Americans favor (and expect) more equal roles in marriage. Is it easy or difficult to break away from traditional roles for females and males? Why?

WEBSITES

www.edc.org/WomensEquity/

The national Women's Educational Equity Act (WEEA) Equity Resource Center works to improve educational, social, and economic outcomes for women and girls.

news:soc.feminism

news:soc.women

Newsgroups are electronic bulletin boards that allow discussion on a variety of topics. These two newsgroups often focus on issues of gender inequality.

www.norgaard.net/newsgroups.htm

This is a convenient list of social science–related newsgroups that you may want to bookmark.

CHAPTER 4: LOVE, DATING, AND MATE SELECTION

In examining mate selection patterns, family scholars note the common practice of Americans to marry homogamously; that is, marriage involving people who share similar social characteristics. Moreover, American mate selection is most often based on romantic love. From an early age, we are socialized to the virtues of love and exposed to many images of love in the mass media, where we learn that people fall in love, marry, and, like the prince and princess of fairy tales, live happily ever after (or until they fall out of love and then separate or divorce).

The three readings in this chapter will explore romantic love and its role in dating and mate selection in the United States. The first article, by Helen Fisher, points out that songs, poems, plays, sculptures, and paintings have portrayed romantic love in Western cultures and traditional societies for centuries. Exactly what is romantic love? Fisher distinguishes psychological, social, and physiological components of love and emphasizes the evolution of attraction, attachment, and detachment in human mating. She proposes that the human tendency to pair up and remain together for about four years reflects an ancestral reproductive strategy to cooperatively rear a single helpless child through infancy.

From a more applied perspective, the next reading presents some practical advice on love and loving. A number of relationship experts suggest that the survival of marriage (or any intimate relationship) depends not on love but on learning necessary skills—problem-solving, communication, empathy, and conflict resolution.

The last article in this chapter examines the attitudes and preferences of African American college students in dating and mate selection. The findings of this empirical study show that skin color and social status are important variables in mate selection. For example, African American males are more likely to favor light-skinned partners than their female counterparts. Females, on the other hand, report that having a good time and getting along with mates are more important than physical attraction.

THE ORIGIN OF ROMANTIC LOVE AND HUMAN FAMILY LIFE

Helen Fisher

Why do people fall in love? And why do some people abandon their partner for another? Helen Fisher, an anthropologist at Rutgers University and author of Anatomy of Love: The Natural History of Monogamy, Adultery, and Divorce, *looks at the the psychological, physiological, and social components of love, monogamy, and divorce.*

"This whirlwind, this delirium of eros," wrote poet Robert Lowell. Poems, songs, novels, operas, plays, films, sculptures, and paintings have all portrayed romantic love in a variety of Western cultures for centuries. The love story of Isis and Osiris was recorded in Egypt more than 3,000 years ago. Ovid composed poems to romantic love in the first century B.C. in ancient Rome. And many other myths and legends about love come from antiquity.

Romantic love also is visible in "traditional" societies. In an examination of 166 cultures, anthropologists William Jankowiak and Edward Fischer found evidence of romantic love in 88 percent of them. People sang love songs. Individ-

Reprinted from Helen Fisher, "The Origin of Romantic Love and Human Family Life," *National Forum: The Phi Kappa Phi Journal*, vol. 76, no. 1 (Winter 1996), ©1996 by Helen E. Fisher, by permission of the publishers.

uals eloped. And the folklore of many societies portrayed romantic entanglements. These scientists attributed the lack of evidence for romantic love in the balance of these cultures to "ethnographic oversight" or lack of access to the folklore of the culture. They concluded that romantic love, which they equate with passionate love, ". . . constitutes a human universal."

What is love? Psychologist Dorothy Tennov devised approximately 200 statements about romantic love and asked 400 men and women at and around the University of Bridgeport, Connecticut, to answer her questionnaire with "true" or "false" responses. From their replies, as well as from over 2,000 personal accounts, Tennov identified a constellation of characteristics common to the condition of "being in love," a state that she calls "limerence" and I call attraction or infatuation.

Limerence begins the moment another individual takes on "special meaning"; it could be an old friend seen in a new perspective or a complete stranger. Infatuation then develops in a characteristic psychological pattern, beginning with "intrusive thinking." Many of Tennov's informants claimed that as the obsession grew, they spent from 85 percent to 100 percent of their waking hours thinking about their beloved. The infatuated person also aggrandized trivial aspects of the adored one in a process Tennov calls "crystallization." Her subjects could list the faults of their love object. But they concentrated on the positive parts of their sweetheart's physical features and personality—confirming what Chaucer said, "Love is blynd."

Tennov's limerent informants also reported specific emotions. Elation was paramount. Hope, apprehension, uncertainty, shyness, awkwardness, fear of rejection, anticipation, and longing for reciprocity also were commonly mentioned. Most interesting, subjects said they felt helpless, that this passion was irrational, involuntary, unplanned, and uncontrollable.

Culture also plays an essential role in infatuation—particularly in whom one chooses. As children we develop specific likes and dislikes in response to family, friends, experiences, and chance associations, so by the teenage years all individuals carry within them an unconscious mental template, or "love map," a group of physical, psychological, and behavioral traits that one finds attractive in a mate. Timing is exceedingly important; people fall in love when they are ready. Barriers seem to enhance infatuation; both men and women like "the chase." And we are often stimulated by someone we find somewhat mysterious.

So culture plays a crucial role in *whom* you find attractive, *when* you begin to court, *where* you woo, and *how* you pursue a potential mate. But parents, teachers, friends, books, movies, songs, and other cultural phenomena do not teach a person *what* to feel *as* he or she falls in love. Instead, like the sensations of fear, anger, and surprise, these emotional responses appear to be generated by brain/body physiology. Psychiatrist Michael Liebowitz is specific about this biochemical response; he theorizes that one feels the elation of infatuation when neurons in the limbic system of the brain (which governs the basic emotions) become either saturated or sensitized by natural amphetamines.

"Love is strongest in pursuit, friendship in possession," Emerson has written. At some point that magic wanes. Tennov measured the duration of limerence from the moment infatuation hit to the moment a "feeling of neutrality" for one's love object began. The most frequent interval, as well as the average, was between approximately eighteen months and three years. Liebowitz hypothesizes that the end of infatuation also is grounded in brain physiology; either the nerve endings in the brain become habituated to the mind's natural stimulants or levels of these amphetamine-like substances begin to drop.

Attachment, Liebowitz proposes, is the second physiological stage of romantic love. As attraction wanes and attachment grows, he hypothesizes that a new chemical system is taking over: the endorphins, peptide neurotransmitters that are chemically related to morphine, giving partners feelings of safety, stability, tranquillity, and peace. Neuroscientist Thomas Insel and others have elegantly shown that other neurotransmitters, oxytocin and vasopressin, are associated with attachment, too.

No one knows how long the attachment phase of love endures. But for some people, love ends. There is often a third stage to romantic encounters: detachment. The physiology that accompanies detachment has never been explored. But I suspect that in some long relationships the brain's receptor sites for the endorphins, oxytocin, vasopressin, and/or other neurochemicals become desensitized or overloaded and attachment wanes, setting up the mind for separation. This is not to suggest that men and women are biologically *compelled* to fall in love, attach, or detach from one another. People regularly maintain long marriages. But divorce is common in societies around the world. And as I collected data on worldwide patterns of marriage, divorce, and remarriage, I came to conclude that the brain physiology associated with attraction, attachment, and detachment evolved as part of our primordial human mating system.

Some 90 percent or more of American men and women in every birth cohort marry; records go back to the mid 1800s. The Demographic Yearbooks of the United Nations list the number of men and women who marry in ninety-seven industrial and agricultural countries; an average of 93 percent of women and 92 percent of men wed by age forty-nine. Marriage is central to life in tribal cultures, too; bachelors and spinsters are rare. Moreover, most men and women in the world are monogamous (one-spouse); they wed only one individual at a time. Many societies permit polygyny. But in most of these cultures only about 10 percent of men actually practice polygyny; even where polygyny is widespread, only about 25 percent of men have several wives at once. Monogamy is a hallmark of the human animal.

This is not to suggest that men and women are faithful to their spouses. "Extra-pair copulations" are common among people, as they are in many other monogamous species. But like polygyny and polyandry, adultery seems to be a secondary *opportunistic* strategy of men and women. Monogamy, or pairbonding, is the rule. Monogamy is not always permanent, however, and it displays several patterns of decay that are relevant to understanding the origins of romantic love and human family life.

Few societies in the world prohibit divorce. The Roman Catholic church banned divorce in the 11th century A.D.; the Incas did not permit divorce either. But with these and a few other exceptions, peoples from Amazonia to Siberia have procedures for divorce, and they do divorce. Several patterns to divorce have purely cultural explanations. Divorce *rates*, for example, correlate with economic autonomy: in those societies where spouses are relatively economically independent, divorce rates are high; where spouses are dependent on one another to make a living and their resources are shared, divorce rates are lower. Economic independence among spouses, as well as many other cultural factors, contributes to the *frequency* of divorce.

But data taken from the Demographic Yearbooks of the United Nations on sixty-two available industrial and agricultural societies for all obtainable years between 1947 and 1989 indicate that human marriages have several patterns of decay that do not correlate with divorce rate. They occur in societies where divorce rates are high and in cultures where divorce is rare. These patterns, I think, are at the heart of our primary human mating system. I shall propose that they evolved— and that these mating habits selected for the char-

acteristic ebb and flow of romantic love.

In many cultures divorces occur most regularly during and around the fourth year of marriage. Men and women tend to divorce while in their twenties, the height of their reproductive and parenting years. Men and women most regularly abandon partnerships that have produced no children or one dependent child. Most divorced individuals of reproductive age remarry. And the longer a marriage lasts, the older spouses get, and/or the more children they bear, the more likely they are to stay together. There are exceptions. But these regularities persist in many industrial, agrarian, and tribal societies.

Why do people fall in love, marry, build a life together, and bear a child, only to abandon their hard-won partnership for another? The evolution of human serial monogamy *during reproductive years* and often *with one dependent child* is best understood within the context of monogamy in other species. Monogamy is rare in mammals; only 3 percent pair up; and they do so under specific circumstances. One is particularly relevant to us: monogamy tends to occur in species where more than a single individual, the female, is needed to rear the young.

The red fox is a good example. The female fox bears as many as five helpless kits; her milk is thin; she must stay in the den to feed them; and she will starve to death unless she has a mate to provision her. The dog fox can rarely collect enough food to feed a harem. But he can provide for a single mate. So a male and female form a pairbond in mid-winter, and together they raise their young. When the kits begin to wander in mid-summer, however, the parents split up to forage independently. *The pairbond lasts only through the breeding season.* Formation of a pairbond in conjunction with a breeding season is common among birds. Most bear immature young or infants that for other ecological reasons need two parents. As a result, over 90 percent of some 9,000 species of birds form pairbonds to rear their broods. But in over 50 percent of these species, the pairbond does not last for life; it lasts only for the breeding season.

Homo sapiens shares traits with foxes and seasonally parenting birds. The modal duration of marriage that ends in divorce, four years, conforms to the traditional period between human successive births, four years. So elsewhere I have proposed that the human *tendency* to pair up and remain together for about four years reflects an ancestral reproductive strategy to cooperatively rear a single helpless child through infancy. And the brain physiology for attraction, attachment, and detachment evolved to fuel this primordial mating system.

Human serial monogamy probably emerged more than four million years ago when our ancestors began to sally forth from the disappearing forests of ancient Africa and walk bipedally through more open terrain. With the evolution of bipedalism, females had to carry their infants in their arms instead of on their backs, increasing their "reproductive burden." Hominid males probably were unable to obtain enough food to sustain a harem in their new woodland/grassland environment; food was spread out and danger constant. But like dog foxes and male birds of many species, they could provide food and protection for a single female. Hence pairbonding *during the infancy of a child* became critical for females and practical for males—and monogamy evolved.

How pairbonding, the core of human family life, emerged was probably relatively simple. Hominid males and females probably first traveled in communities similar to those of common chimpanzees or pygmy chimpanzees, and females regularly developed strong friendships with particular males. Then with time these "special friendships" evolved into longer partnerships that mates sustained through the infancy of their child. Once a juvenile joined a multi-age play group, however, and could be raised by many members of the band, most pairbonds broke up—enabling both partners to choose new mates and rear more young.

Serial monogamy had genetic benefits. Hominids who conceived offspring by varied partners created genetic vitality in their lineages. Males had the opportunity to select younger partners more likely to produce healthier children. And females had the chance to choose mates who

provided better protection, food, and nurturance for them and their forthcoming infants. So despite the social conflicts inherent in changing mates, those who practiced serial monogamy disproportionately survived, passing the brain physiology for attraction, attachment, and restlessness during long relationships, as well as the optimistic drive to seek another partner, across the millennia to us.

Does a red fox feel the euphoria of attraction as he leaps to lick his new mate's face during the breeding season in February? Does a robin feel attachment as he gives his mate a juicy insect at dinnertime? Because birds and mammals share many features of brain anatomy, neurophysiology, and behavior, I hypothesize that the biology for these primary emotions, attraction and attachment, evolved in all avian and mammalian genera to coordinate the ebb and flow of each species' specific breeding system.

Among ancestral humans these emotions evolved specifically to motivate individuals of reproductive age to bond together long enough to rear a single helpless child through infancy, then to find new mates and breed again. Moreover, as a couple aged, as the length of their pairbond increased, and/or as a couple bore successive young, these *flexible* neural circuits helped to sustain pairbonds instead, producing the malleable multi-part human reproductive strategy that is still visible in cross-cultural patterns of marriage, divorce, and remarriage.

With the expansion of the human cerebral cortex more than a million years ago, our ancestors began to build upon this core of primal cyclic reproductive emotions, adding complexity of feeling as well as cultural rituals and beliefs about attraction, attachment, and detachment. And by the time *Homo sapiens sapiens* people were wearing fox-skin coats and ivory beads and drawing beasts and symbols on cave walls in southwestern France, the Pyrenees, and northern Spain some 20,000 years ago, our forebears had developed an intricate, physiologically based constellation of emotions for loving, as well as elaborate traditions to celebrate and curb what European peoples would come to call romantic love.

LOVE LESSONS

Hara Estroff Marano

Relationship experts have devised an array of courses that teach couples how to manage conflict without reciprocating, retaliating, or invalidating their partner. Hara Estroff Marano is a staff writer for Psychology Today.

You and your mate have just had a fight. One of the countless minute, convoluted conversations that busy couples have every day in their push to Get Things Done, each one part spoken word, part signal code, part mind reading, but one that suddenly flares into your own private Bosnia. A simple conversation that started out so expectantly a second before goes off like a grenade in your hands.

Couples' arguments can be so deeply mired in the minutiae of their lives that at times mates may feel like they're locked in their own special hell. But what if most times, without paying any attention, you and your spouse were sliding into a deeply carved groove, having the same argument you've had countless times before? The triggers may be different: socks on the floor, a rude remark to a father-in-law, an oversize phone bill, an unchanged diaper, a puddle of orange juice on the counter, a shrug. When the atmosphere is right, no act is too small to incite hostility.

In couples' myriad fights, despite our glorious individuality, we are all fighting exactly the same fight. Tolstoy, you see, got it wrong. Each couple may be unhappy in its own way, tripping over the particular furnishings of its own house, but every couple *gets* unhappy in the exact same way and for the same reasons. We use the same words. We harden into the same positions. We feel the same alienation. And the same distress. The same processes overtake love in ways that marriage researchers now find extraordinarily predictable.

Yet, it is this very fact—the ritualization of revenge—that now promises to save love. Over the past 20 years, experts have been putting our intimate relationships under the microscope, studying our private reactions by both looking at what goes on between partners and inside them: videotaping every grimace, shrug, and caress, audiotaping every expletive and sigh, and monitoring physiological reactions throughout. They've come to understand why some relationships happily endure, what can make some hellholes of unhappiness, and what, precisely, precipitates divorce, which still claims half of all first marriages, usually within the first seven years.

Psychologists have seen with their own eyes that the overwhelming majority of couples start out with true love and great expectations. But mounting evidence suggests we get into trouble for a very humbling reason. We just don't know how to handle the negative feelings that are the unavoidable by-product of the differences between two people, the very differences that attract them to each other in the first place. Think of it as the friction any two bodies would generate rubbing against each other countless times each day.

Love Survival Skills

As a result, a growing number of researchers and clinicians have come to the conclusion that most unhappy couples don't so much need therapy as they do education. Education in how relationships work, and the specific skills that make them work well. "Having a good relationship is a skill," insists Howard Markman, Ph.D., professor of psychology at the University of Denver, and a longtime marital researcher. Washington, D.C., family therapist Diane Sollee, M.S.W., agrees. "Marriage isn't a disease," she says, "you don't need therapy for it." Sollee is director of the recently formed Coalition for Marriage, Family, and Couples Education, an organization that makes people aware of the new information that can change the odds for marital success. "Couples need to learn a way to stay engaged—not withdraw or attack," adds psychologist Sherod Miller, Ph.D., another pioneer in couples education who practices in Colorado.

This thinking embodies a sea change in the mental health world. For one, it formalizes the idea that the best way to help people is to teach them crucial psychological skills, so-called "psychoeducation." "Psychoeducation is nothing more than giving knowledge to people so they can help themselves," says Sollee. In other words, courses aren't therapy—but they typically have a therapeutic effect. Psychoeducation also flatly rejects the medical model of illness—which sees problems as pathology—because it doesn't fit what are really normal problems of living, however much mental distress they may cause. In addition, it shifts value to prevention so the development of problems that are costly to men, women, and children can be averted.

"We haven't had the revolution we need about love," Sollee insists. "Couples who marry now don't do anything different despite knowing that 50 percent of them will be divorced in a few years. They think their love is so special they'll make it. They don't realize that the survival of marriage is not about love, it's about skills. It's a skill to know how not to escalate a conflict if your relationship isn't working. It's not that you picked the wrong person. You need smart love."

For all the scientifically documentable benefits of preventing marital distress before it starts, Sollee is convinced that marital education is the most romantic thing a couple can do, to stroll hand in hand into a course that will teach them how to keep their love alive. Or the best wedding present parents can give their children. Sollee has put her money where her mouth is; she has herself attended courses and given them as wedding presents to her two sons and their wives.

What couples today need to make a go of relationships is not something they could have readily picked up in their families of origin. "No one has the skills because the world is changing too fast," says Miller. Until recently, when men and women entered relationships, they stepped into rigid roles precast by the culture. "We didn't see our parents make decisions in an open, constructive way," he says. "In my lifetime, couples have gone from role-taking, defined along gender lines, to role-making."

Not only are roles fluid—established by individual couples—but everything is negotiable. "The world is more mobile," says Miller, whose program, Couple Communication, was one of the first. "Information of all sorts impacts families so that they have more choices. In a world that's less routine, to find a context to live in, couples must shift from a reliance on the external—extended family, church—to an internal support system, where they can talk about issues and work out solutions."

Miller began seeing couples conjointly in 1964, well before there was such a thing as family therapy. Quickly he discovered they were relying on the therapist to be the problem-solver. "I saw myself actually *creating* a dependency," he says. "I wanted to teach couples how to be their own best problem-solvers."

For Miller, effective conflict resolution starts with the self—self-awareness, self-caring, self-honesty, knowing what one wants and valuing it enough to speak up for it clearly. "Lots of pathology grows out of not knowing yourself," he says. "Caring is listening to yourself, and owning what you've done and haven't done." Then listen to your partner do the same.

The signature component of Miller's approach is "The Awareness Wheel," a floor-mat map that prompts partners to systematically review the different "zones" of inner information—thoughts, feelings, wants, actions, sensory data—that influence the problems they may have to confront. By physically moving to each zone on the mat, and addressing each other with information appropriate to that zone, couples learn the fundamentals of talking effectively. Especially by getting their wants and feelings out in the open, Miller believes, partners can solve their problems.

"Its simple but powerful," says Miller, who drew on 25 years of research and every school and movement of psychology to create the mat. "In one month, couples can make dramatic changes in the way they relate. The learning isn't just intellectual; it's kinesthetic." And if there's one thing mates need to do, it's learn these techniques through every portal to the brain, so they can access them during times of stress when the natural impulse may be to attack or run away.

"The map also helps couples create a common operating system," Miller says. Most of all, he says it helps a person manage him- or herself— and, pointedly, not the other. "They allow individuals to stay engaged in a situation—connected with themselves and their insides, and their spouse and their spouse's insides," Miller says.

Relationship Enhancement

Around the same time Miller was putting together his ideas, Bernard Guerney, Ph.D., then a young professor of psychology at Penn State, now professor emeritus, and ever a maverick thinker, was coming to the conclusion that all psychotherapy is really psychoeducation. "Therapy is simply education after a problem develops," he says. Having concluded that it was more efficient for couples to help each other resolve their own difficulties, he created a course called

Relationship Enhancement (RE). Its starting point is empathy, or compassion training—learning to see things from a partner's perspective. Empathy, Guerney insists, is what people are really seeking in marriage, and this expectation represents a major break with the past: "People are looking for someone to be emotionally supportive, a friend, a helpmate, a soulmate."

First and foremost in RE is empathic listening, then comes empathic responding. Partners learn how to express themselves in an honest way that helps their mate preserve their self-image without invoking defensiveness. "You need to present your pain—pain your partner has caused—in the context of your love for him or her, so he or she will be willing to make changes," says Guerney. "To convey one's feelings to one's partner is transformative to both."

Guerney, who now runs the National Institute of Relationship Enhancement in Bethesda, Maryland, has come to see that marriage partners typically don't express their needs. Over time, many learn not to ask for what they want—while they secretly wish their partners understood these wants. "Their frustration builds," says Guerney "so then they ask for what they want—but in an attacking way. And that guarantees they won't get it. Hostilities worsen and partners withdraw." Guerney says people have to learn to ask for what they want in a nonthreatening way that's likely to lead to cooperation. "It creates a positive cycle that keeps love alive and growing," he says.

Using the X-ray as a guiding metaphor, Guerney encourages couples to look for feelings and motives their partners haven't expressed. "It's only then they can begin discussing what they can do to help themselves and each other," he says. Guerney describes this as a process of identification, of not emphasizing the differences between people. "We teach people to imagine themselves as the other person."

To help couples get it right, trained coaches work closely and privately with each couple, showing them what to do. "Most people react reflexively," Guerney says. "We help them realize they always have choices in interactions. We slow down the process of responding so that they can see their choices and take control of their relationship."

Guerney's program, like Miller's, has been validated by independent research demonstrating its effectiveness. The evidence shows that RE benefits all partners, while distressed couples make the greatest gains.

Premarital Relationship Enhancement

Where RE fosters identification and shared meaning between partners, Markman has built his course, Premarital Relationship Enhancement Program (PREP), to revolve around their differences. It takes fighting between couples as a given and aims to promote better—and egalitarian—fighting as partners air their gripes and concerns. Not that PREP's premise is that you can say anything you want, any time you want. Markman has established ground rules for handling conflict in ways that he says "protect a marriage from the ravages of poorly handled emotion." His protocol is called The Floor. The structure it imposes on speaking and listening is taught nationally in a series of group lectures that alternate with extensive private coaching sessions.

The technique, says Markman, is deceptively simple. "The Speaker" speaks, usually stating a complaint—without placing blame: It really makes me angry when you don't call and dinner is waiting on the table. "The Listener" doesn't respond or justify him or herself; he or she just demonstrates they've heard the comment by repeating it. "To be heard is a powerful tool by itself," Markman says. "It's at the core of all intimate relationships. You don't even need to solve the problem. In fact, it's critical *not* to resolve things, and just be heard by your partner. People want understanding from each other, not resolution. Couples are really arguing over things from the past. Once they clear the air, things get resolved by means of acceptance." During the private sessions, conducted by trained consultants, couples work on issues they haven't been able to resolve on their own.

If PREP puts most of its emphasis on the containment of negative emotions, it's because, Markman says, that's what takes a great deal of skill training; it's working against biology, which programs us to step up the attack or withdraw altogether. "If couples don't have good skills for handling problems," adds Scott Stanley, Ph.D., a codeveloper of PREP, "the negative overwhelms the positive in their relationships. Over the years, couples don't make time for positive experiences—and they tend not to protect these experiences from conflict. It's important to keep anything negative out of positive time together. It's our belief that with some protection, the positive parts of a relationship can and will flourish."

Handling conflict in a manageable way also fosters couples' commitment to work at their marriage. "For couples about to be married, it prevents an erosion of the positive," Markman says. The trick is being heard by one's partner; it's just damned difficult. We all have a variety of filters—levels of emotional arousal, expectations, fears, cultural beliefs, beliefs acquired in our families of origin, differences in style and pace, a need for self-protection—that distort the unpleasant messages our partners send. What's more, we're usually busy preparing our rebuttal. So what a woman thinks is a perfectly neutral statement may land like a bomb on her husband.

What's more, says psychologist Clifford Notarius, Ph.D., a professor of psychology at Catholic University in Washington, D.C., partners are not good at giving immediate feedback on how their messages are being received. This is especially true of unhappy couples. So Notarius has developed a course that helps couples hear each other, and give and get necessary feedback. But even before that, he bolsters their sense of relationship efficacy, their belief that as a unit they can get through this stuff. He calls his course We Can Work It Out, because it highlights the importance of expecting success. He says his studies show that couples who believe they can resolve their differences remain happy even under stress.

The belief in efficacy can be cultivated, Notarius says, pointing out the very fine line the course treads: "At the same time you want a couple to believe they can work it out, you also want them to feel they can do better."

In paying attention to dimensions beyond

skills, Notarius concentrates on how couples understand their relationships. First he helps them articulate what they want their marriage to look like. Then he shows them the skills to help them get there, because only then will they be motivated to learn.

While the skills component of Notarius's course bears many similarities to PREP—Notarius and Markman were both students of innovative researcher John Gottman, Ph.D., and together and separately pioneered observational studies of how marriages work—it has its differences, too. "The big question," says Notarius, "is how to get people to put into practice what they learn. As a result, we put a coach with each couple 80 percent of the time."

Then there are the big cardboard signs Notarius has couples use. "We're all lousy listeners," he says, "because we're all fragile. We don't want to hear we're the source of our partner's pain." To help people become aware of how their words affect each other, Notarius designates one partner as "the Listener," who holds up reaction cards—large signs with either a plus, minus, or neutral sign—as "the Speaker" speaks. Absent such clear feedback, he says, spouses don't understand why their partner's later response is an attack.

What couples need to focus on, Gottman advises, is their repair attempts. "Everybody messes up," says the University of Washington professor of psychology. "The four horsemen of the marital apocalypse that I identified—criticism, contempt, defensiveness, and stonewalling—are predictors of divorce. Everybody does them to some degree. But some couples deal with them successfully."

Gottman recently summarized his 25 years of research and turned it into the Marriage Survival Kit, a weekend course for couples, taught at the Seattle Marital and Family Institute. He says that what makes couples' attempts at repairing their relationships work is not how they fight but what goes on in everyday, relaxed situations. These situations give partners a positive perspective, so that when they get a blast of negativity from their spouse, they can ignore it and take in only the information in what's being said. In short, it's the

Marriage Survival Kit

John Gottman, Ph.D., a professor of psychology at the University of Washington in Seattle, says his studies show that couples whose relationships remain happy and stable know how to successfully repair problems. His Marriage Survival Kit teaches partners five basic skills for conflict resolution.

1. Use a softened start-up. Present your complaints without criticism. Criticism involves a global attack or blaming of a partner, and only incites defensiveness.

2. Accept influence. Positively take in your partner's attempts to request things of you. In good marriages, both men and women freely give and receive influence from each other. Since women are already good at accepting influence from men, Gottman finds, a husband's role becomes critical in predicting whether a marriage will survive. To the degree that men can accept influence from their wives, marriages succeed.

3. Repair, or put the brakes on, conflict. This means doing anything to halt or reverse negativity. Gottman gives couples a 72-point repair checklist, which includes statements such as "I'm feeling sad," and "Let's start all over again." Even "Will you shut up and listen" is usually a repair attempt.

4. Make use of physiologic soothing. Men are more physiologically aroused during conflict—a factor that often prompts withdrawal, which is deadly for relationships. They will remain engaged in problem-solving only if they or their partners take specific steps to calm them down. One of the best ways to do this is to declare a "time out" during heated discussions, and reconvene after at least 20 minutes of thinking about something else, or nothing at all.

5. De-escalate discord. In good marriages, couples actively de-escalate conflicts by doing things like injecting humor into situations or planting a kiss on their partner's cheek. Unfortunately, this is the one behavior Gottman admits he can't program. It just happens when couples have a positive perspective.

mindless, mundane moments of marriage that are the makers of romance.

Gottman says that in successful marriages, it's in those little moments that so much goes on. Happy couples make what he calls "love maps": They find ways of knowing one another and updating the information regularly. "A fondness and admiration system is active, particularly in the husbands," he says. "Those guys are thinking about the stuff they love and admire in their partners, even when they're not together. If you were to open up their skulls, you'd see they allocate a lot more brain cells to their marriages and the world of their partners than guys who wind up divorced." There's a balance of what Gottman characterizes as "turning towards versus turning away," which builds up the "emotional bank account" of relationships. Partners simply connect in tiny, unremarkable, emotionally neutral moments.

Gottman believes these otherwise unremarkable moments add up and put couples in "positive sentiment override," which in turn determines their disposition when it comes to problem-solving and the success of their repair attempts. So when one partner says something with irritability, the other sees it as neutral. Gottman urges couples—especially men—to see that the irritability or anger behind complaints is really just a form of italics. By positively responding to their partner's irritability, spouses keep their partner's complaints from escalating into criticism. In The Marriage Survival Kit, Gottman teaches couples five basic skills for conflict resolution.

To make sure couples can actually accomplish in their everyday lives what they've learned, Gottman brings them back six months later for a "booster shot," a one-day workshop. He also checks in on them via survey every three months to see how they're faring. Couples still having problems can come back for a special session with a clinician.

Relationship difficulties are resistant to change for a very specific reason, says Falls Church, Virginia, family therapist Lori Gordon, Ph.D. Marriage has a devilish ability to tap into emotional issues from our past, especially from our families

of origin. So Gordon developed Practical Application of Relationship Skills, or PAIRS, which reaches particularly deep and ties the cognitive and emotional components of love to their historical background.

Gordon believes that the past usually manifests itself in hidden expectations and assumptions in relationships. She says that as long as people remain unaware of them, they act as saboteurs to love: "Most unhappy partners feel disappointed, if not outright betrayed, because what they expected to find in their relationship either hasn't happened or stopped happening."

We hand our partner an invisible ledger, displacing onto a current partner the blame for past hurts. We hope they will prove they are not the person who hurt us, while we expect them to make up for previous hurts—hurts that enter our awareness only when we feel frightened or disappointed.

On that ledger are what Gordon calls "love knots," riddles exposing the contradictory nature of our many expectations. And they read like relationship haiku. For example, Love Knot #1: If you really loved me, you would know what I want, and you would do it. Since you don't, you obviously don't care. So why should I care for you, or for what you think, feel, say, want, or do? When you tell me what you want, I won't be very interested. I will be withholding.

Over the 120 hours of PAIRS class time, couples hone their communication skills. In addition to learning how to argue, they also learn how to confide in each other through a structured conversation called the Guide for Dialogue. "It's not enough to work on communication," Gordon says. "You need a cognitive understanding of the way you react to your partner."

Couples who take any of these courses discover that their skills work in other areas—parenting, the workplace, the community. Learning how intimate relationships operate is really a tool for managing the self. Says Markman, "We have to get away from the idea that knowing how to be in a relationship requires therapy. People don't feel bad about going to a ski instructor." Or taking driving lessons. So why should learning how to operate a relationship be any different?

MATE SELECTION PREFERENCES AMONG AFRICAN AMERICAN COLLEGE STUDENTS

Louie E. Ross

Louie E. Ross explores how skin color, social status, and other factors affect the attitudes and preferences of African American college students in dating and future mate selection. Ross is an associate professor in sociology at Fayetteville State University, Fayetteville, North Carolina.

All cultures have rules regarding mate selection. Many societies encourage either homogamy or heterogamy. Homogamy refers to marriage between individuals with similar social and personal characteristics, whereas heterogamy refers to marriage between individuals with different social or personal characteristics. Although there is some freedom in mate selection in American society, the United States is still basically a society whose norms encourage homogamy. Some of the major factors that influence mate selection include socioeconomic status, race, age, and parental and peer pressures.

The purpose of this article is to examine the attitudes and preferences of African American college students toward physical and social status

From Louie E. Ross, "Mate Selection Among African American College Students," *Journal of Black Studies*, vol. 27, no. 4 (March 1997), pp. 554–69; ©1997 by Sage Publications, Inc. Reprinted by permission of Sage Publications, Inc.

related variables regarding dating and future mate selection. Several social status and attractiveness related variables, along with selected background variables (including gender), were analyzed to note relationship patterns. Of particular interest was the importance of skin color or skin tone and social status as mate selection preferences among African American college students. There may be vast differences between attitudes toward mate selection and actual behaviors when selecting mates for marriage. Attitudinal research on skin color and social status preferences as they relate to mate selection on African American populations is lacking.

Historical Notes on African American Mate Selection

During various points in slavery, social factors regarding homogamy, such as economic and class statuses, were somewhat limited because large numbers of slaves had similar social statuses. Social statuses among slaves seems to have been perpetuated by the house and field slave roles, with the house slave carrying the more socially accepted role. Masters often gave house slaves, who were oftentimes mulattoes, slightly better clothes and elevated their status. Many of these house slaves, who were offspring of their masters, had lighter complexions and were told that they were better than their darker-skinned counterparts. Lighter-skinned Blacks also brought higher prices at the slave market and were deemed to have higher social statuses (Russell, Wilson, & Hall, 1992). Although it is well known that not all African Americans were enslaved, this social echelon based on color became an important distinction. The lighter the complexion, the better off he or she was in the eyes of the majority group members. This belief spread and was also internalized among many Blacks.

Research conducted during the 1940s through the 1960s noted how skin tone was related to socioeconomic status, employment, and mate selection among Blacks (Drake & Cayton, 1962). Lighter-skinned Blacks were more favored by Whites because they were closer in appearance to Whites. Different categories of skin color were related to categories of the jobs for which one was eligible (Drake & Cayton, 1962). Lighter-complexioned persons were oftentimes given higher paying jobs and exposed to better opportunities. It was considered better business if lighter workers were hired by Whites. Lighter skin was also positively related to stratification outcomes (e.g., level of education, occupational status, and income) and negatively related to Black awareness (Hughes & Hertel, 1990; Keith & Herring, 1991). The skin color distinction became quite important and a part of ethnocentrism, more specifically, Eurocentrism. Skin color also became a source of status among African Americans and became a part of the fabric of mate selection (Goode, 1982). A premium or mark of status was placed on a woman who was not Black or very dark and for an African American man to marry a light-skinned woman (Zack, 1995).

A Contemporary View of Social Status, Skin Color, and African American Mate Selection

There are many socialization agents regarding preferences in mate selection. Goode (1982) notes that mate selection is controlled by kin or family and that this control is greater as socioeconomic status increases. The family is but one of these socialization agents. Other agents, such as the media, peers, religion, socioeconomic status, and racial socialization, also impart mate selection related scripts to youth. Therefore, many of these scripts become internalized.

The general literature supports differential socialization by gender (Stephan & Stephan, 1990). Buss and Barnes (1986) note that men are more likely than women to prefer mates who were more physically attractive, whereas women are more likely than men to prefer higher levels of education (e.g., college graduates) and those with good potential for high earnings. Both of the latter preferences by women are status related variables. It appears that Black females are socialized either by economic necessity or mobility aspirations to find mates who are perceived as upwardly mobile (Jarrett, 1994).

McAdoo (1988) notes that social statuses for African Americans are in decline due to external pressures such as discrimination and government policies. The children of those who had some advantages, that is, developed skills, acquired land, learned to read, and obtained apprenticeships and formal education, were able to instill into their children the need to continue the upward mobility path. Oftentimes an entire family invested in a selected family member's education (McAdoo, 1988).

In most cultures, women outnumber men. However, the gap between African American women and men is the most extreme in the United States (Guttentag & Secord, 1982). Black females (a) have a much longer life expectancy than Black males, (b) have surpassed Black males in percentage of high school graduates, and (c) have a higher percentage enrolled in college (18–24 years old) (Census Bureau, 1991a).

African American males are also more likely to be both below modal grade or have dropped out at all grade levels compared to African American females (Census Bureau, 1991b). More African American males enter adulthood with increased economic marginality coupled with a number of other structural constraints (e.g., unemployment) that make them less attractive as marriage partners (Tucker & Taylor, 1989). As

African American females enter the marriage market, many may not find eligible mates with similar levels of education, or find a mate at all (Horton & Burgess, 1992). Therefore, costs may outnumber rewards and will reduce the likelihood of a marriage taking place or will reduce the likelihood that a marriage will remain stable. Many African American females will either have to marry down (hypogamy), postpone marriage, or entertain other options, such as marrying someone from another race, marrying someone who is much older or younger, or marrying someone who has previously been married.

In a study by McAdoo (1988), skin color, hair type, and other race related characteristics were deemed important in one-half of her sample. Although skin color preferences still exist, they are not as important as in the past and now seem to be mainly limited to preferences in mates and preferences in employees (McAdoo, 1988). Some lighter-skinned Blacks continue to feel superior and to associate with those with similar appearance. Many continue to use skin color or skin tone as a criterion of status (McAdoo, 1988).

In a 1980 *Ebony* survey, 15% of African American women preferred light-skinned men and 30% of African American men preferred light-skinned women (as cited in Russell et al., 1992). However, in a separate study, 14% of men and 27% of women had actual preferences for lighter-skinned mates (Bond & Cash, 1992).

Conceptual Issues

Much of the mate selection literature seems to be grounded in social exchange, equity, and learning related theories (Murstein, 1986; Stephan & Stephan, 1990). Recent studies have espoused an African American worldview regarding male-female relationships (Asante, 1988). This model emphasizes that Afrocentric cultural values should constitute the foundation of African American relationships. The Afrocentric worldview is rooted in the historical, cultural, and philosophical tradition of African people. Afrocentric relationships encompass spiritual and character values, holistic relationships, and Afrocentric cultural consciousness (Asante, 1987, 1988; Bell, Bouie, & Baldwin, 1990). Human character qualities are stressed over physical characteristics, therefore, Afrocentric relationships may be more healthy and culturally successful for Blacks.

Racial socialization continues to be a powerful tool with regard to values and worldviews. African American youth are said to have been socialized biculturally (Du Bois, 1982) or based on the triple quandary of mainstream, minority, and Black cultural orientations (Boykin & Toms, 1985). The lives of African Americans are significantly shaped by mainstream American society. Mainstream orientations show that youths adapt to and value the Eurocentric cultural system. Mainstream persons may reject varying amounts of the African value system. Minority orientations encompass adaptive reaction, coping styles, and adjustments to the dominant Eurocentric culture that become difficult when coping with the affliction of racism and oppression. Black cultural orientations involve Afrocentric values (Boykin & Toms, 1985). In this conceptual framework, African Americans socialize their children more tacitly and developmentally. Although Boykin and Toms (1985) note the incompatibility between Black and mainstream cultures, African Americans may have to negotiate two or more social worlds simultaneously. Either the mainstream or minority patterns can have negative impact on African Americans and their interpersonal relationships (Bell et al., 1990).

Bell et al. (1990) also note that there are distinct differences between the cultural orientations of African Americans and Whites. The values of power, competition, material affluence, and physical gratification are part of Eurocentric culture (Bell et al., 1990). Euro-American culture has been found to have an overemphasis on physical characteristics.

One such emphasis is on skin color (Bond & Cash, 1992; Keith & Herring, 1991). There is some evidence of discrimination within the African American community based on color (Keith & Herring, 1991). If individuals endorse Eurocentric values, they may depict both themselves as well as other Black males and/or Black females in less than positive ways.

Welsing (1991) addresses the question of Black child socialization by noting that the Black child is brought up in the majority society where inferiorization is stressed. Under the White supremacy system, the darker the skin, the greater the inferiorization pressure asserted by the system. Darker-skinned Black people receive extreme victimization—even from other Blacks.

This skin coloration code established by the global White collective is essential to White genetic survival (Welsing, 1991). This same code causes Black people to say "Don't marry anyone darker than yourself," preferring light-skinned persons over darker-skinned persons as mates. Such socially imposed patterns of thinking yield the Black infant its first direct experience with rejection and negation by the racist social system he or she is born into; this negation will continue for the entire life span (Welsing, 1991).

Hypotheses

Noting the growing patterns of disparity between African American males' and females' levels of education, which is one measure of social homogamy, this study seeks to explore attitudes toward hypogamous and color of skin relationships. Students were asked their (a) willingness to date persons from lower social statuses, (b) preferences to date light-skinned persons, (c) attitudes toward marrying persons perceived as upwardly mobile, (d) willingness to marry persons from lower social statuses, and (e) preferences to marry light-skinned persons. All of the above relate directly or indirectly to a more Eurocentric orientation.

Relationships between background and several dependent variables are expected to differ by gender and socioeconomic status. Specific hypotheses are:

1. Females will differ from males on social status variables (i.e., willingness to date down, etc.) in dating.

2. Males will prefer more physical attributes (i.e., preference to date light-complexioned persons) in dating more than females. Gender is expected to be a strong predictor of the various dependent variables in the analysis.

Methods

Subjects in this study were college students from two historically Black institutions located in the Southeast, one public and one private ($N = 508$). When selecting only African Americans and those who were never-married singles, the final N was 388 (149 males and 236 females, or 39% and 61%, respectively). Students were asked to respond to approximately 25 background variables and almost 100 dependent variables.

Background variables included total family income, father's level of education, mother's level of education, racial (minority group) percentage of neighborhood where respondent was reared, racial (minority group) percentage of high school attended, type of residence (rural or urban), gender, and classification. Dependent variables included willingness to date and marry down, preferences to date and marry light-skinned persons, and preferring a mate who is upwardly mobile.

Bivariate tables will be presented first to offer percentages of each gender related to the various dependent variables. Multiple regression analysis will then be used to analyze the relationship between selected background and the five dependent variables.

Findings

Table 1 shows selected frequencies, based on agreement and disagreement to the eight dependent variables regarding dating and mate selection. Using the chi-square test of significance, significant relationships based on gender were found in 5 of 8 variables: preference to date light-complexioned persons, preference to marry someone with more material wealth than oneself, preference to marry a lighter-complexioned person, willingness to marry a person from a lower social class (than their own), and having a good time and getting along with mate are more important than his or her being attractive (see Table 1).

A correlation table was run to verify strength and direction of the significant relationships (table not shown because it reiterates the findings

Table 1. Breakdown of Dependent Variables by Gender

| Dependent Variable | Percent Agreement | | x^2 | Significance |
	Females	Males		
Would date person with a lower level of education	60.9	75.2	.60	.440
Would prefer to date a light-complexioned person	16.4	33.3	12.54	.000**
Would date person from a lower social class	64.1	70.0	1.25	.263
Prefer to marry someone with more material wealth than myself	60.2	44.0	8.01	.005**
Would prefer to marry a person with light skin	16.8	38.3	19.21	.000**
Would marry a person from a lower social class than my own	49.5	60.8	3.89	.048*
Marriage partner must be upwardly mobile	90.4	85.7	1.41	.235
Having a good time and getting along with my mate are more important than his/her being attractive	88.2	75.5	8.21	.004**

Note: All dependent variables were coded 1 = *strongly disagree*, 2 = *disagree*, 3 = *neither agree nor disagree*, 4 = *agree*, 5 = *strongly agree*. N = 388, df = 1.
*Significant at .05 level. **Significant at .01 level.

in Tables 1 and 2 . . .). Males were more likely than females: (a) to prefer dating light-skinned persons, (b) to prefer marrying a person with light skin, and (c) to be more willing to marry a person from a lower social class than their own. Females were more likely than males: (a) to prefer to marry someone with more material wealth than themselves and (b) to agree that having a good time and getting along with their mates are more important than the person being attractive.

Table 2 sought to ascertain the strongest predictors of groups of dependent variables related to physical attraction and social status. For the skin color related variables, gender was the strongest predictor. That is, being male predicted preference to date and marry lighter-complexioned persons. Being male also strongly predicted having dated lighter-complexioned persons. Father's level of education and racial percentage of the neighborhood were negative predictors of a preference to date lighter-complexioned persons. For each unit increase in the father's level of education, there was a .107 decrease in the preference to date lighter-complexioned persons (controlling for other variables in the model). For each unit increase in the minority percentage of the neighborhood in which reared, there was a .106 decrease in the preference to date a lighter-complexioned per-

son (controlling for other variables in the model).

Only one of the attractiveness related variables was found to be significant. Being female predicted agreement that having a good time and getting along are more important than the mate being attractive (see Table 2).

For the social status related variables, being male significantly predicted willingness to marry someone from a lower social class, having dated females with lower levels of education and having dated females from social classes lower than their own. Mother's level of education was a positive predictor to willingness to marry someone from a lower social class and minority racial percentage of the neighborhood positively predicted willingness to date someone from a lower level of education.

For the mobility related variables, being female predicted that the norm in mate selection is to marry up rather than down. Other significant independents were total family income and rural/urban residence. Students from families with higher levels of income influenced both agreement that the norm is to marry up and that one should marry for love not money, education, jobs, et cetera. Students from higher income families negatively influenced agreement that the person who they marry must be upwardly mobile. Up-

Table 2. Multiple Regression Analysis of Predictor and Dependent Variables

	Gender[a]	Class[b]	Father's Level of Education	Mother's Level of Education	Total Family Income	Racial Percentage of Neighborhood	Rural/ Urban[c]
Skin color related variables:							
If I had a choice, I would prefer dating a light-complexioned person	–.230***	–.044	–.107*	–.083	–.040	–.106*	–.048
If I had a choice, I would prefer to marry a lighter-complexioned person	.247***	.005	.078	.051	.085	.054	.010
I have dated lighter-complexioned persons	–.163**	–.020	–.036	–.031	–.040	.104	–.010
Attractiveness related variables:							
The saying "beauty is only skin deep" applies to me when I am looking for a mate	–.005	.057	.039	.046	.002	.024	–.083
Having a good time and getting along with my mate are more important than him/her being attractive	.133**	.051	.042	.096	.104	–.042	–.053
Social status related variables:							
I would date someone with a lower level of education than myself	–.061	.008	.041	–.007	–.001	.107*	–.050
I would marry someone from a lower social class than my own	–.124*	.039	.018	.149**	–.035	–.056	.044
I have dated someone with a lower level of education than myself	–.187***	.061	.083	.021	–.075	–.007	–.022
I have dated someone from a lower social class than my own	–.124*	.071	.093	.031	.061	.024	–.056
Mobility related variables:							
The norm in mate selection is to marry up rather than down	.156**	.035	–.011	.058	.117*	.019	.040
People should marry for love not money, education, jobs, etc.	.052	–.023	–.003	.054	.107*	–.017	–.109*
The person who I marry must be upwardly mobile	.083	–.068	–.077	.051	–.118*	.033	.098

Note: All dependent variables were coded 1 = *strongly disagree*, 2 = *disagree*, 3 = *neither agree nor disagree*, 4 = *agree*, 5 = *strongly agree*. N = 388.

a. Males coded 0, females coded 1. b. Classification of respondent. Freshman coded 13 to Senior coded 16.
c. Grew up mainly in a rural (coded 1) or urban (coded 2) community. *p < .05. **p < .01. ***p <.001.

ward mobility of the mate was of less concern when total family incomes were higher. Having been reared in a rural rather than urban environment was also associated with agreement that one should marry for love not money, education, jobs, et cetera, (see Table 2).

Discussion

This study sought to clarify the relationship between gender and both physical attractiveness (especially skin color) and social status related variables in terms of mate selection attitudes, preferences, and, to a small extent, behaviors. It was hypothesized that (a) females would differ from males on social status variables (i.e., willingness to date down) in dating and that (b) males would prefer more physical attributes (i.e., preference to date light-complexioned persons) in dating more than females. Gender was also expected to be a strong correlate or predictor of the various dependent variables in the analysis. All of the above were confirmed to an extent. Being female was related to association with most of the social status related variables, just as being male was associated with all of the skin color and physical attractiveness related variables. As a variable, gender was the most significant predictor in the multiple regression analysis.

This study is limited in its generalizability to the larger population. However, the findings support those found in a previous survey. The *Ebony* survey found that 15% of the women and 30% of the men favored a light-skinned partner. In the present study 16.4% of the women and 33.3% of the men favored a light-skinned person to date and 16.8% of the women and 38.3% of the men preferred to marry a person with light skin. This becomes important when almost 4 out of 10 males have such a preference in their future marriage partners. The findings were somewhat opposite to the Bond and Cash (1992) study that found a preference of Black women for lighter-complexioned males.

Attitudes and behaviors are influenced by a myriad of forces or socialization agents. However, there may be differential gender scripts for males and females as shown in the present study.

Russell et al. (1992) noted that socialization and especially the media reinforces both ideal models for beauty and status. It is not unusual for parents to want the best for their offspring. Peer pressure is also strong at the late adolescent to early adulthood ages. Therefore, these young persons look for the best and oftentimes the best does not include intrinsic factors. It includes physical attraction, lighter skin, and higher social statuses. Some concern should be noted with the overall high emphasis on both skin color and social status. There was one exception, however: Females agreed significantly more than males that having a good time and getting along with mates are more important than their being attractive. This finding alludes to agreement to a more intrinsic preference.

Those students from families with higher incomes were less concerned with marrying for money and agreeing that their mates should be upwardly mobile. Therefore, part of the quest of females to neither want to marry someone who is from a lower social class nor to have dated males from a lower social class may be related to their own socioeconomic statuses. That is, many of these females may be from lower socioeconomic statuses themselves.

The minority racial percentage of the neighborhood where respondents grew up seemed to act as a buffer toward preference for lighter skin. That is, the higher the minority percentage in the neighborhood, the less important the preference for lighter skin. Also, the higher the minority percentage in the neighborhood, the more willing respondents were to date persons with lower levels of education. Higher minority percentages in the neighborhood may impart certain social scripts that minimize the importance of the above mate selection preferences.

In revisiting the Afrocentric and triple quandary conceptual frameworks, initial findings support a more Eurocentric leaning; however, results are much more complex. These college students endorse many of the variables related to mainstream orientations, that is, physical attractiveness and skin color. Current findings supported the Buss and Barnes (1986) study that reported that males preferred mates who were high on physical attraction and females preferred mates who were college graduates.

Although direct measures of Afrocentricity and racial socialization were not used in the current study, racial socialization and specifically, socialization toward Afrocentricity, may be effective mediators for such attitudes and behaviors. It is expected that Afrocentricity is negatively related to skin color preferences and perhaps social status (Bond & Cash, 1992; Russell et al., 1992). Certainly a stronger Afrocentric identity should not correlate positively with a preference of lighter skin in dating and mate selection.

As noted by Boykin and Toms (1985), mainstream orientation is vast and overwhelming. We are socialized through hegemony toward the success ethic. Because socialization has its many agents, it is perhaps possible that students can be both mainstream and Afrocentric. Boykin and Toms stressed that African Americans may have to negotiate two or more social worlds simultaneously and that these social world orientations are not necessarily mutually exclusive. Future empirical studies may add clarity to this issue. These studies should examine direct comparisons with Afrocentric variables and other racial socialization mediators to note these relationships (Bond & Cash, 1992). There should be reliable measures of both Afrocentrism and racial socialization. Future studies should also encompass a larger sample to ascertain if findings are the same or different from the present college study.

As McAdoo (1988) noted, the preference of skin color in mate selection, although more historical in nature, continues to be a factor in dating and mate selection in the African American community. It also continues to be a problem in socialization messages from several agents, especially the media. It appears that this socialization may be more tacit than direct; however, the effect is the same.

Social status and the quest for upward mobility appear to be somewhat established in the current study, especially among African American women, just as skin color preference was important to men. These findings shed some light on preferences in mate selection, however, these college students also need to recognize the social, structural, historical, and economic factors that operate against Black families and the Black community. When and if this happens, especially within an Afrocentric related framework, youth may recognize that physical attraction and social status related variables are of lesser importance in future mate selection.

REFERENCES

Asante, M.K. (1987). *The Afrocentric idea.* Philadelphia: Temple University Press.

Asante, M.K. (1988). *Afrocentricity.* Trenton, NJ: Africa World Press.

Bell, Y. R., Bouie, C.L., & Baldwin, J.A. (1990). Afrocentric cultural consciousness and African American male-female relationships. *Journal of Black Studies, 21,* 163–189.

Bond, F., & Cash, T.F. (1992). Black beauty: Skin color and body images among African American college women. *Journal of Applied Social Psychology, 22,* 874–888.

Boykin, A.W., & Toms, F. (1985). Black child socialization: A conceptual framework. In H.P. McAdoo & J.L. McAdoo (Eds.), *Black children: Social, educational, and parental environments.* Beverly Hills, CA: Sage.

Buss, D.M., & Barnes, M. (1986). Preferences in human mate selection. *Journal of Personality and Social Psychology, 50,* 559–570.

Drake, S.C., & Cayton, H.B. (1962). *Black metropolis* (Vol. 1). New York: Harper & Row.

Du Bois, W.E.B. (1982). The *souls of Black folk.* New York: New American Library.

Goode, W.J. (1982). *The family.* Englewood Cliffs, NJ: Prentice Hall.

Guttentag, M., & Secord, P.F. (1983). *Too many women.* Beverly Hills, CA: Sage.

Horton, H.D., & Burgess, N.J. (1992). Where are the Black men? Regional differences in the pool of marriageable Black males in the United States. *National Journal of Sociology, 6,* 3–19.

Hughes, M.G., & Hertel, B.R. (1990). The significance of color remains: A study of life chances, mate selection, and ethnic consciousness among African Americans. *Social Forces, 68*(4), 1–16.

Jarrett, R.L., (1994). Living poor: Family life among single parent, African American women. *Social Problems, 41*(1), 30–49.

Keith, V.M., & Herring, C. (1991). Skin tone and stratification in the Black community. *American Journal of Sociology, 97*(3), 760–768.

McAdoo, H.P. (1988). Transgenerational patterns of upward mobility in African American families. In H.P. McAdoo (Ed.), *Black families.* Newbury Park, CA: Sage.

Murstein, B.I. (1986). *Paths to marriage.* Newbury Park, CA: Sage.

Russell, K., Wilson, M., & Hall, R. (1992). *The color complex: The politics of skin color among African Americans.* New York: Harcourt Brace Jovanovich.

Stephan, C.W., & Stephan, W.G. (1990). *Two social psychologies.* Belmont, CA: Wadsworth.

Tucker, M.B., & Taylor, R.J. (1989). Demographic correlates of relationship status among African Americans. *Journal of Marriage and the Family, 51*, 655–665.

U.S. Bureau of the Census. (1991a). *The Black population in the United States* (Series P-20, No. 448). Washington, DC: Author.

U.S. Bureau of the Census. (1991b). *Household and family characteristics: March 1991* (Series P-20, No. 458). Washington, DC: Author.

Welsing, F.C. (1991). *The Isis papers: The keys to the colors.* Chicago: Third World Press.

Zack, N. (1995). *American mixed race: The culture of microdiversity.* Lanham, MD: Roman & Littlefield.

DISCUSSION QUESTIONS

1. According to Fisher, how is serial monogamy similar to pairbonding among foxes and seasonally parenting birds?

2. What does love mean to you? How do you know when you are in love?

3. What characteristics are you looking for in a future mate? Why? To what extent are your preferences influenced by your parents? By society?

WEBSITES

www.lovemore.com/

Loving More is a national organization that advocates what they term responsible non-monogamy, or polyamory. This can include people involved in an extended family, an open marriage, intimate networks, and other relationship forms.

spider.coba.unr.edu/~ddavis/

If you're interested in participating in research on interpersonal relationships, the Dating Practices Survey out of the University of Nevada, Reno, measures how someone chooses a partner and their behavior during romantic relationships.

CHAPTER 5: HUMAN SEXUALITY/ SEXUAL EXPRESSION

Sexual relationships play a significant role in all societies, and all societies have norms that guide these relationships and control what is considered acceptable sexual activity and what is taboo. Traditionally, in the United States only sexual relations between a married couple were approved. Since the early 1960s, however, attitudes and behaviors regarding sexuality have changed. Today most engaged couples have had sexual experiences before they say "I do," extramarital affairs are reported by a growing number of American men and women in research studies, the sexual double standard that accepts sexual activity for unmarried men but condemns it for unmarried women has diminished, and even within marital intimacy, the primary purpose of sex has changed from "procreation" to "recreation" as both wife and husband seek sexual satisfaction. This chapter will explore several important issues concerning sexuality and sexual expression in today's society.

Premarital sexuality is quite widespread among American teenagers, and young people are having sex earlier than they did in the past. This trend has been accompanied by the gradual postponement of marriage. Since most adolescent sexual activity occurs outside of marriage, teenage pregnancy/parenting is a serious issue today. In her article, Jeannie Rosoff claims that public concern over teenage sexual activity is valid and warranted, because this activity may have destructive consequences for teens such as disease and accidental pregnancy. Rosoff effectively summarizes trends in teen sexuality and pregnancy and emphasizes differences based on income and socioeconomic status.

The second article, by William Grady and associates, is a study of men's perceptions about their role in decision making about sex and contraception, as well as their beliefs about the relative responsibility of men and women for the children they have together. The study finds that most men surveyed perceive gender equality in sexual decision making, contraception, and child rearing.

READING 11
TEENS AND SEX

Jeannie I. Rosoff

In a culture abundant in sexual stimuli, how can American teens be taught to resist the normal biological urges of adolescence? Jeannie I. Rosoff is president of the Alan Guttmacher Institute in New York, a public policy group dedicated to reproductive health issues.

No one can deny that teenage pregnancy is a serious issue. Births to girls too young to care properly for a baby represent both individual and societal tragedies. Yet, society seems unable to develop realistic responses to the problem. This is due, in part, to the fact that rhetoric often serves to obscure the issue.

Indeed, the claims are confusing, if not downright contradictory. Teenage pregnancies are reported to be "soaring," yet their number has remained relatively stable over the last 10 years or so and is considerably lower than in previous decades. "Babies are having babies," trumpet talk show hosts, yet most births to teenagers are to 18- and 19-year-old women. The public, according to opinion polls, believes that the preponderance of the 1,500,000 abortions that take place each year are to teenage girls and that they account, as well, for the majority of births out of wedlock. However these perceptions have come about, the data

From Jeannie I. Rosoff, "Helping Teenagers Avoid the Negative Consequences of Sexual Activity," *USA Today* magazine, May 1996; ©1996 by the Society for the Advancement of Education. Reprinted by permission.

show that they are wrong, on both counts. Yet, teenage pregnancy, while a personal and social problem, routinely is cited both as the end result of all that is wrong in American society and as a major source of all social ills.

Teenage pregnancies and births also are held to be the basis of welfare dependency, and politicians currently are trying to outdo each other in their attempts to alleviate the situation. Among the proposed remedies are restoring the value of sexual abstinence, promoting marriage to make out-of-wedlock pregnancies legitimate, and prohibiting public assistance to teenage mothers under the age of 18 who fail to marry. How many young mothers under 18 actually are receiving welfare checks? Not "hundreds of thousands," as claimed recently by one of the country's most respected newspapers, but 32,000 nationwide. This well may be too many, but could "solving" the problem, assuming that the remedies proposed could do the job, truly be expected to put this country "back on the right track"?

Perhaps what is needed, first, is to define the issue. It is not that many more girls are becoming mothers in their teens than in the past. They are not. Is it that, when they do, they often choose not to marry the father? Even if they do, these youthful marriages are likely to be unstable and impermanent. Is it because they failed to use contraception, or contraception failed them? Or is it because they had sex in the first place, or sex out of marriage?

In U.S. society, much sexual activity does occur outside of marriage. Most Americans today engage in sexual relationships prior to marriage, in between marriages, after divorce or widowhood, or when they choose to remain single altogether, although research shows them to be overwhelmingly faithful to their spouses when in a stable union. It also is a fact that accidental pregnancies are extremely common, some among the married, many more among the unmarried. Of the roughly 4,500,000 pregnancies that take place each year, slightly more than half are unplanned and about 1,500,000 are disruptive or unwanted enough to end in abortion. Given the fact that close to 30% of all births—most to adult women, not teenagers—now occur outside of formal wedlock, it also is clear that an increasing number of women choose to become mothers when marriage is not a likely or promising prospect. Because half of all marriages end in divorce, it tends to blur the differences between the life circumstances of children born in or out of wedlock since the result is increasingly the same—a childhood or a good part of childhood in a single-parent family with its attendant financial and social disadvantages. While these trends are disturbing and a legitimate source of concern, they attract relatively little public ire or condemnation. Neither do they prompt the kind of benign or, alternatively, draconian remedies that sexual activity among teenagers seems to elicit.

Children are not adults. They are, at least under the age of 18, still the legal, financial, and moral responsibility of their parents. Not only their parents, but the community as a whole, have, or should have, a vested interest in their getting a good start in life—acquiring an education, obtaining adequate job training, establishing themselves financially, and, eventually, forming families of their own. They are our collective future and we have a collective investment in their well-being. Sexual activity, with its attendant hazards at all ages—including disease and accidental pregnancy—may have particularly destructive consequences for the very young, shaping prematurely the very course of their lives. Thus, public concern is valid and warranted.

Adolescents today, in spite of their occasional experimentations or temporary rebellions, appear to share their parents' values and aspirations for life. Young people increasingly spend part or all of their childhood in single-parent or "blended" families, and research shows that the deleterious consequences on children, including the likelihood of early sexual activity and pregnancy, are higher in each type. Nowadays, both parents usually work and children tend to have less consistent adult assistance and supervision. The role of the media, particularly television, is pervasive, and the depiction of sex and violence is ubiquitous at virtually all hours of the day. Violence is a commonplace experience in many communities, not in the inner city alone. Drugs often are available at high schools or even at junior high schools.

A large portion—40% of youths aged 15–19—of the country's teenagers live in families that are poor or of low income. Hispanic and black teenagers are substantially more likely than white youths to be at the bottom of the economic ladder, attend substandard schools, fail to graduate from high school, and be unable to pursue further education. Thus, their chances of finding stable and well-paying jobs sometimes are doomed early on. High levels of poverty among children and youths from racial and ethnic minorities, combined with persistent *de facto* segregation in housing and schools, mean that some adolescents, especially African-Americans, grow up in economic and social ghettos where alienation often thrives and education and marriage are not the norm.

Sexual Initiation

It is clear that young people these days are having sex earlier than they did in the past. This has been well-documented in the case of young women on whom information has been collected over the last 20 years. Comparable data for young men and boys is not as plentiful, but, on the whole, they have their first experience with sexual intercourse earlier than girls, a year sooner on average. However, neither are as precocious in their sexual experimentation as the public appears to believe. Still, teenagers are having sex for the first time at younger ages. While initiation of sexual activity during the teenage years has become the norm in the U.S.—as in most developed countries—it should be kept in mind that sex among very young adolescents still is rare and many of the very young girls who have had sex report that they were forced to do so.

Nevertheless, sexual initiation generally has occurred earlier and earlier during the last two decades, with the most significant changes in the behavior of white adolescents. By the end of the 1980s, the differences among youths of different racial, ethnic, and even religious groups had been close to eliminated. This trend toward earlier sexual activity has been accompanied by the gradual postponement of the age of marriage, so that most adolescent sexual activity now occurs outside of marriage. With the median age at marriage approaching 25 for women (and about three years later for men), the interval between the age of puberty and marriage for women has grown from 7.2 years in 1890 to 11.8 years. For men, it is 12.5 years.

The transition from adolescence to full adulthood—usually characterized by entering the labor force full time and setting up one's own household—also has become lengthier. Young people often have to stay in school longer to obtain the same employment opportunities that were available to their parents. There are fewer and poorer job prospects for those who have not completed high school and even for those who have finished high school, but gone no further. Young people who are poor and, within income groups, those who are black or Hispanic, are much less likely than others to graduate from high school on schedule or pursue further education.

So, young people are faced with many contradictory pressures and messages: Get as much education as you can, for as long as you can; establish yourself in a job and achieve financial autonomy; postpone marriage and, at the same time, presumably ignore the biological urges which are normal in adolescence and young adulthood as well as the sexual stimuli that are omnipresent in today's culture. On the whole,

young people cope with these conflicting pressures successfully, and without much help from society. On the other hand, clearly, some succeed better than others in delaying sexual activity until relatively mature and avoiding the potentially harmful consequences of unprotected sex.

The Risks of Being Sexually Active

Within a year, a sexually active teenage girl who does not use contraception has a 90% chance of becoming pregnant. The chances of acquiring a sexually transmitted disease may be even greater since it can result from a single act of intercourse, although some STDs are transmitted more easily than others. While they may not be totally aware of the risks, two-thirds of adolescents use a contraceptive method (usually the condom) the first time they have intercourse. The older the teenager is at the time of first sexual encounter, the more likely he or she is to use a contraceptive. However, most sexually experienced young women delay for a considerable period of time before they consult a medical professional. Roughly 40% wait 12 months after initiating intercourse before they visit a doctor or clinic and obtain more effective contraceptives than over-the-counter methods. Still, most sexually active teenagers utilize some method of contraception and, in general, pill use increases and condom use decreases with age. There are, however, differences among teenagers from different economic backgrounds. Higher-income adolescents are much more likely than those of lower income to use contraceptives. Black and Hispanic youths are less likely to do so than whites, although the differences between whites and blacks are small.

Contrary to popular belief, although their usage is not always perfect, the large majority of adolescents use contraception successfully. Effective use of most contraceptive methods requires motivation, constant attention, and repeated actions that are difficult even for married adults to maintain. It is obviously even more problematic to achieve for others who are not in a stable, predictable type of relationship. Unmarried teenagers, though, appear to do slightly better in preventing an accidental pregnancy than unmarried women in their early 20s and about as well as women in the next age group, 25–29. At all age groups, however, women who are poor or low-income have more difficulty using contraception successfully and, for adolescents in particular, the consequences of not using a method or of using a method ineffectively can be serious indeed.

Over the last two decades, teenage pregnancy rates have gone both up and down, depending on how they are looked at. Reflecting the dramatic rise in the proportion of young women who have had sexual experience in adolescence, the rate increased about 25% between 1972 (when reliable information first became available on the subject) and 1990. Because these teenage women are using contraception earlier and more effectively, the proportion of those who are sexually experienced who become pregnant accidentally actually has declined. Nearly two-thirds of all teenage pregnancies occur among 18- and 19-year-olds. The proportion of sexually active teenagers who become pregnant increases with age because, as they get older, more adolescents become sexually experienced, tend to have intercourse more frequently than their younger sisters, and are more likely to be married (if Hispanic) and/or to want to become pregnant.

Pregnancy rates also vary with race and ethnicity. Black teenagers have a higher pregnancy rate than their Hispanic or white counterparts, due, partially, to the fact that they are still more likely than whites to have initiated sexual activity a little earlier and to be less likely to use contraception or utilize it effectively.

Most teenagers of any race or background actually do not want to get pregnant; 85% of the pregnancies that do occur are unintended. Teenagers are not alone in experiencing high rates of unplanned pregnancies. More than half of all pregnancies among older women are unexpected or "mistimed." Again, income and race or ethnicity make a difference. Pregnancies among higher-income teenagers are more likely to be unintended than those among the less privileged. Among older women, by contrast, those with higher incomes are less likely to have an unintended preg-

nancy than those who are poor or of low income. Hispanic teenagers who become pregnant are somewhat more likely than either blacks or whites to have wanted to do so, or at least not to have cared whether or not they become pregnant.

Dealing with Pregnancy

Obviously, an unmarried woman or girl has only three ways to deal with a pregnancy if the father refuses to marry her or is not known. She can have the baby and raise it herself, give birth and relinquish the infant for adoption, or have an abortion. The overwhelming majority of teenagers faced with these options choose either abortion or going through with the pregnancy and keeping the child. Fifty-three percent of 15- to 19-year-old teenagers who experience an unintended pregnancy have an abortion, compared with 47% of older women facing the same situation. In general, teenagers who are from families that are better off financially are more likely than those from poorer homes to terminate their pregnancies by abortion. The same is true for teenagers whose parents have more education. Those who have a stronger orientation towards the future, with more hopes and aspirations, are more likely to choose to have an abortion.

The age of the male partner also makes a difference. Among the youngest teenagers, who also have partners under the age of 18, 61% have abortions, almost twice the percentage of those whose partner is over 20. This factor is particularly significant since many of the men involved are considerably older than their teenage girlfriends.

When adolescent women become pregnant unintentionally, the path they follow in resolving their dilemma is determined largely by their income and socioeconomic status. Young women from relatively advantaged families generally have abortions, so they can finish their education, get a job or build a career, and establish themselves before they marry and decide to have children. Poor teenagers frequently have abortions as well, but many are not able to avail themselves of this option for financial and other reasons. They also are more likely to have wanted to become pregnant or, probably, not to have cared very much whether they did or not, and to resign themselves to their fate and have the baby if they become pregnant unintentionally. It bears repeating that more than 80% of teenagers who give birth—as distinct from all those who have sex or even those who become pregnant—either are poor or of marginal incomes.

Society can do much—but on the whole has not—to help teenagers avoid the negative consequences of sexual activity. All teenagers need help in postponing the initiation of intercourse, not simply by exhortation, which has been shown to be of very limited use. They need help in acquiring the practical knowledge and skills to help them cope with the glorification of sex in the media, peer pressure, and advances and blandishments on the part of the opposite sex, particularly from older boys and men. All teenagers, when they become involved sexually—as eight in 10 will before they reach the age of 20—need easy access to low-cost, confidential family planning

and STD services. Many also will need easy access to abortion when, as happens so often, contraception fails.

Better coping skills, better and more timely sex education, and improved access to contraceptive, STD, and abortion services will not be sufficient, however, to address the root cause of early childbearing among the disadvantaged teenage women who become parents. For these young women, entrenched poverty, not adolescent pregnancy, is the fundamental issue that must be addressed. Some will have the grit, the inborn talent, and, somehow, garner enough support to escape their circumstances. For most, though, real change in sexual and childbearing behavior will not come unless and until their poverty is alleviated, their schools offer realistic paths to jobs and careers, and their sense of alienation is overcome. In short, it will occur when they develop a sense that their life can, and will if they try, get better. No amount of rhetoric and no laws will change that.

HOW MEN VIEW SEX, CONTRACEPTION, AND CHILD REARING

William R. Grady et al.

Using data from the 1991 National Survey of Men, the authors examine men's perceptions about their roles in relation to those of women in a couple's decision-making about sex, contraception, and child rearing. William R. Grady, Koray Tanfer, and John O.G. Billy are senior research scientists, and Jennifer Lincoln-Hanson is a research assistant, at Battelle Human Affairs Research Centers in Seattle.

Men's involvement in decisions about sex, contraception and childrearing strongly influences sexual and contraceptive behavior,[1] significantly strengthens and reduces discord in relationships,[2] and reinforces a man's responsibility for the children he fathers.[3] Few studies, though, have investigated men's perceptions of their roles and responsibilities regarding decisions about sex, contraception and the raising of children. Furthermore, only recently has such research been identified as being important. High levels of nonmarital childbearing, growing concern about the spread of AIDS and other sexually transmitted

Reproduced with permission of The Alan Guttmacher Institute from William R. Grady, Koray Tanfer, John O.G. Billy, and Jennifer Lincoln-Hanson, "Men's Perceptions of Their Role and Responsibilities Regarding Sex, Contraception, and Childrearing," *Family Planning Perspectives*, vol. 28, no. 5 (September/October 1996), pp. 221–26.

diseases (STDs) and the concomitant increase in the prophylactic use of condoms has led developers of social policy to include men in efforts to prevent pregnancy and STDs. However, most investigations of men's perceptions about their roles and responsibilities have targeted adolescents and other groups of young, unmarried males. Thus, we have little understanding of how married or older men perceive their roles in these decisions.

Current trends in contraceptive method choice suggest that male-controlled methods are increasingly popular. Indeed, the recent rise in contraceptive use among young, unmarried couples is due almost entirely to an increase in the rate of condom use.[4] By 1988, about one-third of married couples were using male methods of contraception, including sterilization,[5] while in a 1991 study, 39% of single men aged 20–39 reported using a condom in the four weeks prior to being interviewed.[6] Clearly, men have an important role in decision-making regarding contraception and family planning.

Research indicates that there has been an increase in the extent to which family planning is considered a joint responsibility. In a study conducted during the 1970s,[7] only about one-third of adolescent males thought that men and women should be equally responsible for contraception.

However, by the late 1980s, more than two-thirds of young men endorsed this belief.[8] Moreover, in the later study, substantially more males thought contraception was solely a male responsibility than thought it a female responsibility. While several other studies have shown that adult males tend to view contraception as a shared decision,[9] only one examined factors that predict such a view: Married men who were older and those who held more egalitarian attitudes were more likely to think that men and women have a shared responsibility for contraception.[10]

There is currently renewed interest in the role of the father in family life, and this is especially so for men raising children outside the context of a marital relationship.[11] Men's attitudes toward parenting responsibilities have a direct bearing on contraceptive behavior:[12] A man is less likely to take responsibility for effective contraception if he lacks a sense of obligation for the children that may result from his sexual behavior.[13] While a very high proportion of adolescent males think that men and women have equal responsibility for the children they have together,[14] there is growing evidence that the fathers of infants born to adolescent mothers are likely to be adults.[15]

In this study, we use data from the 1991 National Survey of Men (NSM) to examine men's perceptions about their role in a couple's decision-making about sex and contraception, as well as their beliefs about the relative responsibility of men and women for the children that they have together. We explore how a man's individual characteristics may affect his perceptions and beliefs, and identify those groups of men who are likely to feel that they have roles and responsibilities that are greater than, less than or equal to those of women. Examining the effects of couple characteristics on men's perceptions helps us to understand how men's views are shaped by both the nature of the relationship in which such decisions are made (e.g., marital or cohabiting) and the characteristics of their partner in that relationship.

Data and Methods

Sample   The 1991 NSM is a nationally representative household survey of men aged 20–39 living in the coterminous United States. The survey was based on a stratified and clustered area probability sample design. Black households were oversampled to ensure adequate representation. The sampling frame contained 17,650 housing units, of which 93% were successfully screened for eligibility. A total of 3,321 in-person interviews were completed (70% of the eligible men). The sample was weighted on the basis of population statistics to account for stratification, clustering and disproportionate sampling, as well as for differential nonresponse.

Since our goal is to examine men's perceptions regarding a man's roles within a sexual relationship, the analyses are restricted to the 2,526 respondents who were in a heterosexual relationship at the time they were interviewed; furthermore, only these men were asked to provide detailed information about their partner's characteristics. Thus, the analyses that follow are based on a sample of 958 black and 1,568 white men.

Measurement   One purpose of the NSM was to develop an understanding of factors influencing a man's decisions about sex, contraception (particularly the use of condoms) and fertility. Thus, men were asked a series of questions regarding their perceptions about both men's and women's roles in these decisions. The analyses presented in this article are based on responses to the following five statements: It is generally the man who decides whether or not the couple will have sex; it is generally the woman who decides whether or not the couple will have sex; it is a woman's responsibility to make decisions about using birth control; it is a man's responsibility to make decisions about using birth control; and men have the same responsibilities as women for the children they father.

When presented with these statements, the respondents were handed a card that displayed a five-point scale (with one representing "strongly disagree," three representing "neutral" and five representing "strongly agree") to indicate their level of agreement with the statements. We cross-tabulated responses to the first two statements to create a combined, three-category measure of perceptions about whether decisions about sex were male-oriented, egalitarian, or female-oriented. Men who indicated a higher level of agreement with the male-focused statement than with the female-focused statement were considered to have a male-oriented perception. Men who indicated a higher level of agreement on the female-focused statement were considered to have a female-oriented perception. Those who registered equal levels of agreement on both items were considered to have an egalitarian orientation. Thus, a respondent who disagreed with the statement that it is generally the man who decides when a couple has sex, and also disagreed that it is generally the woman who decides, was considered to have an egalitarian orientation on the contraceptive measure. A similar procedure was used with the third and fourth statements to assess perceptions about contraceptive decision-making.

The item capturing beliefs about responsibility for the children that men and women have together is not based on a combination of two separate questions. Thus, it is not exactly comparable to the combined measures used to examine the other dimensions. Moreover, a very high proportion of men (87%) strongly agreed with the statement that men and women have the same responsibilities for their children. Thus, in the multivariate analyses, this item was collapsed into a dichotomous outcome variable (strongly agree vs. not strongly agree). . . .

Results

Eighty-eight percent of the men in the sample were white and 12% were black; 8% were of Hispanic origin. Thirty percent of the men were 35 and older, and 19% were in the 20–24 year age-group. Two-thirds of the men were married and living with their spouse, while 11% were cohabiting and 23% had a regular partner. Only 11% of the men in the sample had not completed high school, and 22% had completed college. One-third of the men were Catholic, 36% were non-conservative Protestant and 16% were conservative Protestant. Partners were somewhat younger than the men; 21% were 35 and older, and 25% were younger than 25. However, partners were more likely to have had a previous marriage:

Twenty-one percent of the partners had been previously married, compared to only 9% of the male respondents.

Only 9% of men registered stronger agreement with the statement that it is generally the man who decides whether the couple will have sex than with the statement that it is generally the woman who decides this. In contrast, 30% reported stronger agreement with the female orientation than with the male orientation. Sixty-one percent of men registered equal levels of agreement with both statements.

Fifteen percent of men registered stronger agreement with the statement that it is a man's responsibility to make decisions about contraception than with the statement that it is a woman's responsibility to make these decisions. This is significantly higher than the 7% who indicated greater agreement with the statement that it is a woman's responsibility, and is consistent with recent research examining the perceptions of male adolescents.[16] Seventy-eight percent of respondents reported an egalitarian orientation on this measure.

Shown below are the weighted percentage distributions of responses to the two composite measures of men's perceptions:

Measure	Female oriented	Egali-tarian	Male oriented
Decisions about sex	29.9	60.8	9.3
Contraception	6.5	78.2	15.2

A very high proportion of men (87%) strongly agreed with the statement that men have the same responsibility as women for the children they father, a finding that is also consistent with prior research with adolescents.[17] An additional 8% of men indicated that they somewhat agreed with the statement. In contrast, 5% of men disagreed with the statement or were neutral (not shown).

Decisions About Sex Table 1 presents the standardized probabilities derived from the multinomial logit analysis of the composite measure on decisions about sex. Men's race, age and prior marital history had no significant impact on the relative scoring of the male and female orientations. Hispanic origin, in contrast, had a large impact. Specifically, Hispanic men were substantially more likely than non-Hispanic men to have a male-dominant scoring pattern (.20 vs. .10). They were also less likely than other men to endorse a female-dominant scoring pattern (probabilities of .20 and .36, respectively).

Cohabiting males were more likely than either married men or single men with a regular partner to have a female-dominant scoring pattern (.43 vs. .36 and .35, respectively) and were less than one-half as likely to exhibit a male-dominant scoring pattern. Education was negatively related to the likelihood of scoring the two orientations equally (.61 for men with eight years of education compared with .48 for men with 16 years of education) and was positively related to the likelihood of scoring the male orientation higher: The probability that men with 16 years of education indicated greater agreement with the male orientation was twice that of the probability among those with only eight years of education (.14 vs. .06). Nonetheless, for all levels of education, men with nonegalitarian perceptions were more likely to endorse a female than a male orientation.

Among religious subgroups, conservative Protestants had the highest probability of scoring both orientations equally (.66) and the lowest probability of having a female-dominant scoring pattern (.24). For other Protestants, this pattern was reversed: These men had a probability of .55 of scoring both orientations equally, compared to a probability of .36 of having a female-dominant response pattern. Catholics were the least likely to have a male-dominant scoring pattern (.08), and those men whose religion was categorized as "other or none" were the most likely to have this pattern (.12).

Whether a man's partner was Hispanic had no significant impact on his scoring patterns. However, partner's previous marriage did influence the pattern of scores. Men with a previously married partner were less likely than men with a never-married partner to score both orientations equally (.49 compared with .55) and were more likely to have a female-dominant scoring pattern

(.43 compared with .36). Men with highly educated partners were more likely than those with less educated partners to score the measures equally and less likely to exhibit a male-dominant scoring pattern. The effects of partner's religion were not statistically significant.

Decisions About Contraception   Table 1 also presents results of the analysis of the composite contraceptive responsibility measure. Black men were significantly more likely than white men to have a female-dominant scoring pattern (.16 vs. .06) and were less likely than white men to have a male-dominant scoring pattern (.11 vs. .19). Hispanic origin, in contrast, was associated with an elevated probability of egalitarian scoring and a reduced likelihood of either a male-dominant or female-dominant scoring pattern.

Older age was associated with a less egalitarian scoring pattern: The probability of scoring the two measures equally was .80 at age 20 compared with .67 at age 40. This was due primarily to an increase in the likelihood of female-dominant scoring among older men. A prior marriage was associated with an increased likelihood of having an egalitarian scoring pattern and with a decreased likelihood of a male-dominant scoring pattern. Currently married and cohabiting men were more than twice as likely as unmarried, noncohabiting men to have a female-dominant scoring pattern.

Education was positively related to the likelihood of a male-dominant scoring pattern and was negatively related to the likelihood of a female-dominant scoring pattern. For example, men with 16 years of education were much less likely than men with eight years of education to have a female-dominant scoring pattern (.02 vs. .17). Additionally, men in the category of "other or no religion" had the lowest probability of a male-dominant scoring pattern.

Having a partner of Hispanic origin significantly increased the likelihood of a female-dominant scoring pattern, while having an older partner decreased the likelihood of a female-dominant scoring pattern: Thus, a man with a 40-year-old partner was only about one-fourth as likely as a man with a 20-year-old partner (.03

Table 1. Standardized Probabilities, by Men's Orientations Regarding Decisions About Sex and Contraception, According to Demographic Characteristics of the Respondent and His Partner

Characteristic	Decisions about sex			Decisions about contraception		
	Female	Egalitarian	Male	Female	Egalitarian	Male
RESPONDENT						
Race[3]						
Black	.354	.570	.076	.164	.732	.105
White	.355	.550	.095	.060	.747	.194
Hispanic origin[2,3]						
Yes	.199	.599	.202	.035	.854	.111
No	.355	.550	.095	.060	.747	.194
Age at interview[3]						
20	.373	.551	.076	.033	.802	.165
30	.355	.550	.095	.060	.747	.194
40	.335	.546	.118	.106	.674	.220
Previously married[3]						
Yes	.338	.552	.110	.039	.838	.123
No	.355	.550	.095	.060	.747	.194
Relationship status[1,4]						
Married, living with spouse	.355	.550	.095	.060	.747	.194
Cohabiting	.427	.532	.040	.056	.756	.188
Regular partner	.346	.557	.097	.028	.718	.253
Completed education (in years)[2,4]						
8	.326	.610	.063	.172	.682	.146
12	.355	.550	.095	.060	.747	.194
16	.376	.484	.140	.019	.747	.253
Religion[2,3]						
Catholic	.313	.606	.081	.048	.775	.177
Conservative Protestant	.238	.662	.099	.046	.773	.181
Other Protestant	.355	.550	.095	.060	.747	.194
Other/none	.258	.627	.116	.046	.850	.104
PARTNER						
Hispanic origin[4]						
Yes	.425	.500	.075	.176	.645	.177
No	.355	.550	.095	.060	.747	.194
Age at interview[4]						
20	.358	.532	.110	.122	.668	.210
30	.355	.550	.095	.060	.747	.194
40	.351	.567	.083	.028	.801	.171
Previously married[1]						
Yes	.427	.493	.079	.060	.747	.192
No	.355	.550	.095	.060	.747	.194
Completed education (in years)[2,4]						
8	.362	.502	.136	.038	.703	.259
12	.355	.550	.095	.060	.747	.194
16	.342	.593	.066	.091	.769	.140
Religion[3]						
Catholic	.308	.609	.083	.065	.778	.157
Protestant	.355	.550	.095	.060	.747	.194
Unknown	.288	.670	.043	.103	.616	.281
Other/none	.282	.591	.126	.108	.684	.208

Note: For decisions about sex, [1] = $p \leq .05$ and [2] = $p \leq .01$; for decisions about contraception, [3] = $p \leq .05$ and [4] = $p \leq .01$.

compared with .12) to display a female-dominant scoring pattern. Partner's age was also positively related to egalitarian scoring. Partner's education, in contrast, was positively associated with a female-dominant scoring pattern among respondents and negatively associated with a male-dominant scoring pattern.

Finally, men with Catholic partners had the highest probability of an egalitarian scoring pattern (.78), and those who did not know their partner's religion had the lowest probability of such a pattern (.62). These men also had the lowest and highest probabilities (.16 and .28, respectively) of exhibiting a male-dominant scoring pattern.

Responsibilities for Children   Table 2 presents the results of the binomial logit analysis of men's beliefs regarding responsibility for the children they father. Hispanic origin was significantly and positively related to the belief that both sexes have an equal responsibility for their children ($p < .01$). Men with Hispanic partners, however, had a lower probability of strongly agreeing with the statement about equal responsibility than those whose partners were not Hispanic (.73 compared with .87, $p < .01$).

Men who were previously married were more likely than other men to strongly agree that both sexes have equal responsibility for their children (.94 vs. .87, $p < .05$). In contrast, men with previously married partners were less likely to have a strong level of agreement (.82 vs. .87, $p < .05$). No other characteristic of either the man or his partner had a significant impact on this belief.

Discussion

Most men perceive a couple's decision-making regarding sexual behavior and contraception as an egalitarian process. Sixty-one percent of men currently in a heterosexual relationship view decisions about sex as a shared responsibility and 78% view decisions about contraception in this way. Moreover, men are highly likely to perceive that the responsibility for children is a shared effort: Nearly 90% of men strongly endorse such a belief.

Among men who are not egalitarian in their views, decisions about sex are likely to be perceived as a woman's domain, whereas decisions

Table 2. Standardized Probabilities of Men Strongly Agreeing That They Have the Same Responsibility as Women for Their Children, by Demographic Characteristics of the Respondent and His Partner

Characteristic	Probability
RESPONDENT	
Race	
Black	.844
White	.869
Hispanic origin[2]	
Yes	.950
No	.869
Age at interview	
20	.856
30	.869
40	.881
Previously married[1]	
Yes	.939
No	.869
Relationship status	
Married, living with spouse	.869
Cohabiting	.901
Regular partner	.878
Completed education (in years)	
8	.858
12	.869
16	.879
Religion	
Catholic	.859
Conservative Protestant	.858
Other Protestant	.869
Other/none	.890
PARTNER	
Hispanic origin[2]	
Yes	.725
No	.869
Age at interview	
20	.833
30	.869
40	.899
Previously married[1]	
Yes	.818
No	.869
Completed education (in years)	
8	.861
12	.869
16	.877
Religion	
Catholic	.874
Protestant	.869
Unknown	.907
Other/none	.831

[1]$p \le .05$. [2]$p \le .01$.

about contraception are likely to be perceived as a man's responsibility. Men with nonegalitarian perceptions are three times as likely to have a female-dominant orientation towards sexual decisions as to express a male-dominant one, but they are twice as likely to register a male-dominant orientation toward contraceptive responsibility as to have a female-dominant view.

Race, while unrelated to the perception of either male dominance or female dominance in the sexual decision-making process, is significantly related to perceptions of relative responsibility for contraception. Black men are more likely than men of other races to view the decision to practice contraception as a woman's responsibility and less likely to view it as a man's responsibility. In comparison, men of Hispanic origin are more likely than non-Hispanics to perceive men as dominant in sexual decision-making and are also more likely than non-Hispanics to indicate that men and women have an equal responsibility regarding contraception. Being black has no significant effect on the level of agreement that both sexes share responsibilities for their children, whereas Hispanic origin is related to stronger agreement in this area. Having a Hispanic partner has no impact on a man's perception of who makes decisions about sex, but it is associated with a perception that women bear a greater responsibility for the decision to use contraceptives and with lower levels of agreement that men and women have the same responsibilities for their children.

Age is unrelated to perceptions of male or female dominance in sexual decision-making. However, older men are more likely than younger men to view women as governing contraceptive decision-making. Men with older partners, in contrast, are less likely than those with younger partners to view women as controlling these decisions. This may reflect a shift by women, as they age, away from the use of oral contraceptives and toward either coitus-dependent methods or male sterilization.[18]

A man who has been previously married is more likely than other men to have egalitarian views about the responsibilities of parenthood. However, if a man's partner has been previously married, he is less likely to hold these views. This may reflect perceived differences between men and women in the kinds of experiences they have in dealing with former spouses who are the parents of their children or differences in their expectations about these experiences. Such expectations may be more salient for men who have already experienced a marital dissolution. Previously married men are also more likely to feel that there is joint responsibility in contraceptive decision-making, a relationship that may reflect prior cooperative involvement in such decisions.

Cohabiting men are less likely than their married or noncohabiting peers to view either men or women as primarily responsible for sexual decision-making. This is consistent with research indicating that those in cohabiting relationships have a less traditional sexual ideology, and that cohabiting women initiate sex more often than women in marital relationships.[19] Cohabiting men are also most likely to indicate perceived gender equality in the responsibility for contraceptive use. Unmarried, noncohabiting men, in contrast, are more likely than men in coresidential unions to indicate male dominance in contraceptive decision-making, a pattern that may reflect the greater use of condoms for disease prevention among such men.

A man's educational attainment is positively associated with his perceptions of dominance in decisions regarding both sex and contraception. Men whose partners are highly educated, however, are more likely to perceive that decisions about sex are egalitarian, and they are also more likely to perceive that women have greater responsibility in contraceptive decision-making. These findings are consistent with a relative power hypothesis that suggests that the higher the status of the man, the more likely he is to view himself as the dominant decision-maker, while the higher the status of his partner, the more likely he is to adopt a view of her as either an equal or as the dominant decision-maker.[20]

Conservative Protestants are the most likely to perceive men and women as egalitarian and the least likely to adopt a female-oriented view concerning whether a couple will have sex. This is consistent with a conservative view of gender roles and of the family, a view that increasingly accepts sexuality as a positive, mutual aspect of a marital relationship, yet still tends to favor patriarchal authority.[21] That men who are affiliated with a Christian denomination are more likely than non-Christians and those with no religious affiliation to adopt a male-dominant orientation toward contraceptive decisions may derive from proscriptions against abortion that lead such men to take greater responsibility over contraceptive decisions, to insure that an unintended pregnancy does not occur.[22]

Men who do not know their partner's religious affiliation are very likely to perceive that contraceptive use is a male responsibility. Not knowing the religious affiliation of one's partner may be an indicator of poor communication in the relationship, which also reduces the likelihood of joint decision-making.

Several issues should be kept in mind when interpreting the results presented here. The data are based on perceptions about the behaviors and responsibilities of men and women in general; men's responses therefore reflect ideology more than actual behaviors or the true division of responsibilities in their own relationships. Thus, while about 30% of the men in our sample indicated that the woman generally decides whether or not a couple will have sex, it cannot be assumed that the partners of these men actually exert greater decision-making power regarding sex. Similarly, although a very high proportion of men indicated that men and women have equal responsibility for decisions about contraceptive use, it seems unrealistic to assume that they are all involved equally with their partners in those decisions. Yet, it is likely that such attitudes and perceptions are strongly influenced by an individual's own behavior.

Personal attitudes and perceptions shape sexual and contraceptive decisions. Numerous studies have shown that a woman's partner has a major effect on her sexual, contraceptive and fertility behavior.[23] Yet partners may have appreciable differences in their sexual values, and more importantly,

one partner's perception of the other's values may be inaccurate.[24] Effective contraceptive behavior may depend on joint decision-making to minimize the consequences of such misperceptions.[25]

The impact of such misperceptions extends beyond their implications for unintended pregnancy to other issues of reproductive health, including the risk of STD and HIV infection. The importance of partner influence underscores the need to include men in interventions to reduce unintended pregnancies and STDs. Yet the prevailing policy and program emphasis on women as the key figures in these decisions often unjustly and unwisely excludes men.

The results reported in this article add to our knowledge about how men perceive their role in decisions about sex and contraception, as well as how they view their parental responsibilities. They also show how men's perceptions and views are shaped by their own characteristics, the characteristics of their partner and the nature of their relationship. Despite the limitations discussed above, the information provided here is useful for understanding the sexual and contraceptive behavior of men, and instrumental for efforts to increase their participation in family planning and reproductive health decisions.

NOTES

1. J. Burger and H. Inderbritzen, "Predicting Contraceptive Behavior Among College Students: The Role of Communication, Knowledge, Sexual Anxiety and Self-Esteem," *Archives of Sexual Behavior*, 14:343–350, 1985; W.B. Miller, "Why Some Women Fail to Use Their Contraceptive Method: A Psychological Investigation," *Family Planning Perspectives*, 18:27–32, 1986; J. Inazu, "Partner Involvement and Contraceptive Efficacy in Premarital Sexual Relationships," *Population and Environment*, 9:225–237, 1987; and M. Gerard, C. Breda and F.X. Gibbons, "Gender Effects in Couple Sexual Decision Making and Contraceptive Use," *Journal of Applied Social Psychology*, 20:449–464, 1990.

2. I.L. Reiss, *Journey Into Sexuality*, Prentice-Hall, Englewood Cliffs, N.J., 1986, pp. 235–236; and P. Blumstein and P. Schwartz, *American Couples*, William Morrow, New York, 1983.

3. L.J. Beckman, "Husbands' and Wives' Relative Influence on Fertility Outcomes," *Population and Environment*, 7:182–197, 1984.

4. F.L. Sonenstein and J.H. Pleck, "The Male Role in

Family Planning: What Do We Know?" unpublished manuscript, The Urban Institute, Washington, D.C., 1994.

5. W.D. Mosher and W.F. Pratt, "Use of Contraception and Family Planning Services in the United States, 1988," *American Journal of Public Health,* 80:1132–1133, 1990.

6. K. Tanfer et al., "Condom Use Among U.S. Men, 1991," *Family Planning Perspectives,* 25:61–66, 1993.

7. J.H. Pleck, F.L. Sonenstein and S.O. Swain, "Adolescent Male's Sexual Behavior and Contraceptive Use: Implications for Male Responsibility," *Journal of Adolescent Research,* 3:275–284, 1975.

8. S.D. Clark, Jr., L.S. Zabin, and J.B. Hardy, "Sex, Contraception and Parenthood: Experience and Attitudes Among Urban Black Young Men," *Family Planning Perspectives,* 16:77–82, 1988; and F. L. Sonenstein and J. H. Pleck, 1994, op. cit. (see reference 4).

9. W. Marsiglio, "Husbands' Sex Role Preferences and Contraceptive Intentions: The Case of the Male Pill," *Sex Roles,* 12:22–31, 1985; W. Marsiglio and E.C. Menaghan, "Couples and the Male Birth Control Pill: A Future Alternative in Contraceptive Selection," *Journal of Sex Research,* 56:278–284, 1987; and F.L. Sheean, S.K. Ostwald and J. Rothenberger, "Perceptions of Sexual Responsibility: Do Young Men and Women Agree?" *Pediatric Nursing,* 12:17–21, 1986.

10. W. Marsiglio and E.G. Menaghan, 1987 op. cit. (see reference 9).

11. S.K. Danzinger and N. Radin, "Absent Does Not Equal Uninvolved: Predictors of Fathering in Teen Mother Families," *Journal of Marriage and the Family,* 52:536–642, 1990; H.P. Gershenson, "Redefining Fatherhood in Families with White Adolescent Mothers," *Journal of Marriage and the Family,* 45:591–599, 1983; and A.D. Greene, C. Emig and G. Hearn, "Improving Federal Data on Fathers: A Summary of the Town Meeting on Fathering and Male Fertility, March 27, 1996, Washington, D.C.," Child Trends, Inc., Washington, D.C., unpublished report, 1996.

12. B. Major et al., "Male Partners' Appraisals of Undesired Pregnancy and Abortion: Implications for Women's Adjustment to Abortion," *Journal of Applied Social Psychology,* 22:599–614, 1992; and W. Marsiglio, "Male Pro-

creative Consciousness and Responsibility: A Conceptual Analysis and Research Agenda," *Journal of Family Issues,* 12:268–290, 1991.

13. Ibid.

14. F.L. Sonenstein and J.H. Pleck, 1994, op. cit. (see reference 4).

15. D.J. Landry and J.D. Forrest, "How Old Are U.S. Fathers?" *Family Planning Perspectives,* 27:159–161 & 165, 1995.

16. S.D. Clark, Jr., L.S. Zabin and J.B. Hardy, 1988, op. cit. (see reference 8); and F.L. Sonenstein and J.H. Pleck, 1994, op. cit. (see reference 4).

17. Ibid.

18. W.R. Grady et al., "Contraceptive Switching Among Currently Married Women in the United States," *Journal of Biosocial Science,* Vol. 11, Supplement, 1989, pp. 114–132.

19. P. Blumstein and P. Schwartz, 1983, op. cit. (see reference 2).

20. I.L. Reiss, 1986, op. cit. (see reference 2); C. Saflios-Rothschild, "The Study of Family Power Structure: A Review 1960–1969," *Journal of Marriage and the Family,* 32:522–539, 1970; and ———, *Love, Sex, and Sex Roles,* Prentice-Hall, Englewood Cliffs, N.J., 1977.

21. W.V. D' Antonio, "Family Life, Religion, and Societal Values and Structures," in W.V. D' Antonio and J. Aldous, eds., *Families and Religions,* Sage Publications, Beverly Hills, Calif., 1983, pp. 81–108.

22. Ibid.

23. S.S. Brown and L. Eisenberg, eds., *The Best Intentions: Unintended Pregnancy and the Well-Being of Children and Families,* National Academy Press, Washington, D.C., 1995.

24. L.J. Severy, "Couples' Contraceptive Behavior: Decision Analysis in Fertility," address delivered at the annual meeting of the American Psychological Association, Toronto, Aug. 28, 1984.

25. L.J. Severy and S.E. Silver, "Two Reasonable People: Joint Decision-Making in Contraceptive Choice and Use," in L.J. Severy, ed., *Advances in Population Psychosocial Perspectives Vol. 1,* Jessica Kingsley Publishers, London, 1994, pp. 207–227.

DISCUSSION QUESTIONS

1. What types of sexual stimuli are omnipresent in today's culture? Is it possible for teenagers to ignore the sexual messages that bombard them? Why or why not?

2. Who should be primarily responsible for contraceptive use, the male, the female, or both? Why?

3. The second article in this chapter points out that men perceive gender equality in sexual decision making, contraception, and child rearing. Do these perceptions match actual behaviors? If men agree that they have the same responsibilities as women for contraception and child rearing, then why do women still shoulder most of these responsibilities?

WEBSITES

www-rci.rutgers.edu/~sxetc/

SEX, etc., is a website written and produced by teens about issues related to love, sex, abstinence, contraception, AIDS, STDs, drugs and drinking, and other topics. The goal is to provide teens with solid information to help them make good decisions.

www.hsph.harvard.edu/organizations/healthnet/contra/topic16.html

Harvard's Global Reproductive Health Network website offers a wealth of information on reproductive health and rights, including this page on contraception options for men.

PART III

THE MARRIAGE EXPERIENCE

CONTENTS

PART III: THE MARRIAGE EXPERIENCE

CHAPTER 6: MARRIAGE AND PARTNERSHIPS
    READING 13: THE FUTURE OF MARRIAGE   103
    READING 14: THE CASE FOR GAY (AND STRAIGHT) MARRIAGE   108
    READING 15: DOES YOUR MARRIAGE PASS THE TEST?   114

CHAPTER 7: MARRIAGE: COMMUNICATION AND POWER
    READING 16: WOMEN, MEN, AND MONEY   119
    READING 17: BUT WHAT DO YOU MEAN?   122

CHAPTER 8: FAMILIES AND WORK: FACING THE ECONOMIC SQUEEZE
    READING 18: MOTHERS IN THE LABOR FORCE   128
    READING 19: IS YOUR FAMILY WRECKING YOUR CAREER?   130
    READING 20: MOONLIGHT AND CHILD CARE   137

CHAPTER 6: MARRIAGE AND PARTNERSHIPS

Marriage is considered to be the most intimate of human relationships. It is through marriage that many people attempt to fulfill their emotional, material, and sexual needs. Research indicates that Americans are poorly prepared for marriage, and it is not uncommon for persons to enter the marital relationship with unrealistic expectations. Likewise, "being married" is not an easy task, and people today recognize that couples must consciously work to sustain satisfying and rewarding marriages.

The sexual revolution and the women's movement have transformed many of our traditional images of marriage. Consequently, there is growing concern in the United States with the marital institution. A number of social trends are cited by critics as evidence that marriage is not what it used to be: divorce rates are high; people are waiting to marry until an older age; and marriage is no longer a prerequisite for parenthood. Yet we see from the readings in this chapter that marriage is still popular in our society. The vast majority of Americans still consider marriage an appropriate and desirable arrangement for adults, and over 90 percent of Americans will marry at least once in their lifetime. Family scholars speculate that in the future a new form of marriage is likely to emerge that corresponds with other societal changes.

Frank Furstenberg discusses the future of marriage in the first reading. He predicts that marriage, although changing, is not going to disappear. While the traditional marital roles—husband providing financial support and wife providing domestic services—are no longer valid, the symmetrical marriage with companionship and shared responsibilities is now the desired form for both women and men.

The second reading, "For Better or Worse" by Jonathan Rauch, questions the function of marriage. Rauch argues that neither love nor children can be the defining element of modern marriage. Instead he proposes that marriage (either heterosexual or homosexual) serves the purpose of settling males and caretaking.

Most married people desire a stable and satisfying marriage. The last article in this chapter provides a quick ten-item marriage test and discusses some of the warning signs that a marriage is in trouble.

READING 13
THE FUTURE OF MARRIAGE

Frank F. Furstenberg Jr.

Women's increased economic independence, modern contraception, and financial demands have led Americans to evaluate marriage outside of traditional constraints. Today, many married couples expect less financial security but more companionship and shared work. Change always creates stress, but in the end, a new form of marriage could emerge that will carry Americans into a new era of family life. Frank F. Furstenberg Jr. is the Zellerbach Family Professor of Sociology at the University of Pennsylvania.

It's clear that the institution of family is undergoing a major overhaul. Perhaps you've recently been to a wedding where the bride and groom have invited their former spouses to join the festivities. Or maybe a family member told you that your 37-year-old unmarried cousin is pregnant by artificial insemination. Or you heard that your 75-year-old widowed grandfather just moved in with his 68-year-old woman friend. To those of us who grew up in the 1950s, the married-couple family is beginning to look like the Model T Ford.

Public concern over changes in the practice of marriage is approaching hysteria. An avalanche of books and articles declares that the American family is in a severe state of crisis. Yet little agreement exists among experts on what the crisis is about, why it has occurred, or what could be done to restore confidence in matrimony. I believe that the current situation falls somewhere between those who embrace the changes with complete sanguinity and an increasingly vocal group who see the meltdown of the so-called traditional family as an unmitigated disaster.

Social scientists agree that we have seen a startling amount of change in nuptial practices in the past half century. The shift is producing an especially striking contrast from the 1940s, because the period just after World War II was a time of remarkable domestication. The post-war period followed several decades of turbulence in marriage patterns initiated by rapid urbanization during World War II, and the Great Depression.

Many of the complaints about family life in the 1990s sound an awful lot like those voiced in the 1950s, an era we look upon with nostalgia. We often forget that the current gold standard of family life—the family built upon an intimate marital relationship—was regarded with great suspicion when it made its debut. The middle-class nuclear family that became the norm at mid-century was a stripped-down version of the extended families of previous decades. Kingsley Davis observed that a host of social ills could be traced to this new form of family: ". . . The family union has been reduced to its lowest common denominator—married couple and children. The

Reprinted, with permission, from Frank F. Furstenberg Jr., "The Future of Marriage," *American Demographics*, June 1996; ©1996 American Demographics, Inc., Ithaca, New York.

family aspect of our culture has become couple-centered with only one or two children eventually entering the charmed circle," he wrote.

Ernest Burgess, one of the most respected sociologists of his generation, wrote in 1953 that urbanization, greater mobilization, individualization, increased secularization, and the emancipation of women had transformed the family from an institution based on law and custom to one based on companionship and love. Despite believing that the changes taking place in the family were largely beneficial to society, Burgess acknowledged that enormous pressure would be placed on the marital relationship to meet new expectations for intimacy. Burgess and Davis correctly predicted that divorce would rise because of the tremendous strain placed on couples to manage the growing demands for congeniality and cooperation.

Marriage is not in immediate danger of extinction, though. In 1960, 94 percent of women had been married at least once by age 45. The share in 1994 was 91 percent. In other words, the vast majority of Americans are still willing to try marriage at some point. What has changed from the 1960s is when, how, and for how long.

The median age at marriage has risen from a low of 20.3 for women and 22.8 for men in 1960, to 24.5 for women and 26.7 for men in 1994. The proportion of women never married by their late 20s tripled from a historical low of 11 percent in 1960 to a high of 33 percent in 1993. The divorce rate among ever-married women more than doubled between the early 1960s and late 1980s, although it has since leveled off.

The number of children living in married-couple families dropped from 88 percent in 1960 to 69 percent in 1994. Divorce plays a role in this decline, but much of the rise in single-parent families results from the sharp increase in nonmarital childbearing. The proportion of births occurring out of wedlock jumped from 5 percent in 1960 to 31 percent in 1993. While some of these births occur among couples who are living together, the vast majority are to single parents.

The increase in single-parenthood due to divorce and out-of-wedlock births may be the most

The Trade-Offs of Ending a Marriage

Recently separated women are more likely to perceive improvement in their parenting and social lives than in their financial well-being.

(percent of separated women who say selected aspects of their life are somewhat or much better than in the year before they separated, 1992–93)

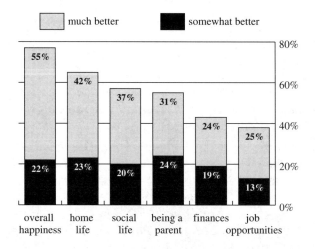

Note: Separated women are those who split from their husbands since the last survey was taken in 1987–88.

Source: National Survey of Families and Households, 1992–93.

telling sign that Americans are losing confidence in marriage. Ironically, some of today's most vitriolic political rhetoric is directed toward gay couples who want the right to marry, just as the cultural legitimacy of marriage has been declining.

What has transformed societal attitudes toward marriage so that young people delay it, older people get out of it, and some skip it altogether? Before attempting to answer these questions, a few cautions are in order. Demographers and sociologists, like climatologists, are pretty good at short-term forecasts, but have little ability to forecast into the distant future. In truth, no one can predict what marriage patterns will look like 50 years from now.

Virtually no one foresaw the "marriage rush" of the 1940s that preceded the baby boom. And few predicted the sudden decline of the institution in the 1960s. If our society alternates periods of embracing and rejecting marriage, then we could be poised on the cusp of a marriage restoration. It's doubtful, however, because most of the forces that have worked to reduce the strength of marital bonds are unlikely to reverse in the near future.

The biggest stress on marriage in the late 20th century is a transition from a clearcut gender-based division of labor to a much less focused one. For a century or more, men were assigned to the work force and women to domestic duties. This social arrangement is becoming defunct. Women are only moderately less likely than men to be gainfully employed. Even women with young children are more likely than not to be working. In 1994, 55 percent of women with children under age 6 were currently employed, compared with 19 percent in 1960.

Women's participation in the labor force has reduced their economic dependency on men. The traditional bargain struck between men and women—financial support in exchange for domestic services—is no longer valid. Men now expect women to help bring home the bacon. And women expect men to help cook the bacon, feed the kids, and clean up afterward. In addition, the old status order that granted men a privileged position in the family is crumbling.

These dramatic alterations in the marriage contract are widely endorsed in theory by men and women alike. The share of both who say their ideal marriage is one in which spouses share household and work responsibilities has increased since the 1970s, according to the 1995 Virginia Slims Opinion Poll. Yet in practice, moves toward gender equality have come with a price. Both men and women enter marriage with higher expectations for interpersonal communication, intimacy, and sexual gratification. If these expectations are not met, they feel freer than they

Mom Learns to Juggle

Married mothers of preschoolers are more likely than all mothers to be in the labor force.

(labor force participation rate of mothers with children younger than age 6 at home for all women aged 16 and older and for married women, 1975–94)

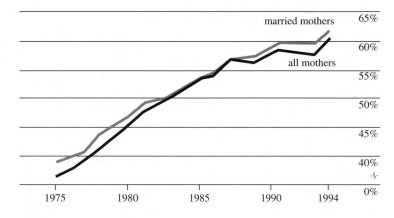

Source: Bureau of Labor Statistics

once did to dissolve the relationship and seek a new partner.

Being out of marriage has its downside, too, of course. About four in ten recently separated women say they are worse off financially than they were while married, according to the 1992–93 National Survey of Families and Households. This longitudinal study asked women who separated from their husbands since the previous survey in 1987–88 to evaluate several aspects of their lives. At the same time, 43 percent of separated women say their finances are better than during marriage.

Ending an unhappy marriage obviously brings about other positive changes. If it didn't, people wouldn't divorce. Being a single parent isn't easy. Yet more than half of separated women say that being a parent is better than before their split-up; 52 percent say care of children is better. Sixty-five percent say their overall home life is better, and 49 percent say their leisure time has improved. This may not mean they have more leisure time than while married, but perhaps the quality of that time is more fulfilling.

The increase in the share of women who work

is not the only reason why Americans readily leave marriages that don't suit them. Legal reform and social trends have made divorce and nonmarital childbearing easier and more acceptable. Safe, affordable contraception enables couples to engage in sex outside of marriage with minimal risk of pregnancy. Women's college-enrollment rates have risen sharply in the past two decades, while public policies and societal attitudes have helped increase their involvement in politics and government. These changes have spurred women to greater autonomy. Each has affected marriage in a different way, but they have all worked in concert toward the same result: to make marriage less imperative and more discretionary.

Some Americans vigorously object to this "take-it-or-leave-it" approach to marriage on moral grounds, hoping to reverse the course of recent history by restoring "traditional" family values. Yet changes in the practice of marriage are not peculiar to the U.S. The decline of marriage as it was practiced in the 1940s in the United States has occurred in virtually all Western societies.

The rise of delayed marriage, divorce, and out-of-wedlock childbearing disturbs the moral sensibilities of many observers. Others may not object on moral grounds, but they fear that the by-products of intimate relationships—children—are no longer safeguarded by the family. Their fears are well-founded. A great deal of research shows that children are disadvantaged by our society's high level of marital flux.

A wealth of data shows that married men and women have lower incidences of alcohol-related problems and other health risks than do divorced and widowed people. Men especially seem to enjoy health benefits from marriage. Experts believe this is because wives often monitor health behavior, and because marriage provides incentives for men to aver high-risk behaviors.

Marriage gives all parties involved an economic boost. In fact, stable marriages could be perpetuating the growing division in American society between the haves and have-nots. Marriage, quite simply, is a form of having. Children growing up with both of their biological parents are likely to be more educated, and to have better

The Perfect Family, 1974–95

Both men and women are more likely now than 20 years ago to say an egalitarian marriage is ideal, but they are also more likely to favor alternatives to marriage.

(percent distribution of respondents' ideal lifestyle, by sex, 1974 and 1995)

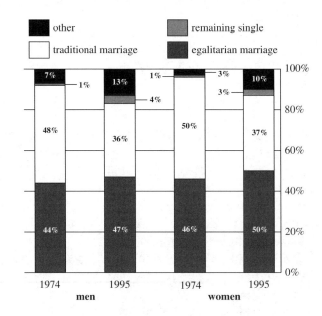

Source: 1995 Virginia Slims Opinion Poll

job skills and a more secure sense of themselves. Thus, they enter adulthood with greater chances of success and a greater likelihood of finding a mate with a similar profile.

This does not mean, however, that children are better off with married parents. Some think that men and women today lack the capacity to sacrifice for children as they did a generation ago. Maybe they do. But if sacrifice means remaining in a stressful, hostile, and abusive environment, it's not necessarily worth it. Even so, I doubt if failure to compromise one's own needs for the good of others is the main reason why fewer couples are getting married and staying married.

In my research on low-income families, I hear men and women talking about the virtues of marriage. Nearly all endorse the idea that children are better off when they grow up with both biological parents, although this is probably said in the context of assuming that the marriage is a "good" one.

Plenty of young people have seen "bad" marriages as they've grown up, which has given them an understandable fear of committing themselves and children to such a situation. "Most of my girlfriends, they got married when they was 20," says one woman. "Now they divorced. They got children. Fathers don't do nothing for them, so then, it was a toss-up. Either to go ahead and start out on the wrong foot or get on the right foot and then fall down." In other words, if you plan to have children, it may not matter too much whether you get married first, because you may not get anything out of the marriage, either financially or emotionally.

Although women may not depend on men's economic support as much as they used to, they still expect something out of the bargain. Young adults in low-income populations feel that they don't have the wherewithal to enter marriage. It's as if marriage has become a luxury consumer item, available only to those with the means to bring it off. Living together or single-parenthood has become the budget way to start a family. Most low-income people I talk to would prefer the luxury model. They just can't afford it.

Marriage is both a cause and a consequence of economic, cultural, and psychological stratification in American society. The recent apparent increase in income inequality in the U.S. means that the population may continue to sort itself between those who are eligible for marriage and a growing number who are deemed ineligible to marry.

There is little to suggest that marriage will become more accessible and enduring in the next century. The unpredictability and insecurity of the job market is likely to have an unsettling effect on marriage in the short term by making marriage a risky proposition, and in the long term by generating larger numbers of people who are the products of unstable family situations. Men are making some progress in taking on household tasks, including child care, but women still shoulder most of the burden in families, causing continued marital stress.

While this may sound unduly pessimistic, marriage may change for the better if people are committed to making the institution work, albeit in a new format. The end of the 20th century may eventually be recognized as the period when this new form of family—the symmetrical marriage—first appeared.

It's no longer noteworthy to see a man pushing a stroller or for preschoolers to be just as curious about mommy's job as daddy's. As with many social trends, well-educated couples appear to be leading the way in developing marriages based on equal sharing of economic and family responsibilities. It may be a little easier for them, too, because they are more likely to have the resources to hire people to do the things they choose not to do themselves.

The move toward symmetry may be more challenging for average Americans of more modest means. Couples who work split shifts because they can't afford child care may be sharing the economic and household load, but they don't spend much time with their spouses. Single parents who have no one with whom to share the load might have little sympathy for couples who argue about whose turn it is to do the dishes, but at least they are spared the arguing. Single people supporting themselves may feel that their finances are strapped, but when a married person loses his or her job, more than one person is adversely affected.

I am often struck by the fact that we have generous ways—both public and private—of aiding communities beset by natural disasters. Yet we do practically nothing for the same communities when a private industry abandons them, or when their young people can't find work, no matter how hard they look. Restoring marriage to an institution of enduring, compassionate relationships will require more than sanctimonious calls for traditional, communitarian, and family values. We should back up our words with resources. This includes moving toward a society that offers secure, remunerative jobs, as well as better child-care options and more flexible schedules so people can accept those jobs. Otherwise, the institution of marriage as we knew it in this century will in the 21st century become a practice of the privileged. Marriage could become a luxury item that most Americans cannot afford.

THE CASE FOR GAY [AND STRAIGHT] MARRIAGE

Jonathan Rauch

Jonathan Rauch reviews the arguments for and against gay marriage. Rauch is a contributing editor to the National Journal, *a guest scholar to the Brookings Institution, and author of several books concerned with the issues of free thought and speech.*

Whatever else marriage may or may not be, it is certainly falling apart. Half of today's marriages end in divorce, and, far more costly, many never begin—leaving mothers poor, children fatherless and neighborhoods chaotic. With timing worthy of Neville Chamberlain, homosexuals have chosen this moment to press for the right to marry. What's more, Hawaii's courts are moving toward letting them do so. I'll believe in gay marriage in America when I see it, but if Hawaii legalizes it, even temporarily, the uproar over this final insult to a besieged institution will be deafening.*

Whether gay marriage makes sense—and

---

*As of 1998, the issue of gay marriage was still being argued in the Hawaiian legislature and courts.

Reprinted from Jonathan Rauch, "For Better or Worse?" *The New Republic*, May 6, 1996, by permission of the author.

whether straight marriage makes sense—depends on what marriage is actually for. Current secular thinking on this question is shockingly sketchy. Gay activists say: marriage is for love, and we love each other, therefore we should be able to marry. Traditionalists say: marriage is for children, and homosexuals do not (or should not) have children, therefore you should not be able to marry. That, unfortunately, pretty well covers the spectrum. I say "unfortunately" because both views are wrong. They misunderstand and impoverish the social meaning of marriage.

The Purpose of Marriage

So what is marriage for? Modern marriage is, of course, based upon traditions that religion helped to codify and enforce. But religious doctrine has no special standing in the world of secular law and policy (the "Christian nation" crowd notwithstanding). If we want to know what and whom marriage is for in modern America, we need a sensible secular doctrine.

At one point, marriage in secular society was largely a matter of business: cementing family ties, providing social status for men and economic support for women, conferring dowries, and so on. Marriages were typically arranged, and "love" in the modern sense was no prerequisite. In Japan, remnants of this system remain, and it works surprisingly well. Couples stay together because they view their marriage as a partnership: an investment in social stability for themselves and their children. Because Japanese couples don't expect as much emotional fulfillment as we do, they are less inclined to break up. They also take a somewhat more relaxed attitude toward adultery. What's a little extracurricular love provided that each partner is fulfilling his or her many other marital duties?

In the West, of course, love is a defining element. The notion of lifelong love is charming, if ambitious, and certainly love is a desirable element of marriage. In society's eyes, however, it cannot be the defining element. You may or may not love your husband, but the two of you are just as married either way. You may love your mistress, but that certainly doesn't make her your spouse. Love helps make sense of marriage emotionally, but it is not terribly important in making sense of marriage from the point of view of social policy.

If love does not define the purpose of secular marriage, what does? Neither the law nor secular thinking provides a clear answer. Today marriage is almost entirely a voluntary arrangement whose contents are up to the people making the deal. There are few if any behaviors that automatically end a marriage. If a man beats his wife, which is about the worst thing he can do to her, he may be convicted of assault, but his marriage is not automatically dissolved. Couples can be adulterous ("open") yet remain married. They can be celibate, too; consummation is not required. All in all, it is an impressive and also rather astonishing victory for modern individualism that so important an institution should be so bereft of formal social instruction as to what should go on inside of it.

Secular society tells us only a few things about marriage. First, marriage depends on the consent of the parties. Second, the parties are not children. Third, the number of parties is two. Fourth, one is a man and the other a woman. Within those rules a marriage is whatever anyone says it is.

Perhaps it is enough simply to say that marriage is as it is and should not be tampered with. This sounds like a crudely reactionary position. In fact, however, of all the arguments against reforming marriage, it is probably the most powerful.

Call it a Hayekian argument, after the great libertarian economist F.A. Hayek, who developed this line of thinking in his book *The Fatal Conceit*. In a market system, the prices generated by impersonal forces may not make sense from any one person's point of view, but they encode far more information than even the cleverest person could ever gather. In a similar fashion, human societies evolve rich and complicated webs of nonlegal rules in the form of customs, traditions and institutions. Like prices, they may seem irrational or arbitrary. But the very fact that they are the customs that have evolved implies that they embody a practical logic that may not be apparent to even a sophisticated analyst. And the web of custom cannot be torn apart and reordered at will because once its internal logic is violated it falls apart. Intellectuals, such as Marxists or feminists, who seek to deconstruct and rationally rebuild social traditions, will produce not better order but chaos.

So the Hayekian view argues strongly against gay marriage. It says that the current rules may not be best and may even be unfair. But they are all we have, and, once you say that marriage need not be male-female, soon marriage will stop being anything at all. You can't mess with the formula without causing unforeseen consequences, possibly including the implosion of the institution of marriage itself.

However, there are problems with the Hayekian position. It is untenable in its extreme form and unhelpful in its milder version. In its extreme form, it implies that no social reforms should ever be undertaken. Indeed, no laws should be passed, because they interfere with the natural evolution of social mores. How could Hayekians abolish slavery? They would probably note that slavery violates fundamental moral principles. But in so doing they would establish a moral platform from which to judge social rules, and thus acknowledge that abstracting social debate from moral concerns is not possible.

If the ban on gay marriage were only mildly unfair, and if the costs of changing it were certain to be enormous, then the ban could stand on Hayekian grounds. But, if there is any social policy today that has a fair claim to be scaldingly inhumane, it is the ban on gay marriage. As conservatives tirelessly and rightly point out, marriage is society's most fundamental institution. To bar any class of people from marrying as they choose is an extraordinary deprivation. When not so long ago it was illegal in parts of America for blacks to marry whites, no one could claim that this was a trivial disenfranchisement. Granted, gay marriage raises issues that interracial marriage does not; but no one can argue that the deprivation is a minor one.

To outweigh such a serious claim it is not enough to say that gay marriage might lead to bad things. Bad things happened as a result of legalizing contraception, but that did not make it the wrong thing to do. Besides, it seems doubtful that extending marriage to, say, another 3 or 5 percent of the population would have anything like the effects that no-fault divorce has had, to say nothing of contraception. By now, the "traditional" understanding of marriage has been sullied in all kinds of ways. It is hard to think of a bigger affront to tradition, for instance, than allowing married women to own property independently of their husbands or allowing them to charge their husbands with rape. Surely it is unfair to say that marriage may be reformed for the sake of anyone and everyone except homosexuals, who must respect the dictates of tradition.

Faced with these problems, the milder version of the Hayekian argument says not that social traditions shouldn't be tampered with at all, but that they shouldn't be tampered with lightly. Fine. In this case, no one is talking about casual messing around; both sides have marshaled their arguments with deadly seriousness. Hayekians surely have to recognize that appeals to blind tradition and to the risks inherent in social change do not, a priori, settle anything in this instance. They merely warn against frivolous change.

So we turn to what has become the standard view of marriage's purpose. Its proponents would probably like to call it a child-centered view, but it is actually an anti-gay view, as will become clear. Whatever you call it, it is the view of marriage that is heard most often, and in the context of the debate over gay marriage it is heard almost exclusively. In its most straightforward form it goes as follows (I quote from James Q. Wilson's fine book *The Moral Sense*):

> A family is not an association of independent people; it is a human commitment designed to make possible the rearing of moral and healthy children. Governments care—or ought to care—about families for this reason, and scarcely for any other.

Wilson speaks about "family" rather than "marriage" as such, but one may, I think, read him as speaking of marriage without doing any injustice to his meaning. The resulting proposition—government ought to care about marriage almost entirely because of children—seems reasonable. But there are problems. The first, obviously, is that gay couples may have children, whether through adoption, prior marriage or (for lesbians) artificial insemination. Leaving aside the thorny issue of gay adoption, the point is that if the mere presence of children is the test, then homosexual relationships can certainly pass it.

You might note, correctly, that heterosexual marriages are more likely to produce children than homosexual ones. When granting marriage licenses to heterosexuals, however, we do not ask how likely the couple is to have children. We assume that they are entitled to get married whether or not they end up with children. Understanding this, conservatives often make an interesting move. In seeking to justify the state's interest in marriage, they shift from the actual presence of children to the anatomical possibility of making them. Hadley Arkes, a political science professor and prominent opponent of homosexual marriage, makes the case this way:

> The traditional understanding of marriage is grounded in the "natural teleology of the body"—in the inescapable fact that only a man and a woman, and only two people, not three, can generate a child. Once marriage is

detached from that natural teleology of the body, what ground of principle would thereafter confine marriage to two people rather than some larger grouping? That is, on what ground of principle would the law reject the claim of a gay couple that their love is not confined to a coupling of two, but that they are woven into a larger ensemble with yet another person or two?

What he seems to be saying is that, where the possibility of natural children is nil, the meaning of marriage is nil. If marriage is allowed between members of the same sex, then the concept of marriage has been emptied of content except to ask whether the parties love each other. Then anything goes, including polygamy. This reasoning presumably is what those opposed to gay marriage have in mind when they claim that, once gay marriage is legal, marriage to pets will follow close behind.

But Arkes and his sympathizers make two mistakes. To see them, break down the claim into two components: (1) Two-person marriage derives its special status from the anatomical possibility that the partners can create natural children; and (2) Apart from (1), two-person marriage has no purpose sufficiently strong to justify its special status. That is, absent justification (1), anything goes.

The first proposition is wholly at odds with the way society actually views marriage. Leave aside the insistence that natural, as opposed to adopted, children define the importance of marriage. The deeper problem, apparent right away, is the issue of sterile heterosexual couples. Here the "anatomical possibility" crowd has a problem, for a homosexual union is, anatomically speaking, nothing but one variety of sterile union and no different even in principle: a woman without a uterus has no more potential for giving birth than a man without a vagina.

It may sound like carping to stress the case of barren heterosexual marriage: the vast majority of newlywed heterosexual couples, after all, can have children and probably will. But the point here is fundamental. There are far more sterile heterosexual unions in America than homosexual ones. The "anatomical possibility" crowd cannot have it both ways. If the possibility of children is what gives meaning to marriage, then a post-menopausal woman who applies for a marriage license should be turned away at the courthouse door. What's more, she should be hooted at and condemned for stretching the meaning of marriage beyond its natural basis and so reducing the institution to frivolity. People at the Family Research Council or Concerned Women for America should point at her and say, "If she can marry, why not polygamy?"

Obviously, the "anatomical" conservatives do not say this, because they are sane. They instead flail around, saying that sterile men and women were at least born with the right-shaped parts for making children, and so on. Their position is really a nonposition. It says that the "natural children" rationale defines marriage when homosexuals are involved but not when heterosexuals are involved. When the parties to union are sterile heterosexuals, the justification for marriage must be something else. But what?

Now arises the oddest part of the "anatomical" argument. Look at proposition (2) above. It says that, absent the anatomical justification for marriage, anything goes. In other words, it dismisses the idea that there might be other good reasons for society to sanctify marriage above other kinds of relationships. Why would anybody make this move? I'll hazard a guess: to exclude homosexuals. Any rationale that justifies sterile heterosexual marriages can also apply to homosexual ones. For instance, marriage makes women more financially secure. Very nice, say the conservatives. But that rationale could be applied to lesbians, so it's definitely out.

The end result of this stratagem is perverse to the point of being funny. The attempt to ground marriage in children (or the anatomical possibility thereof) falls flat. But, having lost that reason for marriage, the anti-gay people can offer no other. In their fixation on excluding homosexuals, they leave themselves no consistent justification for the privileged status of *heterosexual* marriage. They thus tear away any coherent foundation that secular marriage might have, which is precisely the opposite of what they claim they want to do. If they have to undercut marriage to save it from homosexuals, so be it!

For the record, I would be the last to deny that children are one central reason for the privileged status of marriage. When men and women get together, children are a likely outcome; and, as we are learning in ever more unpleasant ways, when children grow up without two parents, trouble ensues. Children are not a trivial reason for marriage; they just cannot be the only reason.

Domesticating Men

What are the others? It seems to me that the two strongest candidates are these: domesticating men and providing reliable caregivers. Both purposes are critical to the functioning of a humane and stable society, and both are much better served by marriage—that is, by one-to-one lifelong commitment—than by any other institution.

Civilizing young males is one of any society's biggest problems. Wherever unattached males gather in packs, you see no end of trouble: wildings in Central Park, gangs in Los Angeles, soccer hooligans in Britain, skinheads in Germany, fraternity hazings in universities, grope-lines in the military and, in a different but ultimately no less tragic way, the bathhouses and wanton sex of gay San Francisco or New York in the 1970s.

For taming men, marriage is unmatched. "Of all the institutions through which men may pass—schools, factories, the military—marriage has the largest effect," Wilson writes in *The Moral Sense*. (A token of the casualness of current thinking about marriage is that the man who wrote those words could, later in the very same book, say that government should care about fostering families for "scarcely any other" reason than children.) If marriage—that is, the binding of men into couples—did nothing else, its power to settle men, to keep them at home and out of trouble, would be ample justification for its special status.

Of course, women and older men don't generally travel in marauding or orgiastic packs. But in their case the second rationale comes into play. A second enormous problem for society is what to do when someone is beset by some sort of burdensome contingency. It could be cancer, a broken back, unemployment or depression; it could be exhaustion from work or stress under pressure. If marriage has any meaning at all, it is that, when you collapse from a stroke, there will be at least one other person whose "job" is to drop everything and come to your aid; or that when you come home after being fired by the postal service there will be someone to persuade you not to kill the supervisor.

Obviously, both rationales—the need to settle males and the need to have people looked after—apply to sterile people as well as fertile ones, and apply to childless couples as well as to ones with children. The first explains why everybody feels relieved when the town delinquent gets married, and the second explains why everybody feels happy when an aging widow takes a second husband. From a social point of view, it seems to me, both rationales are far more compelling as justifications of marriage's special status than, say, love. And both of them apply to homosexuals as well as to heterosexuals.

Take the matter of settling men. It is probably true that women and children, more than just the fact of marriage, help civilize men. But that hardly means that the settling effect of marriage on homosexual men is negligible. To the contrary, being tied to a committed relationship plainly helps stabilize gay men. Even without marriage, coupled gay men have steady sex partners and relationships that they value and therefore tend to be less wanton. Add marriage, and you bring a further array of stabilizing influences. One of the main benefits of publicly recognized marriage is that it binds couples together not only in their own eyes but also in the eyes of society at large. Around the partners is woven a web of expectations that they will spend nights together, go to parties together, take out mortgages together, buy furniture at Ikea together, and so on—all of which helps tie them together and keep them off the streets and at home. Surely that is a very good thing, especially as compared to the closet-gay culture of furtive sex with innumerable partners in parks and bathhouses.

The other benefit of marriage—caretaking—clearly applies to homosexuals. One of the first things many people worry about when coming to terms with their homosexuality is: Who will take care of me when I'm ailing or old? Society needs to care about this, too, as the AIDS crisis has made horribly clear. If that crisis has shown anything, it is that homosexuals can and will take care of each other, sometimes with breathtaking devotion—and that no institution can begin to match the care of a devoted partner. Legally speaking, marriage creates kin. Surely society's interest in kin-creation is strongest of all for people who are unlikely to be supported by children in old age and who may well be rejected by their own parents in youth.

Gay marriage, then, is far from being a mere exercise in political point-making or rights-mongering. On the contrary, it serves two of the three social purposes that make marriage so indispensable and irreplaceable for heterosexuals. Two out of three may not be the whole ball of wax, but it is more than enough to give society a compelling interest in marrying off homosexuals.

There is no substitute. Marriage is the *only* institution that adequately serves these purposes. The power of marriage is not just legal but social. It seals its promise with the smiles and tears of family, friends and neighbors. It shrewdly exploits ceremony (big, public weddings) and money (expensive gifts, dowries) to deter casual commitment and to make bailing out embarrassing. Stag parties and bridal showers signal that what is beginning is not just a legal arrangement but a whole new stage of life. "Domestic partner" laws do none of these things.

I'll go further: far from being a substitute for the real thing, marriage-lite may undermine it. Marriage is a deal between a couple and society, not just between two people: society recognizes the sanctity and autonomy of the pair-bond, and in exchange each spouse commits to being the other's nurse, social worker and policeman of first resort. Each marriage is its own little society within society. Any step that weakens the deal by granting the legal benefits of marriage without also requiring the public commitment is begging for trouble.

So gay marriage makes sense for several of the same reasons that straight marriage makes sense. That would seem a natural place to stop. But the logic of the argument compels one to go a twist further. If it is good for society to have people attached, then it is not enough just to make marriage available. Marriage should also be *expected*. This, too, is just as true for homosexuals as for heterosexuals. So, if homosexuals are justified in expecting access to marriage, society is equally justified in expecting them to use it. I'm not saying that out-of-wedlock sex should be scandalous or that people should be coerced into marrying. The mechanisms of expectation are more subtle. When grandma cluck-clucks over a still-unmarried young man, or when mom says she wishes her little girl would settle down, she is expressing a strong and well-justified preference: one that is quietly echoed in a thousand ways throughout society and that produces subtle but important pressure to form and sustain unions. This is a good and necessary thing, and it will be as necessary for homosexuals as heterosexuals. If gay marriage is recognized, single gay people over a certain age should not be surprised when they are disapproved of or pitied. That is a vital part of what makes marriage work. It's stigma as social policy.

If marriage is to work it cannot be merely a "lifestyle option." It must be privileged. That is, it must be understood to be better, on average, than other ways of living. Not mandatory, not good where everything else is bad, but better: a general norm, rather than a personal taste. The biggest worry about gay marriage, I think, is that homosexuals might get it but then mostly not use it. Gay neglect of marriage wouldn't greatly erode the bonding power of heterosexual marriage (remember, homosexuals are only a tiny fraction of the population)—but it would certainly not help. And heterosexual society would rightly feel betrayed if, after legalization, homosexuals treated marriage as a minority taste rather than as a core institution of life. It is not enough, I think, for gay people to say we want the right to marry. If we do not use it, shame on us.

DOES YOUR MARRIAGE PASS THE TEST?

Florence Isaacs

A test developed by a marriage therapist gives couples the opportunity to identify potential trouble spots in their marriage. Florence Isaacs is a freelance writer who specializes in relationships. She is the author of Toxic Friends/True Friends.

SHE: He travels a lot for work and if he *is* home, all he does is play with his computer. When I discuss the kids, he barely listens. Our sex life is nonexistent. I've talked to him and he promises to change, but a week later, he's back to his old ways. It's hopeless.

HE: I'm on overload, trying to make a living and save enough to put two kids through college. I don't drink or gamble; I'm faithful. But she never gets off my back.

We've all had battles with our spouses. But there's a difference between normal fights that occur in any marriage and chronic problems that weaken a relationship and leave it fragile, says Martin V. Cohen, Ph.D., a New York City marriage therapist. Discord chips away at a relationship over time and can set you up for serious trouble.

"Spouses often deny problems until they're out of control and can become vulnerable to crises like extramarital affairs and separations. But if issues are spotted early, they can often be addressed while still manageable," says Dr. Cohen.

He has identified 10 warning signs of possibly serious trouble. To detect and help couples deal with them before they cause irreparable damage, Dr. Cohen has developed a series of questions he asks his patients. They're designed to bring issues out in the open, and help couples begin to work on what may be troubling their marriage.

The evaluation that follows, adapted from the questions [on p. 115], can help target areas that may need attention in your relationship.

The Answers

1 ANSWER: NO. Satisfied partners tend to look at the big picture and be more tolerant of minor annoyances. So if you find yourself making a mountain out of a molehill, be aware that troubled couples can often feel irritable about everything. When you collect grievances, it's easy to explode at cigar ashes on the rug. They may seem like just one more indication your wishes or needs aren't taken seriously.

If you *have* grown grouchy, reflect on what you may be more deeply distressed about, advises Dr. Cohen. Is it the spot on the carpet—or a basic dissatisfaction, such as the sense you're getting very little out of the relationship and feel helpless to make changes?

2 ANSWER: NO. There's nothing wrong with daydreaming even about being single again or being pursued by an appealing man [or woman]; the issues are frequency and the intensity of the accompanying feelings. Fantasy can be

Reprinted from Florence Isaacs, "Does Your Marriage Pass the Test?" *Woman's Day*, July 16, 1996, by permission of the author.

Marriage Checkup

1. Do you frequently feel impatient with your partner and irked at everything he [or she] says and does?
   __Yes __No

2. Do you often fantasize about what your life would be like without your partner?
   __Yes __No

3. Do you hesitate to confide in your spouse and share private thoughts because you fear they will be used against you in the next argument?
   __Yes __No

4. Are you sexually turned off by your spouse? Do you feel you don't want him [or her] to touch you?
   __Yes __No

5. Do you and your partner find pleasant ways to surprise each other?
   __Yes __No

6. Do you and your partner seem to have little to say to each other?
   __Yes __No

7. When something goes wrong, can you and your mate usually work together to solve the problem, rather than fight?
   __Yes __No

8. Do you feel closer to friends or parents than to your spouse?
   __Yes __No

9. Do you and your partner laugh and have fun together?
   __Yes __No

10. Do you feel lonely in your marriage?
    __Yes __No

---

a stimulant or an escape, and if you need to escape from your marriage regularly, something is missing.

Study your fantasies, Dr. Cohen advises. Are they primarily about sex or exciting adventures, or are they about intimate heart-to-hearts? Your fantasies can tell you much about what you may be yearning for and not getting in your marriage.

3 ANSWER: NO. Happy couples trust each other and feel safe sharing their deepest feelings. That's intimacy. If you *are* holding back confidences, is the fear justified? Or are you afraid your trust *might* be abused?

Sometimes the problem stems from your earlier history. Perhaps another [partner] or a good friend once betrayed you; that, however, doesn't mean your spouse will, too. On the other hand, if [your partner] has made it painful to share thoughts and feelings, talk to him [or her] about the consequences (that it kills intimacy)—and about fighting fair.

Check your own behavior, too. Suppose the two of you are arguing about the checkbook. If you retaliate by saying, "You always want things your way. Look at the blowup you had with the office manager," you've derailed the discussion and made it impossible for him [or her] to respond reasonably. [Your partner] trusted you by revealing a problem at work and you used it against him [or her].

4 ANSWER: NO. There are normal peaks and valleys in sexual enjoyment in any marriage. But sex is also a form of intimacy and often a barometer of how people feel about each other. If sex used to be an important part of your relationship but no longer, realize that this may signal emotional withdrawal.

Ask yourself, "What's the real turnoff?" Is sex being used as a vehicle for punishment or to express dissatisfaction with something else? Are you feeling angry or depressed? Depression can kill desire, but it can be treated; anger can be discussed.

5 ANSWER: YES. Surprise is giving pleasure. It involves spontaneity, creativity, willingness to take risks. The unexpected helps keep marriage exciting. If you feel you and your partner rarely surprise each other, it may be a sign of thoughtlessness, suggesting the relationship isn't a high priority. This can occur even in a good-faith marriage, when partners are naive about what it takes to nurture a relationship.

The first step toward change is awareness. Surprise can range from a new sexual position to a special wine for dinner to an unplanned, "Let's park the kids with Grandma overnight and get away."

6 ANSWER: NO. Partners who feel close can easily express what's in their minds—and hearts—to one another. If conversation with your spouse is difficult, it may be a sign of emotional distance and, sometimes, buried resentment. You may be censoring what you say to each other—possibly because you fear being judged, or worse, rejected.

To start talking, choose a safe topic, one you know you can discuss without hostility. Try sharing a loving concern about the children or [your spouse's] parents, such as, "I'm worried about your dad's high blood pressure." How can you broach a touchy subject that makes you angry? Open it only when you feel calm, and stick to positive suggestions, avoiding criticism.

7 ANSWER: YES. One mark of a strong marriage is the ability to handle crises together in a constructive way.

If you can't work together, you may be focusing on who's at fault, not the conflict itself. Try a new approach. Take one small piece of the problem at a time and talk in terms of, "Let's," instead of 'You" or "I." It takes courage, humility and a certain degree of intimacy to say, "Let's see if we can do something about this," says Dr. Cohen.

8 ANSWER: NO. In a happy marriage, partners are good friends as well as lovers. There's nothing wrong with having other separate supports—they're positive. But if you feel closer to other people than to [your spouse], it can be a sign of a limited marital relationship and often causes conflict.

Beware of putting others first and excluding your spouse, even in small ways. Let's say you're on the phone for a long time with your mother and [your partner] asks, "Who did you talk to?" You reply, "Nobody." Or [your spouse] asks, "What did you talk about?" and you answer, "Nothing." We've all done this, yet it can make a spouse feel left out and consequently resentful.

9 ANSWER: YES. Fun and laughter are signs of closeness. You can allow yourself to feel vulnerable, be playful, take a chance on acting silly. If you can't let go and be free with each other, intimacy may be missing. To reclaim it, realize that time together takes planning. You can't rely on spontaneity. Busy spouses need to schedule events and rituals—or time gets gobbled up.

10 ANSWER: NO. Lonely means "without company." Happy couples usually don't feel lonely because they know they have companionship—each other. If you are chronically lonely, it can indicate a lack of connection or a sign of depression. Have you stopped trying to share feelings? You may secretly wish that your partner should share first, but somebody has to take the lead. When couples can't discuss a problem, it may be time for professional help.

What the Answers Mean

Your answers offer a broad review of your marital relationship. If you've identified potential trouble spots, take the opportunity to explore issues with your [spouse]. (You might start by showing him [or her] this article to initiate discussion.) Tell [your partner] how you feel and see if the two of you can make improvements. In the process, both of you may find some perceptions are less than accurate. It's quite common to misinterpret what a partner is doing and to overreact.

If you need coaching, acknowledge that it's a sign of strength to seek help—not weakness. Says Dr. Cohen, "If the trouble isn't long-standing, short-term marriage therapy can often point you in the right direction."

DISCUSSION QUESTIONS

1. What is the price of gender equality in marriage?

2. Discuss arguments for and against gay and lesbian marriages.

3. How has the definition of marriage changed at the end of the twentieth century? Is marriage still viewed as a permanent, lifelong commitment? Why or why not?

WEBSITES

www.couples-place.com/

The Couples Place provides information and skills training for married and unmarried couples.

www.xq.com/hermp/

Marriage Project—Hawaii is a website devoted to making same-sex marriages legal in the state of Hawaii.

www.poey.demon.co.uk/links.htm

A broad and useful collection of links for the marriage and family therapist.

CHAPTER 7: MARRIAGE: COMMUNICATION AND POWER

The degree and quality of marital interaction is an important factor in a marriage's success or failure. This chapter focuses on two types of marital interaction studied by family scholars: the power environment of marriage and marital communication.

Nearly all married couples experience power struggles in their day-to-day interactions. In some instances, one spouse dominates the other when it comes to decision making. In others, decisions are more equally shared. Power issues can lead to conflict and dissatisfaction in marriage. The resource theory of power proposes that the spouse with more resources has more power in decision making. Traditionally, men were the breadwinners and their economic power was dominant. But what about today? More wives now work outside the home and bring home a paycheck. Kim Clark's article examines the issue of who "wears the pants" when wives earn more money than their husbands. With an estimated 29 percent of working wives outearning their husbands, Clark points out that role (and power) reversal is often a difficult issue for such couples.

To help resolve conflict and enrich the intimate relationship, good communication skills are necessary. Communication is seen as the cornerstone of any intimate relationship, and countless books and magazine articles offer advice to help spouses and partners learn how to communicate effectively. Good communication does not come naturally or easily. When married couples (or even co-workers) have communication breakdowns, the author of the second article, Deborah Tannen, suggests that part of the reason may be gendered patterns of communication. She illustrates how conversational differences exist between men and women: Women's talk is more inclusive and nurturing, while men's talk is more competitive.

WOMEN, MEN, AND MONEY

Kim Clark

The changing economy is bringing more women into the workplace and many of them, especially upper-income women, outearn their husbands. This inequity in earning can create problems in some marriages. Kim Clark is a staff writer for Fortune.

Aha. Money. It's probably the only thing that complicates life between the sexes as much as sex. And when a woman makes more of it than her man, life *really* gets complicated. Even the most liberated man can feel threatened by a woman who earns more than he does. And even the most well-adjusted couples say they have to work extra hard to keep their relationships happy if the woman has the higher salary.

A surprisingly large percentage of women bring home their family's big paycheck. They're not just single moms. Elizabeth Dole, Katie Couric, and Queen Elizabeth outearn their spouses. Statistics compiled by the Department of Labor show that, in all, 29% of working wives—10.2 million women—make more than their husbands, a figure that has grown by nearly 35% since 1988. Among upper-income women, the numbers are much higher. A recent Catalyst survey of 460 female executives at Fortune 1,000

companies found that three-quarters of the married women outearned their spouses. Why is this happening when women, on average, pull down only 66% of their male counterparts' wages? There are several reasons: Women are better educated than they used to be, more of them are working full-time, and equal-opportunity laws have broken down many workplace barriers that held them back.

Despite the growing numbers, couples attempting to adjust to a shift in economic power often find it too touchy to talk about honestly. Jo-Ann Ghio is director of information services for Arbor Software in Sunnyvale, California. As she rose in her company, her husband seemed proud and supportive, especially in public. "But inside it bothered him," she says now. The couple grew apart, but never discussed the root of their problems. "I was afraid to talk about it," says Ghio. "I didn't want to say things that were embarrassing to him." Now divorced, Ghio is finally able to talk about her story. That's how she discovered she is surrounded by women secretly straining to achieve the balance she lost. "We are a silent sisterhood," she says. Men don't talk about it when their wives earn more because they're afraid other men will sneer at them, and women don't talk about it because they don't want to embarrass their men. Or themselves. "If we're successful, society thinks we ought to be connected with somebody just as successful," says Ghio. "If we're not, something's not quite right."

Reprinted from Kim Clark, "Women, Men, and Money," *Fortune*, August 5, 1996, by permission of *Fortune* magazine.

A psychiatric administrator from Philadelphia says that when she brought home her first big paycheck, her salesman husband took it to ensure that he maintained control of the family finances. As her career flourished, he began insulting her. "He had to play down my job," she says. "He would tell me I was stupid or lazy." Then he started hitting her—something he had done early in their relationship but that she thought had been solved with counseling. "He wanted to keep me in my place," she says. The woman moved out and filed for divorce.

Coping with Success

Violence is comparatively rare in affluent households, but studies show that whenever men earn significantly less than their wives, they are more likely to react violently. Ron Levant, a Boston psychologist and co-author of *Masculinity Reconstructed*, says he's counseling a growing number of men in all socioeconomic classes who are having trouble coping with their wives' success. "There is a lot of emotional and physical abuse," he says. Others retaliate in subtler ways—drinking more or having an affair. Even Levant, who says he wouldn't mind if his wife outearned him, admits he'd have trouble making a sacrifice, such as moving, to further her career. "It would be hard," he says. "I'd have to get into therapy."

Financially successful single women lament that it can be a romantic disaster to reveal their salaries to prospective mates. But men can't always be blamed for the problems in these relationships. Anne Gingras, co-owner of a $32 million computer consulting business in Orinda, California, knows she scared men away by saying she expected them to be comfortable with her success. "I dress in designer clothes," she says. "I drive a Jaguar, and I would compare his car with mine. I couldn't date a man who drove a Geo." It took a while, but she thinks her selection technique is effective: She's happy with her boyfriend of eight years, who earns less than a quarter of her income. "He's got other qualities," she says. Plus he drives an Acura.

Judith Wallerstein, a psychologist and co-author of *The Good Marriage*, says her research shows that relationships in which one partner derives most of his or her self-esteem from a career or income are likely to have trouble adapting to a shift in economic power. Aside from choosing the right mate in the first place, Wallerstein offers women more practical help for making the role reversal work. It sounds a lot like the advice a therapist would give a man in a traditional relationship, the difference being that women have to practice it over and over—far more than most men would do.

First, says Wallerstein, a high-earning woman must be supersensitive to a man's feelings. If her career requires a sacrifice from him, "she's got to say, 'I adore you; how can we make up for it?'" Second, she needs to acknowledge his support in private and in public, reassuring him that she couldn't have succeeded without him. Finally, she should never throw her money around during an argument; disputes must be resolved based on what's fair and realistic.

Making It Work

Women who carefully follow this advice—and fall in love with a secure man—won't necessarily find bliss, but at least they have a chance. When Jim Campbell and Elizabeth Mackey married in 1978, says Campbell, "We figured we'd get our MBAs and do yuppie-type things." Their plans changed after son Alex was born in 1981. Mackey was rising rapidly on Wall Street and loved her work. Campbell, less enamored of his, quit and took a sales job he could do from home while caring for Alex. Mackey has since moved to another position as head of CD-ROM acquisitions for Simon & Schuster. Campbell and a friend opened a trophy shop in Briarcliff Manor, New York. His wife's earnings have allowed them to buy a nice house and send Alex to private school. Campbell, proud of his relationship with his son, says life has turned out better than he expected: "I'm happy."

Mackey, who travels frequently, is both grateful for—and a little jealous of—her husband's close ties to Alex. She says the biggest problem caused by their disparity in income is disputes over household chores. While the couple long ago hired out tasks like cleaning and laundry, they are now debating whether they can afford to hire someone to do the bigger jobs, like painting the house. "My weekends are my downtime," says Mackey. "And I loathe having to ask Jim, after he's already worked half of Saturday, to come home and do more work."

Nancy and Frank Dickey resolved that debate years ago. Lower your standards, hire somebody, and be done with it. Nancy, an associate professor of medicine at Texas A&M and chair of the board of the American Medical Association, earns more money than Frank, but he may have more prestige: He's a high school football coach in the country's most football-crazed state. Nancy says she sometimes feels guilty that, because of her job and their family (they have three children), Frank didn't pursue openings that would have required a move. Says Frank: "That's a bunch of bahooey."

Any regrets over jobs he's passed up are more than balanced by the advantages he says he's gotten from Nancy's career. He has a terrific team physician, for example, and her prosperity has given him a freedom most coaches envy—to bench the unathletic sons of school board members. Frank acknowledges that he sometimes feels isolated in the world of Texas macho. Men ask him: "How can you let her gallivant all over?" But he says Nancy has mastered the art of making the Dickeys seem like a traditional couple.

For now it may be easier for everyone to keep up appearances. But all signs indicate that this trend has legs, that the changing economy will bring more—and better-educated—women into the work force. Inevitably, more of them will outearn their husbands. Eventually, both sexes may be able to take comfort in the numbers.

BUT WHAT DO YOU MEAN?

Deborah Tannen

Deborah Tannen, an expert on the different conversational styles of men and women, lists seven common conversation traps that keep men and women apart at work and at home. Tannen is a prolific author and professor of linguistics at Georgetown University.

Conversation is a ritual. We say things that seem obviously the thing to say, without thinking of the literal meaning of our words, any more than we expect the question "How are you?" to call forth a detailed account of aches and pains.

Unfortunately, women and men often have different ideas about what's appropriate, different ways of speaking. Many of the conversational rituals common among women are designed to take the other person's feelings into account, while many of the conversational rituals common among men are designed to maintain the one-up position, or at least avoid appearing one-down. As a result, when men and women interact—especially at work—it's often women who are at the disadvantage. Because women are not trying to avoid the one-down position, that is unfortunately where they may end up.

Here, the biggest areas of miscommunication.

Reprinted from Deborah Tannen, "But What Do You Mean?" *Redbook*, October 1994 (which article was adapted from *Talking from 9 to 5*, by Deborah Tannen; ©1994 by Deborah Tannen), by permission of William Morrow & Company, Inc.

1. Apologies

Women are often told they apologize too much. The reason they're told to stop doing it is that, to many men, apologizing seems synonymous with putting oneself down. But there are many times when "I'm sorry" isn't self-deprecating, or even an apology; it's an automatic way of keeping both speakers on an equal footing. For example, a well-known columnist once interviewed me and gave me her phone number in case I needed to call her back. I misplaced the number and had to go through the newspaper's main switchboard. When our conversation was winding down and we'd both made ending-type remarks, I added, "Oh, I almost forgot—I lost your direct number, can I get it again?" "Oh, I'm sorry," she came back instantly, even though she had done nothing wrong and I was the one who'd lost the number. But I understood she wasn't really apologizing; she was just automatically reassuring me she had no intention of denying me her number.

Even when "I'm sorry" *is* an apology, women often assume it will be the first step in a two-step ritual: I say "I'm sorry" and take half the blame, then you take the other half. At work, it might go something like this:

A: When you typed this letter, you missed this phrase I inserted.

B: Oh, I'm sorry. I'll fix it.

A: Well, I wrote it so small it was easy to miss.

When both parties share blame, it's a mutual face-saving device. But if one person, usually the woman, utters frequent apologies and the other doesn't, she ends up looking as if she's taking the blame for mishaps that aren't her fault. When she's only partially to blame, she looks entirely in the wrong.

I recently sat in on a meeting at an insurance company where the sole woman, Helen, said "I'm sorry" or "I apologize" repeatedly. At one point she said, "I'm thinking out loud. I apologize." Yet the meeting was intended to be an informal brainstorming session, and *everyone* was thinking out loud.

The reason Helen's apologies stood out was that she was the only person in the room making so many. And the reason I was concerned was that Helen felt the annual bonus she had received was unfair. When I interviewed her colleagues, they said that Helen was one of the best and most productive workers—yet she got one of the smallest bonuses. Although the problem might have been outright sexism, I suspect her speech style, which differs from that of her male colleagues, masks her competence.

Unfortunately, not apologizing can have its price too. Since so many women use ritual apologies, those who don't may be seen as hard-edged. What's important is to be aware of how often you say you're sorry (and why), and to monitor your speech based on the reaction you get.

2. Criticism

A woman who cowrote a report with a male colleague was hurt when she read a rough draft to him and he leapt into a critical response—"Oh, that's too dry! You have to make it snappier!" She herself would have been more likely to say, "That's a really good start. Of course, you'll want to make it a little snappier when you revise."

Whether criticism is given straight or softened is often a matter of convention. In general, women use more softeners. I noticed this difference when talking to an editor about an essay I'd written. While going over changes she wanted to make, she said, "There's one more thing. I know you may not agree with me. The reason I noticed the problem is that your other points are so lucid and elegant." She went on hedging for several more

sentences until I put her out of her misery: "Do you want to cut that part?" I asked—and of course she did. But I appreciated her tentativeness. In contrast, another editor (a man) I once called summarily rejected my idea for an article by barking, "Call me when you have something new to say."

Those who are used to ways of talking that soften the impact of criticism may find it hard to deal with the right-between-the-eyes style. It has its own logic, however, and neither style is intrinsically better. People who prefer criticism given straight are operating on an assumption that feelings aren't involved: "Here's the dope. I know you're good; you can take it."

3. Thank-Yous

A woman manager I know starts meetings by thanking everyone for coming, even though it's clearly their job to do so. Her "thank-you" is simply a ritual.

A novelist received a fax from an assistant in her publisher's office; it contained suggested catalog copy for her book. She immediately faxed him her suggested changes and said, "Thanks for running this by me," even though her contract gave her the right to approve all copy. When she thanked the assistant, she fully expected him to reciprocate: "Thanks for giving me such a quick response." Instead, he said, "You're welcome." Suddenly, rather than an equal exchange of pleasantries, she found herself positioned as the recipient of a favor. This made her feel like responding, "Thanks for nothing!"

Many women use "thanks" as an automatic conversation starter and closer; there's nothing literally to say thank you for. Like many rituals typical of women's conversation, it depends on the goodwill of the other to restore the balance. When the other speaker doesn't reciprocate, a woman may feel like someone on a seesaw whose partner abandoned his end. Instead of balancing in the air, she has plopped to the ground, wondering how she got there.

4. Fighting

Many men expect the discussion of ideas to be a ritual fight—explored through verbal opposition. They state their ideas in the strongest possible terms, thinking that if there are weaknesses someone will point them out, and by trying to argue against those objections, they will see how well their ideas hold up.

Those who expect their own ideas to be challenged will respond to another's ideas by trying to poke holes and find weak links—as a way of *helping*. The logic is that when you are challenged you will rise to the occasion: Adrenaline makes your mind sharper; you get ideas and insights you would not have thought of without the spur of battle.

But many women take this approach as a personal attack. Worse, they find it impossible to do their best work in such a contentious environment. If you're not used to ritual fighting, you begin to hear criticism of your ideas as soon as they are formed. Rather than making you think more clearly, it makes you doubt what you know. When you state your ideas, you hedge in order to fend off potential attacks. Ironically, this is more likely to *invite* attack because it makes you look weak.

Although you may never enjoy verbal sparring, some women find it helpful to learn how to do it. An engineer who was the only woman among four men in a small company found that as soon as she learned to argue she was accepted and taken seriously. A doctor attending a hospital staff meeting made a similar discovery. She was becoming more and more angry with a male colleague who'd loudly disagreed with a point she'd made. Her better judgment told her to hold her tongue, to avoid making an enemy of this powerful senior colleague. But finally she couldn't hold it in any longer, and she rose to her feet and delivered an impassioned attack on his position. She sat down in a panic, certain she had permanently damaged her relationship with him. To her amazement, he came up to her afterward and said, "That was a great rebuttal. I'm really impressed. Let's go out for a beer after work and hash out our approaches to this problem."

5. Praise

A manager I'll call Lester had been on his new job six months when he heard that the women reporting to him were deeply dissatisfied. When he talked to them about it, their feelings erupted; two said they were on the verge of quitting because he didn't appreciate their work, and they didn't want to wait to be fired. Lester was dumbfounded: He believed they were doing a fine job. Surely, he thought, he had said nothing to give them the impression he didn't like their work. And indeed he hadn't. That was the problem. He had said *nothing*—and the women assumed he was following the adage "If you can't say something nice, don't say anything." He thought he was showing confidence in them by leaving them alone.

Men and women have different habits in regard to giving praise. For example, Deirdre and her colleague William both gave presentations at a conference. Afterward, Deirdre told William, "That was a great talk!" He thanked her. Then she asked, "What did you think of mine?" and he gave her a lengthy and detailed critique. She found it uncomfortable to listen to his comments. But she assured herself that he meant well, and that his honesty was a signal that she, too, should be honest when he asked for a critique of his performance. As a matter of fact, she had noticed quite a few ways in which he could have improved his presentation. But she never got a chance to tell him because he never asked—and she felt put down. The worst part was that it seemed she had only herself to blame, since she *had* asked what he thought of her talk.

But had she really asked for his critique? The truth is, when she asked for his opinion, she was expecting a compliment, which she felt was more or less required following anyone's talk. When he responded with criticism, she figured, "Oh, he's playing 'Let's critique each other'"—not a game she'd initiated, but one which she was willing to play. Had she realized he was going to criticize her and not ask her to reciprocate, she would never have asked in the first place.

It would be easy to assume that Deirdre was insecure, whether she was fishing for a compliment or soliciting a critique. But she was simply talking automatically, performing one of the many conversational rituals that allow us to get through the day. William may have sincerely misunderstood Deirdre's intention—or may have been unable to pass up a chance to one-up her when given the opportunity.

6. Complaints

"Troubles talk" can be a way to establish rapport with a colleague. You complain about a problem (which shows that you are just folks) and the other person responds with a similar problem (which puts you on equal footing). But while such commiserating is common among women, men are likely to hear it as a request to *solve* the problem.

One woman told me she would frequently initiate what she thought would be pleasant complaint-airing sessions at work. She'd talk about situations that bothered her just to talk about them, maybe to understand them better. But her male office mate would quickly tell her how she could improve the situation. This left her feeling condescended to and frustrated. She was delighted to see this very impasse in a section in my book *You Just Don't Understand*, and showed it to him. "Oh," he said, "I see the problem. How can we solve it?" Then they both laughed, because it had happened again: He short-circuited the detailed discussion she'd hoped for and cut to the chase of finding a solution.

Sometimes the consequences of complaining are more serious: A man might take a woman's lighthearted griping literally, and she can get a reputation as a chronic malcontent. Furthermore, she may be seen as not up to solving the problems that arise on the job.

7. Jokes

I heard a man call in to a talk show and say, "I've worked for two women and neither one had a sense of humor. You know, when you work with men, there's a lot of joking and teasing." The show's host and the guest (both women) took his comment at face value and assumed the women this man worked for were humorless. The guest said, "Isn't it sad that women don't feel comfortable enough with authority to see the humor?" The host said, "Maybe when more women are in

authority roles, they'll be more comfortable with power." But although the women this man worked for *may* have taken themselves too seriously, it's just as likely that they each had a terrific sense of humor, but maybe the humor wasn't the type he was used to. They may have been like the woman who wrote to me: "When I'm with men, my wit or cleverness seems inappropriate (or lost!) so I don't bother. When I'm with my women friends, however, there's no hold on puns or cracks and my humor is fully appreciated."

The types of humor women and men tend to prefer differ. Research has shown that the most common form of humor among men is razzing, teasing, and mock-hostile attacks, while among women it's self-mocking. Women often mistake men's teasing as genuinely hostile. Men often mistake women's mock self-deprecation as truly putting themselves down.

Women have told me they were taken more seriously when they learned to joke the way the guys did. For example, a teacher who went to a national conference with seven other teachers (mostly women) and a group of administrators (mostly men) was annoyed that the administrators always found reasons to leave boring seminars, while the teachers felt they had to stay and take notes. One evening, when the group met at a bar in the hotel, the principal asked her how one such seminar had turned out. She retorted, "As soon as you left, it got much better." He laughed out loud at her response. The playful insult appealed to the men—but there was a trade-off. The women seemed to back off from her after this. (Perhaps they were put off by her using joking to align herself with the bosses.)

There Is No "Right" Way to Talk

When problems arise, the culprit may be style differences—and *all* styles will at times fail with others who don't share or understand them, just as English won't do you much good if you try to speak to someone who knows only French. If you want to get your message across, it's not a question of being "right"; it's a question of using language that's shared—or at least understood.

DISCUSSION QUESTIONS

1. When wives earn more money than their husbands, why do neither of them feel comfortable talking about it? When husbands make more money than their wives, is the same true? Why or why not?

2. Can couples in intimate relationships share too many thoughts and feelings with each other? Is there such a thing as being too open and honest in marriage? Why or why not?

3. Deborah Tannen claims that women and men really do speak different languages. If we accept Tannen's arguments, are we buying into existing myths and stereotypes about men and women? Why or why not?

WEBSITES

www.georgetown.edu/faculty/tannend/
Author and psychologist Deborah Tannen's home page at Georgetown University.
http://www.familytrack.com/irc.htm
Family Track, a commercial site, provides a list of links on their Interpersonal Relations page. Many of these links address the issue of communication among couples.

CHAPTER 8: FAMILIES AND WORK: FACING THE ECONOMIC SQUEEZE

Shifts in the U.S. economy and in women's place within it are re-shaping the connection between families and work. The mass entry of women (most of whom are married and/or have children) into the labor force is one of the most significant social trends of this century. Consequently, most children grow up today with working mothers; in fact, having a stay-at-home mom is considered a luxury since economic necessity propels most women into employment. The two-paycheck family is quickly becoming the norm in our society.

Because men have not responded to women's employment by significantly increasing their domestic and child-rearing responsibilities, employed women must perform a daily balancing act, juggling the demands of family and employer. As a result, working women get less sleep, have less leisure time for themselves and their children, and experience much stress. This chapter explores the family and work dilemma and how workplace policy choices such as child care, parental leave opportunities, and flexible schedules could alleviate some of the current strains on families.

The first reading presents statistics on the increased number of mothers in the labor force. Most American women with children under age eighteen at home are labor force participants.

The second article discusses how the demands of families and the business world are often incompatible. The author, Betsy Morris, points out that today's ideal employee is always available—to work extra hours, to take the unexpected business trip—which directly conflicts with the needs of families, especially children. Career paths often require the highest investment of time and energy just when child rearing is most intensive.

Parents' struggle to find child care that fits their work schedule has become a prominent issue in recent years. The third reading addresses the growth in the number of employees who work nontraditional hours (i.e., shifts other than eight-to-five) and the failure of child care providers to accommodate these workers during evening/night hours. Many of these workers are mothers of young children.

READING 18
MOTHERS IN THE LABOR FORCE

Shannon Dortch

Shannon Dortch, senior editor for American Demographics *magazine, examines recent studies that show an increase in the number of working mothers.*

Being a mother means many things, from changing diapers to answering questions about the wonders of the universe. For most American women with children under age 18 at home, it also means having a job. More than 68 percent of women aged 16 and older with children at home were labor force participants in 1994, according to new data from the Bureau of Labor Statistics. That's a slight increase from the previous year, when the rate was 67 percent, and a significant rise from 47 percent in 1975. Labor force participants either have a job or are actively looking for one.

Even with the demands of parenting and running a household, mothers have higher labor force participation rates than women as a whole. The overall rate for women aged 16 and older, whether they are mothers or not, was about 59 percent in 1995, up slightly from 58 percent the previous year. One reason why mothers are more likely than average to work or want to work is because of their age. Mothers with children under age 18 at home are roughly aged 15 to 54, which

is also the prime age span for labor force participation.

Mothers of Young Children

The likelihood of a mother working increases with the age of her youngest child. Mothers with a child under age 3 were the least likely of all mothers to be in the labor force in 1994, at 57 percent. Mothers with only school-aged children aged 6 to 17 have significantly higher labor force participation rates than their counterparts with preschoolers, at 76 percent in 1994.

Holding down a job is probably more difficult for mothers of preschool children than those whose youngest child spends his or her days at school. Women with children under age 6 at home generally must arrange child care for them, unless they have a nonworking spouse who watches the kids. Married mothers of children under age 6 have slightly higher labor force participation rates than all mothers of preschool children, 62 percent in 1994, compared with 60 percent on average. "This may partly be because married women have husbands with whom they can share the care of a child," says Howard Hayghe, an economist with the Bureau of Labor Statistics.

Married mothers of young children are much more likely now than in the 1970s to be in the labor force. But that doesn't hold true for divorced mothers of preschoolers. Their labor force participation rates have been fairly steady since 1975;

Working with Preschoolers

Divorced mothers of young children are more likely than their married or never-married counterparts to work.

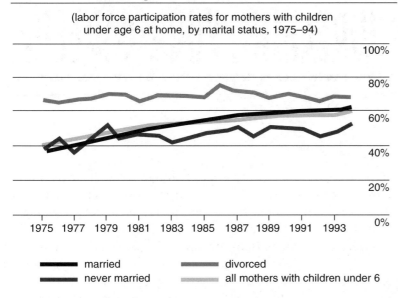

(labor force participation rates for mothers with children under age 6 at home, by marital status, 1975–94)

married
never married
divorced
all mothers with children under 6

Source: Bureau of Labor Statistics

68 percent were working or looking for work in 1994. While married mothers may have some choice in their decision to work or not work, many divorced mothers work out of necessity, Hayghe says.

Never-married mothers with children under age 6 at home are the least likely of all mothers of young children to be in the labor force. This is partly due to their age. They are typically younger than married or divorced mothers, and young women generally have lower labor force participation rates than their older counterparts. Rates for never-married mothers of preschoolers have risen, to 52 percent in 1994 from 46 percent two years earlier. But it's unclear whether this is a true trend or a result of changes in survey methodology, Hayghe says.

In 1994, the Bureau of Labor Statistics changed the wording of some questions asked by the monthly Current Population Survey in an effort to capture more complete information on labor force status. "In the older survey, it appeared that some women didn't understand we were asking them about any kind of employment—not just full-time employment," he says. "We'll have to wait for a few years to see what happens after 1994."

IS YOUR FAMILY WRECKING YOUR CAREER?

Betsy Morris

Ambitious two-income couples are discovering that the demands of corporate America are taking a toll on their family lives. Betsy Morris, a writer for Fortune *magazine, looks at how some in an affluent Atlanta suburb are coping with success.*

Set aside the talk of family values for a minute, and let's be frank. How valuable are families, really? Once upon a time, a family was a corporate prerequisite. A man (there were hardly enough corporate women to count) wasn't in the right circles if he didn't have a wife and three kids. He couldn't get onto the right boards or into the right clubs. No children? What a shame. And a wife was so important that she was often under scrutiny on her husband's route up the ladder. Families mattered. Not to have one was considered strange. Un-American.

Today, in the corridors of business as elsewhere, families are getting more lip service than ever. Being on the right side of work and family issues—having the proper programs, letting Mom or Dad slip out to watch a T-ball game—is very PC. But corporate America harbors a dirty secret. People in human resources know it. So do a lot of CEOs, although they don't dare discuss it. Families are no longer a big plus for a corpora-

tion; they are a big problem. An albatross. More and more, the business world seems to regard children not as the future generation of workers but as luxuries you're entitled to after you've won your stripes. It's fine to have the kids' pictures on your desk—just don't let them cut into your billable hours.

In the 1980s there was the career-killing Mommy Track. In the 1990s there's the Parent Track, and it's a killer too. Several studies indicate that well-educated men with working wives are paid and promoted less than men with stay-at-home wives, possibly because they can't clock as much face time. In a 1995 survey at Eli Lilly & Co., just 36% of workers said it was possible to get ahead and still devote sufficient time to their families—and Lilly has a reputation as one of the most family-friendly companies. Corporate manuals would do well to carry a warning: *Ambitious beware. If you want to have children, proceed at your own risk. You must be very talented, or on very solid ground, to overcome the damage a family can do to your career.*

And vice versa. Your career, in fact, may be doing even more damage to your family. The casualties are high and rising in Morningside, a quiet, leafy Atlanta neighborhood just down the road from where I live. Morningside is full of prim Tudor houses, crisscrossed by sidewalks, anchored by parks, dotted with playgrounds. It looks like the storybook family neighborhood—and it probably is about as storybook as it gets. But here, be-

Reprinted from Betsy Morris, "Is Your Family Wrecking Your Career (and Vice-versa)," *Fortune*, March 17, 1997, by permission of *Fortune* magazine.

hind the family-friendly trappings, elementary school teachers debate whether they should quit assigning homework because working moms and dads are too tired or busy—or both—to handle it. Here families are smaller as parents decide they can't afford or cope with—or both—more children. Here husbands try to reconcile their own ambitions with the post-traditionalist expectations of wives who may be working even harder than they are. And both spouses wonder: Will the company write them off if they do what it takes to keep their families intact?

The Price of Ambition

"We are making it less likely for people to have families," says Rosalind C. Barnett, a research psychologist and author of *She Works/He Works*. "It is just too punitive. There is no formal child care. There is no institutional support. It is hugely expensive." Whether business may be inadvertently penalizing families "is really the question of the 1990s," says Linda K. Stroh, associate professor of organizational development at Chicago's Loyola University.

Corporations, of course, have always demanded single-mindedness from employees. Ambitious men have historically been required to work long hours, miss dinners, and forgo time with their kids to get ahead. The reason the right wife was once so important to a man's career was that she provided the stay-at-home support that allowed him to concentrate on work. But the women's movement and powerful economic forces ended all that. As incomes began to stagnate in the early 1970s, it has taken a second earner to keep the standard of living of even the most affluent households from falling behind. Now, in 84% of married couples, both the husband and wife work. And in an interesting turn of events, the ultimate male status symbol is not a fancy car or a fancy second home or a wife with a fancy career. You've really made it, buddy, if you can afford a wife who doesn't work. She may be a drag on earnings, but she provides a rare modern luxury: peace on the home front.

The modes and rhythms of the 24-hour global company have only heightened the conflict between corporate values and family values. In a world built on just-in-time, the ideal employee is the one who's always available, not the one who's constantly torn. In a world that's a village, the corporate hero is the one free to fly to Singapore on a moment's notice, not the poor schlep who has to get home to relieve the nanny. In the wired world of ubiquitous communication, where work has become an insatiable maw devouring every waking hour—and many sleeping ones too—the model worker is the one who can best feed the beast.

The demands of this new economy wreak havoc on family routines that are the bulwark of childhood. One parent—or both—may vanish for days with little warning, because travel has become a critical component of even mundane jobs. The family dinner has disappeared in many homes as parents work long past the time little tummies start to growl; bedtime slippage follows to give Mom and Dad time—which may or may not be "quality time"—with the kids. The long, unpredictable hours lead to kaleidoscopic child care arrangements. Many households have not one but several babysitters; parents need a flow chart to keep it all straight.

Never mind the debate over day care. Today's parents are even more worried about how kids will be affected by the stress and crammed-to-bursting schedules in their own house. A recent report by the Carnegie Council on Adolescent Development found that kids spend significantly less time in the company of adults than a few decades ago. About one-third of all adolescents have contemplated suicide; half are at moderate or high risk of abusing drugs, failing in school, getting pregnant, or otherwise seriously damaging their lives. While the risks are exacerbated by poverty, "in survey after survey, young adolescents from all ethnic and economic backgrounds lament their lack of parental attention and guidance," the report found.

"Kids are highly stressed," agrees Carrell Dammann, a psychologist who has practiced in Atlanta for 25 years and whose patients come mostly from corporate and professional families. "If parents don't give them enough time, don't set norms and limits, adolescents turn to drugs and alcohol to fill the emptiness." As for younger children, Dammann wonders how they are affected by parents whose unpredictable movements necessitate staying in touch with the kids by beeper. "The one thing that's essential in early childhood is a sense of security. Children who don't have it are going to be anxious."

Companies are trying to help. To their credit, many offer flexible schedules, job sharing, and personal leaves. Some have gone the extra mile to establish on-site day care; others provide personal valet services to buy groceries, birthday presents—even plan the birthday party. While all that relieves some symptoms of the work and family dilemma, it doesn't alleviate the structural problems: the hierarchical and often unforgiving way in which work is organized; the pace of the managerial career path, which requires the highest investment of time just when child rearing is most intense; the emphasis on face time as a measure of dedication and commitment.

"Historically we looked at whose cars were in the parking lot at 7 P.M., and we made the assumption that they belonged to corporate heroes hard at work," says Randall Tobias, the CEO of Eli Lilly. "In truth, some of those people were probably poorly organized or spending time on the wrong things. We have to get more focus off measuring activity and onto measuring results—not the number of hours put in but what gets produced." As for the struggle of working families, says Tobias, who has begun to advocate out-of-the-box thinking on the subject, "I'm not sure a lot of corporate America understands."

Success in Morningside

Morningside is a microcosm of the dramatically altered world of work and family. Like America itself, it began as an agrarian community. In the 1920s, when businesses became more industrial, it became one of Atlanta's first suburbs; fathers left for jobs in the city while mothers stayed home. As Atlanta grew and its demographics changed, Morningside turned into an eclectic in-town neighborhood with all kinds of families: traditional, gay, childless, dual career.

Now, as in so many places across the land, moms and dads leave here each morning headed not just for the nearby headquarters of BellSouth, Coca-Cola, and Georgia-Pacific, but for Richmond, Chicago, Hong Kong.

Houses in Morningside typically cost $250,000 and range up to $450,000. It's an expensive place to live by Atlanta standards, but not one of the showiest. People aren't here to impress. Instead they are paying for what families used to have: community. Neighbors serve as extended family; schools are within walking distance; commutes are blessedly short.

Morningside is a good place to study the odd mismatch between today's well-trained women and the traditional infrastructure that still undergirds work. Over on Wildwood Road live Karen Sukin, 32, and Brad Slutsky, 33, once the bright young stars of the Atlanta law scene. They met in college at Brown University. Her grades were slightly higher than his, but he scored in the 99.6th percentile on the LSAT, a tenth of a percentage point ahead of her. Both were hotshots during their summer internships at Kilpatrick & Cody. Brad eventually went to work for the silk-stocking firm of King & Spalding, while Karen chose its major competitor, Alston & Bird. Since then their work paths have veered in very different directions.

Soon after joining Alston & Bird, Karen got some advice: If she wanted a family, she should wait until after making partner. It was kindly advice and probably politically sound. But it didn't make sense to her. She had grown up in Billings, Montana, with three siblings, and family was important to her. She didn't want to be too old when she had her children; she didn't want to take the risk she might not get pregnant. "It takes a lot of energy to have kids," she says, sitting in the living room of her two-story brick house, sparsely furnished in Little Tikes. "I didn't want to be having babies in my 40s."

Biologically her argument was sound. But it held no weight in the world of law. When Isaac was born almost five years ago, Karen was counseled to come back full-time and slip home early if she needed to. She tried but felt guilty. So she scaled back to a part-time 40-hour week, which enabled her to get home for dinner. When Lauren was born a year and a half later, that was barely acceptable, and then only on the grounds that it seemed wise to get her childbearing out of the way as efficiently as possible. When she became pregnant with Sarah, who was born a year ago, people were politely incredulous: "You could see it in their faces," recalls Karen. "The reaction was, 'But you have enough already. You have a boy and a girl, and that's all you're entitled to.'"

Somewhere Karen fell off the partnership track. At the end of last summer she stopped working altogether. "Commitment is the big word at law firms," she says. "Commitment is what makes you a partner. That means working long hours, as well as spending your evenings and all your other available time building your career. I just can't do that now." But she misses work and told the firm she hopes to return in a few years.

While Karen has dropped out, her husband has worked 60 to 80 hours a week since joining King & Spalding seven years ago. Brad, who made partner last year, rarely gets home for dinner, and he works many weekends. Summer before last, he went five months without a day off. He spends free nights on outside activities that might help build his practice. He sees his children in the morning before getting to the office at 9. "I miss a lot," he says wistfully. He moved to Morningside, which is ten minutes from his office, to cut down on commuting time and to be able to slip home to see his children at lunch. But most days he eats lunch at his desk.

Brad feels pressure from peers and clients. "You always have to be available for a client," he says. "I think about who I would want handling a serious problem for me. I would want someone devoted to the problem—not someone working on it when it's convenient." With Karen off the track, Brad feels more pressure too, to support and educate his children. And of course he feels guilty—about not seeing his kids, about Karen not working. "She's an extremely intelligent person," says Brad. "She's a great lawyer. You wish there were a setup where what she is doing is more acceptable."

Lawyers have always worked hard. But, says Karen, "I don't think partners today worked nearly as much when they were younger as we do now. Nor were there the same expectations. There's no way a generation ago that men were expected to devote all their waking hours to work. Brad and I talk about it a lot. We think it's because we're at the bottom of the baby-boom generation. We're fungible."

High Expectations

It's true that this generation has provided corporate America with an army of workers, an unprecedented number of them unencumbered. Young people are delaying marriage and children with a vengeance. One-third of women and one-half of men ages 25 to 29 have never married—an all-time high. The percentage of childless women has risen from 10% of 40- to 45-year-olds in 1976 to 17.5% in 1994, another all-time high. Some of this childlessness is due to infertility, but a lot is due to choice: opting out of the complications and expense. Birthrates, which have rebounded slightly to about two per woman after falling to a low of 1.8 a decade ago, are buoyed largely by immigrant groups.

The commitment of today's workers dovetails nicely with the voracious appetites of business. At global Coca-Cola, fast-track employees had better be prepared to move around. At BellSouth, even departments like customer service and computer support work round-the-clock. "People tell me that if they're working less than 50 hours a week, they aren't carrying their load," says Elaine Rubin, a therapist who grew up near Morningside and now directs the employee assistance program for BellSouth. Rubin says she sees far fewer cases of drug and alcohol abuse that such programs were designed to handle, and many more cases of work and family stress. Says Rubin: "I keep hearing that employees are being asked to work smarter, work harder. Their supervisors keep thinking it is an issue of time management."

No one is better at managing time than working couples with children. But only the most deluded would describe themselves as both standout managers and adequate parents. (Can anyone be a standout parent?) Nancy Nicholl-Hasson and Marty Hasson live on Cumberland Road in Morningside. Nancy, 32, is a project manager in the chemical division of Georgia-Pacific. Marty, 40, is a sales rep for Ribelin Sales, a Dallas-based distributor of chemical products. Both their jobs require travel. Both struggle constantly to avoid shortchanging either their employers or their daughter Claire, 2. . . .

To that end, they have developed some complex rules. Explains Nancy: "An overall premise of our relationship is that neither of our careers is dominant; both are valuable and have a major impact for our family." Each spouse must give the other as much notice as possible of a trip. If trips conflict, says Nancy, "we have to assess which one is more important." If one spouse forgets to notify the other, he or she has to cancel the trip. "I think we have done a great job of being fair to each other," says Nancy.

Marty has a different take, one that is typical of life in two-career households everywhere: "There is always a wall of defense, an attack of offense. I say: 'I'm going out of town.' She says: 'I'm going out of town and coming back the same day. Think how stressful that is.' I say: 'Well, I've got an early morning meeting.'" Often they coordinate travel schedules five to eight weeks out. Sometimes they get competitive: "I had that day before you did," one of them will say.

"If I come home late," Marty continues, "Nancy says, 'Pick up,' and rightly so. She's dead tired. And she's had Claire all evening. But maybe I've just had three days of insanity, so I say, 'You want me to do what?' What generally results is an argument. Most of the time you attribute it to two tired people who love each other but who don't have enough time together."

Balancing Work and Family

For all its politically correct talk, the corporate world seems strangely impervious to the pressures on working families. "People have always had to make choices about balancing work and family," says John Clendenin, chairman of Bell-South. "It has always been a personal issue, and

individuals have to solve it." Trouble is, the solution has gotten much harder. In the past two decades the growth in personal incomes has slowed, and in some cases declined. Incomes of even the wealthiest men have increased by only 16.7% since 1975. At the same time, the big-ticket expenses of family life—a house, a car, a college education—have soared.

The median income of families rose only 6.7% in real terms between 1979 and 1994, even though women more than doubled their time in the work force, according to a 1995 survey by the Massachusetts Institute for a New Commonwealth. "For families to maintain their standard of living, it has been essential for women to get in the labor market and stay there longer," says Katherine S. Newman, a professor of public policy at Harvard. "This is not pin money. It is not fulfillment of stated ambitions. This is driving economic necessity."

Well, yes and no. The second income often lets families splurge on luxuries—an expensive car, an exotic vacation, private school for the kids. But in most cases it is not a question of to have or not to have a BMW. With women contributing a large chunk of the income in the most affluent families, subtracting their paychecks would require not just giving up luxuries but making the decision to be downwardly mobile.

As economic realities have changed, so has the nature of work. Forget 9 to 5. Forget weekends. At companies that try to accomplish more, in less time, with fewer people, work becomes all consuming. More than 2,000 *Fortune* readers surveyed in 1995 said they spent, on average, 57 hours a week working and commuting.

Working parents often fret about the career consequences of being a conscientious parent or a diligent enough partner to keep a marriage on track. How and when, they wonder, will they have to pay a price for leaving the office in time to get home for dinner? Vince Luciani and his wife, Dana, live with 22-month-old Gabriel in a pretty brick house at the eastern end of Morningside—a labor of love Vince has been renovating brick by brick with his father-in-law. Dana, 33, a senior vice president and in-house consultant for

NationsBank, left a killer job at Andersen Consulting because of its less family-friendly environment. Vince, 34, is the assistant manager of audio engineering at a Panasonic plant that makes car radios. Next month he will begin a new job as president of Smart Devices Inc., which makes movie theater audio equipment.

In both the old job and the new, Vince has weighed whether his strong commitment to family might put him on the Daddy Track. Since Gabriel's birth, he has tried to leave work by 5:30 or 6 P.M., at least an hour earlier than normal in his department, to make the hourlong commute home to see his son before bedtime. To compensate, Vince arrives early, skips lunch, and doesn't take any of the smoking breaks common at the plant. "I've tried to position myself to have a life," says Vince. "You work in order to have a family. Work is important, but family is important too." He explained this to his boss, who seemed to understand, despite the reputation that Japanese executives have of being even less family-friendly than their American counterparts. But, says Vince, "I worried a lot. I didn't know what the long-term consequences would be."

He still doesn't. Although his new job is only a 20-minute commute, enabling him to work a longer day, he is being groomed to run the business, and he'll be working for a man who puts in long hours. Once again, Vince confronted the issue directly, telling his new boss that he wants to help raise his son. "I didn't want to set the expectation that I would be at the office till 11 P.M.," says Vince. "He says he understands. Time will tell."

Making Compromises

Working parents often find they must make compromises that change their career aspirations, their family expectations—or both. Bert Hogeman, 40, is a lawyer at BellSouth, the kind of dedicated corporate soldier who takes a portable fax to the beach. Until a year and a half ago he was general counsel for BellSouth's international operations, spending as much as two weeks of every month overseas. Sometimes he would leave for the office in the morning to discover he'd be heading overseas that afternoon. "It was all very exciting," says Bert, whose wife, Lori, is a clinical social worker at Hillside, an adolescent treatment hospital in Morningside.

But it was hell on Lori and Kaitlin, nearly 8. "Lori never issued an ultimatum," says Bert. "But there was chronic complaining and unhappiness." Says Lori, 39: "I would say, 'Just be a garbage collector. Just stay home.' I was angry at Bell-South for saying, 'You go now; you don't have a choice.'" Kaitlin would ask her mother why Daddy didn't say goodbye. Once, when a friend asked what her father did, Kaitlin responded: "Well, he works in an airplane." Increasingly Bert felt left out of the family. "I went to Kaitlin's school one day, and I overheard one of her friends say, 'Kaitlin, I didn't think you had a daddy,' which made me feel like a worthless individual. Lori would function very well without me, and I didn't like it. Not that I wanted them to be missing me all the time. But I wanted to feel that I was necessary."

Because of all the traveling, Bert and Lori came to a critical decision: They wouldn't have more children. It had taken a long time and numerous infertility treatments to conceive Kaitlin. At some point, Lori says, "it got to be too late. We didn't want to go through it all again." She worried, too, about her ability to devote enough time to a second child. "I said to Bert, 'I'm 38 years old, and you're not home half the time. I'm raising this child—I'd be raising two children—alone. I can't imagine what it would be like.'" At the hospital where she works, Lori is confronted daily with a basic truth about children: Whether they come from $300,000-a-year households or welfare households, they need time and attention.

In the fall of 1995, Bert became the legislative and regulatory counsel for BellSouth's U.S. business. The new job eased his family pressures and at the same time enhanced his career. But, says Bert, "this hasn't been without a cost. I really wanted—and still want—a larger family. We made a decision, reluctantly on my part, not to have another child. To me that's almost an incalculable price to pay. It makes me aggravated and sad at times. We have a great child, and if we can only have one, she's the best one to have. But I wanted to have a little boy. If we don't have a boy to carry on the Hogeman name, it comes to an end. I really wanted to have a son."

The people who teach in Morningside's classrooms and preach from its pulpits, the educators and ministers who try to maintain the traditional rhythms of neighborhood institutions, are distressed by what they see. At Morningside Elementary School, Beth Burney often has a hard time getting her fifth-graders to do homework. "Their parents are so busy working," she says. "By the time they get home, have dinner, and clean up, it's so late that there's no time for homework." It's not that Burney can't relate. She has two children, and after a day of teaching, she has barely enough energy for a Monopoly game.

One parent recently told Burney it wasn't right to assign homework when families have so little time together. Such remarks have prompted soul-searching among Morningside teachers. Is it appropriate? If not, should the school day be extended? On the one hand, homework is an important way to teach children responsibility. On the other, says Burney, "when I was a child, homework would take up only a small part of my free time. I got home from school at 2:30. Now kids don't get home until dinner. They have no time to play." Burney worries about 10-year-old kids whose schedules seem every bit as full as their parents': "Some of them need little date-books." Burney says her students seem needier than those in years past. And they are more easily distracted, more often fatigued. "Just as adults get scattered, children get scattered," she says.

Over at Morningside Presbyterian Church, pastor Coile Estes worries too. Her beautiful brick church, shaded by magnolias, is within walking distance of most of the neighborhood. But increasingly she says there is no such thing as sanctuary in her parishioners' lives. Between jobs and families, they have little time for church and less for reflection. Wednesday nights have traditionally been church night, especially in the South. "But it just doesn't work here," says Estes. Even on Sundays she sees the encroachment of T-ball practice and birthday parties, as families squeeze in on weekends what they have no time for during the week. "A lot of employers don't appreciate a balanced life," says Estes. "I hear that from my people all the time." Preacher that she is, Estes calls up a lesson from the Bible. "Even Jesus had to pull away from his preaching and performing of miracles to rest and relax, to have some private time and prayer."

Parents who have spent their prime years torn between career and kids say that ultimately something has to give. For many it will be the work. Employees committed to more family time will switch jobs, redefine their career paths, become free agents in the workplace. Down the road, there is hope in trends beginning to play out in corporate America: Technology, now so often an enemy of family time, may eventually become its savior, not only by enabling employees to do more work from home but also by eliminating some offices altogether and permanently altering the way business gets done. "I do think we are at a turning point," says Ellen Gabriel, a partner at Deloitte Touche who is leading a companywide effort to retain and advance women. "Work has to change for parents to raise healthy kids and to be healthy, contributing employees."

On some level corporate America must know this. Because even if it doesn't much care about families, it surely cares about a brain drain. Companies that don't do more to let parents be parents will begin to lose them. People who want children will find a better way.

READING 20
MOONLIGHT AND CHILD CARE

Shelly Reese

As increasing numbers of employees are working nonstandard hours, they are creating a need for safer, affordable nighttime child care options. Shelly Reese is a staff writer for American Demographics *magazine.*

Terry Witt says she doesn't know what she would have done over the past four years if her employer, Toyota Motor Manufacturing, hadn't offered around-the-clock child care at its Georgetown, Kentucky, plant. Child care is scarce in the tiny town, and her family lives an hour away, so Witt relied on Toyota to care for her son for three years while she worked the night shift. Although Witt was able to switch to the day shift last fall, she continues to use Toyota's facility. It's convenient, inexpensive—she pays $75 a week—and the only center open when she drops Matthew off at 6 a.m.

Witt is one of the lucky few with access to around-the-clock child care. While no one knows exactly how many 24-hour centers exist, the Women's Bureau of the U.S. Labor Department estimates there are only about a dozen offered by private employers, employer consortiums, and employer-community partnerships.

That supply is a thin shadow of the need. More than 14 million Americans—nearly one in five full-time workers—worked nontraditional hours in 1991, according to the Women's Bureau. Many of those are mothers of young children. In 1990, about 7.2 million women with 11.7 million children under age 15 worked full- or part-time jobs with nonstandard hours, according to a recent study by the bureau.

Shift work is growing fastest in the service sector, which is heavily reliant on female employees. More than four in ten service employees of both sexes currently work nonstandard hours, such as early mornings, nights, and weekends. And the trend is expected to accelerate in coming years.

Seventy percent of the fastest-growing occupations in the U.S. have a disproportionate number of female employees and require more than 40 percent of their workers to work nonstandard hours, according to a study by Harriet Presser of the University of Maryland. These jobs, which include nurses, restaurant workers, and cashiers, are expected to account for almost 19 percent of the overall projected growth in employment through the year 2002, according to the study.

Although child care is a consideration for both sexes, its availability and quality often have a more profound effect on female workers. Unmarried and divorced mothers are more likely than fathers to have custody of their children, while married women are more likely than their male counterparts to have a working spouse. That

Reprinted, with permission, from Shelly Reese, "Moonlight and Child Care," *American Demographics*, August 1996; ©1996 American Demographics, Inc., Ithaca, New York.

Working Nights and Weekends

Three in ten employed men and women with part-time schedules work nonstandard hours.

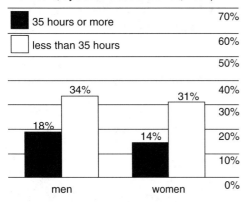

(percent of employed adults aged 18 and older who work other than fixed daytime hours, by sex and hours worked, 1991)

■ 35 hours or more
□ less than 35 hours

men: 18% (35 hours or more), 34% (less than 35 hours)
women: 14% (35 hours or more), 31% (less than 35 hours)

Source: *Demography*, Population Association of America, Silver Spring, MD.

means they're less likely to have someone at home ready to watch the kids.

A Growing Problem

Parents have always struggled to find child care that fits their work schedules, but the problem has become more of an issue in recent years. Marguerite Sallee, president and CEO of CorporateFamily Solutions, a Nashville-based child-care center operator, attributes growing attention to off-hours child care to workers' growing willingness to discuss child-care problems. The search for good-paying jobs has also increased workers' willingness to relocate to new cities where they don't have family and friends to provide child-care support, Sallee says.

But bringing attention to the issue doesn't solve the underlying problems associated with it. Child care is expensive, and many workers with nonstandard schedules have low to moderate incomes. "The biggest problem is the economics of child care," says Sallee, whose firm operates the Toyota center in Georgetown, Kentucky. "The normal supply-demand equation does not apply. If a parent can't write a big check, the supply is not going to be created."

Companies such as Toyota that step in to fill the void struggle with economic considerations as well. Popular as Toyota's center is with parents like Witt, most second-shift workers opt to have their children sleep at home or at a relative's if possible. As a result, the center operates at 100 percent capacity during the day, but is just over 30 percent full at night.

For many companies, low utilization at night makes around-the-clock care unfeasible from a business standpoint. It may take strong incentives, such as tax breaks, to encourage companies to gear up for the growing number of shift workers needing nighttime child care, Sallee says. "It's a very real and growing problem, and it's getting to the point of a potential crisis."

DISCUSSION QUESTIONS

1. What types of changes are needed in the business world to make home and work demands more compatible?

2. How does the existence of a spouse affect the stress that an employed woman experiences as she juggles family and work responsibilities?

3. From a child's perspective, what is it like to have working parent(s)? What are the advantages? Disadvantages? How do children respond to having employed parent(s)? Do they respond differently to a working father compared with a working mother? Explain your answer.

WEBSITES

epn.org/idea/welfare.html
epn.org/idea/welf-bkm.html
The Electronic Policy Network provides links to news articles and organizations with a liberal and progressive viewpoint. The first of these addresses is to their Welfare and Family page.

www.cyfc.umn.edu/
The University of Minnesota's Children, Youth, and Family Consortium (CYFC) is an excellent place to find information and resources on children, youth, and families. The following pages are links to sites that specifically address the topic of work and family:

http://www.cyfc.umn.edu/worklinks.html
http://www.cyfc.umn.edu/Work/studentlinks.html

PART IV

PARENTS AND CHILDREN

CONTENTS

PART IV: PARENTS AND CHILDREN

CHAPTER 9: TO PARENT OR NOT TO PARENT
READING 21: FEMINISM AND THE FAMILY   142
READING 22: BALANCING ACT   148
READING 23: THE MOTHER MARKET   155
READING 24: NEW MOTHERS, NOT MARRIED   162

CHAPTER 10: RAISING CHILDREN
READING 25: NORMAL FAMILIES: RESEARCH ON GAY AND LESBIAN
    PARENTING   169
READING 26: THE LOST ART OF FATHERHOOD   174
READING 27: THE CHANGING MEANINGS OF SPANKING   176

CHAPTER 11: OTHER FAMILY RELATIONSHIPS
READING 28: GRANDPARENTS RAISING GRANDCHILDREN   190
READING 29: CARING FOR AGING PARENTS   197
READING 30: THE SIBLING SYNDROME   200

CHAPTER 9: TO PARENT OR NOT TO PARENT

Years ago, people seldom questioned whether they would become a parent; they simply assumed that they would have children, just as their parents did. Prior to the development of effective methods of contraception, children were the consequence of sexual activity, and parenthood was considered a duty of married couples. Often, to be married and childless required an explanation. Today major changes are taking place in regard to parenthood. While most people, particularly most women, are still taught that having children and being a parent is one of the most important achievements in life, parenting, like marriage, is more optional and individualized. Parenthood now involves more choices—whether to have children or not, how many children to have, and when to have them.

The readings in this chapter explore several emerging trends in parenthood, for example, delayed parenthood, smaller families, and the growing number of births occurring out of wedlock.

Mary Ann Glendon, in the first reading, discusses how issues such as raising children and caring for elderly parents are no longer just "women's issues." She suggests that parenting and family responsibilities must be top priorities in people's lives and that people must be recognized and rewarded for quality parenting.

The next reading addresses how important it is for companies, both large and small, to develop and implement family-friendly programs. Child care referral, flextime, and job sharing benefit working parents, and in turn, companies with family-friendly policies benefit from more productive, loyal employees.

Pregnancy and childbirth products and services are big business in the United States. As the number of American women in their peak childbearing years declines and as mothers get older, birthrates decline. The third article looks at how fewer babies means more aggressive maternity/childbirth marketing by hospitals, other health providers, and manufacturers who are competing for paying customers.

While U.S. birthrates have been declining and leveling off over the past thirty years, the out-of-wedlock birthrate has soared. The authors of the last reading in this chapter propose that increased availability of contraception and abortion and the demise of "shotgun marriage" have contributed to this increase in unwed motherhood.

READING 21
FEMINISM AND THE FAMILY

Mary Ann Glendon

The feminist ideology of the 1970s gives little guidance in addressing the issues that face marriage, motherhood, and family life in the 1990s. Mary Ann Glendon, a law professor at Harvard University, encourages both men and women to actively participate in politics, thereby working to solve social issues and facilitate change. This reading is adapted from a talk given by Glendon to the Berkshire County Pregnancy Assistance Association.

In September 1995, I had the honor of heading the Vatican delegation to the United Nations' Fourth Conference on Women held in Beijing. The conference's mandate was "Action for Equality, Development, and Peace." To what extent the conference advanced that mandate is open to question. I will try to explain why we seem to have seen so little progress toward those goals.

Beijing and the Old Feminism

As news reports indicated, there were actually two women's conferences in China in September 1995: the official UN conference where delegates and negotiators from 181 member states produced the final version of the document known as the Beijing Program of Action; and a larger, more

Reprinted, with permission, from Mary Ann Glendon, "Feminism and the Family: An Indissoluble Marriage," *Commonweal*, February 14, 1997; ©1997 by the Commonweal Foundation.

colorful, unofficial conference held several miles away. This second conference was the NGO conference (nongovernmental organizations). The official conference was attended by 5,000 persons; the NGO conference was attended by 30,000.

The word "conference" in both cases is somewhat misleading. UN conferences would be more accurately described as dispersed negotiating sessions. Their main aim is to put the final touches on a document that has been circulating for years in draft form. To do this, the delegates split up into groups to go over different sections of the document, paragraph by paragraph, trying to reach consensus on the final text that will be submitted for approval when the whole group comes together on the last day. As for the so-called NGO conference with its 30,000 participants, you wouldn't be far wrong if you translated "conference" in that setting as "lobbyists' headquarters," and "NGO" as "special-interest group."

Like most UN conference documents, the statement that emerged after two weeks of negotiations was a set of nonbinding guidelines for future action. The Beijing statement set a UN record for length at 125 pages, single-spaced. The document contains many very fine proposals regarding women's access to education and employment, and the feminization of poverty. But it is marred by two serious defects.

The first is that the best parts of the Beijing program—especially the ones I just mentioned—are the most likely to remain dead letters because they require funding. If there was anything that united the rich countries at Beijing, it was their successful fight to keep out any language that would commit them to back up their fine promises with material resources.

The second defect also involves something that was left out. It is nothing short of amazing, in a world where over eight out of ten women have children, that a 125-page program of action produced at a *women's* conference barely mentions marriage, motherhood, or family life!

The reaction of most women to this document, I suspect, would be similar to that of a young Nigerian law student who wrote me recently. She couldn't afford to go to the conference, but she tried to follow it closely from afar. She was disappointed, she said, that the conference had paid so little attention to the problems that the majority of the world's women struggle with on a daily basis. She was surprised, for example, that the section on women's health was focused almost entirely on women's reproductive systems. She wondered why it didn't address the health of the whole woman, particularly the problems of poor nutrition, sanitation, and tropical disease that have a disproportionate impact on women. (Keep in mind that women and girls compose 70 percent of the world's poverty population.)

And even the treatment of reproductive health in the document is strange, since it focuses almost entirely on birth control and abortion—as though reproductive health did not include pregnancy and childbirth.

Women's Ideology of the '70s

How are these omissions to be explained? For the answer, you only have to look at the original draft document prepared by the UN Committee on the Status of Women. In the few places where the drafting committee mentioned marriage, motherhood, or family life, these aspects of women's lives were described in a negative way—as sources of oppression, or as obstacles to women's progress. In other words, what we had to work with in Beijing was a document whose defects corresponded rather closely to the defects of 1970s' feminism. A negative attitude toward

men and marriage and the same lack of attention to the problems of women who are mothers were starkly evident.

The conference document is not legally binding. It is in the form of "international standards" against which UN member states are supposed to measure their conduct. So why all the fuss and lobbying about a set of nonbinding guidelines?

The main reason is this: Government agencies and private foundations tend to use these UN documents (I should say, selected parts of these documents) to justify the way they run their foreign and domestic programs. That means that, when they announce policies and set conditions, they don't have to invoke the modern version of the golden rule ("We've got the gold, so we make the rules"). It sounds so much better to say: "We follow guidelines established by international consensus." *But the bottom line is that millions of people's lives are affected by a kind of rule-making as far removed as possible from public scrutiny and democratic participation.*

That fact makes these UN conferences magnets for all sorts of special-interest groups, especially those who want to do an end-run around ordinary political processes. It's tempting for them to try to plant their agendas in a long, unreadable document, behind closed doors at a conference held in some faraway place. (When I say closed doors, I mean that literally. All the negotiating sessions in Beijing were closed to the public and the press.)

The Beijing conference offers two lessons for those of us who are concerned with women's issues in the '90s. First, beware of policies manufactured far away from public scrutiny, and without input from the people most concerned. Second, it seems to me the conference was more about the women's ideology of the '70s than about women's issues in the '90s. Beijing was like a Woodstock reunion. Moreover, it showed that the handwriting is on the wall for the peculiar form of feminism that held sway in the 1960s and 1970s. And the message on the wall is the same that was written in the Book of Daniel: "You have been weighed in the balance and found wanting."

That point was reinforced for me by the conversations I had with my students when I returned from Beijing. The very first question the women law students asked had never occurred to me. "What was the average age of the women at the conference?" Looking back, I realized that there was almost no one there under forty. Most were in their late forties, fifties, or sixties. Many, like Bella Abzug and Betty Friedan, were older.

Incidentally, I find it amusing that the attitudes of my women students' toward legendary figures like Abzug and Friedan are similar to the way my generation thought about Susan B. Anthony and the suffragettes. We admired them for securing the vote for women, but we didn't identify with them. To us, they seemed quaint, and a bit strange. Similarly, my students seem grateful to the second-wave women's movement for the educational and employment opportunities they now enjoy, but they're ready to move on to new frontiers. In the opinion polls of the '90s, when women are asked, "Do you consider yourself a feminist?" two-thirds of American women answer no. What's even more striking is the response of younger women. Among college women in their twenties, four out of five say they do not consider themselves feminists.

What is the message that large majorities of women are sending to organized feminism? Betty Friedan herself, I believe, has read it correctly. The message seems to be that official feminism hasn't been listening to the women who are too busy to be in movements, that it is out of touch with the real-life concerns of most women today. In a recent *New Yorker* article, Friedan urges feminists to wake up to the fact that "the most urgent concerns of women today are not gender issues but jobs and families." And whom did we see on the cover of *Time* magazine as the key voter in the 1996 elections? An exhausted, frazzled, working mother. The issue on her mind? Job and family.

I've observed a similar shift in attitude even among my career-oriented law students. Law schools were strongholds of feminism in the late '70s when women were a minority. But now that women make up nearly half the student body (and are more representative of the female popu-

lation), I hear much more concern about how you can have a decent family life without suffering excessive career disadvantages. And, most significant of all, in my view, is that this worry seems to be bothering the young men almost as much as it concerns the women.

The signs of shifting attitudes among men lead to a point I'll discuss later on: the sense in which women's issues of the '90s are everybody's issues. But first, it must be noted that many issues confront men and women in significantly different ways, especially where the women concerned are, or hope to be, mothers. Let me give you some examples of that differential impact.

Women's Issues of the '90s

A major issue for the women's movement of the 1970s was the "gender gap" between men's and women's wages. You may recall we used to hear that for every dollar earned by a man, a woman made 60 cents. Today, women's opportunities have improved to the point where there is virtually no gender gap between the earnings of women and men *who have made similar life choices*. Among young adults who have never had children, women's earnings are now nearly 98 percent of men's earnings.

But something is wrong with that picture. Why do we talk about women in the abstract when the great majority of women (about 85 percent in the United States) are mothers? The women who are disadvantaged in the workplace are not women in the abstract, but women who are raising children. And the real income gap in this country is between child-raising families and other types of households.

Another good example of the different form that the work-family dilemma takes for men and women is what happens when a child-raising family is broken up by divorce. (Keep in mind here that the majority of all divorces, 57 percent, involve couples with children under sixteen.) There is no doubt that the rise in divorce has had a disproportionate effect on women. After divorce it is nearly always the mother who remains primarily responsible for the physical care of the children; the father's standard of living typically rises, while that of the mother and children declines—in all too many cases below the poverty line.

To put it another way, motherhood in our society is a pretty risky occupation. Ironically, women in the abstract have never had more rights, but rarely has the position of mothers been more precarious. Women have tried to protect themselves and their children against the risks they face in two ways: They're having fewer children, and they're maintaining at least a foothold in the labor force even when their children are very young. But that strategy still does not protect them very well against what we might call the four deadly Ds: disrespect for unpaid work in the home; disadvantages in the workplace for anyone who takes time out for family responsibilities; divorce; and destitution, a condition that afflicts so many female-headed families.

As if that were not enough, many women now find themselves facing what might be called "Work-Family Dilemma II": no sooner has the last child left home than the needs of aging parents start the process of juggling job and family responsibilities all over again.

A New Set of Problems

The fact is that we are in a situation where the experience of past generations gives little guidance. Now that most women are in the labor force, no one has yet come up with a good solution to the problem of who performs the caretaking work for children and for the elderly that women used to do, for free. The idea of some social conservatives is that women should "just stay home" (unless they're welfare mothers, in which case off to work they must go). I can't help thinking that the "just stay home" idea is a bit like what the chicken said to the pig when they were trying to think what they could give Old MacDonald for a birthday present. The chicken said: "How about a nice breakfast of bacon and eggs—I'll provide the eggs and you give the bacon." You can see why the pig was not enthusiastic about that division of labor.

Another set of problems that will have a disparate impact on women is just beginning to come into view. Thanks to medical advances, we have never had such a large elderly population. As you know, that group includes more women than men. At the same time, we know that much of the burden of supporting that population will fall on the shoulders of a labor force that is growing proportionately smaller.

Against that background, a real concern about the assisted-suicide movement is the pressure that is going to be exerted on elderly people in failing health to cease using up scarce resources. When you consider that three out of four poor Americans over sixty-five are women, you can see that this is yet another issue that is everybody's issue, but that will affect women in a special way. It is sobering to think that more than two-thirds of the people Dr. Jack Kevorkian has helped to die are women.

Assisted suicide also involves the political problem mentioned earlier in connection with Beijing—the question of who settles whose hash. The "right to die" (like the right to abortion) is being pushed mainly by the kind of people who are accustomed to having a lot of control over their lives. The outcome of the debate over this issue is likely to be determined by judges—who are also people who are used to having a lot of control over their lives.

To privileged folks, the right to die may look like an aspect of personal freedom—a way of feeling in control until the very end. In the case of such people, it may well work out that way. But how is it going to work out for the less fortunate, the people who are in the most danger of being regarded as burdensome to their families and a drag on the taxpayers of the welfare state? What is a "right to die" for some may well become a "duty to die" for others. And if that happens, women, again, will be most affected.

Consider the ways in which, despite the disparate impact on women, all these problems are everybody's problems. One of the main sources of discontent with the old feminism was the way it set women and men at odds with one another. Now we're beginning to realize that we're all in this thing together. In the world of work, men as well as women are increasingly chafing under pressures to put the demands of the job ahead of the needs of their families. Both men and women are increasingly realizing that feminists have always had a strong point when they complained that society gives little respect or security to people who make sacrifices for their children and families. Ironically, the '70s feminists bought into that disrespect. By treating marriage and motherhood as obstacles to women's progress, they actually helped to reinforce the idea that the only work that counts is work for pay outside the home.

But while feminists were maintaining, correctly, that society doesn't respect work in the home, things were changing in the workplace outside the home. In all too many ways the new globalized economy is sending the same message to working men and women that society once sent to homemakers: that they and the work they do are not worthy of much respect.

Monsignor George Higgins, a longtime advocate of the rights of workers, asked some important questions in a recent speech. When a profitable company "downsizes," doesn't that tell dedicated employees that their years of service don't really count for much? When employees' wages stagnate while their companies prosper, aren't working people being told that their effort and skill aren't valued? And when benefits like health insurance and pensions are cut back, doesn't that tell working people that nobody cares what happens when they get sick and old? To those questions, you might add: What scale of values rewards some CEOs to the tune of $200 million a year (head of Disney) while moms and dads must work harder than ever to counter a relative decline in real family income?

Building a Decent Family Life

All these are men's and women's issues. They are family issues. They are issues about what kind of society we want to try to hand on to future generations. Something is wrong when most jobs are too rigidly structured to accommodate family responsibilities. Something is wrong when we frame laws and policies as though human beings existed to serve the economy, rather than the other way round. In the long run, that's not even good for the economy. To spell out the obvious: a healthy economy requires a certain kind of work force, with certain skills and qualities of character. And those qualities—honesty, a work ethic, and the ability to cooperate with others—are going to be acquired, for the most part, in the nation's families or not at all.

Having said that, it is not easy to imagine what can be done about all this. Some factors, such as worldwide economic developments, may be outside the control of any one country. Other factors, let's admit it, are more related to the materialistic excesses of a consumer society than to basic family needs. We Americans do have a tendency to want to "have it all." But anyone who has tried to combine work and family life knows that we can't have it all. You're always shortchanging somebody somewhere—one day it's the job, the next it's your spouse, or your children. The grown-up question is not can all our dreams come true. The real question is whether we can do better than we're doing now. Is it possible to harmonize women's and men's roles in social and economic life with their desires (and their children's needs) for a decent family life?

I would say it's possible—but that the prospects are dim, unless society as a whole is prepared to recognize that when mothers and fathers raise their children well, they are not just doing something for themselves and their own children, but for all of us. Governments, private employers, and fellow citizens would all have to recognize that we all owe an enormous debt to parents who do a good job raising their children under today's difficult conditions. There's something heroic about the everyday sacrifices that people have to make these days just to do the right thing by their nearest and dearest.

What Is to Be Done?

The above observations bring me to the realm of politics. I want to focus on one basic problem: the problem of how American men and women can gain a say in the decisions that shape their lives and livelihoods—a voice in our jobs, in our children's education, in our communities, and in the direction our country is taking.

Is that problem soluble? A glance around the

social landscape is not particularly reassuring. Something is terribly wrong when Americans from every viewpoint and every walk of life are beginning to feel that the forces that govern our economic and political lives have spun out of control; and when parents feel that they are losing the struggle for the hearts and minds of their own children.

There has been much speculation about why Americans seem uninterested in voting and in the electoral process generally. That disaffection just might have something to do with the perception that both political parties are out of touch with citizens' deepest concerns. Reporting on political party finances shows that that common perception isn't uninformed. Both political parties are heavily financed by big business—the Democrats by the kinds of businesses that make their livings from government, and the Republicans by the kinds of businesses that just want government to butt out. Yes, the Democrats throw a few crumbs to working men and women. Yes, the Republicans throw a few crumbs to those who are concerned about the moral fabric of society. But it's been a long time since either party has done much for constituents whose main concerns are a decent job and decent conditions for raising a family.

My one suggestion for a possible solution to this problem is likely to make many people groan, but I can see no other alternative. Simply put, more of us have to take a more active role in politics. Frustration with a distant, unresponsive government is nothing new in America. Indeed, this nation was founded in the rejection of unre-

sponsive government. The constitutional convention in Philadelphia produced an ingenious design for a republic with democratic elements. (Not a pure democracy, but a republic in which the democratic elements were extremely important.) To protect those democratic elements, the Bill of Rights specified that all powers not expressly delegated to the federal government, or forbidden to the states, are reserved to the states and the people. That's the forgotten part of the Bill of Rights—the Tenth Amendment. You'll wait a long time before you hear a peep about the powers reserved to the people from the groups that are self-appointed defenders of our civil liberties. Yet what liberty is more basic than the freedom to participate in setting the conditions under which we live, work, and raise our families?

Now it seems that many people are tempted to give up on the idea that we, especially at the local level, can help to make things better. They're tempted to give up on the idea that we could ever take back democratic institutions; that we could ever restore decision-making power to the many who have the most to lose from the few who have the most to gain. But, to be honest, the women and men who have gone before us often faced much greater challenges than we do now. Do we really want to be the generation who didn't even try to turn things around? After all, this isn't Eastern Europe where the men and women who toppled authoritarian regimes are now struggling to build democratic government from scratch. We have the machinery at hand. We've had it for over 200 years. It's rusty, but it's there. Let's use it.

READING 22
BALANCING ACT

Marlene Lozada

Flexible work days, child care referral, job sharing, paternity leave—these are just some of the policies businesses are adopting to accommodate the swelling number of parents they employ. Three of every four U.S. employees are parents; in 1994, these working parents had 1.7 million children in child care programs before and after school. Traditional one-income families are no longer the norm, and working America is having to make some changes. Marlene Lozada is an associate editor at Techniques *magazine.*

The timid five-year-old turns the corner toting a fresh bag of microwave popcorn—this should hold him until dinner. Suddenly a chorus of voices breaks out.

"Andreeeww!"

"Hey-a Andrew!"

"Andrew! How 'bout some popcorn?"

"Yeah, I'm hungry!"

"Don't give it to 'em Andrew! Charge 'em for it!"

His big blue eyes get bigger and he quickly turns to muffle a giggle in his father's leg. Andrew Kicinski is used to this crowd his dad, Gary, calls coworkers at *USA Today Baseball Weekly* in Arlington, Virginia. He's known most of them for

years. They're friendly, funny and best of all they've got a lot of neat stuff to play with.

It's about six o'clock on a Friday evening and several of the *Baseball Weekly* staff are working. Gary Kicinski, operations editor since the publication started up nearly six years ago, looks over a story on his computer screen. His son, Andrew, is working just as hard right next to him, using a publishing program to create a brilliant masterpiece on his screen.

"It's about half and half for necessity and fun," Kicinski says about his son coming to work with him. "As he got older he became more aware of what I do and where I work and where [my wife] Kate works. He likes to come over now because he's become computer literate and I have a couple of software applications he can play with. The other half is out of necessity. For example, if Kate needs to go to a business dinner and I still have to work, I'll pick him up [from day care] and bring him back to the office while I finish up."

USA Today Baseball Weekly is published by Gannett, one of the top-grossing U.S. publishing companies, according to *Fortune* magazine. Perhaps more important to some Gannett parents is its eleventh appearance on *WorkingMother* magazine's 100 best companies for working mothers in 1996. But maybe Gannett should be listed in just one magazine for doing good business, because several studies show a work environment that fosters happy employees is crucial to a healthy bottom line.

From Marlene Lozada, "Balancing Act," *Techniques*, vol. 72, no. 1 (January 1997), pp. 14–19, 64–65. Reprinted with permission from *Techniques* magazine; ©1997 American Vocational Association.

Weighing the Options

Employees who must miss work to care for their children cost U.S. companies $3 billion a year, according to The Conference Board, a New York research firm. To counter this loss more and more companies—bigger and much smaller than Gannett—are contracting with child care resource and referral services. Employees with this benefit can get help with all the research they would have had to do during business hours— which day care centers are convenient for them, the different features of each, their costs and hours of operation. Employees save time and can feel more at ease with the facility they've chosen for their child.

It seems logical that if employees aren't worrying about the care their children are receiving, they will be more productive at work. But there are no hard numbers to prove this.

"There is a growing body of research that connects family-friendly programs to greater productivity, loyalty and initiative," says Robin Hardman, director of communications for the Families and Work Institute in New York. "They also result in a lot of employee recruitment and retention positives. It's very hard to come up with hard data types of numbers in this area, but there is a growing body of evidence, most of it anecdotal. When you're talking to employers, you tend to hear them say things like, 'My employees are happier. They're more productive. We respect their need to fulfill their responsibilities and they're eager to do whatever they can to respect ours.'"

Andrew Kicinski has been going to the Rosslyn Children's Center in Arlington Virginia, since he was three months old. Gary Kicinski says he and his wife feel good about leaving Andrew there, and it's not far from the *USA Today* building. Elise Forrester, who works in Gannett corporate services, also has a son at the Rosslyn Children's Center. When she had her baby 18 months ago, she opted to take about three months off. Gannett allows parents to use a week of paid sick leave and then 8 to 10 weeks of paid or partially paid short-term disability depending on how long they've been with the company.

"I consider [Gannett] very family-friendly," Forrester says. ". . . The policies give the managers every opportunity to allow you to do what you need to do."

During her pregnancy Forrester also took advantage of "Right from the Beginning," a prenatal care program operated through "Health-Works," Gannett's health and fitness program. A nurse answered Forrester's questions and made suggestions for good prenatal care throughout her pregnancy.

"It was nice to have a nurse, [someone] other than my own doctor to compare notes with," Forrester says.

But Gannett's prenatal program is definitely butter in the world of family-friendly programs.

A more common policy is "flextime," which Gannett also practices. Flextime allows employees to adjust work days to accommodate family responsibilities. For example, a parent who needs to get a child to school in the morning may work later to make up for the later start.

"Implementing family-friendly programs in the workplace is really putting more responsibility in the hands of workers to get the job done," Hardman says. "A manager isn't going to be watching over you from nine to five. It's managers saying, 'We're not as concerned when you come and go, but that you get the job done.' It's putting more responsibility in the hands of employees and that should be a relief to managers. And it makes employees feel better about their jobs."

Where there's flextime in a workplace there's usually job sharing, which means two employees can share a full-time position by working different days or hours. Usually the sharing employees will receive either part-time benefits or prorated full-time benefits. Job sharing tends to be more popular among working mothers, but family-friendly policies in general are aimed at both parents.

"There are ways that men and women need specialized supports in the workplace," Hardman says. "But if you focus on gender you may lose track of the fact that everybody has work-family issues."

Hardman says emergency child care services also have become prevalent among businesses with family policies. In this case, companies usually arrange for in-home child care if, for example, the child's school is closed because of inclement weather. This typically is a contracted service, and sometimes the employee may be asked to contribute a small fee.

"Programs that are *consciously* family-friendly are still pretty rare," Hardman says. "A lot of companies might have flextime, for example, but they might not have it for that reason. Big companies are more likely to have formal policies and programs. But sometimes small companies by their nature are more flexible."

Real People, Real Results

Small companies may not be able to afford such full-scale packages. But these efforts almost always start small. Ford Motor Company's new and improved family-friendly policies got off the ground in 1993. And while Ford Motor Company is even bigger than Gannett, its family-friendly seed germinated at a smaller subsidiary, the North Penn facility of Ford Electronics and Refrigeration in Lansdale, Pennsylvania. This branch is part of Ford's Automotive Components Division.

The Work/Family Initiative Task Force at the North Penn facility got a burst of energy when a new employee joined in 1993. Lisa Farnin, a manufacturing engineer and project leader, wanted to help create a comfortable environment for addressing family concerns as they related to work. For several months, on their own time, Farnin and the task force researched other companies' family-friendly policies and the concerns of their fellow employees.

"We were trying to find out what other companies were doing and then see what made sense to our company—using common sense and good business sense," Farnin says. "We really tried to look through what to propose and why it would work."

When all the homework was done, the task force came up with seven suggestions—part-time work options, child care resource and referral service, flextime, job sharing, family sick days (for staying home with a sick child), emergency child care and paid paternity/adoption leave. And in a clever stroke, the task force chose to make its presentation to plant manager Dudley Wass and employee manager Larry Stewart in Ford format, following the procedures it uses for analyzing and improving production.

Not only were Wass and Stewart impressed, but the presentation research joined an ongoing corporate effort. Since then Ford and the United Auto Workers have started a joint fund for improving dependent care around their plants, and Ford CEO Alex Trotman chairs a work/life steering committee.

By early 1994 North Penn adopted five of the task force's ideas—part-time work, job sharing, child care resource and referral, flextime and the use of personal days for paternity leave for both birth parents and adoptive parents. And while they didn't entirely plan it this way, Farnin and her husband, Paul, had their first baby that fall. Now Farnin is enjoying the benefits she helped create. She is working a reduced schedule, about 75 percent of her full-time job.

"I work typically three to three-and-a-half days [a week] and it's working out quite well," Farnin says. "It's been a wonderful balance as a mom, wife, student and worker. And I work hard to make it work."

Farnin also is pursuing a computer science master's degree at Villanova University. She's on track to finish her degree in another semester, and her second baby is due around that time.

Constance Wimbley, an accounting clerk at First Tennessee Bank in Alcoa, handles her work-family balancing act with a little help from her friends. Wimbley, who has a five-year-old daughter, works in a department of 10 people, six of whom have children. They all take advantage of their flexible schedules to accommodate each other's needs. Wimbley says First Tennessee's family-friendly policies have created a comfortable work environment for discussing work-family concerns.

"It's very easy because we're a team," she says. "It makes me feel good about where I work. I can be myself and I can set a good example for my team."

First Tennessee was the smallest U.S. company to make the first *Business Week* top 10 list for

Should Employers Help with the Kids?

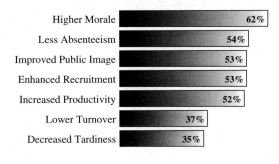

Higher Morale — 62%
Less Absenteeism — 54%
Improved Public Image — 53%
Enhanced Recruitment — 53%
Increased Productivity — 52%
Lower Turnover — 37%
Decreased Tardiness — 35%

◄ **The Pros**
In a survey of 139 companies, employers ranked the advantages and difficulties of offering child care services as a job benefit. These services included on- and off-site child care, emergency child care and child care resource and referral service, which saved employees 10 to 15 hours of work.

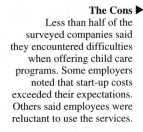

The Cons ▶
Less than half of the surveyed companies said they encountered difficulties when offering child care programs. Some employers noted that start-up costs exceeded their expectations. Others said employees were reluctant to use the services.

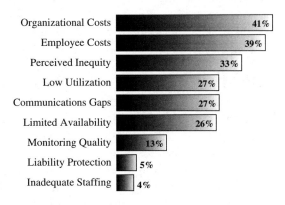

Organizational Costs — 41%
Employee Costs — 39%
Perceived Inequity — 33%
Low Utilization — 27%
Communications Gaps — 27%
Limited Availability — 26%
Monitoring Quality — 13%
Liability Protection — 5%
Inadequate Staffing — 4%

Source: The Conference Board, "Work-Family Roundtable, Child Care Services," 1995.

family-friendly programs last September. Competing with corporate giants like Merrill Lynch, Hewlett-Packard and Motorola, which also were on the list, First Tennessee Bank outscored them all. *Business Week* noted the effectiveness of First Tennessee's worker teams, flexible schedules and the family-friendly culture throughout the company.

Wimbley's manager, Becky Tipton, has been with First Tennessee for more than 20 years. She says managers used to work with employees individually, but an official program really helped foster a company-wide culture change.

"We definitely have changed our culture," says First Tennessee Bank Vice President Pat Brown. "It was a matter of letting everyone know it's okay to be flexible. We worked to give managers the tools to evaluate workplace flexibility requests."

Tipton was one of 1,000 managers who participated in a three-day seminar. She learned about child care resource and referral services as well

as similar services to help employees choose doctors and lawyers.

"We did a lot of role playing, too," Tipton recalls. "We would have a script. For example, this employee is coming to you with this problem. Then we would decide what to tell them, how to counsel them and what else to do for that employee. We also brainstormed ways to determine how the business needs of the company could be met and still have what the employee needed."

A recent survey of 1,000 managers by MC Associates, a management consulting group in Philadelphia, Pennsylvania, found that a "lack of balance between work and personal life" was a top reason new managers fail, according to the *Wall Street Journal*. In September's *HRMagazine,* Edward Betof of MC Associates said managers who "place high value on what's going on at home and how they're spending their life outside work" will see a significant negative effect on their performance if "they can't get those areas under control to their satisfaction."

Brown says about 50 percent of First Tennessee's 8,000 employees have children under 18. When she began working on the family-friendly project in 1992, it was supposed to comprise 10 percent of her job for three months. Now it has become a permanent part of her job, and she works with a staff of four.

"In an internal survey, 94 percent [of employees] say the family-friendly program meets or exceeds their expectations," Brown says. "We feel it's improved our attention to customers . . . our [customer] retention rate is higher—and the longer you keep your customers, the more profitable they become to you."

Combating the Fear Factor

Developing and implementing family-friendly programs is quite a feat, but they benefit no one if employees are reluctant to use them, says Hardman. She says companies and managers must ease employees' fears that they might appear unproductive or undedicated if they take advantage of these benefits.

"We [at the Families and Work Institute] concentrate on trying to find out and inform companies about what those fears are and how that can really hurt them," Hardman says. "If employers introduce flex hours and then employees are afraid to take them, that's a waste of time and energy. Our studies show that it's not enough to just introduce the idea. You really need a constant push from management."

First Tennessee uses its office newsletters to keep employees informed and to share success stories related to family-friendly programs. Gannett's Working Parents Group has seen positive results from its lunchtime speaker series. The group will bring in, for example, an expert on car safety for children who's willing to speak for free. Fliers posted in all elevators invite employees to bring their lunches to the event. Gannett provides the space for an hour and refreshments—a convenient and inexpensive service, which brings up another point—employees aren't the only ones who can be afraid of family-

friendly programs. Many times a company's upper management believes a family-friendly program will cost too much. The Conference Board report found that employers favor resource and referral services because "start-up costs are low and many parents' needs are met by the assistance," according to *HRMagazine.*

Brown says reluctant companies should look at the cost of *not* responding to work and family issues. "If you have people walking out the door or people who are not being productive on the job because of work and family issues, then you're not helping your bottom line."

First Tennessee Bank made a $100,000 commitment when it decided to revamp its family-friendly policies, which include a work and family resource service, sick-child care and flexible scheduling. Brown estimates the bank spent between $70 and $100 on each of the 1,000 managers who went through training. She says First Tennessee's work and family resource service—which provides information about child care, medical care, legal services and continuing education—runs about $15 to $20 per employee. First Tennessee Bank also teamed with a local hospital and several local businesses to share the cost for sick-child care, which amounts to about $10,000 a year. Brown adds that the bank breaks about even here because those parents are able to work.

"There is a perception that [family-friendly programs] cost a lot of money," says Ellen Bankert, an associate director for the Center on Work & Family at Boston University. "Most of the stuff doesn't cost a lot of hard dollars and cents. The most difficult part is making the cultural change."

That was Tracy Grant's biggest challenge when she became a working mother. Business graphics editor for *The Washington Post,* Grant had twin boys [in 1996].

"This job in my pre-pregnancy and pregnancy days was 55 to 60 hours a week," Grant says. "About six months into my pregnancy I went to my boss and said I didn't see how I could come back to this job."

Grant was used to working long days and irregular hours—anything less seemed inadequate.

She even thought about returning to her old copy desk position so she could have regular hours, but the *Post* was willing to be flexible.

"If you're well-respected, well-liked and you're doing your job well, use it," Grant advises working parents. "I used the fact that they needed me and wanted me in this job to structure something that would work for me. I had worked very hard, very long hours, I had produced well and so it was sort of a pay-back time. They were very willing to do that."

Grant's supervisors decided to make the most of her time by shaving some technical and copy editing duties from her job. Grant now works more closely with a copy editor, who makes minor edits and changes to the graphics Grant creates. Now, without a change in salary or benefits; she works from 10 a.m. to about 6:30, but getting used to it hasn't been easy, Grant says.

"I worried about [seeming undedicated]," Grant says. "That was my paranoia. There was a time when I first came back [to work] that I felt like the only conversations I had with my supervisors were about the boys. I thought, 'Do they only see me as a mother of twins now?' But they were asking about [Andrew and Christopher] because they were a novelty."

Soon after speaking with her boss about her concerns, Grant's fears were alleviated. Having been back at work for nearly six months, she's become accustomed to her new schedule and lifestyle. She and her husband, Bill, hired a nanny to care for the twins during the work day.

"I enjoy my job greatly," Grant says. "And I enjoy my career. But if the moon were made of blue cheese and I could do whatever I wanted, I would probably work two to three days a week and be more of a stay-at-home mom. But I'm in the same situation that a ton of people are. [A family] just can't make it on one salary."

Nearly 70 percent of Americans believe companies should give employees help with child care, according to The Conference Board report. Half of the companies in the study say they will implement family-friendly services in the future.

Federal legislation also may help the family-friendly movement gather steam. In 1993 President Bill Clinton signed the Family and Medical Leave Act, which allows employees to take up to 12 weeks of unpaid leave every year provided:

• they work for a private employer with 50 or more employees within 75 miles of their workplace, the federal government or a state or local government and

• they have worked for that employer for one year and at least 1,250 hours during the previous year.

This leave allows employees to:

• care for newborn or newly adopted children,

• care for children, parents or spouses who have serious health conditions or

• recover from their own serious health condition.

The Women's Legal Defense Fund in Washington, D.C., provides a free FMLA fact sheet and other related materials.

"On the positive side, [FMLA] drew attention to family issues at the federal policy level," Bankert says. "That was really a first. On the down side, it's created more administrative procedures than it needed to."

Reaping the Benefits

William M. Mercer Inc., an employee benefits consulting firm in New York City, recently surveyed employers and found 64 percent attributed increased employee morale to family-friendly programs. Nearly half of the more than 800 employers surveyed said their programs helped increase productivity and decrease absenteeism. About three of every four employers said family-friendly programs helped recruiting efforts. Three-fourths also said flexible work scheduling was their most important family-friendly feature.

"I have a lot of sympathy for parents who don't have the scheduling flexibility that I have," Kicinski says. "I'm home for dinner four days a week, which is probably more than a lot of dads can say. Especially in journalism, a lot of people don't have the luxury of having Saturdays and Sundays off. All in all, I've got it pretty good."

Wimbley at First Tennessee says she appreciates just knowing she has a family-friendly workplace to fall back on when she needs it. "I never have to worry when it comes to my baby," she says about her five-year-old daughter Chelsea. "If you work for a company that doesn't pay much attention to you, that just treats you like a number, then you're not going to produce really good work for that company. [My advice to parents interviewing for jobs] is, go research the companies and see what they have to offer. Talk to people in personnel about your concerns."

Ninety-four percent of the companies surveyed by Mercer said they offer flexible scheduling. Of those, 38 percent offer flextime and 26 percent allow job sharing. Eighty-six percent of the surveyed employers said that "a company cannot remain competitive in the '90s without addressing the issue of the balance between an employee's work and personal life."

Like Kicinski and his son Andrew, Wimbley also brings Chelsea to work when she needs to. As an added family-friendly bonus, their children are being exposed to jobs and the workplace at an early age.

"[Andrew] understands that I work with words on a computer and the newspaper is the product," Kicinski says. ". . . he understands that work is important to [me and my wife] and that it's not something to be feared. I know he knows for sure that if we didn't work we wouldn't be able to buy him as many toys. He's definitely gotten down that work equals money equals toys."

THE MOTHER MARKET

Patricia Braus

The twenty-first century will bring new challenges to organizations that market prenatal and maternity services, including fewer new moms, the end of childbearing for baby boomers, more minority mothers, and cost-conscious health care providers. Patricia Braus is a contributing editor of American Demographics *magazine.*

Picture a bridal show in Atlanta, Georgia, teeming with brides-to-be, their even more anxious mothers, and dreamy younger sisters. You're approaching a booth that has a small television perched on a table. You have already seen videotapes hawking silver services and honeymoon resorts, but this one is different. Moving closer, you're transfixed by the screen.

It's a live birth. The booth is sponsored by Atlanta Women's Specialists, a group of doctors and midwives who want your business after the honeymoon.

Welcome to the anything-but-squeamish new world of marketing childbirth services. Not long ago, most things having to do with childbirth were only discussed in private. Today, childbirth is so much an element of public life that fashionable southern brides gravitate to films of the process.

The products and services of reproduction and childbirth are now sold by maternity specialists to working women who tend to be demanding, intelligent customers. Sales in this most womanly category have increased dramatically over the last decade, as the huge baby-boom generation has moved through its childbearing years. Oral contraceptives were a $930 million market in 1990; 1995 sales are estimated at $1.5 billion by the research firm Find/SVP. Retail sales of feminine-hygiene products in the U.S. have increased from $1.5 billion in 1989 to $1.8 billion in 1993, according to Packaged Facts.

But now the market is changing. As the first baby-boom women reach their 50th birthdays and enter menopause, childbirth marketers may find it necessary to take more aggressive approaches to maintain sales growth. The Atlanta Women's Specialists booth is an example of this new, more direct approach.

The movie goes from showing the live birth to scenes of the practice with the doctors and midwives at work. "It's intriguing," says Lisa Borders Marbury, administrator for the practice. It just "draws people in. After a trade show, we get 20 to 30 new patients in the next month."

Efforts like Marbury's are not traditional and perhaps not suited to other markets. "We're not leading edge, we're bleeding edge," she says proudly. But most organizations that sell health services to young women will have to become more aggressive as their patient base changes in the next decade.

Changes in the mother market will include slow growth in the numbers of women of child-bearing age in most U.S. markets, along with a declining number of women in the peak years for childbearing. The overall market—the number of U.S. women aged 15 to 44—will increase from about 59 million in 1990 to 60 million in 2000, then remain unchanged until 2005. Yet the number of women in their peak childbearing ages, 20 to 34, is predicted to fall from 31 million in 1995 to 28 million in 2000 and 2005. The number of women aged 20 to 34 will not rebound to its 1995 level until after the year 2015, according to Census Bureau projections.

The annual number of births in the U.S. exceeded 4 million between 1989 and 1993, but it dropped just below 4 million in 1994 and is not expected to break that mark again until the year 2008. After 2008, births may rise again as the 69 million children of baby boomers born between 1977 and 1994 begin having children themselves. In the year 2018, births are projected to exceed 4.5 million.

The birth rate is also expected to fall through the late 1990s. Birth rates hit a postwar peak in 1957, when 25.3 babies were born for every 1,000 people in the population. But decline has been fairly steady since then with a brief upswing from 1988 to 1991. The rate stood at about 15.6 per 1,000 in 1995, and the Census Bureau expects it to sink to a record low of 13.9 in 2026. Fewer babies means more than just a tougher market for hospitals. It means fewer customers for childbirth-related products, including drugs used in labor and delivery, products to help breast-feeding mothers, baby formula, and diapers.

While the national trend is for slow growth or stagnation, the number of births in some markets may continue to grow rapidly, while others could see absolute declines. The Northeast and the Midwest should see their population of 18-to-44-year-old women drop steadily until the year 2010, but western states may see a steady increase in this group. Southern states are expected to see their population of women aged 18 to 44 increase until the year 2000, then decrease to 1995 levels in 2010.

Table 1. States of Birth

Fast-growing and southern states have the highest birth rates; slow-growing and northern states have the lowest.

(top and bottom states for birth rate per 1,000 residents, 1994)

TOP		BOTTOM	
state	birth rate	state	birth rate
1. Utah	20.1	40. North Dakota	13.5
2. California	18.1	41. Rhode Island	13.5
3. Alaska	17.6	42. Wyoming	13.5
4. Texas	17.5	43. Wisconsin	13.4
5. Arizona	17.4	44. New Hampshire	13.3
6. New Mexico	16.7	45. Iowa	13.1
7. Hawaii	16.6	46. Pennsylvania	13.0
8. Nevada	16.4	47. Montana	12.9
9. Illinois	16.1	48. Vermont	12.7
10. Georgia	15.7	49. West Virginia	11.7
11. Louisiana	15.7	50. Maine	11.6
12. Mississippi	15.7		
Total U.S.	15.2		

Source: National Center for Health Statistics

Birth rates will continue to vary by region. Some hospitals will see increasing numbers of babies if they are in a market where the population is younger than average or includes a high share of racial or ethnic minorities. Utah had the nation's highest birth rate in 1994, with 20.1 babies born for every 1,000 residents. In this case, nonminority Mormons are responsible for high birth rates. Maine had the lowest birth rate, with 11.6 per 1,000.

Higher birth rates among Hispanics, blacks, and some other groups will run counter to a national slowdown in births among non-Hispanic whites. The number of children born to minority women is often higher than it is for non-Hispanic white women, but this isn't the only reason for the minority baby boom. The median age of Hispanic and Asian immigrants is below that of native-born Americans, so large numbers of these minority women are likely to be young adults in the midst of their childbearing years.

Hispanic-American birth rates, at 25.5 per

1,000 people, were higher in 1994 than the national birth rate was in 1957. Hispanics were about 16 percent of estimated U.S. births in 1995, and are expected to make up 17.5 percent by the year 2000 and 19 percent by 2005. In many southern and western states, Hispanic births could approach or exceed a majority of the total.

Births to Asians are also expected to continue climbing. Asian Americans were slightly more than 4 percent of estimated U.S. births in 1995; they are expected to make up 5 percent in 2000 and 5.3 percent in 2005. In California and some large urban markets, their share will be far greater.

Blacks will also maintain above-average birth rates. But the Census Bureau predicts that black birth rates may decline in the future, mainly because this group has not been absorbing large numbers of young adults from other countries. In 1994, the birth rate for blacks was 19.5 births per 1,000 people, compared with 14.4 per 1,000 whites.

The growing number of births to racial and ethnic minorities means that multicultural marketing will be increasingly important to the success of family-planning products and services. Some maternity centers in the U.S. are placing Spanish-language advertising on radio and TV, and marketers of childbirth and related reproductive-health products are also placing ads in local and national publications for black Americans. The 1995 campaign for the contraceptive Depo-Provera, for example, included many magazines with heavy black readership.

A New Generation of Moms

The last woman of the baby-boom generation could give birth in about 2014, when she turns 50. Until then, baby boomers will steadily cede the childbearing world to the smaller generation of 44 million Americans born between 1965 and 1976. Marketers must be attuned to the different values of mothers who belong to this generation, often called the "baby bust" because of its relatively small size.

One way to look at these values is to consider what demographers call the "cohort effect," or the traits that develop in groups according to influences during the formative years of 17 to 21.

Table 2. Moms Get Older

The number of births to women under age 30 declined 10 percent between 1980 and 1994, but births to women aged 30 and older increased 88 percent.

(thousands of U.S. births, by age of mother, 1980, 1990, 1994)

	1980	1990	1994
15 to 29	2,887	2,893	2,596
30 to 34	550	886	906
35 to 39	141	318	372
40 to 44	23	50	64
Total	3,612	4,158	3,953

Note: Numbers do not sum to total because a small number of births are to women under age 15 or over 44.

Source: National Center for Health Statistics

Baby-boom women came of age during the heyday of the women's health movement, when young people were encouraged to question authority. They saw the birth of the modern environmental movement, with its emphasis on "natural" products. The popularity of patient-controlled health products and services such as home pregnancy tests and "natural" childbirth is no coincidence.

Baby-bust women matured at a time when the "natural" label could be found on everything from clothing to candy, so they may not attach as much significance to the term—or they may take it for granted. They were more likely to be treated by women physicians, and more likely to be raised by working mothers, than were baby boomers. The decreasing demand for "natural" childbirth and the growing interest in female obstetrician-gynecologists stems largely from the baby bust's preferences.

The challenge for childbirth marketers is to serve both generations until about 2005, then craft new messages for the huge generation of baby boomers' children. The 69 million-member generation known as the "echo boom" or "the next baby boom" is aged 2 to 19 in 1996. This group will dominate the childbearing market in the first decade of the 21st century. The news events and cultural trends of the next ten years will help determine the values and attitudes of this generation throughout their lives.

Childbirth Meets Managed Care

Hospitals generally don't give anything away. But in late 1995, Tampa General Health Care announced it would be cutting the price of its rooms from over $200 per night to zero for any woman who gave birth in the hospital. The free room is available for 48 hours after their medical discharge, so new mothers can enjoy inpatient care for themselves and their newborns, even though insurance won't cover the cost.

Tampa General's gamble started after Fred Karl, the retired chief executive officer and a father of seven, decided that something had to be done for women like his youngest daughter. She gave birth at another hospital and was sent home after 12 hours. "She was a wreck," says Claudia Mahoney, director of women's and children's services at Tampa General. Karl's announcement galvanized interest in the hospital, triggering media coverage and a swell of customer interest. "It ended up being a good marketing plan, but I don't think that was the idea," says Mahoney.

Tampa General loses money on the extra night's stay. But its willingness to launch the program is a measure of the importance of childbirth services to hospitals. Childbirth is a lucrative procedure that provides bread-and-butter income and future patient loyalty. Thirty-eight percent of all hospital patients have their first relationship with a hospital through childbirth services, says consultant Ruthie H. Dearing, president of Dearing and Associates in Spokane, Washington. Hospitals see it as a crucial opportunity to make a good first impression.

Likewise, obstetrician-gynecologists and family practitioners see childbirth as nine months of steady visits that can be the introduction to a lifelong relationship with a family. Among midwives, childbirth is the only source of business and referrals.

Pregnant women are a prize for health-care providers, and competition for them has intensified with the rise of health-maintenance organiza-

Figure 1. Moms Go West

The number of 18-to-44-year-olds will decrease nationally, but it should increase in the West.

(projected millions of 18-to-44-year-olds for U.S. regions, 1995, 2000, and 2010)

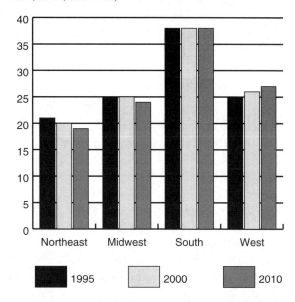

Source: Census Bureau, Current Population Reports, Series P25-111

tions (HMOs) and other managed-health-care plans. Hospitals across the country have opened new maternity units so they can compete with other hospitals for managed-care contracts. Knowing what pregnant women want out of childbirth services gives some of the competitors a powerful advantage.

The maternity experience has changed drastically in the last decade. During the 1980s, childbirth marketers promoted everything from steak dinners and champagne for new parents to family birthing rooms. Today, new kinds of approaches are required for mothers who are more diverse, less interested in frills, and more interested in receiving high-quality care at a low price.

In addition, the rules of managed-care plans are having a powerful and growing effect on childbirth services. Managed care can dictate how and when women choose their physicians and midwives, what hospitals they use, and how long they stay at the hospital. Health providers in this environment must walk a tightrope, appealing to a more discriminating clientele while keeping costs down.

In 1988, about 29 percent of Americans with private health insurance were enrolled in managed-care plans. By 1993, most Americans with private health insurance were enrolled in managed care, and the proportion continues to grow. One result has been a sharp decrease in the average hospital maternity stay, from 4.1 days in 1970 to 2.6 days in 1992.

Managed care makes it essential for maternity marketers to give women a positive feeling about their hospital before pregnancy begins. "Anything that will influence decisions at insurance enrollment helps," says Mary Anne Graf, president of Health Care Innovations Inc. market research group in Salt Lake City, Utah. This makes traditional advertising less important than in the past, while highly targeted media such as billboards and direct mail become more important.

The need to appeal to women early is especially important in childbirth services, because women form general impressions of their local hospitals well before their first bout of morning sickness. And it is especially important for hospi-

Figure 2. Moving Moms Along

The average birth meant 4.1 hospital days in 1970, but 2.6 days in 1993.

(average days of stay for hospital deliveries, by delivery method, 1970–93)

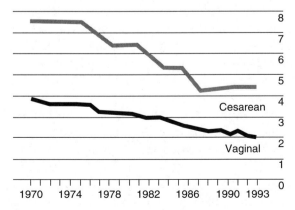

Source: National Hospital Discharge Survey

tals, because most women (58 percent) choose their hospital first and their physician second, according to consultant Ruthie Dearing. "If you're going to market your hospital, your customer is currently looking in her lover's eyes. She's not pregnant yet," says Sally Rynne, president of Women's Healthcare Consultants in Evanston, Illinois.

Although much has changed in marketing childbirth services to women, many of the basics still apply in every market, whether or not managed care is a factor. Marketers across the country continue to follow three key strategies.

First, they conduct market research by holding focus groups and conducting surveys of women. This is the most reliable way to track the specific services women want in a specific market. "The [preferences] are different for every area and for every age group," says Maxine Brinkman, director of women's and children's services for North Iowa Mercy Health Center. "We have to listen to our customers."

Second, they promote educational programs, including a full range of childbirth classes. "Educational programs bring folks into the system," says Kris Powell of Anne Arundel Medical Center.

Third, they draw public attention to new programs. "Every time something [we do] is in the news, we book new patients," says Terry Mullady Guymon, manager of women's health services at the Women's Health Center of Christ Hospital and Medical Center in Tinley Park, Illinois.

Relationship Marketing

The most effective hospital marketing programs develop links to women that last for years. Relationship marketing can include everything from educational programs to membership programs, urgent care services, and children's centers.

One innovative program pursues healthy women in San Antonio, Texas. The Methodist Health Care System offers men and women membership in its WomanPlus program for $10. The program provides discounts at stores and restaurants, offers members the chance to take free health classes, provides free transportation to the hospital, and gives some discounts on hospital services.

When WomanPlus was launched in 1987, Methodist Hospital lagged behind competitors in the childbirth market. Eight years later, the hospital is the top San Antonio provider of childbirth services, says Geoffrey Crabtree, vice president of strategic planning and market services. "It gives us a relationship to you," he says. "In building that relationship over a period of time, we hope you'll remember us."

The hospital has used the information from the WomanPlus membership form to compile a massive record of individual health profiles, from which it develops demographic and lifestyle profiles of its current and likely customers. The database's value goes far beyond childbirth marketing, says Crabtree. For example, Methodist General can now send information by mail to women of menopausal age about services for this group.

Methodist General's system requires top-of-the-line computer capability. Smaller hospitals and obstetric practices have found lower-tech ways to reach out to potential customers that are just as effective. Many hospitals send out newsletters to former patients and likely future prospects, for example. Bellevue Woman's Hospital in Niskayuna, New York, also sends educators to junior high schools to give programs on puberty, nutrition, and pregnancy awareness. When the girls' soccer team at the local high school won the state championship, the hospital held a reception and gave the girls warm-up jackets. Support of local girls reminds the community about the hospital and its two freestanding primary-care women's health centers.

What Pregnant Women Want

The essence of relationship marketing is customizing a product or service to satisfy the unique wants of individuals. And what pregnant women of the 1990s seem to want, more than anything else, is options. While most expectant women are not choosing drug-free childbirth, those who do are an important segment in some markets. It isn't the rule for a woman to request that small children and other family members be allowed to visit freely during her labor, but it does happen—and it is a popular option among

Figure 3. Minority Moms

After 2020, minority women will account for the majority of births.

(percent distribution of births by race and Hispanic origin,* 1990 and middle-series projections for 2000–2050)

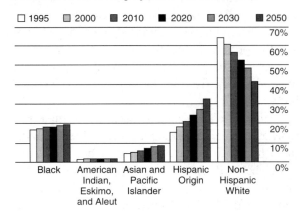

*Persons of Hispanic origin may be of any race.

Source: Census Bureau

Hispanic families. This demand for options during birth is one reason why the number of certified nurse midwives in the U.S. has more than doubled since 1980, to more than 5,000 in 1995. Virtually all nurse midwives are women, and many women choose them out of a desire for woman-to-woman care.

The popularity of midwives is likely to increase as managed care responds to the less-expensive cost of midwifery, and as women choose women practitioners. One sign of this is the heavy dependence on nurse midwives by Kaiser Permanente, the massive HMO based in California. More than 90 percent of Kaiser's pregnant patients choose midwives with an obstetrician backup when given a choice, according to Find/SVP.

The future of childbirth services will be increasingly competitive. In most markets, hospitals and health providers will compete for a stable number of pregnant women. Any expansion of efforts to attract pregnant women will need to be financed by increased market share, because managed care will make it harder to raise the price of maternity services in most markets.

While managed care presses for cost savings, women's demands for the best possible birth experience will remain high. Yet even this creates new opportunities in health care. The increasingly short hospital stays mandated by insurers give hospitals, family practitioners, obstetrician-gynecologists, and midwives many opportunities to market after-delivery care to help with breast feeding and other needs. In the 21st century, the boundaries of maternity care will go well beyond the hospital or physician's office, changing what women want and expect when they give birth.

NEW MOTHERS, NOT MARRIED

George A. Akerlof and Janet L. Yellen

An increase in the availability of contraceptives and abortion and an erosion of the custom of "shotgun marriages" have combined to increase the rate of out-of-wedlock births. George A. Akerlof is a senior fellow in the Brookings Economic Studies program and professor of economics at the University of California at Berkeley. Janet L. Yellen is on the Board of Governors of the Federal Reserve System.

In 1970 a permanent cure to poverty in America seemed on the horizon. Federal poverty warriors appeared to be gaining ground, and decisions by state courts regarding abortion and by state legislatures regarding the availability of contraception seemed to be giving poor families the tools to control the number and the timing of their children. The dream of eliminating poverty, however, has remained unfulfilled. Not only have U.S. poverty rates stayed stubbornly constant over the intervening 25 years, but also poor families have seen their lot worsen as huge increases in single-parent families—more and more headed by unmarried mothers—have led to the feminization of poverty in America.

Since 1970, out-of-wedlock birth rates have soared. In 1965, 24 percent of black infants and

Reprinted from George A. Akerlof and Janet L. Yellen, "New Mothers, Not Married," *The Brookings Review*, Fall 1996, by permission of the Brookings Institution, Washington, D.C.

3.1 percent of white infants were born to single mothers. By 1990 the rates were 64 percent for black infants, 18 percent for whites. Every year one million more children are born into fatherless families. If we have learned any policy lesson well over the past 25 years, it is that for children living in single-parent homes, the odds of living in poverty are great. The policy implications of the increase in out-of-wedlock births are staggering.

Searching for an Explanation

Efforts by social scientists to explain the rise in out-of-wedlock births have so far been unconvincing, though several theories have a wide popular following. One argument that appeals to conservatives is that of Charles Murray, who attributes the increase to overly generous federal welfare benefits. But as David Ellwood and Lawrence Summers have shown, welfare benefits could not have played a major role in the rise of out-of-wedlock births because benefits rose sharply in the 1960s and then fell in the 1970s and 1980s, when out-of-wedlock births rose most. A study by Robert Moffitt in 1992 also found that welfare benefits can account for only a small fraction of the rise in the out-of-wedlock birth ratio.

Liberals have tended to favor the explanation offered by William Julius Wilson. In a 1987 study, Wilson attributed the increase in out-of-wedlock births to a decline in the marriageability of black men due to a shortage of jobs for less educated men. But Robert D. Mare and Christopher

Winship have estimated that at most 20 percent of the decline in marriage rates of blacks between 1960 and 1980 can be explained by decreasing employment. And Robert G. Wood has estimated that only 3–4 percent of the decline in black marriage rates can be explained by the shrinking of the pool of eligible black men.

Yet another popular explanation is that single parenthood has increased since the late 1960s because of the change in attitudes toward sexual behavior. But so far social scientists have been unable to explain exactly how that change came about or to estimate in any convincing way its quantitative impact. In recent work we have been able to provide both.

The Answer: No More Shotgun Marriages

In the late 1960s and very early 1970s (well before *Roe v. Wade* in January 1973) many major states, including New York and California, liberalized their abortion laws. At about the same time it became easier for unmarried people to get contraceptives. In July 1970 the Massachusetts law prohibiting the distribution of contraceptives to unmarried people was declared unconstitutional. We have found that this sudden increase in the availability of both abortion and contraception—we call it a reproductive technology shock—is deeply implicated in the increase in out-of-wedlock births. Although many observers expected liberalized abortion and contraception to lead to fewer out-of-wedlock births, the opposite happened—because of the erosion in the custom of "shotgun marriages."

Until the early 1970s, shotgun marriage was the norm in premarital sexual relations. The custom was succinctly stated by one San Francisco resident in the late 1960s: "If a girl gets pregnant you married her. There wasn't no choice. So I married her."

Since 1969, however, the tradition of shotgun marriage has seriously eroded (see table 1 for the trend from 1965 through 1984). For whites, in particular, the shotgun marriage rate began its decline at almost the same time as the reproductive technology shock. And the decline in shotgun marriages has contributed heavily to the rise in the out-of-wedlock birth rate for both white and black women. In fact, about 75 percent of the increase in the white out-of-wedlock first-birth rate, and about 60 percent of the black increase, between 1965 and 1990 is directly attributable to the decline in shotgun marriages. If the shotgun marriage rate had remained steady from 1965 to 1990, white out-of-wedlock births would have risen only 25 percent as much as they have. Black out-of-wedlock births would have increased only 40 percent as much.

What links liberalized contraception and abortion with the declining shotgun marriage rate? Before 1970, the stigma of unwed motherhood was so great that few women were willing to bear children outside of marriage. The only circumstance that would cause women to engage in sexual activity was a promise of marriage in the event of pregnancy. Men were willing to make (and keep) that promise for they knew that in leaving one woman they would be unlikely to find another who would not make the same demand. Even women who would be willing to bear children out-of-wedlock could demand a promise of marriage in the event of pregnancy.

The increased availability of contraception and abortion made shotgun weddings a thing of the past. Women who were willing to get an abortion or who reliably used contraception no longer found it necessary to condition sexual relations on a promise of marriage in the event of pregnancy. But women who wanted children, who objected to abortion for moral or religious reasons, or who were unreliable in their use of contraception found themselves pressured to participate in premarital sexual relations without being able to exact a promise of marriage in case of pregnancy. These women feared, correctly, that if they refused sexual relations, they risked losing their partners. Sexual activity without commitment was increasingly expected in premarital relationships.

Advances in reproductive technology eroded the custom of shotgun marriage in another way. Before the sexual revolution, women had less freedom, but men were expected to assume responsibility for their welfare. Today women are more free to choose, but men have afforded themselves the comparable option. "If she is not willing to have an abortion or use contraception," the man can reason, "why should I sacrifice myself to get married?" By making the birth of the child the physical choice of the mother, the sexual revolution has made marriage and child support a social choice of the father.

Many men have changed their attitudes regarding the responsibility for unplanned pregnancies. As one contributor to the Internet wrote recently to the Dads' Rights Newsgroup, "Since the decision to have the child is solely up to the mother, I don't see how both parents have responsibility to that child." That attitude, of course, makes it far less likely that the man will offer marriage as a solution to a couple's pregnancy quandary, leaving the mother either to raise the child or to give it up for adoption.

Before the 1970s, unmarried mothers kept few of their babies. Today they put only a few up for adoption because the stigma of unwed motherhood has declined. The transformation in attitudes was captured by the *New York Times* in 1993: "In the 'old days' of the 1960s, '50s, and '40s, pregnant teenagers were pariahs, banished from schools, ostracized by their peers or scurried out of town to give birth in secret." Today they are "supported and embraced in their decision to give birth, keep their babies, continue their education, and participate in school activities." Since out-of-wedlock childbearing no longer results in social ostracism, literally and figuratively, shotgun marriage no longer occurs at the point of the shotgun.

The Theory and the Facts

The preceding discussion explains why the reproductive technology shock could have increased the out-of-wedlock birth rate. How well do the data fit the theory?

In 1970 there were about 400,000 out-of-wedlock births out of 3.7 million total births (see table 1). In 1990 there were 1.2 million out-of-wedlock births out of 4 million total. From the late 1960s to the late 1980s, the number of births per unmarried woman roughly doubled for whites, but fell by 5–10 percent for blacks. The fraction of unmarried women rose about 30 percent for whites, about 40 percent for blacks. The fertility rates for married women of both races declined rapidly (also, of course, contributing to the rise in the out-of-wedlock birth ratio).

If the increased abortions and use of contraceptives caused the rise in out-of-wedlock births, the increase would have to have been very large relative to the number of those births and to the number of unmarried women. And as table 1 shows, that was indeed the case. The use of birth control pills at first intercourse by unmarried women jumped from 6 percent to 15 percent in just a few years, a change that suggests that a much larger fraction of all sexually active unmarried women began using the pill. The number of abortions to unmarried women grew from roughly 100,000 a year in the late 1960s (compared with some 322,000 out-of-wedlock births) to more than 1.2 million (compared with 715,000 out-of-wedlock births) in the early 1980s. Thus the data do support the theory.

Indeed, the technology shock theory explains not only the increase in the out-of-wedlock birth rate, but also related changes in family structure and sexual practice, such as the sharp decline in the number of children put up for adoption. The peak year for adoptions in the United States was 1970, the year of the technology shock. Over the next five years the number of agency adoptions was halved from 86,000 to 43,000. In 1969, mothers of out-of-wedlock children who had not married after three years kept only 28 percent of those children. In 1984, that rate was 56 percent; by the late 1980s it was 66 percent.

Unlike the other statistics we have mentioned, the shotgun marriage rate itself underwent only gradual change following the early 1970s. Why did it not change as dramatically as the others? For two reasons. The first is that shotgun marriage was an accepted social convention and, as such, it changed slowly. It took time for men to recognize that they did not have to promise marriage in the event of a pregnancy in exchange for sexual relations. It may also have taken time for women to perceive the increased willingness of men to leave them if they demanded marriage. As new expectations formed, social norms readjusted, and the shotgun marriage rate began its long decline.

In addition, the decreasing stigma of out-of-wedlock childbirth reinforced the technology-driven causes for the decline in shotgun marriage and increased retention of out-of-wedlock children. With premarital sex the rule, rather than the exception, an out-of-wedlock childbirth gradually ceased to be a sign that society's sexual taboos had been violated. The reduction in stigma also helps explain why women who would once have put their baby up for adoption chose to keep it instead.

One final puzzle requires explanation. The black shotgun marriage ratio began to fall earlier than the white ratio and shows no significant change in trend around 1970. How do we account for that apparent anomaly? Here federal welfare benefits may play a role. For women whose earnings are so low that they are potentially eligible for welfare, an increase in welfare benefits has the same effect on out-of-wedlock births as a decline in the stigma to bearing a child out-of-wedlock. The difference in welfare eligibility between whites and blacks and the patterns of change in benefits—rising in the 1960s and falling thereafter—may then explain why the decline in the black shotgun marriage ratio began earlier than that for whites. Because blacks on average have lower incomes than whites, they are more affected by changes in welfare benefits. As a result, the rise in welfare benefits in the 1960s may have had only a small impact on the white shotgun rate but resulted in a significant decrease in the black shotgun marriage rate.

Policy Considerations

Although doubt will always remain about the ultimate cause for something as diffuse as a change in social custom, the technology shock theory does fit the facts. The new reproductive technology was adopted quickly and on a massive scale. It is therefore plausible that it could have accounted for a comparably large change in marital and fertility patterns. The timing of the changes also seems, at least crudely, to fit the theory.

From a policy perspective, attempts to turn the

Table 1. America's Reproductive Technology Shock, 1965–84

	1965–69	1970–74	1975–79	1980–84
Births (thousands)				
Total	3599	3370	3294	3646
White	2990	2760	2660	2915
Black	542	583	540	590
Birthrates per 1000 married women, age 15–44				
White	119.4	103.6	93.1	94.5
Black	129.1	110.3	93.3	90.6
Birthrates per 1000 unmarried women, age 15–44				
White	12.7	12.6	13.7	18.9
Black	91.0	94.6	85.5	81.7
Women married, age 15–44 (percent)				
White	67.8	65.3	61.6	58.8
Black	55.9	52.9	45.2	39.9
Out-of-wedlock births (thousands)				
Total	322	406	515	715
White	144	166	220	355
Black	189	230	280	337
Women age 16 with sexual experience (percent)				
White	13.8	23.2	28.1	32.8
Black	35.0	42.3	50.8	49.9
Unmarried women using the pill at first intercourse (percent)				
Total	5.7	15.2	13.4	NA
Abortions, unmarried women, age 15–44 (thousands)				
Total	88	561	985	1271
First-birth shotgun marriage rate (percent)				
White	59.2	55.4	45.7	42.0
Black	24.8	19.5	11.0	11.4
Adoptions (thousands)				
Total	158	156	129	142
Ratio of adoptions to births to mothers not married within three years of birth				
Total	49.0	38.4	29.0	19.8

Source: George A. Akerlof, Janet L. Yellen, and Michael L. Katz, "An Analysis of Out-of-Wedlock Childbearing in the United States," *Quarterly Journal of Economics*, May 1996.

technology clock back by denying women access to abortion and contraception is probably not possible. Even if it were, it would almost surely be counterproductive. In addition to probably reducing the well-being of women who use the technology, such measures could lead to yet greater poverty. With sexual abstinence rare and the stigma of out-of-wedlock motherhood small, denying women access to abortion and contraception would probably increase the number of children born out-of-wedlock and reared in impoverished single-parent families. On the contrary, efforts should be made to ensure that women can use the new technologies if they choose to do so.

Finally, if the technology shock theory does explain the rise in single motherhood, cuts in welfare as currently proposed would only further immiserize the victims. Such cuts would have little impact on the number of children born out-of-wedlock while impoverishing those already on welfare yet further. Instead, policy measures to make fathers pay to support their out-of-wedlock children would not only directly contribute to the well-being of children, but also tax men for fathering such children, thereby offsetting at least partially the change in terms between fathers and mothers. Such measures deserve serious policy consideration.

DISCUSSION QUESTIONS

1. How is parenthood promoted in our society? What messages do we receive about parenthood from television or magazine advertising? Is there a tendency to glamorize parenthood in our society? Why or why not?

2. Are the providers of maternity/childbirth products and services more concerned about the needs of expectant mothers or "the bottom line" (i.e., profits)? Explain your response.

3. The authors of the last reading suggest that increased availability of contraception and abortion have led to higher rates of out-of-wedlock births. If women were denied access to abortion and contraception, would this reduce the number of out-of-wedlock births in our society? Why or why not?

WEBSITES

www.babycenter.com/
Babycenter.com is an excellent commercial parenting page that focuses exclusively on pregnancy and infant raising.

www.parentsplace.com
ParentsPlace.com combines chat rooms, reading material, and links to other sites.

CHAPTER 10: RAISING CHILDREN

Concern for the welfare of children comes from all quarters in the United States today, there is great concern over children, as well as controversy over how much parenting children need and what constitutes "quality" parenting. Empirical research shows that having a reliable, loving, and consistent person in a child's life is important for their development. But does that person have to be the mother? Some family critics argue that women's departure from full-time mothering has led to an increase in social problems such as youth crime, drug abuse, teen pregnancy, and poverty. Others counter with the claim that traditional parenting arrangements are no longer appropriate in today's society.

Raising children in a society that has become more competitive, dangerous, and uncertain is no easy task. In fact, parenting is probably the most difficult, and thankless, job that people can take on. This chapter focuses on several important aspects of modern-day parenting.

Gary Sanders's article examines the research on gay and lesbian parenting. Citing research findings that clearly contradict four myths commonly associated with homosexuals, the author claims that gays and lesbians can be effective parents.

While most people now believe that fathers need to be more involved with their children, two opposing trends in fatherhood styles have emerged in recent years. Some fathers have extended their familial roles beyond that of breadwinners and have become more heavily involved in child rearing. Other fathers deny responsibility for their children, refusing to support them emotionally and/or financially. The second reading looks at the latter. With the divorce rate and number of out-of-wedlock births rising, absent fathers are a growing problem in our society.

The third reading explores another controversial aspect of parenting: Should parents use spankings when disciplining their children? The author, Phillip Davis, discusses how the meaning of "spanking" has changed over the years and how the traditional child-rearing issue has become a contemporary child-protection controversy.

NORMAL FAMILIES: RESEARCH ON GAY AND LESBIAN PARENTING

Gary Sanders

According to many experts, sexual preference has little to do with being a parent. Gary Sanders addresses four common myths that argue against gay and lesbian parenting. Sanders is the associate director of the Family Therapy Program and director of the Human Sexuality Program at the Faculty of Medicine at the University of Calgary, Canada. He is also a practicing therapist, working with families, adolescents, and couples.

Recently, the newspapers in Edmonton, Alberta, were filled with the story of the refusal of the Provincial Child Welfare System to allow a woman, who had been a highly regarded foster mother to more than 70 children, to receive further foster child placements when it was discovered that she was in a lesbian relationship. The government officials stated that only traditional, "normal" families were appropriate as foster parents. The officials defined "normal" as "a family with a mother and a father."

One of the great myths about families is that

Reprinted from Gary Sanders, "Normal Families: Gay and Lesbian Parenting," *In the Family*, January 1998, by permission of *In the Family*.

gay and lesbian people do not have children or families, either by reproduction or by adoption. The designation "normal family" has historically been co-opted by a heterosexual married union with offspring. However, M.A. Gold and colleagues, in the 1994 article "Children of Gay or Lesbian Parents" in *Pediatrics in Review,* point out that in the United States, fewer than one third of children live in a so-called traditional family, with a working father, homemaking mother and one or more children. Therefore, the understanding of "normal" family has grown to include single-parent families, families that are blended (i.e., remarried with children), and families that are led by one or two parents who are lesbian- or gay-identified. Despite the enlargement of the notion of family to include this diversity, the right wing often speaks of a "threat to family values" by gay and lesbian parents, despite lack of research support.

Four Common Myths

Dr. Lorne Warneke of the University of Alberta has written extensively on this issue, including a 1997 amicus brief entitled "When Virtually Normal is Normal Enough: Homosexual Orientation and Parenting." He outlines four myths that are used to support a prejudicial and unfounded position against gay and lesbian people being effective parents. It is useful to examine those myths and then the research on gay and lesbian parenting that addresses each one.

Myth #1: Homosexuality Is Only a Chosen Lifestyle

Common sense suggests that an individual does not choose a homosexual orientation, because it is unlikely anyone would consciously choose to be vilified and denigrated by centuries of persecution. Some women and men have chosen to be lesbian and gay for various reasons, but the majority of homosexuals don't choose to have homosexual attractions; it is simply a fact of their existence. Research on gay men shows that sexual orientation occurs long before conscious choice is even available for an individual's action and/or awareness. Recent research is indicating that homosexuality has a degree of biologic predetermination. However, whether it is biologically predetermined or culturally instilled through as yet too complicated processes of early development, what is known is that one's affiliative sexual orientation is indelible, just as one's concept of self as male or female is indelible.

There is a significant amount of research data to support claims of a biological basis for male homosexuality. For example, writer Chandler Burr's 1996 book, *A Separate Creation,* goes into great depth on the question of research regarding the existence of a "gay gene" described by Dean Hamer and colleagues in a 1993 *Science* article, "A Linkage Between DNA Markers on the X Chromosome and Male Sexual Orientation." The hypothesis that there is a "gay gene" was also explored by Simon Levay in his book *The Sexual Brain,* and in his article, "The Evidence of Biological Influence on Male Homosexuality," published in *Scientific American* in 1994. Even before Levay and Hamer came out with their findings, others such as D. Swaab and M. Hofman had published research on biological differences between heterosexual and gay men in a 1990 issue of the journal *Brain Research.* (Research on lesbians has not been done because systemic sexism minimizes research on women.)

Myth #2: Gay and Lesbian People Are Psychologically Maladjusted

The concept of homosexual orientation, as well as the concept of heterosexuality, is a fairly recent creation, according to historian Jonathan Katz in his book *The Invention of Heterosexuality.* It was a German lawyer, Karl Heinrich Ulrichs, who published a series of booklets in 1864, who first coined the term homosexual. The term was incorporated into the English vocabulary just before the turn of the century. Ulrichs suggested that homosexuals are normal people, that homosexuality is inborn, and that sexual relationships between members of the same sex are based on love. He went on to argue that homosexuals should have the right to marry one another. Magnus Hershfield, a famous early-twentieth-century German sexologist, also believed that homosexuality was inborn and a normal of variant sexual expression. However, it was Sigmund Freud, in his famous "Letter to an American Mother" of a gay son, who spoke to the inherent normality of gayness and published the first widespread professional disagreement with the myth of homosexuality as pathological. The Kinsey reports of 1948 and 1949 on the sexual behavior of men and women showed that homosexuality was omnipresent, although at one-tenth the rate of heterosexuality. Yet it was the classic studies by Evelyn Hooker that demonstrated that homosexuals and heterosexuals could not be differentiated by a battery of psychological personality tests when read blind by trained professionals. In other words, individuals with a homosexual orientation were as normal in terms of psychological makeup and emotional maturity as heterosexuals. Other studies have been done to reaffirm her findings of normal psychological development and the fact that there is no higher incidence of mental illness in gay or lesbian persons compared to heterosexuals. Some of those include M. Weinberg and C. Williams's 1974 work, *Male Homosexuals: Their Problems and Adaptations,* a 1971 article in the *Journal of Abnormal Psychology* by N. Thompson and colleagues entitled "Personal Adjustment of Male and Female Homosexuals and Heterosexuals," an even earlier study—1969—in the *British Journal of Psychiatry* by J. Hopkins called "The Lesbian Personality" and others.

Once the major professional organizations of the mental health field declassified homosexuality as a mental disorder, a process that began back in 1973 with the American Psychiatric Association, the official consensus in the field has been that homosexuality should not be seen as a condition that necessitates change, "conversion" or any pathologizing. In fact, the American Pediatric Association stated that trying to change gay or lesbian sexual orientation would be unethical and grounds for malpractice. Therefore, the idea that gay and lesbian people are somehow less mentally healthy, well-adjusted, or able to cope compared to their heterosexual brothers and sisters can be put to rest for good. Of course, as with any group, some persons who are gay and lesbian may have psychiatric or psychological disorders, but this occurs no more or less often than in the rest of the population.

Myth #3: Gay and Lesbian People Cannot Be Good Parents

This myth is often touted by those with homophobic and heterosexist agendas; however, not only does the research refute this belief, it also points out that, in fact, gay and lesbian people can be equally as good at parenting as heterosexuals. Seldom in the area of psychological, sociological, anthropological, psychiatric, and medical research has there been such agreement amongst researchers as there is on this issue.

There has been considerable research done in the area of parenting abilities of gays and lesbians, the effects on children of being raised by gays and lesbians and studies comparing heterosexual parents with lesbian and gay parents. M. Kirkpatrick has shown in an article in the *Journal of Homosexuality,* "Clinical Implications of Lesbian Mother Studies," that findings from studies comparing lesbian and heterosexual mothers show no difference with respect to maternal attitude. In a 1981 article in the *American Journal of Orthopsychiatry,* "Children's Acquisition of Sex-Role Behavior in Lesbian Mother Families," B.

Hoeffer indicated that lesbian and heterosexual mothers are very similar with respect to childrearing and maternal interest. Fiona Tasker and colleagues conducted a longitudinal study of 25 young adults from lesbian families compared to 21 young adults raised by heterosexual single mothers and, as their 1991 *Family Law* article revealed, they discovered that the former compared to the latter as well-adjusted psychologically, both in terms of well-being and of family identity and relationships. Lesbian mothers on average are found to be as child-oriented, warm and responsive, nurturing and confident with their children as were their heterosexual counterparts. Lesbians may even do a better job in some cases—there have been findings that show that lesbian mothers after divorce are more likely to ensure their children have male role models compared to heterosexual mothers.

As for gay fathers, F.W. Bozett compared parenting between gay and heterosexual fathers in a 1989 review of the literature in the *Journal of Homosexuality,* and found no differences between the two groups in terms of problem-solving and providing recreation for their children. Gay fathers were found to be less traditional, demonstrated greater nurturing, had more investment in the parental role, and were more positive about this, than heterosexual fathers. These findings have been backed up by several research studies by J. Bigner and R. Jacobsen. Charlotte Patterson, in her comprehensive review of the subject of children raised by gays or lesbians ("Children of Lesbians and Gays," in a 1992 issue of *Child Development*) writes, "There is no evidence to suggest the psychosocial development among children of gay men or lesbians is compromised in any respect relative to that among offspring of heterosexual parents." She goes on to say, "Indeed, the evidence to date suggest that home environment provided by gay and lesbian parents are as likely as those provided by heterosexual parents to support and enable children's psychosocial growth." Bigner and Jacobsen conclude, "There is no evidence that being gay is a liability as far as parenting is concerned"; and "it appears that gay fathers are at least equal to heterosexual fathers in the quality of their parenting."

While there is a long bibliography of research that upholds the idea that lesbians and gays can make fine parents, there is no evidence to suggest that gays and lesbians are less capable than heterosexuals with respect to parenting skills and attitudes. There has only been one researcher, Paul Cameron, who has repeatedly spoken, written, and published on this point; however, he was discredited by his own professional associations as having fabricated his research on gay and lesbian parenting to fit with his preconceived homophobic belief system. Despite his being dismissed from his professional association and discredited by his scientific peers, there are those with an agenda of intolerance and prejudice who continue to cite his writings as if they had credence.

Two additional fears are often raised by those who are opposed to gay and lesbian parenting: One is that there may be a higher preponderance of gay and lesbian children because their parents are openly lesbian and gay. Despite the inherent heterosexist and homophobic premise that more lesbian or gay children would be undesirable, the concern is not supported in any research. For instance, researcher R. Green, in his 1978 article in the *American Journal of Psychiatry,* "Sexual Identity of 37 Children Raised by Homosexual or Transsexual Parents," and J.M. Bailey and colleagues, in their 1995 article in *Developmental Psychology,* "Sexual Orientation of Adult Sons of Gay Fathers," and—most recently—S. Golombok and F. Task, in the 1996 article in *Developmental Psychology,* "Do Parents Influence the Sexual Orientation of Their Children: Findings from a Longitudinal Study of Lesbian Families," showed the incidence of homosexuality in offspring of gay and lesbian people, or those raised by gay and lesbian people, as being no different than in the general population.

A second worry is that children raised by gay and lesbian parents will show emotional or social maladjustment because of stigmatization. This is based on the assumption that children of homosexual parents may be more likely to experience social trauma due to stigmatization, social isolation, parental divorce, and being raised in a single-parent household. All the studies found that the children of gay fathers or lesbian mothers have normal peer relationships, develop close friendships and do not suffer adversely from stigmatization because of having a parent who happens to be homosexual. We must certainly expect that the children of gay parents will have to cope with prejudice, misunderstanding, and possibly even negative peer reactions. But then, so may the children of African American parents, poor Appalachian parents, divorced parents, and parents with physical impairments. The fact that a child's parents are different from the majority of white, middle-class, unimpaired parents is not usually considered an appropriate reason for removing a child from a home. Therefore, sexual preference should not be any different in this respect.

Myth #4: Children of Gay or Lesbian Parents Are at Greater Risk for Sexual Abuse

This myth can easily be jettisoned since no research whatsoever supports it. It seems that the myth is perpetuated by two mistaken beliefs: first that there is a higher incidence of pedophilia amongst gay men than in the heterosexual population, and secondly, that therefore gay fathers are more likely to abuse their sons.

As regards the incidence of pedophilia, interestingly, there appears to be proportionally fewer homosexual pedophiles than heterosexual pedophiles. Three key studies bear this out: C. Jenny and colleagues' 1994 article in *Pediatrics,* "Are Children at Risk for Abuse by Homosexuals?"; D.E. Newton's 1978 article in *Adolescence,* "Homosexual Behavior and Child Molestation: A Review of the Evidence"; and A. Groth and H.J. Birnbaum's 1978 study in *Arch Sexual Behaviors,* "Adult Sexual Orientation and Attraction to Underage Persons." Additionally, the research indicates that sexual molestation of children is essentially a heterosexual act with familial incest almost always being father-daughter in type. Even in those situations where a boy is sexually interfered with by a father, the father is disproportionally self-identified as heterosexual.

Warneke sums up the relevant recent literature

on the issue of gay and lesbian parenting by saying: "With almost boring repetition, the conclusions of all the major studies, reviews and opinions of experts in the field were virtually the same. All of this is best summarized by B. Maddox in a classic article where she stated, 'What does sexual preference have to do with the need to love and care for children? Not much, according to studies and interviews with married and divorced homosexuals.'"

THE LOST ART OF FATHERHOOD

Dan Fost

As the United States faces a crisis of father-lessness, some groups are campaigning for ways to make fathers more involved and responsible. Dan Fost is a staff writer for American Demographics *magazine.*

On the day of the Million Man March [in October 1995], President Clinton addressed an audience at the University of Texas. While he focused on race relations, the president digressed at the end of his speech. "The single biggest social problem in our society may be the growing absence of fathers from their children's homes because it contributes to so many other social problems," said Clinton.

Clinton's call represents one more thrust in a movement with growing national momentum: the push for fatherhood. The Million Man March, the National Fatherhood Initiative, books, conferences, think tanks, and football stadiums full of Promise Keepers all aim to improve men's participation in their children's lives.

"There certainly has been an increased recognition that we are faced with a crisis of father-lessness in the U.S.," says David Blankenhorn, president of the Institute for American Values in New York City and author of *Fatherless America:*

Confronting Our Most Urgent Social Problem. Blankenhorn also co-founded the National Fatherhood Initiative, an advocacy group based in Lancaster, Pennsylvania. "At the broadest level, we're trying to change our culture," says group director Wade Horn.

The group's best estimate is that nearly 40 percent of American children currently don't live with their biological fathers. The consequences of these absences can be severe. Seventy percent of juveniles in state reform institutions grew up with one or neither parent. Forty-three percent of adult inmates grew up in single-parent homes, mostly without dads. Thirty percent of children living with never-married mothers and 22 percent with divorced mothers repeat a grade, compared with 12 percent of those living with both biological parents.

The National Fatherhood Initiative aims to tackle the issue through several channels in addition to the public service messages it already produces. Using religious and civic groups already in place, the initiative hopes to instill them with its message of paternal participation. The group also thinks laws should be changed to slow the rate of divorce, welfare reform should encourage fathers' participation, and schools should adopt father-specific curricula in family-life courses. Companies need to become "father-friendly," giving fathers time off through paternity leave, flex-time, and telecommuting options.

The problem of absent fathers will not turn

Living Without Dad

Black children are most likely to have absent fathers.

**(percent of white and black children under age 18
who do not currently live with a father, 1960–93)**

	1960	1970	1980	1990	1993
WHITE	8%	9.6%	15.7%	18.0%	19.3%
BLACK	31%	39.2%	55.9%	58.7%	61.4%

Source: Census Bureau

around overnight. "There's a tendency for expectations to be too simplistic," says Michael Lamb, head of social and emotional development at the National Institute for Child Health and Human Development in Bethesda, Maryland. Even so, Lamb views efforts toward more engaged fathers as "positive developments."

Blankenhorn acknowledges that change will come slowly, but notes the swift rate at which the debate has shifted. A seminal point arrived in May 1992, when then–Vice President Dan Quayle made his famous "Murphy Brown" speech, criticizing the television character for her decision to have a child out of wedlock. The speech drew ire from people who saw it as an attack on the valiant efforts of single mothers rather than as a criticism of uninvolved fathers. Yet a mere three years later, advocates for single mothers are saying that fathers should help care for their children. "Consciousness-raising has

been achieved," says Blankenhorn.

Few suggest that parental styles return to the "good old days." "It's a mistake to say we need to go back to some earlier version of fatherhood," says Wade Horn. "Thirty years ago, fathers were around, but the roles they played were restricted and contributed to the trend toward absent fathers."

The phenomenon has its positive flip side. Horn sees fatherlessness as a broader trend, but he also notes a "minor trend toward more responsible fatherhood." These are the men who go through Lamaze classes, read books to their kids, and even stay home while Mom takes on the role of breadwinner.

Although many absent fathers will never become superdads, there are lots of things businesses, governments, and communities can do to help men become more active parents, says David Popenoe, sociology professor at Rutgers University and author of *Life Without Father*. Although he dislikes Sweden's welfare model, he praises its policy that permits new fathers to take up to 15-month job leaves. "Most workplaces [in the U.S.] don't have a clue kids are there who have to be taken care of," he says.

The negative signals men pick up from employers, ex-wives, teachers, and others may help fuel their lax parenting. But in *New Expectations: Community Strategies for Responsible Fatherhood*, James Levine and Edward Pitt of The Fatherhood Project at New York City's Families and Work Institute cite examples of programs that have substantially increased fathers' involvement. The best strategy, they say, is simply to assume that fathers will be involved with their children.

THE CHANGING MEANINGS OF SPANKING

Phillip W. Davis

Phillip W. Davis, a sociologist at Georgia State University, reviews five decades of coverage in magazines and newspapers on the issue of spanking. He finds that traditional arguments about spanking have been supplemented by new criticisms that reflect cultural concerns about abuse.

The general consensus is that adults in the past treated children in ways that seem especially harsh by today's standards (e.g., deMause 1974; but see also Pollock 1983). In fact, "whipping" children with buggy whips, cat-o'-nine-tails, riding crops, plough lines, sticks, switches and rods, as well as hair brushes and the "maternal slipper," did not generally lose favor in the United States until the 1830s, when "spanking" became more popular (Pleck 1987). Since then, the topic of spanking has arisen repeatedly in public and private arenas, with ministers, popular childrearing experts, researchers, parents, media representatives, and even politicians debating whether spanking is too harsh.

Some critics argue for national legislation such as that found in Sweden and a few other European countries banning all physical punishment of children, but the issue has not led to much activity among policymakers. Even though many critics

link spanking and physical punishment with child abuse, policymakers have generally resisted treating physical discipline as abuse (Nelson 1984: 127). As a columnist wrote decades ago, "Despite years of debate on the matter, 'spanking' remains a fighting word" (D. Barclay 1962).

Why examine the debate over spanking? . . . I am interested in the links between children and social problems. By looking at this particular debate, I think that we can better understand how seemingly simple matters of childrearing often involve complex, changing, and competing ideas about the essential nature of children and their appropriate place in society. I also think that we can see how the social meanings of a seemingly simple practice such as spanking can emerge, develop, and shift as one kind of social issue transforms into another.

There have always been controversies over how best to deal with children (Elkin and Handel 1989). As those controversies develop, the key themes, issues, and definitions associated with the problem frequently change. Take child care. The debate in the popular press over daycare shifted in its key concerns over time (Cahill and Loseke 1993), and issues of institutional sponsorship arose only after attention shifted from the desirability of daycare to its availability (Klein 1992). Or take child abuse. First "discovered" and publicized by medical experts, its meanings have changed since the 1960s in response to claims by a widespread child-protection movement (Best 1990; Johnson 1985; Nelson 1984).

Researchers usually ignore the spanking controversy, focusing instead on spanking behavior. Most define spanking as a kind of physical punishment, perhaps the "prototypical" punishment (Sears, Maccoby, and Levin 1957), although Straus (1991a:134) recently defined physical punishment as a "legally permissible physical attack." Sociologists have focused on spanking's developmental effects for the child's conscience and aggressive behavior (Steinmetz 1979), its uneven distribution by social class (Duvall and Booth 1979; Erlanger 1974), the widespread cultural approval for the practice (Straus, Gelles, and Steinmetz 1980), how often people spank (Wauchope and Straus 1990), the influence of religious fundamentalism on attitudes towards physical punishment (Ellison and Sherkat 1993; Wiehe 1990), and the role of physical punishment in shaping juvenile and adult deviance (Erlanger 1979; Straus 1991a).[1]

Spanking, however, is more than mild physical punishment to make children behave. It is also the focus of competing ideas, beliefs, and vocabularies put forth by critics and advocates in a debate over spanking's definition, appropriateness, and implications. There is a long history of religious and secular justifications for spanking (Grevens 1991). Beliefs that spanking is natural, normal, and necessary form a "spare the rod ideology" that may perpetuate the practice (Straus, Gelles, and Steinmetz 1980). Trivializing terms such as "smack," "spank," and "whack" are at the heart of a rhetoric of punishment that presupposes the legitimacy of parental authority and makes assumptions about the impersonality of adult motivation (Harding and Ireland 1989; Maurer 1974). Spanking is a socially constructed reality; it means what people say it means.

Controversial topics such as spanking cause people to trade competing images and moral vocabularies. They look selectively at certain parts of the "problem" and not at others. They also name and characterize the problem in the course of making claims and counterclaims about its essential nature, typical features, and social implications (Best 1990; Miller and Holstein 1993; Spector and Kitsuse 1987). Sometimes, they identify types of people with certain characteristics and moral qualities as part of the problem (Loseke 1993).

My purpose . . . is to compare the traditional defense of spanking with the emergent criticism of spanking, identifying the claims and counterclaims spanking's advocates and critics have made in the popular press since mid-century. I also want to link both formulations to wider cultural influences. I will limit my focus to the debate over spanking by parents, recognizing that there is a parallel debate about spanking in schools. In general I argue that the debate over spanking has become more complex in its themes and vocabularies. New definitions of spanking supplement older ones, and what was once primarily a childrearing issue has become a child-protection issue as well.

Data and Materials

My research strategy involves an ethnographic content analysis (Altheide 1987) of newspaper and popular magazine articles that either focus on spanking or consider spanking in the course of discussing something else. This kind of analysis is appropriate when the research goal is to document and understand social meanings. First, I examined articles indexed in *The Reader's Guide to Periodical Literature* (RGPL) between 1945 and 1993. I chose articles spanning nearly half a century because I wanted to compare more recent statements about spanking with older arguments. The RGPL listed "spanking" as a subject category for those years and also referred readers to "corporal punishment" for specific articles. Most of the 142 articles listed under "corporal punishment" dealt with paddling in the schools; only 47 (33 percent) focused on spanking by parents. The RGPL excludes most religious periodicals, although it indexes a few (e.g., *Christianity Today* and *U.S. Catholic*). I also searched RGPL for the same years under "children—behavior and training," collecting more items on spanking and screening many pieces on discipline to see if they addressed spanking in any way.

To sample newspaper coverage of spanking, I

searched the *New York Times Index* from 1945 to 1993, collecting articles and columns listed under "corporal punishment" or "children—care and training." I also searched a computerized index of seven major newspapers from 1985 to 1993 under the subject "spanking." I collected over 100 magazine articles and over 80 newspaper articles and columns about spanking

Not all of these articles are by self-identified advocates or critics. Many summarize the debate, often presenting what are described as the "pros" and "cons" of spanking. Others are news reports about conference activities or research reports having to do with spanking. The reactions and opinions of pediatricians, sociologists, psychologists, childrearing "experts," and others are incorporated into many articles, usually couched in terms of their support or rejection of spanking. Occasionally, a magazine or newspaper article inspired letters to the editor criticizing or applauding the article, and I collected these as well.

Large-city newspapers and mainstream magazines are but one arena or claimsmaking setting in which contrasting ideas and images of spanking appear.[2] Of course, these materials do not reveal what is written in small-city newspapers, religious magazines and pamphlets, childrearing manuals, parent-education texts, and abolitionist pamphlets. We also miss what is said on radio and television shows and in other popular cultural sources.[3] Debates over spanking also occur in semipublic arenas such as churches and parent-education classes and in private arenas where parents, children, and others formulate their own claims about spanking as an issue in their everyday lives.[4]

My materials represent a mix of primary and secondary claims (Best 1990:19). Most newspaper articles present the secondary claims of reporters, recasting the claims of the "experts" interviewed for the story. Editorial and letter writers, however, as well as family columnists, take sides and write as primary claimsmakers—champions or critics of spanking. Most magazine articles also present primary claimsmaking by advocates or critics exhorting readers to support or condemn spanking. They also tend to rely

heavily on the opinions of experts and the findings of researchers in making their case. Written to sway an audience, these materials are an example of what Lofland (1976:113) calls "mediated exhortatory encounters." The readily available data are "frozen in print."

This paper begins by identifying themes associated with traditional defenses of spanking and noting how critics traditionally respond to those defenses. I take up the newer critiques of spanking that have appeared since the early 1970s, arguing that spanking is compulsive, violent, and abusive. Finally, I identify some of the likely influences on the development of these newer meanings and discuss the implications of these changes for understanding spanking and the social transformation of social issues.

Traditional Defenses of Spanking

Spanking's advocates traditionally use a rhetoric and vocabulary that paints spanking as the reasonable reaction of responsible parents to their wayward children. They claim that spanking is (1) the sign of nonpermissiveness; (2) anticipatory socialization; (3) God's will; (4) a morally neutral childrearing tool; and (5) a psychic release.

The Sign of Nonpermissiveness   Advocates often present spanking as an answer to the problem of permissive parents who are responsible for much of the "youth problem." The argument is that parents' lax attitudes result in the "undercontrol" of their children who go on to become delinquents, hippies, political activists, liars, cheaters, and thieves who lack respect for authority. In this view, failure to spank becomes the standard or benchmark of nonpermissiveness. The close association of nonspanking and the "permissive" label is clear in an interview with Dr. Benjamin Spock:

> He laughs when the subject of permissive child-raising is brought up, and how he is often blamed for the recent youth rebellions in this country: "In the first place, as anybody who has read my books knows, I was never permissive," he said. "I never said that parents shouldn't spank their children. To some par-

ents, spanking is a natural way of making children behave. I would never tell them not to spank," he added. (Klemesrud 1970)[5]

Advocates also argue that character flaws lie behind the permissiveness of parents who do not spank; they lack the courage and responsibility that spanking is said to require. Parents who don't spank have neglected their responsibilities, taken the easy way out, or let themselves be duped by experts into taking a scientifically progressive but unwittingly troubled path. One father wrote how he and his wife started out permissive, despite his "itching palm." Finally they decided to try some real "action":

> More than once, the palm of my hand itched, but our textbook made it plain that the ultimate parental weapon, physical discipline, was arbitrary and old-fashioned. . . . Eight years of "permissiveness" had made my boy a liar, and an unrepentant and defiant one at that. "All right," I said heavily, realizing there was no alternative, "over my knee!". . . George is 13 now and in the intervening five years, I don't think I have had to spank him more than three or four times. Once my wife and I steeled ourselves to substitute action for pleading words, we had no hesitations about spanking Linda, or Johnny as he grew older. (Conway 1955)

This statement suggests that spanking requires an admirable degree of decisiveness, in contrast to the inadequacy of permissive nonspankers who follow textbooks advising parents to use pleading words. Textbooks, experts, and scientists are part of the "new enlightenment" that appeals to permissive parents with disastrous effects:

> As the new enlightenment spreads its gentle glow in more and more of our modern American homes, the infant emperor is scientifically nurtured into a demanding little tyrant who relatives and neighbors detest . . . free to develop into a youthful vandal, a car-thief, a thrill-sadist, or perhaps just into an arrogant boor, too selfish for an enduring marriage. (Kilbourne 1958)

Anticipatory Socialization   A second claim is that spanking effectively prepares children for the tribulations of life and the vagaries of adulthood. Some advocates argue that children will profit from spankings once they enter the real world, a world that is characteristically more difficult and demanding than family life. Although the idea that physically harsh treatment somehow hardens and toughens children, especially boys, is centuries old (deMause 1974; Grevens 1991), it is the hard realities of an industrialized world that these modern advocates care about. One father described spanking as a sign of caring:

> To have rules for behavior without the threat of physical punishment is like having laws without jails. . . . Better to punish children than to be indifferent to them, since it is the neglected child who is more likely to grow up to be a problem. A father who spanks can at least be said to care. . . . May I say that life spanks us all for mistakes which, had they been caught in time by a parent who cared enough to correct them, need never have happened? (Dempsey 1958)

Another advocate wrote that going "back to the hairbrush" prepares children for life's "booby-traps":

> The "permissive" parents have to suffer through the uncurbed tantrums and general hell-raising of their offspring. . . . And the poor kids, when they eventually break out of the cocoon of an undisciplined childhood, are completely unprepared for the fenced-in and booby-trapped pattern of conventional adult life. (*Colliers* 1951)

This statement appeals to the idea that modernity and nonspanking are an unfortunate combination and that old-fashioned approaches better prepare children for the confinements of adult life.

God's Will   When religious themes appear in the materials I examined, it is usually when authors mention "biblical sanctions" as a traditional argument for spanking. Some ministers are quoted in support of spanking, but they are just as likely to emphasize effectiveness as divine sanction. James Dobson, author of *Dare to Discipline* and *James Dobson's New Dare to Discipline*, writes from the standpoint of Christian fundamentalism and is notorious among critics for his advocacy of spanking and switching: "I think we should not eliminate a biblically sanctioned approach to raising children because it is abused in some cases" (Neff 1993).

Although the definition of spanking as a "biblically sanctioned approach" figures prominently in the fundamentalist Christian press (Grevens 1991), it is relatively uncommon in the materials I examined. More often, articles make passing mention of religious themes or mention them in setting up a more secular discussion. Most people probably believe that the phrase, "spare the rod and spoil the child" comes from the Bible, but it first appeared in a poem by Samuel Butler published in 1664 (Gibson 1978:49).

A Morally Neutral Childrearing Tool Advocates often refer to spanking as a tool, technique, or method, writing about it as if its "use" were but the impersonal and mechanical application of a morally neutral procedure. The virtues of this technique are said to include speed, efficiency, and efficacy. Spanking creates obedience and respect with minimum effort and without long, "dragged-out" discussions. These claims contend that the good child is an obedient child and that faster techniques are superior to slower ones. Defining spanking as a tool or method suggests that spankers are purposive rather than aimless and depicts spanking as a logical activity rather than an emotional outburst. The overall image of parents who spank is that their "applications" are part of a method that is reasonable, systematic, and even merciful:

> Why spank? Simply because there are times when spanking is the easiest, best method of correction—best for the children, easiest for me. I believe in spanking because it works! (Bramer 1948)

> A spanking is concrete enough to be effective, soon over, and more merciful than a prolonged bout or clash of wills. (English and Foster 1950)

The definition of spanking as a childrearing tool or technique is especially clear in the widespread claim by advocates in the popular press that spanking should be used as a "last resort," only after other, presumably less harsh, efforts have failed. The rhetoric of "last resorts" implies that spankers possess the knowledge and ability to mete out penalties of varying severity in the proper sequence.

A Psychic Release Another common contention is that spanking resolves particular conflicts by somehow allowing parents and their children to start over, because it "clears the air." The popularity of this phrase no doubt derives from its use in Spock's popular *Baby and Child Care,* first published in 1945. Some authors elaborate on the phrase, claiming that spanking frees children from guilt by providing them with an opportunity for repentance or offers a cathartic release of the parent's tension and anger. One parent wrote:

> One salubrious effect of spanking, which is often overlooked by those who hold out for other methods of punishment, is the resulting feeling of expiation. . . . A child likes to feel that "it's all over now," that he's paid the price for his bad behavior, the slate's clean, the air clear, and the fresh start made. (Bramer 1948)[6]

Advocates also contend that parents who don't spank will find other, less healthy, ways of expressing their anger:

> This is frequently the best reason for doing it—tensions that might otherwise remain bottled up are given a therapeutic release. While it is true that the child is not happy about this, he might be far less happy with a father who restrains his temper at the cost of continued irritability. (Dempsey 1958)

If they don't become neurotically guilty, insecure, or repressed, parents may erupt later and do greater harm to the child, for all their progressive efforts to conform to the new psychology.

The Critics Respond Critics of spanking claim that these traditional defenses are flawed for a variety of reasons. They argue that, rather than preventing youth problems, spanking creates them. For one thing, spanking makes children untrustworthy:

Few children feel as kindly toward a parent after a spanking as they did before. In time, bitter resentment, antagonism and strained child-parent relationships develop. To escape spankings, many a child develops into a sneak, a cheat or a liar. (Hurlock 1949)

Critics also claim that, although spanking may "work" in the immediate situation, its effects are highly limited: "It's true that a spanking can, very occasionally, work wonders with the child who has gotten a bit frisky, but it usually causes rebellion and resentment instead, especially in a preteen" (Kelly 1989). They also argue that, while it may be effective, it is effective for the wrong reason. Instead of complying voluntarily out of respect based on reason, children who are spanked comply out of fear. Critics claim that spankers are irresponsible, because they are avoiding the harder but superior alternatives. Spankers worry too much about teaching the values of respect and authority, oblivious to the fact that spanking really teaches the legitimacy of aggression, brute strength, and revenge. Critics also contend that spanking can easily escalate. A physician answered questions about spanking in his *McCall's* column:

> Q: *Should I hit my child back when he hits me?*
>
> A: No, you should not. If you strike him back, you are simply teaching him that the only way to respond in anger is by physical blows, and it may turn into a fist fight. (Seen 1957)

Critics argue that the true meaning of discipline involves teaching children the lesson of self-control, whereas "physical discipline" only teaches them "might makes right."

In sum, since mid-century advocates and critics in the popular press have been invoking several different meanings of spanking. Advocates claim that children are "underdisciplined," that they need to be spanked, that parents who do not spank are mollycoddling their children, that being spanked doesn't harm children, and that nonspanking parents are irresponsible. Critics respond that spanking is futile at best and counterproductive at worst. In this traditional debate, advocates emphasize the drawbacks of permissiveness as a cause of delinquency and rebellion, and critics argue that discipline should involve teaching and self-control.

Emergent Meanings

The traditional claims about spanking persist. Popular experts, columnists, researchers, professionals, and parents still argue for or against spanking by talking about effectiveness, lessons, psychic release, preparation, and permissiveness. Spanking is still said to work or not work, to counter permissiveness or encourage aggression, to reflect concern for the child's well-being or indicate a lack of self-control, to clear the air or breed resentment. Although claims about delinquency prevention and rhetoric about the woodshed have generally faded from view, along with worries about hippies and the youth rebellion, most of the other claims appear routinely in contemporary materials. One recent letter to a magazine, for example, echoes older claims: "Spanking is immediate, sharply focused, and lets everyone get on with their lives. It should be used sparingly and only as a last resort. But believe me, it can be effective." (*U.S. Catholic* 1993). But spanking's critics bring newer, supplementary meanings to the debate, meanings that coincide with changing concerns and arguments borrowed from debates over other issues.

Spanking Is Compulsive The critics' first new claim is that spanking is compulsive, habit-forming, or addictive. This claim depicts parents as people who have lost their autonomy by becoming dependent on a highly satisfying behavior that they can abandon only with considerable difficulty. Critics compare spanking to smoking, because both practices are legal, harmful, and habitual. A mother described the day she decided to "kick the habit": "It was akin to the evening I found myself digging through a trash basket for a half-smoked cigarette butt and decided to quit smoking. And like the days that followed that decision, kicking the spanking habit proved to be tough" (Hyde 1980). A psychologist extended the analogy:

People who smoke claim that it makes them feel better and helps them to relax; parents who spank their children also feel better by getting out their anger. . . . There is liberal evidence that both are fraught with potential harm. Of course, most people who smoke never get cancer, and most children who are excessively spanked do not become delinquent. Yet for those who are affected, it is a serious matter indeed. (Welsh 1985)

Others associate spanking and smoking, because, given the widespread criticisms of each, they are increasingly secretive practices. Responding to a report that time out is more popular with parents than spanking, for example, one pediatrician was skeptical, saying that "spankers today are like closet smokers" (*Atlanta Journal/Constitution* 1993). A therapist and father asks spankers why they "reach for spanking, much as an alcoholic or drug addict reaches for their fix? . . . It takes great diligence to cultivate a new way of being and prevent the old addiction from taking hold again" (Dale 1993). Spanking in this rhetorical vein is an irrational attachment to a druglike experience. The attachment is so intense for some spankers that their "recovery" may require changes in their being.

Spanking Is a Demeaning, Violent Act   Critics in the popular press routinely echo the view of most family violence researchers that spanking is a form of violence. Critics frequently quote researchers such as Murray Straus and Richard Gelles in their articles. They describe spanking as an act of violence that models violent behavior for the child and teaches children that violence is socially acceptable. Penelope Leach, an extremely popular British author, argues for no spankings and fewer time outs in the name of clear thinking and nonviolence: "a spanking humiliates and devalues the whole child, overwhelms thought with anger, and demonstrates that physical violence is a good way to solve problems" (Leach 1992). A newspaper columnist points to the lessons in violence that spanking teaches: "Spanking demeans parents as well as children by presenting violence as an acceptable way to solve problems" (Ashkinase 1985). Other critics define spanking as an

assault. In a *Psychology Today* reader survey on spanking and physical punishment, "one woman said that hitting a child should be considered assault: 'It gives the message that size and power make abusive behavior acceptable'" (Stark 1985). For critics, spanking is a prime example of minor violence that later causes adult violence, especially by those who experience frequent, severe spankings as children.

Spanking Is Abusive   With increasing frequency, newspaper and magazine articles interweave references to spanking and abuse, although the nature of the claimed connection varies considerably. I found no flat statements that "spanking is child abuse," but one article noted: "Parents Anonymous, a group for parents who want to avoid abusing their children, recently declared that any physical punishment is emotionally abusive and should not be sanctioned" (Lehman 1989). Some critics argue that spanking is associated with future abuse by the spanked child:

> Clearing the air with a quick spank sometimes *seems* to halt the progress of a deteriorating situation. . . . Nevertheless, the short-term utility must be weighed against the real possibility, gleaned from clinical evidence, that corporal punishment is not associated, in the long run, with self-discipline; rather, it is associated with the abuse of the child of the next generation. (Katz 1980—emphasis in original)

Others emphasize that a "fine line" separates spanking and abuse, a line that is too easily crossed. The notion of fine lines appears frequently in professional writings, and its popularization has been successful:

> You should never hit your children, even when you've reached the end of your rope because that's exactly when you are the least in control of yourself. Lines can blur and a hitting can turn into real, if unintentional, child abuse. (Schlaerth 1993)

In discussing "The Three Cardinal Rules of Good Discipline" (don't insult or demean your child, don't forget that you are a role model, and "spare the rod, period"), a psychologist concludes: "Worst of all, for many grown-ups, the line between physical punishment and child abuse can become blurred with frightening ease" (Segal 1986).

The Advocates Respond   Advocates have had little say about the idea that spanking is a compulsion, but they take issue with critics who claim it is violent or abusive. They go about this in various ways. Some claim that critics are less concerned about raising children than they are about social appearances. One professor emeritus of English wrote in a *Wall Street Journal* commentary (with the headline, "The Bottom Line on Spanking"):

> My wife recalls that when she misbehaved as a child, her mother cut a switch from a tree in the backyard and whaled her with it then and there. Any mother so thwacking today would be condemned. . . . Joan Beck, a nationally syndicated columnist, equates corporal punishment in schools with child abuse. Thus has political correctness befogged one of civilization's most useful ways to raise the young. . . . I do not recommend beating children. . . . Spanking a child is but a single act—among many—that supports civilized behavior against the natural barbarism of the American brat." (Tibbetts 1992)

Not only does he imply that critics worry more about political correctness than raising children, but also he writes about thwacking and spanking as if they were the best hope of turning back the barbaric child. Lest his defense of thwacking is taken to mean he is insensitive, he issues a disclaimer about beatings. Several days later the paper printed 10 letters about the article. Only three favored "thwacking," echoing the refrain that "It didn't hurt me" and the idea that the only alternative is permissiveness. One writer said he started out a spanker, got trendy, and then resumed:

> Several years ago, however, I suffered a nasty bout of enlightened guilt. Trendy psychologists almost had me convinced I was a child abuser causing long term damage to my kids. I was almost ready to confess my sins and flog myself in front of the American Academy of Pediatrics. (Bell 1992)

Another put a twist on a contemporary theme by suggesting that the unspanked child may be an unguided child and that parents who don't spank may be guilty of "neglect."

In his syndicated column William Raspberry reacted to the publicity given a 1989 conference on physical punishment.[7] After a disclaimer, he ridiculed the idea that spanking and abuse are different points on the same continuum:

> Well, it's time to confess. My parents, for all their surface warmth and respectability, were into physical cruelty—child abuse, to put it plainly. You see, they spanked their children. I'm no advocate of child abuse, but it strikes me that the experts at Wingspread . . . are guilty of what might be called the fallacy of the false continuum. . . . Child abuse—the depressingly frequent incidents of child battering—is, for these experts, just another point on a continuum that begins with spanking. . . . Ordinary fanny dusting, to which some parents resort when more intelligent approaches fail, teaches children that violence is an acceptable way of settling disputes. . . . I think these experts are nuts. (Raspberry 1989)

The columnist notes that other approaches are more intelligent but also normalizes spankings by calling them "ordinary." His vocabulary pits "fanny dustings" against abuse, making light of what the critics take too seriously—spankings, after all, are only a light brushing of an unimportant part of the child's body. He also claims that people who confuse something inconsequential with something as important as violence are irrational and not to be taken seriously. A letter to the editor complained:

> I object to Columnist William Raspberry's characterization that we are "nuts" to link spanking to child abuse. . . . Without love, hitting children—no matter how euphemistically described—very easily becomes severe child abuse. (Hare 1989)

Some writers make increasingly sharp distinctions between spanking and abuse, between "an occasional swat" and spankings, or between rare swats and corporal punishment. They then discuss the differences these distinctions represent, emphasizing how rare swats are more defensible and less incriminating than the other things. One columnist reporting on a conference noted, for example: "Several specialists left the door open for that rare swat of a child who repeatedly endangers himself" (Lehman 1989). The occasional swat was also the topic of a syndicated column after Lady Di spanked Prince William, age 8, when he wouldn't stay at her side during his school's sports day in 1990. The writer wondered whether such a swat is the same as corporal punishment:

> The incident has revived debate over how parents should respond when their children misbehave and whether there is a difference between corporal punishment and a rare swat from a loving parent. . . ."She sounds pretty human," said Dr. T. Berry Brazelton. . . . "What Princess Di did, and what I probably would have done too, is to react in a way that lets the boy know that you really mean it," he said. "All of my kids will tell you that I've swatted them on the bottom when I've been upset with them." He added that he sees this as different from unacceptable physical punishments like planned or protracted spankings. (Kutner 1990)

The headline for the story in a different paper was, "Crowning Blows," comically suggesting that Lady Di's action was relatively unimportant. Advocates who use phrases such as the "occasional swipe" rhetorically suggest that there are important differences between what critics argue is so damaging and what is an inconsequential if not valuable practice. Some advocates tell parents just what to do so that they will not be considered abusive:

> Spank only for a few specific offenses, such as blatant disrespect and defiance. . . . John Rosemond, in his Knight News Service newspaper column "Parent and Child," gives these guidelines: "With no threats or warnings, spank with your hand, not a wooden spoon, paddle, belt or switch. A spanking is not more than three swats to the child's rear end. *A swat to any other part of the child's body is abuse*." (Oliver, 1987—emphasis added)

This statement tells readers what to spank with, how many times to spank, and where to spank. Not only does it promote a bottoms-only definition of spanking, but also it equates "a swat to any other part" with abuse.

Discussion

I have examined spanking as a controversial topic rather than a behavior. Spanking remains a fighting word, and what people are fighting about is both complex and changing. I have identified arrays of older and newer meanings of spanking in a long-lived controversy filled with fluid, shifting claims by spanking's advocates and critics. In the course of formulating, defining, and characterizing spanking over time, a topic traditionally approached as a childrearing issue in a debate over "what works" is now also a child-protection issue in a debate over whether spanking is violent and abusive.

I have shown that advocates and critics employ rhetorical formulations that define and characterize spanking in ways meant to resonate deeply among readers, exhorting them to accept or reject "good old-fashioned" spankings. Advocates of spanking extol its virtues in the name of tradition, effectiveness, efficiency, and responsibility, defining it essentially as a tool, technique, or method for making children behave. Spanking is said to offer an antidote to the youth problem, release tension for both parent and child, and prepare children for life's hardships. Advocates generally ignore or trivialize children's suffering, portray nonspankers as irresponsible, and cite their own positive personal histories as spanked children. Critics counter that spanking ironically promotes, rather than deters, misbehavior. They contend that it is usually an expression of the parent's anger and frustration and teaches children that violence and aggression are acceptable. More recent critics also define spanking as a bad habit, an act of violence, and a form of abuse. All too often, they argue, spanking leads to abuse later in life or is closely linked to the abuse of the spanked child.

In the context of increasingly broad definitions of child abuse, some advocates argue for narrow definitions of spanking (e.g., bottom-only). Narrow definitions, as well as distinctions between planned spankings and the occasional smack, are ways of maintaining a "place" for spanking on the list of what parents can rightfully do to their children without lapsing into a new category of "putative person" (Loseke 1993). Otherwise, the moral character of spankers is vulnerable to allegations of being "old-fashioned" if not sadistic. To look at their rhetoric, advocates seem to embrace the notion of being old-fashioned, but they ridicule the idea that there is something incriminating about a normal form of discipline.

Activities in wider professional, scientific, religious, and political contexts have no doubt prompted and shaped these changing meanings for spanking. Psychological research and popular writings on aggression in the 1950s and 1960s challenged behaviorist assumptions about the role of punishment. Some well-publicized studies provided dramatic ironies such as the finding by Sears, Maccoby, and Levin (1957) that physical punishment for aggressive behavior is associated with more, not less, aggression by children. Many of these scholarly ideas and facts made their way into articles and stories in the popular press.

Moreover, in the 1960s and early 1970s, the development of a modern child-protection movement, the discovery of child abuse, and the continuing emergence of violence as a major policy issue led to a series of controversies associated with the idea that children are increasingly "at risk" (Wollons 1993). As these issues developed, spanking was mentioned, and sometimes its importance was highlighted. Working for the National Commission on the Causes and Prevention of Violence, for example, Stark and McEvoy (1970) wrote about spanking alongside fist fights, vigilantism, police violence, assassination, and military violence. In his influential book on child abuse, David Gil (1970) stressed how approval of physical punishment creates a cultural climate in which abuse can flourish. Both studies received national media attention.

There has also been a convergence of interests and activities among anticorporal punishment and antiabuse organizations. Organizations such as the National Coalition to Abolish Corporal Punishment in Schools, the National Center for the Study of Corporal Punishment and Alternatives, and End Violence Against the Next Generation, although they focus on educational settings, regularly point to spanking and physical punishment by parents as an analogous issue (Hyman 1990).[8] The National Committee for the Prevention of Child Abuse (NCPCA) has been actively seeking the primary prevention of child abuse through pamphlets, surveys, and press releases about physical punishment and spanking since the mid-1980s.[9]

We cannot make a flat statement that the newer meanings of spanking are now dominant. The themes in the newer debate suggest only a partial transformation of the traditional childrearing issue into a contemporary child-protection controversy. There is certainly the potential for definitions related to abuse to become dominant. Whether the transformation proceeds further depends in part on the discourse, resources, and activities of advocates and critics in organizational, political, media, and movement contexts.

Activities in medical settings will have an impact. The Centers for the Study of Disease Control instituted a division for the study of domestic violence in 1992. The June 1992 issue of the *Journal of the American Medical Association* was devoted to family violence and included an article on spanking as a form of corporal punishment. Some physicians now claim that "corporal punishment is child abuse," (Leung, Robson, and Lim 1993:42). These medical developments, if they are recognized by the press, policymakers, and agency officials, should encourage spanking's association with child abuse.

Other activities are likely to inhibit the ascendance of abuse meanings. Religious action groups are sensitive and alert to any move to broaden definitions of abuse to include spanking, or to remove existing legal protections of parents who use "reasonable physical discipline." We may see other spanking-related controversies develop as groups organize to resist further involvement by the state in family matters (Johnson 1986). In addition, some critics promote the idea that spanking is really a civil rights issue, and civil rights organizations may make spanking part of their agenda. Their constructions of the problem might easily bypass the issue of abuse or make it secondary to the issue of discrimination on the basis of age. Similarly, critics campaigning for state and national legislation comparable to that in Sweden may successfully promote the association of spanking with the violation of human or children's rights rather than child abuse. Finally, it is likely that child-protection officials will continue to warn that their limited resources should be reserved for "truly" abused children. Whether spanking ever fully becomes a child-protection issue, these emergent meanings challenge the assumptions that spanking is natural, normal, and necessary on a fundamental level.

NOTES

1. Some critics argue that these studies overemphasize the importance of physical punishment and fail to appreciate the importance of context, inequality, authority, and control (Kurz 1991; Loseke 1991; see also Straus 1991b).

2. Ibarra and Kitsuse (1993) point to at least three settings where claimsmaking rhetoric occurs: media, academic, and legal-political. Advocates and critics of spanking have made their points in each arena, with considerable crossover. Researchers, for example, appear in the press when interviewed about their findings.

3. The highly rated television show "20/20" did a segment on spanking in October 1992 and reran it in July 1993. In addition to interviewing Murray Straus, noted family violence researcher at the University of New Hampshire, the show included videotape of children in four families being "spanked." The gist of the segment was that experts condemn the practice and recommend alternatives. Spanking is said to be "wrong" and interviewer John Stossel tells one set of parents, "It's almost as if you're abusive, that you're cruel" (ABC News, 1992).

4. Elsewhere I examined situations when strangers debate spanking and punishment in the context of one person trying to stop another from hitting a child (Davis 1991).

5. Spock later modified his position and, by 1988, he explicitly rejected the practice, stating that spanking and punishment were linked to the nuclear arms race and increasing rates of murder, wife abuse, and child abuse (Grevens 1991:95–97).

6. The assumption that spanking spares the guilty child is also found in the 1962 version of the Children's Bureau booklet, "Your Child from One to Six." The text refers to mild physical punishment as superior to prolonged disapproval and scolding with the advantage that, "a mild physi-

cal punishment can actually relieve the child who wants to shed his guilty feelings."

7. The Wingspread Conference in Racine, Wisconsin, was sponsored by the University of Wisconsin and the American Academy of Pediatrics' Provisional Committee on Child Abuse. Conference activities led to a call to stop parents from using physical punishment (Haueser 1990:68).

8. Two new organizations devoted to the abolition of all physical punishment of children are EPOCH (End Physical Punishment of Children) and EPOCH-USA. The former started in 1989 in the United Kingdom, soon after that country legislatively abolished corporal punishment in its public schools in 1986. EPOCH-USA started in 1990 (Haeuser 1990).

9. Daro and Gelles (1992) believe the surveys show that such public awareness and education campaigns are effective in reducing the overall amount of physical punishment and promoting the belief that physical punishment can be injurious.

REFERENCES

ABC News. 1992. "20/20 Transcripts." *Journal Graphics, Inc.* October 30.

Altheide, D.L. 1987. "Ethnographic Content Analysis." *Qualitative Sociology* 10:65–77.

Best, J. 1990. *Threatened Children: Rhetoric and Concern about Child-Victims.* Chicago: University of Chicago Press.

Cahill, S., and D. Loseke. 1993. "Disciplining the Littlest Ones." *Studies in Symbolic Interaction* 14: forthcoming.

Daro, D., and R.J. Gelles. 1992. "Public Attitudes and Behaviors with Respect to Child Abuse Prevention." *Journal of Interpersonal Violence* 7:517–31.

Davis, P.W. 1991. "Stranger Intervention into Child Punishment in Public Places." *Social Problems* 38:227–46.

deMause, L. 1974. "Our Forebears Made Childhood a Nightmare." *Psychology Today* 8 (April):85–87.

Duvall, D., and A. Booth. 1979. "Social Class, Stress and Physical Punishment." *International Review of Modern Sociology* 9:103–17.

Elkin, F., and G. Handel. 1989. *The Child and Society: The Process of Socialization,* 5th ed. New York: Random House.

Ellison, C., and D. Sherkat. 1993. "Conservative Protestantism and Support for Corporal Punishment." *American Sociological Review* 58:131–44.

Erlanger, H.S. 1974. "Social Class and Corporal Punishment in Childrearing: A Reassessment." *American Sociological Review* 39:68–85.

———. 1979. "Childhood Punishment Experience and Adult Violence." *Children and Youth Services Review* 1:75–86.

Gibson, I. 1978. *The English Vice: Beatings, Sex and*

Shame in Victorian England and After. London: Duckworth.

Gil, D. 1970. *Violence Against Children: Physical Abuse in the United States.* Cambridge, MA: Harvard University Press.

Grevens, P. 1991. *Spare the Child.* New York: Knopf.

Harding, C., and R. Ireland. 1989. *Punishment: Rhetoric, Rule, and Practice.* New York: Routledge.

Haeuser, A.A. 1990. "Can We Stop Physical Punishment of Children?" *Education Digest* 56 (September):67–69.

Hyman, I.A. 1990. *Reading, Writing, and the Hickory Stick: The Appalling Story of Physical and Psychological Violence in American Schools.* Lexington, MA: Lexington Books.

Ibarra, P., and J. Kitsuse. 1993. "Vernacular Constituents of Moral Discourse: An Interactionist Proposal for the Study of Social Problems." Pp. 21–54 in *Constructionist Controversies: Issues in Social Problems Theory,* edited by G. Miller and J. Holstein. Hawthorne, NY: Aldine de Gruyter.

Johnson, J. 1985. "Symbolic Salvation: The Changing Meanings of the Child Maltreatment Movement." *Studies in Symbolic Interaction* 6:289–305.

———. 1986. "The Changing Concept of Child Abuse and Its Impact on the Integrity of Family Life." Pp. 257–75 in *The American Family and the State,* edited by J. Peden and F. Glahe. San Francisco: Pacific Research Institute for Public Policy.

Klein, A.G. 1992. *The Debate over Child-Care: 1969–1990.* Albany: State University of New York Press.

Kurz, D. 1991. "Corporal Punishment and Adult Use of Violence: A Critique of 'Discipline and Deviance'," *Social Problems* 38:155–61.

Leung, A., W. Robson, and S. Lim. 1993. "Corporal Punishment." *American Family Physician* 47:42–43.

Lofland, J. 1976. *Doing Social Life.* New York: Wiley.

Loseke, D.R. 1991. "Reply to Murray A. Straus: Readings on 'Discipline and Deviance'," *Social Problems* 38:162–66.

———. 1993. "Constructing Conditions, People, Morality, and Emotions: Expanding the Agenda of Constructionism." Pp. 207–16 in *Constructionist Controversies,* edited by G. Miller and J. Holstein. Hawthorne, NY: Aldine de Gruyter.

Maurer, A. 1974. "Corporal Punishment." *American Psychologist* 28:614–26.

Miller, G., and J. Holstein (eds.). 1993. *Constructionist Controversies: Issues in Social Problems Theory.* Hawthorne, NY: Aldine de Gruyter.

Nelson, B. 1984. *Making an Issue of Child Abuse.* Chicago: University of Chicago Press.

Pleck, E. 1987. *Domestic Tyranny: The Making of Social Policy against Family Violence from Colonial Times to the Present.* New York: Oxford University Press.

Pollock, L. 1983. *Forgotten Children: Parent-Child Relations from 1500–1900.* New York: Cambridge University Press.

Sears, R., E. Maccoby, and H. Levin. 1957. *Patterns of Child Rearing.* White Plains, NY: Row, Peterson.

Spector, M. and J.I. Kitsuse. 1987. *Constructing Social Problems.* Hawthorne, NY: Aldine de Gruyter.

Stark, R., and J. McEvoy. 1970. "Middle-Class Violence." *Psychology Today* 4 (November):52–65.

Steinmetz, S. 1979. "Disciplinary Techniques and Their Relationship to Aggressiveness, Dependency, and Conscience." Pp. 405–38 in *Contemporary Theories about the Family,* edited by W. Burr, R. Hill, F. Nye, and I. Reiss. New York: Free Press.

Straus, M. 1991a. "Discipline and Deviance: Physical Punishment of Children and Violence and Other Crime in Adulthood." *Social Problems* 38:133–52.

———. 1991b. "New Theory and Old Canards about Family Violence Research." *Social Problems* 38:180–97.

Straus, M., R. Gelles, and S. Steinmetz. 1980. *Behind Closed Doors.* New York: Doubleday.

Wauchope, B., and M. Straus. 1990. "Physical Punishment and Physical Abuse of American Children." Pp. 133–48 in *Physical Violence in American Families,* edited by M. Straus and R. Gelles. New Brunswick, NJ: Transaction Books.

Wiehe, V.R. 1990. "Religious Influence on Parental Attitudes toward the Use of Corporal Punishment." *Journal of Family Violence* 5:173–86.

Wollons, R. 1993. "Introduction." Pp. ix-xxv in *Children at Risk in America: History, Concepts, and Public Policy,* edited by R. Wollons. Albany: State University of New York Press.

DISCUSSION QUESTIONS

1. If women returned to full-time mothering, would this ease the current social ills of our society? Why or why not?

2. What does it mean to be a father today? Do young men today have different expectations of the father role than their fathers? Why or why not?

3. What arguments justify spanking children? What arguments justify not spanking? Will you spank your children? Why or why not?

WEBSITES

www.fathersworld.com
Father's World is a site devoted to supplying information, resources, support, and education for all types of fathers and their families.

www.pflag.org
www.glpci.org
Parents, Families, and Friends of Lesbians and Gays and the Gay and Lesbian Parents Coalition International are organizations providing advocacy, education, and support for gay, lesbian, bisexual, and transgendered persons.

www.aacap.org/factsfam/
The American Academy of Child and Adolescent Psychiatry has developed a series of papers called Facts for Families, providing concise and up-to-date information on issues that affect children, teenagers, and their families. Examples include "Children and TV Violence" and "Talking to Your Kids About Sex."

www.ed.gov/pubs/parents.html
The U.S. Department of Education publishes a wealth of material, including electronic versions of popular pamphlets and brochures, designed to address parents' concerns about their children's education.

CHAPTER 11: OTHER FAMILY RELATIONSHIPS

Although parents typically are the major influence on their children's development, other family members also play important roles. For instance, the vast majority of American children have siblings, and what they learn from their sister(s) and brother(s) can range from cooperation and empathy to competition and dominance. Likewise, grandparents and other members of the extended family can also affect the child's socialization, especially if they spend quite a bit of time together. This chapter will highlight several of these special family relationships.

The first article focuses on the topic of grandparents raising grandchildren. Historically, grandparents stepped in and took care of dependent grandchildren following the death, divorce, or abandonment of the parent(s). Today, however, a growing number of American grandparents are assuming parenting responsibilities in response to dysfunctional parents who are unable or unwilling to nurture their own children due to child abuse or neglect, mental illness, incarceration, or drug addiction. The article discusses the major challenges facing this diverse group of grandparent caregivers and their grandchildren.

Another type of stress associated with caregiving is experienced by adult children caring for aging parents. The second reading points out that caring for an elderly parent can be painful, frustrating, and overwhelming. Yet, at the same time, there can be unexpected rewards, especially if five common mistakes can be avoided.

The average American today has two or three siblings. (This may include full, half-, or stepsiblings.) Brothers and sisters share a lifelong bond. Diane Crispell documents how siblings continue to support each other, emotionally and financially, even when they live great distances apart, and how siblings influence us and our decisions throughout our lives.

READING 28
GRANDPARENTS RAISING GRANDCHILDREN

Nancy M. Pinson-Millburn et al.

Children and youths are being raised by grandparents in greater numbers than would be expected by choice or by chance. These new households represent a transfer of childrearing responsibilities from an absent or incapacitated parent to an older adult who could also be at risk for disability. The authors, Nancy M. Pinson-Millburn, Ellen S. Fabian, Nancy K. Schlossberg, and Marjorie Pyle, are all associated with the Center of Human Services Development in the Department of Counseling and Personnel Services at the University of Maryland, College Park.

Historically, the assumption of a parenting role by the grandparent has been tied to life events, such as death, divorce, or abandonment; the parent was no longer in the picture and the grandparent stepped in to care for the dependent children. Although this pattern has by no means disappeared, we are now seeing more and more cases of dysfunctional parents who remain "in the picture" but are unable or unwilling to nurture their own children.

These parents may be substance abusers, victims or perpetrators of physical or sexual violence, or sufferers of emotional or neurological disorders that render them incapable of parent-

Excerpted from Nancy M. Pinson-Millburn, Ellen S. Fabian, Nancy K. Schlossberg, and Marjorie Pyle, "Grandparents Raising Grandchildren," *Journal of Counseling and Development*, vol. 74 (July/August 1996), pp. 548–51, 553–54. Reprinted by permission of the authors.

ing. They may also be HIV-positive, enrolled in drug treatment programs, or incarcerated (Barry, 1991; Dressel & Barnhill, 1991; Lambert, 1989). In all cases, these particular parents have inadvertently triggered the advent of a grandparent assuming parenting responsibilities.

In perhaps the most comprehensive analysis available on the status of grandparent caregivers, Rinck and Charnow (1993) sound both a challenge and an alarm to our policy makers and legislators. Within the last decade alone, there has been a 40% increase in these households across the United States (Minkler, Driver, Roe, & Bedeian, 1993), with a disproportionate presence among African American families. These grandparents are faced with multiple problems: their own declining health, the incapacity of their children, and the possibility that their grandchildren could also be disabled or dysfunctional.

The children and youths who become members of these new families are at great risk of psychiatric as well as developmental disorders (Beardslee, Bempora, Keller, & Klerman, 1983). If the parent is mentally ill, perceived by the child as neglectful or cruel, absent without explanation, incarcerated, or involved with drugs, these children are affected deeply. Unlike their peers who may have experienced the more "acceptable" traumas of parental death or divorce, these youngsters are harder to console and more likely to withdraw or act out.

Minkler and Roe (1993) described the onset of

this new caretaking role for these grandparents as often sudden, and sometimes unwelcome. As the last resort, when the state insists on out-of-home placement "in the best interests of a neglected child," the distant grandparents are expected to juggle work responsibilities, a smaller income, and a household not geared to child care (McAdoo, 1990). When the grandparent moves in, with or without the parent present, other problems surface that are almost always associated with anxieties about the incapacitated parent, the restrictions imposed by the system (access to food stamps, Aid to Families with Dependent Children, or Medicaid for their grandchildren), and the increased prevalence of their own health problems.

Not only must these caregivers confront their own failing health, they must also face bureaucratic nightmares. A study announced by the American Association of Retired Persons' (AARP, 1994) Women's Initiative also confirmed this view and pointed out that grandparents are continually at war with unfriendly laws and officials in their search for the most basic entitlements for their grandchildren. That study reported that in those households headed by grandparents, about one third have no parent present and reflect an estimated 723,000 midlife and older adults caring for grandchildren.

Many of these grandparents have volunteered for these roles without realizing the stresses of raising children in the 1990s. Child management problems, combined with their own aging, exert unexpected pressures, with social isolation, financial difficulty, and health problems becoming primary concerns. . . .

A New Kind of Household

What triggers the advent of a grandparent assuming the head of household role? We have suggested that an absent, ill, or failing parent is the contemporary cause, but what distinguishes this multigenerational household from others formed in the past?

As recently as 30 years ago, families would have described themselves as purposeful caregivers of the aging relative or the orphaned child; the parenting role remained intact. Today, we are

finding that more parents are less able to function in the face of increased social, emotional, and economic pressures—pressures against which their own parents have apparently built some sort of immunity.

A number of factors are frequently cited as causes for the biological parent's "disappearance" from this household. . . . The following observations are associated with the creation of grandparent-caregiving households:

1. An increase in drug abuse (particularly, crack cocaine) by young mothers and a parallel decrease in funding of treatment programs have created a catch-22: Infants with serious developmental problems are now being raised by their grandparents and young mothers remain vulnerable to their addiction (Davis, 1995).

2. Children born to young parents who are unable to care for them and children born out of wedlock to parents of any age are more likely to become part of these new households (Downey, 1995).

3. Reasons given by grandparents for the formation of these new families are substance abuse by parents (44%), child abuse or neglect (28%), teenage pregnancy or parent failure to handle children (11%), death of parent (5%), unemployment of parent (4%), divorce (4%), and other reasons (4%), including HIV/AIDS (Woodworth, 1994).

Poverty is both a cause and an effect of these new family formations. Although children are the poorest population, they are closely followed by adults over 65 in low socioeconomic rankings. These families, then, are more likely to be poor and to become even poorer (Downey, 1995; National Council on Aging, 1995).

Therefore, if we exclude factors of terminal illness, discrimination based on race or ethnicity, irreversible disability, and the poverty that may result from unemployment or illiteracy, the creation of these new families has taken place because of circumstances that make it impossible for the parents to assume or continue the expected parenting roles. These circumstances have inevitably been followed by consequences transforming this family unit and its members.

The Caregiver Challenge

These grandparent caregivers represent an extraordinary challenge to the theorist. . . . As O'Reilly and Morrison (1993) have observed, what might be described as predictable life changes for others in their age group (such as job advancement, retirement, or more leisure time) simply do not occur on schedule for grandparents raising grandchildren, if they occur at all. This brings us to the question of the capacity of these adults to cope with the immensity of a life transition that is usually unexpected and has no guarantees of success.

In studying this population, we are faced with a paradox: the necessity of understanding an increasing number of grandparents raising grandchildren and the difficulty of categorizing such a diverse group of adults. For example:

1. Some grandparents are 40 years old, others 50, some 80. In other words, there is no one age that represents grandparents.

2. There is no single pattern of household arrangements. To illustrate, more than 1 million households are headed by single grandparents with a median income of $18,000 a year. Many more grandparents are part-time caretakers, and other grandparents live in three-generation families in which they assume major caregiving responsibilities. Some grandparents have legal custody; others have no legal rights. Some grandparents are poor, but others have financial resources.

3. There is no specific time that caregiving might last. For some, it is for life. For others, it is intermittent or short-lived.

4. Ethnic composition of these households shows that 12% of all African American children are living with grandparents, with 6% of Hispanic children and 4% of Anglo American children similarly situated. Each ethnic group has different expectations about caregiving and different sets of experiences. And, of course, individuals within each ethnic group have different sets of expectations.

Given the diverse life span the grandparent represents, current theories of adult development are inadequate in describing the challenges and needs of this population. Many are based on models that explain behavior as a function of the individual's age and stage of life, providing merely a one-dimensional way of viewing individuals in today's pluralistic society. Instead, a more inclusive approach to understanding the changes in the lives of grandparent caregivers is necessary.

Before we propose or recommend such an approach, it is important to examine the effect of these roles on current caregivers. What are the most notable characteristics of this life change, and how can any current theory accommodate these characteristics?

The Effect of Caregiving on Grandparents

It is generally expected that parents will assume direct responsibility for raising their own children, and although grandparents play a major role—either as buffers, family historians, occasional caretakers, or as fun-loving, unambivalent stabilizers—they are not seen as the primary caretakers and socializers. It is, therefore, an "off-time" and unexpected transition (Neugarten, 1979). It is off-time for the grandparents to be raising infants, young children, and adolescents. Moreover, transitions occurring at unexpected times can be very stressful.

Assuming parenting responsibility off-time, when social timetables would assume a more passive, benign role for grandparents, changes everything about the grandparents' lives: leisure, friendships, work, health, and finances. In other words, their roles are changed from a "love then leave" grandparent to parent substitute on call 24 hours a day; the routines of their lives are totally changed; relationships with family and friends are altered; and their assumptions about themselves and their lives are in flux. Basically, there is little, if any, time for self. The unexpected loss of freedom to be able to "do what I want to do" was a persistent theme of the Minkler and Roe study (1993, p. 60) of grandmothers who were raising their grandchildren as a result of the parents' drug addiction. As one woman reported, "I feel I've been cheated. I'm not ready for the rocking chair, but if I want to go out with friends, I can't. I feel like something has been stolen from me" (Minkler & Roe, 1993, p. 60).

The psychological consequences of this transition are enormous. Often, grandparents are gaining a grandchild but losing their own child. In addition, grandparents are facing double jeopardy as they question their own sense of inadequacy: What have they done wrong to have children who cannot care for their own children, and are they competent enough to deal with raising children again?

The emotional response is often grief—grief for the loss of their children through death, addiction, unemployment, child neglect or abuse, or some other psychological or physical disability; and grief for their own loss of freedom to realize their own dreams.

Most of what is reported is negative. For example, many grandparents report feelings of isolation and frustration with the legal, health, education, and welfare systems that offer little support and set up obstacles to be overcome. However, many report positives, saying they feel useful, needed, and as if they "matter." Mattering, a concept defined by Rosenberg, refers to feeling needed, noticed, and depended on. Rosenberg and McCullough (1981) suggested that people need to feel they matter, and not feeling appreciated, noticed, and attended to can result in depression, sadness, or, in the case of adolescents, even delinquent behavior. In this instance, mattering can be for "better or worse." It can help grandparents feel useful and needed. However, for many it can mean that they matter too much and are pulled in too many directions by several generations.

Most literature on stress and burnout associated with caregiving focuses on adult children caring for aging parents (Myers, 1989; Zarit, 1989). The few studies about stress and burnout associated with grandparent caregivers emphasize a strong correlation with physical and emotional health and only secondary effects on work roles. Minkler, Roe, and Price (1992), for example, found that observable declines in physical health were reported in one third of the population of grandparents they studied after caregiving began. They also found that more than 51% of their sample complained of joint swelling and stiffness,

41% reported severe back problems, and 25% cited heart trouble.

Minkler's (1994) later findings confirmed that grandmothers downplayed the severity of their health problems in an effort to convey that they were "up to" the task. In that study, further probing revealed that moderate to severe health problems did in fact exist, but there was "no time" for these women to check with their doctors.

The depressed or disabled caregiver may also be particularly vulnerable to alcoholism or other sedating substances, such as tranquilizers. Helwig and Holicky (1994) proposed treatment based on changing self-perceptions, reducing stress, and challenging the myths and stereotypes about disability that are too readily adopted as self-fulfilling. Hulnick and Hulnick (1989) agreed. They saw disability in a family member or members as a functional limitation that can be a curse or an opportunity. Whether this limitation is referring to the body, the mind, or the emotions is less relevant than what is perceived as possible and meaningful to that affected family member.

Jacobson (1993) warned against the social and professional "overselling" of depression as a disease to these grandparents. He pointed out that aging itself is distressing because it brings a person closer to the end of life and that it is normal to be a little depressed about that knowledge. Instead, he and Heller (1993) both pointed out that the assumption of these vitally important roles as caregivers is the best kind of therapy for mild depression because it confirms this adult's value to his or her new family.

It is safe to conclude that physical and emotional responses to these stressors are highly interrelated in these grandparents. Any stamina or resiliency they demonstrate is more likely a function of their determination, as opposed to their innate reserves. They are, by and large, wearing thin. They also report losing heart in a society that has not recognized their importance.

The Effect on Grandchildren

Every 8 seconds, a child drops out of school; even 26 seconds, a child runs away from home; every 47 seconds, a child is abused or neglected;

every 67 seconds, a teenager has a baby; every 7 minutes, a child is arrested for a drug offense; every 36 minutes, a child is killed or injured by a gun; and every day 135,000 children bring their guns to school (Gibbs, 1990. p. 42).

These statistics underscore the notion of America's youths as children at risk. The children and youths who are being raised by grandparents are also children at risk, and as such might experience and encounter the social problems and issues described above. However, it is equally important to make the point that all grandparent caregivers and their grandchildren do not fit these descriptions. Solomon and Marx (1995) found that children raised by grandparents fared better across health, academic, and behavioral dimensions than did those being raised by a single parent. Indeed, many of these grandparents have enthusiastically taken up their role in parenting, and many of their grandchildren are in stable, loving, and structured environments. It has been established, however, that this population of grandchildren is at higher risk for developmental delays and potentially serious emotional problems than children in general. We know also that these grandparent caregivers are trying to provide the kind of nurturance that could offset some of these risks, at no small cost to themselves. In fact, the love and care now being provided to these children may be superior to what their parents were able to offer in the past. Nonetheless, these children represent a major challenge to our schools (Capuzzi & Gross, 1989; McWhirter & McWhirter, 1989; Rice & Meyer, 1994; Thompson & Sherwood, 1989).

What behavior or what combination of events leads to these challenges? The following contributing factors serve as common denominators.

Contributing Factor 1: Parents Abusing Drugs and Alcohol   By far, the major contributing factor to the creation of grandparent households is the inability of parents to provide care because of their serious drug and/or alcohol abuse problems. Unfortunately, the greatest risk factor for a host of disabilities and behavioral problems among these children is parental drug abuse.

Potential problems experienced by grandchil-

dren include the following:

- They may be born with birth defects and fetal alcohol syndrome. Both of these pre- and postnatal complications can result in learning disabilities, mental retardation, and disabilities such as cerebral palsy.
- They may have a higher incidence of attention deficit disorders. There is an increased predisposition among children of substance-abusing parents to have attention deficit hyperactivity disorder.
- They may have a higher incidence of emotional and psychiatric disorders, resulting in placement in special education programs.
- They may also abuse drugs and/or alcohol. The majority of people in treatment for alcohol and drug abuse have had chemically dependent parents or relatives.
- They may have a higher incidence of teenage pregnancy.
- They may demonstrate poor academic achievement and have a higher incidence of school dropout.

Contributing Factor 2: Parents Who Are Incarcerated   Frequently, parents are imprisoned for drug-related crimes, and the children face similar circumstances to those described above. However, there is a unique set of risk factors for these children that deserves attention.

Potential problems experienced by grandchildren include the following:

- They may exhibit emotional and behavioral problems as a result of intermittent or long-term parental incarceration.
- They may experience shame and isolation among other family members and peers.
- They may be victims of social stereotyping on the part of school or other agency or social service personnel.
- They may experience posttraumatic stress disorder in terms of managing the stress associated with what caused the parental imprisonment. For example, children may have seen their parents shot, arrested, or taking drugs.

Contributing Factor 3: Parents Who Abuse or Neglect Their Children   Another contributing circumstance is parental abuse or neglect. Here, school personnel encounter the serious problems of children who have been the victims of sexual abuse and/or physical or emotional abuse.

Potential problems experienced by grandchildren include the following:

- They may manifest psychiatric symptoms such as depression or agitation.
- They may manifest behavioral disorders and inadequate coping skills.
- They may be extremely depressed and/or suicidal.
- They may never have developed skills of independent living.
- They may have poor or inadequate social supports.
- They may experience other psychiatric disorders such as developmental delays, anxiety disorders, and posttraumatic stress disorder.

Contributing Factor 4: Parents Who Have Died from AIDS, Other Illnesses, or Accidents
In some cases, children are raised by their grandparents because their parents are either too sick with HIV/AIDS or have died from the disease. In other cases, single parents may have died from other illnesses (such as alcoholism or drug overdoses) or an accident.

Potential problems experienced by grandchildren include the following:

- They may be HIV-positive.
- They may have to deal with the social and peer stigma associated with HIV and AIDS.
- They may be dealing with loss and bereavement issues.
- They may experience feelings of shame and guilt, depending on the cause of the parents' deaths. . . .

The Future of Grandparent Households

To predict with any certainty that these new grandparent households will thrive and multiply in the decades ahead is risky at best. This is true because we cannot forecast the legal standing of the grandparent caregiver, nor can we assign an absolute delivery of basic social and financial resources. On the other hand, we can be fairly sure that grandparents and other elders will become the caregivers of choice when their children can no longer function. These adult children, along with other family members, increasingly view the options of foster care or institutionalization for minor children as last resorts. They are far more likely to choose, when they are able, their own parents as caregivers. The reasons given for this choice of a substitute parent are many: proximity, economics, dependency, and sometimes, love and respect. Courts and grandparents themselves might specify still other reasons, such as the capacity of the grandparents on both physical and financial grounds and their genuine desire to help resolve a crisis situation.

If these experienced elders are living longer— and they are—they are no less vulnerable to an adult child's plea for assistance. At best, they see themselves as rescuers of their grandchildren and become revitalized in that pursuit. At worst, they see themselves continuing as enablers for their own troubled children in patterns established years before. Or they may recognize this opportunity as a chance to correct earlier parenting mistakes and, in so doing, forgive themselves for real or imagined inadequacies as parents.

What kind of future can we foresee for these families in the next century? According to the most conservative estimates, there will be more frail or disabled very old people and more vigorous young-old people within the total U.S. population. These twin phenomena will come about primarily because of advances in medical science and nutrition that both prolong and enrich life.

The twenty-first century grandparent caregiver will most likely be drawn from the second population: typically between 50 and 70 years old and in fair to good health. These households will reflect a growing trend in the 1990s: the presence of the parent, usually the mother, in this multigenerational family. This household will face the same challenges in child rearing but will have become more skilled in accessing scarce resources through established community networks.

REFERENCES

American Association of Retired Persons. (1994, October). Barriers to raising grandchildren. *AARP Bulletin, 35,* (9), p. 3.

Barry, E.M. (1991, September). Grandparent caregivers: The need for services and support. *State Bar Association of California Newsletter,* pp. 5–6.

Beardslee, W.R., Bempora, J., Keller, M.B., & Klerman, G. (1983). Children of parents with major affective disorders: A review. *American Journal of Psychiatry, 240,* 825–832.

Capuzzi, D., & Gross, D. (Eds.). (1989). *Youth at risk: A resource for counselors, teachers, and parents.* Alexandria, VA: American Counseling Association.

Davis, E. (1995, March). Untitled presentation to Mini-White House Conference on Grandparents Raising Grandchildren. University College, University of Maryland, College Park, MD.

Downey, T. (1995, March). Untitled presentation to Mini-White House Conference on Grandparents Raising Grandchildren. University College, University of Maryland, College Park, MD.

Dressel, P.L., & Barnhill, S.K. (1991, November). *Three generations at economic risk: Imprisoned African-American women and their families.* Paper presented at the meeting of the Gerontological Society of America, San Francisco.

Gibbs, N. (1990, October 8). Shameful bequests to the next generation. *Time,* 42–47.

Heller, K. (1993). Prevention activities for older adults: Social structures and personal competencies that maintain useful social roles. *Journal of Counseling & Development, 72,* 124–130.

Helwig, A., & Holicky, R. (1994). Substance abuse in persons with disabilities: Treatment considerations. *Journal of Counseling & Development, 73,* 227–233.

Hulnick, M., & Hulnick, R. (1989). Life's challenges: Curse or opportunity? Counseling families with disabilities. *Journal of Counseling & Development, 68,* 166–170.

Jacobson, S. (1993, April). Overselling depression to the old folks. *The Atlantic Monthly,* 46–51.

Lambert, B. (1989, July 17). AIDS legacy: A growing generation of orphans. *The New York Times,* pp. A-1, B-5.

McAdoo, H.P. (1990). A portrait of African-American families in the United States. In S. Rix (Ed.), *The American woman 1990–91: A status report* (pp. 77–93). New York: Norton.

McWhirter, J., & McWhirter, E. (1989). Poor soil yields damaged fruit: Environmental influences. In D. Capuzzi & D. Gross (Eds.), *Youth at risk: A resource for counselors, teachers, and parents* (pp. 19–40). Alexandria, VA: American Counseling Association.

Minkler, M. (1994, March). Grandparents as parents: The American experience. *Aging International, 21,* 24–28.

Minkler, M., Driver, D., Roe, K., & Bedeian, K. (1993). Community interventions to support grandparent caregivers. *The Gerontologist, 33*(6), 807–811.

Minkler, M., & Roe, K.M. (1993). *Grandmothers as caregivers: Raising children of the crack cocaine epidemic* (Family Caregiver Applications Series: Vol. 2). Newbury Park, CA: Sage.

Minkler, M., Roe, K.M., & Price, M. (1992). The physical and emotional health of grandmothers raising grandchildren in the crack cocaine epidemic. *The Gerontologist, 32,* 5752–5761.

Myers, J.E. (1989). *Adult children and aging parents.* Dubuque, IA: Kendall Hunt.

National Council on Aging. (1995). Public policy agenda: 1995–1996. In W.E. Oriol (Ed.), *Perspective on aging* (Vol. 24, pp. 1–32). Washington, DC: Author.

Neugarten, B.L. (1979). Time, age, and the life cycle. *American Journal of Psychiatry, 136*(7), 887–894.

O'Reilly, E., & Morrison, M.L. (1993). Grandparent-headed families: New therapeutic challenges. *Child Psychiatry and Human Development, 23,* 147–160.

Rice, K., & Meyer, A. (1994). Preventing depression among young adolescents: Preliminary process results of a psychoeducational intervention program. *Journal of Counseling & Development, 73,* 145–152.

Rinck, C., & Charnow, M. (1993). *Grandparent caregivers: A concept paper.* Unpublished manuscript, National Council on Aging, Washington, DC.

Rosenberg, M., & McCullough, B.C. (1981). Mattering: Inferred significance and mental health among adolescents. In R. Simmons (Ed.), *Research in community and mental health* (Vol. 2, pp. 163–182). Greenwich, CT: JAI Press.

Solomon, J., & Marx, J. (1995). "To grandmother's house we go": Health and school adjustment of children raised solely by grandparents. *The Gerontologist, 35,* 386–394.

Thompson, R., & Sherwood, A. (1989). Female, single, and pregnant: Adolescent unwed mothers. In D. Capuzzi & D. Gross (Eds.), *Youth at risk: A resource for counselors, teachers, and parents* (pp. 195–225). Alexandria, VA: American Counseling Association.

Woodworth, R. (1994, September 8). *Grandparent-headed households and their grandchildren: A special report.* Washington, DC: AARP Grandparent Information Center.

Zarit, S.H. (1989). Do we need another stress and caregiving study? *The Gerontologist, 29,* 147–148.

CARING FOR AGING PARENTS

Virginia Morris

Annually, family members provide $300 billion in free care to loved ones who are chronically ill or disabled. Virginia Morris, a freelance writer, discusses five common mistakes not to make in caring for aging parents.

You knew they would get old. Still, when you first notice your mother's unsteady gait or get a call that your father has had a stroke, the realization comes as a shock. Your parent is mortal and will not be around forever. Then comes an even bigger jolt: The person who always looked after you now needs your help.

No one plans on taking care of an aging parent. No one sets aside time or energy for the task. But as baby boomers move into their fifties—and their parents turn seventy and eighty—more and more of us are facing this responsibility. And it can be a daunting one. The job triggers all sorts of unsettling emotions, including guilt, helplessness, frustration, anxiety and intense sibling rivalry. It can also resurrect the parent-child power dance—a struggle you thought you had long outgrown.

Caring for an elderly parent is never easy, but it can be made much more manageable if you remember not to treat them like backward children—and avoid these other common mistakes.

Mistake # 1

"My parents are still independent, so I don't have to think about this yet."

Planning is one of the most important things you can do, both for your parents and yourself. If you put it off, you may find yourself scrambling to locate community services in the midst of a crisis, making hasty and uninformed decisions about vital financial and medical issues or, worse, going to court to gain the legal right to manage the care of a parent who is too confused or ill to make decisions for himself.

The crucial three Make sure your parent has an up-to-date will, a durable power of attorney and advance directives. Without a will, the state will decide how assets and belongings are to be divided. A durable power of attorney is a simple document that gives you or someone else the right to handle your parent's financial and personal affairs should she ever be unable to handle them herself. Advance directives, which include both a power of attorney for health care and a living will, outline your parent's wishes concerning life-sustaining medical care and give someone the authority to make medical decisions, if necessary.

Critical conversations Be sure to talk with your parent about housing, finances, medical care and personal care. Where would your father want to live if he could not stay in his home? Will he be able to pay for nursing-home care? If you had to decide about your mother's medical care, how would she want you to weigh the choices? How does she feel about hospice care or aggressive medical intervention?

None of this is easy. But confront your fears, and try to break the code of silence. Even if your parent cuts off the conversation, you have planted a seed that may take root.

When raising an issue, try to be diplomatic as well as direct. Explain that you want to respect your parent's wishes, but that you need to know what they are. Then listen. Don't immediately voice your thoughts. If the direct approach is uncomfortable, raise an issue in regard to your own planning ("I just had my will revised, and I was wondering if yours is up to date") or discuss a friend who faced a related problem ("What do you think of that life-care center that the Goodwins moved into?").

If your parent refuses to talk and the issue is pressing, ask a sibling or other relative, a trusted friend or a professional, such as a doctor, lawyer or minister, to intervene. Your parent may be more willing to listen to someone else.

Vital research Learn about local services and housing options *before* your parent needs them. Many of the best life-care and assisted-care residences have waiting lists. Start by calling the area agency on aging or the Alzheimer's Association (800-272-3900), if appropriate.

Mistake # 2

"She did everything for me, so I should do everything for her."

The I-must-do-it-all syndrome is the easiest trap to fall into and the hardest one to climb out of. Don't let yourself get sucked up in the emotional eddy of feeling resentful about having to do so much, guilty that you aren't doing more, and even guiltier for feeling resentful. Scrambling to do more than you can handle will jeopardize your health, your marriage, your friendships, your career—even your sanity.

Setting limits Zero in on exactly what else you think you should be doing, then assess whether your goals are realistic. Accept that you can't make your mother well, protect her from all risks or transform her relationship with your father.

Then determine what you *can* do. Provide some financial guidance? Call on a regular basis? Set up your father's house to make it safer? Try not to worry about what others think or what a friend is doing for her parent.

Enlisting help Let go of the reins. Recruit neighbors, church volunteers, friends, siblings and other relatives. Use community services, such as meal delivery, transportation and adult day care. If you can afford it, hire a professional, known as a geriatric-care manager, to oversee some aspects of your parent's care.

Mistake # 3

"My brother doesn't do his share for Mom."

When a parent needs care, childhood rivalries may be revived and new arguments born. The one who is shouldering the majority of the day-to-day care feels put upon because the others aren't more helpful. The siblings who live at a distance may feel guilt-ridden about their lack of involvement and irritated that they are made to feel that way. All of this wastes valuable energy and actually gets in the way of your parent's care.

A family meeting Open the lines of communication. Whatever the situation, hold a family meeting, whether it's an informal discussion after Sunday supper or a structured meeting with a family counselor, social worker or clergyman, and have a detailed agenda. If the family is spread out geographically, schedule a meeting during a holiday or, if there's really no way to get together, arrange a conference call.

Your parents should be present, unless they are incapacitated, and the discussion should focus on their current and future needs, who will help with what and, if there are deep conflicts, how siblings can work together. (You might arrange visits so you don't run into each other, for example.) Give each person a chance to talk—get a timer if necessary—and pull the conversation back to the point any time it strays.

The first meeting may be rough. Don't give up. Meet again. And remember, just airing views and acknowledging that you need to work together is an accomplishment.

Mistake # 4

"I'm the parent now."

You're driving your parent to appointments, sitting with her for the first morning of adult day care, tying shoelaces, buying spill-proof cups and diapers. This is starting to feel a lot like parenthood. But it's not.

It's true that the familiar parent-child relationship has shifted. There may be times when you have to be forceful with your parent: Perhaps taking away the car keys if your father is a danger on the roads and refuses to stop driving, or disconnecting the stove if your mother repeatedly forgets to turn off the burners. Remember, though, he has a right to have his needs, opinions and preferences honored. He has a right to make choices and take risks.

If your father is making decisions that you think are foolish—he won't move out of an isolated living situation and into a senior housing complex, for example—try to understand why he feels the way he does. Point out the reasons that you feel he should act differently, and if necessary, get others to help persuade him. If he still won't budge and is mentally competent, you may simply have to live with his decision and then get someone to visit him, perhaps a senior companion. Or you might hook up with a meal-delivery program or hire help for the house.

Whatever you do, your job is not to control your parent's life but to help him maintain control of it.

Mistake # 5

"I'll take time for myself later; right now Mom needs me."

If you are providing hands-on care with any regularity, you must make time for yourself. If you become depressed, sick or just plain exhausted—as many caregivers do—what use will you be to your parent, or to anyone else for that matter?

Take breaks. Carve out escape time that is solely for you. If a relative or neighbor can't fill in for you, scout out volunteers in the community or look into hiring someone on an hourly basis. Ask nursing homes in your area as well; some will take people in for a week or two.

Don't cut off contact with close friends, for they provide invaluable emotional support. When friends can't help, join a support group. Having hobbies and pastimes may seem indulgent, but they can help calm and revive you.

If you're not with your parent regularly, worry alone can exhaust you. Set aside thirty minutes a week to think clearly about your parent's needs, your feelings or anything that troubles you. Then, when you start fretting at two A.M., tell yourself you will think about it during your worry time, and shut off the light.

Finally, let yourself laugh. It may seem disrespectful when your parent is frail, but it's not. Rent a funny video, buy a humor book or get together with a silly friend. Laughter is a great healer.

Caring for an aging parent can be painful, frustrating and overwhelming, but there are often unexpected rewards. This is your parent, after all, and no matter how he might infuriate you at times, no one will ever love you in quite the same way. Helping him now is an opportunity to say things you might not have said otherwise and to care for him in ways you may never have before. When it's all over, you may be glad you had this chance.

READING 30
THE SIBLING SYNDROME

Diane Crispell

While exploring the bonds between siblings, Diane Crispell, executive editor of American Demographics *magazine, discusses how these lifelong ties fuel marketing strategies, especially for greeting card companies and long-distance carriers.*

Since Louisa May Alcott wrote a semi-autobiographical story about four sisters in 1869, *Little Women* has been filmed five times. Laura Ingalls Wilder's autobiographical account of four sisters growing up in a *Little House on the Prairie* became one of the most popular family dramas in TV history. *Seven Brides for Seven Brothers* and *Rainman* are two movies separated by vast differences in style, yet they tell the same story of brothers looking out for each other.

The relationships people share with siblings are often the longest-lasting they will ever have. Siblings are there from the beginning, and they are often still around after parents, and even spouses and children, are gone. In some societies, brothers and sisters have rigidly defined responsibilities within the family network. American siblings of the 1990s don't have such formal obligations to each other, but they continue to conform to deeply rooted social norms. They also share genuine emotional and economic ties.

Over the past two generations, sibling relationships in the United States have become a tangle of steps and halves created by multiple marriages. Although the average baby-boom woman today has half as many children as her mother did, her children have almost as many siblings as she does. These quasi-siblings don't necessarily grow up together, and they are often a generation apart. On the other hand, sibling-like bonds can also develop between unrelated people, and extended families further complicate the picture. Well-educated people are more likely than others to make long-distance moves, so a better-educated population suggests looser family ties. But physical closeness and emotional closeness are not one and the same thing. Far-flung siblings can and do share intense bonds.

Siblings share things other than assistance and emotional support. They spend money on each other. The average adult sibling estimates spending an average of $610 on brothers and sisters in the past year, finds a survey conducted for *American Demographics* by Maritz Marketing Research of Fenton, Missouri. In return, however, these adults say they receive about $230 in gifts and cash from their siblings during the same time period.

Whether or not we like to admit it, our siblings influence us throughout our lives. Directly or indirectly, deliberately or involuntarily, they affect the choices we make about careers and mates, as well as the way we manage our health, finances, and purchase decisions. Sometimes we ask for their advice about the person we're dating, whether a job offer sounds good, and whether a brand of shampoo might suit us. But even when we don't ask, they tell us. Marketers and others who approach consumers through their sibling ties are playing to a solidly forged and rarely broken link.

Staying in Touch

The average American today has two or three siblings. Many middle-aged baby boomers have at least two full brothers and sisters, while young adults are more likely to have a mixture of full, half-, and stepsiblings. Older adults are likely to have lost one or more siblings to death, but 55 percent of those aged 65 and older have two or more surviving brothers or sisters, according to the 1992–93 National Survey of Families and Households (NSFH).

One in five Americans aged 65 and older had no living siblings in 1993, but nearly everyone has or had a brother or sister at some point. Just 5 percent of all adults have never had a sibling of any type, finds the 1994 General Social Survey (GSS), while 29 percent have or had five or more, including step-, half-, and adopted siblings. Ninety-five percent of adults under age 65 currently have at least one living brother or sister, finds the NSFH. Overall, 85 percent of siblings, living or dead, are or were full brothers or sisters, according to GSS respondents. The proportions for half-, step-, and adopted siblings are 9 percent, 5 percent, and 1 percent, respectively. Older adults are likely to have more full siblings. Young adults are likely to have acquired multiple siblings through blended families.

There are exceptions, of course. Clara Henderson of Mesa, Arizona, is a widow in her mid-60s. Her father's first wife died in childbirth with her fifth baby; he remarried and had five more children. Clara is one of the younger siblings in a still-living group of eight who range in age from 59 to 92. She moved in with her oldest half-brother a couple of years ago after his wife died.

Few adults live with brothers and sisters, but many have siblings nearby. Those with just one

Keeping in Touch

Elderly people are twice as likely as average to never see their brothers and sisters.

(percent of adults who see any siblings at selected intervals, by age, 1992–93)

	not at all	once to several times a year	one to four times a month	two or more times a week
TOTAL, 18 and older*	9.4%	42.7%	29.8%	18.1%
25 to 34	3.8	31.8	33.9	30.5
35 to 44	7.4	44.2	31.6	16.9
45 to 54	11.4	51.3	25.7	11.6
55 to 64	10.8	45.5	32.2	11.5
65 to 74	17.7	47.4	23.8	11.2
75 and older	19.2	46.6	24.1	10.1

*Note: 18 to 24 not broken out separately due to small sample size and unreliability of data

Source: National Survey of Families and Households

brother or sister tend to stick closer together; 11 percent live within 2 miles of their brother or sister, 28 percent live 3 to 25 miles away, and 27 percent can get there in an hour or a day's drive, at a distance of 26 to 300 miles. In contrast, of those with two or more siblings, just 3 percent have one within 2 miles, and 63 percent have at least one who lives more than 300 miles away. This distribution by distance varies little by age, although 25-to-34-year-olds with multiple siblings are more likely than average to have one nearby. The proportion of Americans who have a brother or sister living more than 300 miles away rises with age, peaking at 70 percent for those aged 75 and older.

Physical distance can put a crimp in face-to-face contact between adult siblings, which is why telephone contacts are more common. Even so, 7 percent of brothers and sisters never talk to a sibling. Forty-four percent talk at least once a month, 29 percent several times a year, and 20 percent twice a week or more.

Sibling contacts rarely remain constant through the years; instead, they ebb and flow as adulthood takes brothers and sisters in different directions. When Linda Hinkin was 22, she and her husband moved to Florida from their hometown near Flint, Michigan. They relocated to Virginia for several years, then moved to upstate New York four years ago. Her older sister Laurie still lives near her parents in Michigan with her husband and two children.

Now in their late 30s, the two sisters talked on the phone and saw each other infrequently during much of their young adulthood. "We'd talk maybe twice a year, but when we did, we'd be on the phone for an hour or more at a time," says Linda. Laurie finally graduated from college a couple of years ago, and Linda went to Michigan for the ceremony. "I went as a surprise, which delighted her," says Linda. "We'd already begun talking more frequently, but it was a sort of turning point. We've made a commitment to be in touch about every month," says Linda. "And Laurie came to visit this summer, without her family. It was the first time she initiated a visit."

The more siblings people have, the more likely they are to have contact with at least one of them. Just 6 percent of those with four or more siblings never see any of them, compared with 16 percent of those with one brother or sister.

Sibling ties weaken slightly with age, too. Nineteen percent of people aged 75 and older with at least one living sibling never see a brother or sister, versus just 4 percent of those aged 25 to 34. Eleven percent never talk to a sibling on the phone, versus 5 percent of those aged 25 to 34. Young adults have the most frequent contact, and middle-aged people are most likely to see siblings occasionally. The most common amount of sibling phone contact for adults in all age groups is one to four times a month; 44 percent call a brother or sister this frequently. Young adults are no more likely than average to talk this often on the phone, probably because they are more likely to talk in person.

It's understandable that younger adults have more contacts with siblings, especially before they shift their attention to spouses and children. But siblings aged 55 and older also have more contact when they are single and/or childless, ac-

Sibling Headcount

Most adults have two or three living siblings. Only boomers are most likely to have at least four.

(percent distribution of adults by number of living siblings, including step- and half-, by age, 1992–93)

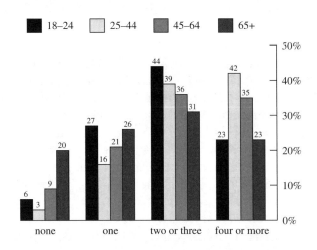

Source: National Survey of Families and Households

cording to Ingrid Arnet Connidis of the University of Western Ontario in London, Ontario, Canada. As with younger siblings, this may be partly because they have fewer competing relationships, and also because they feel more obligation.

Better-educated siblings have less contact than average because they are more likely to live farther away from each other. However, they demonstrate a stronger-than-average emotional bond to the sibling with whom they share the closest relationship, although this closeness doesn't necessarily extend to other siblings. Connidis speculates that this is because better-educated siblings are more likely to have a relationship based on affection rather than on mutual economic need.

Helping Hands

Marvin and Joe Brown are brothers in their 30s who live a few miles apart and see each other about once a week. Yet Marvin doesn't characterize their relationship as a primarily social one. "We get together for pizza sometimes, but mostly we help each other out," he says. Marvin is an electrician, and Joe is an auto mechanic. These skills naturally play into the kind of assistance they give each other. "I bought a motor home last year," says Marvin. "The first time we took it out, someone rear-ended us." Having a brother with a garage came in handy.

Proximity plays a big role in the types of help people request from their siblings. Also, people don't call on brothers for the same kind of help as they do sisters, and they don't look to brothers nearly as often as sisters.

Spouses or partners are the helpers of first resort in most situations. People often turn to parents, children, and close friends before siblings, but brothers and sisters aren't a last resort, either. Adults are most likely to say they would first turn to a son if they needed help with a household or garden task, according to the 1986 General Social Survey. Brothers rank third. If more brothers lived nearby, as the Brown brothers do, their ranking might be higher.

Although siblings don't rank first as helpers in any particular situation, sizeable minorities of adults say that a brother or sister is a first or second choice in six situations measured by the General Social Survey. Twenty-three percent would turn first or second to a sibling if they were very upset with their spouse or partner; 20 percent if they were depressed; 19 percent to borrow money; 18 percent to help out during an illness; 17 percent to get advice; and 16 percent with household chores.

Sharing Good Times and Bad

People aged 45 and older are much less likely to spend any money on siblings, according to the Maritz survey. One in four aged 46 to 54 reports no spending in the past year, as do almost half of those aged 65 and older. Although young adults,

Lending a Hand

People look to sisters for emotional support and brothers for physical help.

(persons to whom adults would first run for help in selected scenarios,* four top-ranking choices, 1983–87)

	first	second	third	fourth
Heavy chores	son	best friend	brother	daughter
Help when sick	mother	daughter	best friend	sister
Borrow big sum of money**	father	mother	other relative	best friend
Upset with spouse/partner	best friend	clergy	mother	sister
Talk to when depressed	best friend	sister	mother	daughter

*Excluding spouses/partners
**Excluding banks

Source: General Social Survey

who tend to have lower incomes, spend the smallest average amount on siblings, they are most likely to spend anything at all. Just 6 percent of those aged 18 to 24 spent nothing in the past year, and the share who spent $1,000 or more is an average 12 percent.

Adults aged 45 to 54 are the most likely to have spent at least $1,000 on siblings in the past year, 15 percent. The average sibling aged 45 to 54 spent $854 on brothers and sisters, and those aged 35 to 44 spent $685. Those aged 55 to 64 spent $1,140. The amount drops sharply after age 65, to $300. However, people aged 45 to 54 estimate that they got about $300 worth from siblings in the past year, versus $70 for those aged 55 to 64.

Much of the money goes for birthday and holiday cards and gifts. Eight in ten respondents to the Maritz survey currently exchange cards with siblings, and three in four exchange gifts. Sisters are more likely than brothers to say they make these kinds of exchanges. Like men, young adults are not noted for their letter-writing tendencies, and those aged 18 to 24 are no more likely than average to exchange cards with siblings, although they are more likely to exchange gifts.

One in ten adult siblings used to send each other cards, and 14 percent used to exchange gifts, but have given up the effort. Marvin Brown says that "it got too hard to buy for everyone." He and Joe have 3 other brothers and 2 sisters, the 7 siblings have a total of 16 children, and the extended family is truly extensive. "One of my aunts had 14 kids," says Marvin. "My grandmother has 105 great-grandchildren."

Clara Henderson faces the same problem. "We don't exchange holiday gifts because there are just too many people," she says. "But I always bring gifts when we visit people—flowers, wine—that sort of thing." Clara also has an unusual way to keep in touch with both siblings and extended family. "We've had a family chain letter going for about 75 years now," she says. "Each household reads it, adds their own information, and sends it to the next one on the list."

Even if they don't write letters, most siblings exchange greetings to mark special occasions, and they often choose cards that specifically relate to the sibling relationship. Cards addressed directly to sisters and brothers are an ongoing large segment of the market, says Kathy Bernetich, executive director of editorial studios at American Greetings Corporation in Cleveland. "Birthday cards are the biggest sellers for siblings," says Bernetich. Cards for brothers and sisters cover the gamut of sibling relationships, and their approaches range from "very best friends" to messages for those who feel no more than a social obligation.

One in ten adults never exchanges cards or gifts with siblings. The share is highest among the elderly, who are least likely to be in touch with siblings. Older people are also least likely to take trips with brothers and sisters. Overall, about half of adults spend vacation time with brothers and sisters. One in four has done so at some point as an adult, and the same share has never done so. The share of elderly people who have never vacationed with adult siblings is twice as high as for young adults, 37 percent versus 17 percent, despite the fact that younger people are more likely to have step- and half-siblings with whom relationships might seem more tenuous.

Those aged 45 to 54 are more likely than others to have vacationed with adult siblings in the past, and 45 percent continue to make the effort. "Joe and I used to do a lot of stuff together before

Rates of Exchange

Young adults are more likely to exchange gifts than cards with siblings, but a majority of adults of all ages do both.

(percent of adults who currently exchange birthday/ holidays cards and gifts with siblings, by age, 1996)

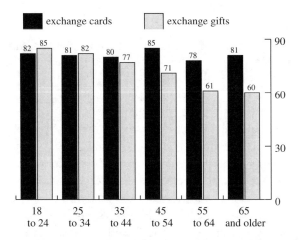

Source: Maritz Marketing Research, Fenton, MO

we got married," says Marvin Brown. Many would consider that they still do. The two brothers, who live in upstate New York, have taken trips to nearby Saratoga Springs and Niagara Falls. With one of their sisters, they are planning a midwestern camping trip this summer, complete with spouses and children.

Some of the money exchange between siblings is financial assistance, but this is a rare expression of the sibling relationship. Overall, just 6 percent of adults give monetary help to siblings, finds the Maritz survey. One might think of the Depression generation as a group of people who early in life learned to pull together for the good of the family. But 94 percent of people aged 55 to 64 say they have never financially assisted siblings, compared with 83 percent of adults under age 55 and 91 percent of those aged 65 and older.

Those born during the Depression years are also least likely to have ever called upon siblings for help with child care or assisted their siblings with the same task. Overall, 81 percent of all adults have never been involved with their siblings in the realm of child care. But 92 percent of those aged 55 to 64 never traded child-care help with siblings, perhaps because they raised their children in the 1950s when parents rarely divorced, mothers rarely worked, and women expected no help in the domestic sphere. People aged 25 to 34 are in the greatest need of child-care assistance today, and one in five currently gives or receives help of this kind to or from siblings. So do 10 percent of those aged 35 to 44. Those aged 45 to 54 or 65 and older are most likely to have been involved with siblings and child care in the past.

Some people trust brothers and sisters to care for their children not only in life, but in the event of their death. Nearly one in four currently names a sibling or siblings in some capacity in a will, as guardians for children, trustees of money, and/or executors of the will itself. The share peaks at 32 percent for those aged 45 to 54. The share is noticeably lower for young adults, many of whom don't have wills. Older adults may be less likely to name siblings in wills because they assume that by the time they die, their brothers and sisters may not be around to take care of things, either. The same reasons probably explain why those aged 45 to 54 are most likely to name siblings on life insurance policies, at 22 percent, while younger and older adults are less likely. On average, 16 percent of adults currently list siblings as beneficiaries.

The Power of Family Ties

Some aspects of sibling relationships remain a mystery. It's clear that women exhibit stronger sibling bonds, but it is difficult to determine how much of this is due to societal norms that encourage women to maintain family relationships and how much is due to true familial feeling. Likewise, conventional wisdom, in some instances supported by valid research, holds that oldest siblings are authoritative, middle siblings are mediators, and youngest siblings are free-spirited. But these generalities don't apply across the board. Differences among brothers and sisters are determined by factors other than birth order, including

Not-So-Mutual Aid

Adults say they give more to brothers and sisters than they get in return.

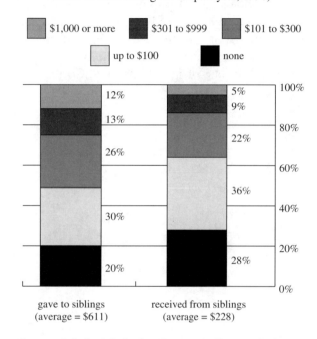

(percent distribution of adults by estimated amount of money and gifts given to and received from siblings in the past year, 1996)

Source: Maritz Marketing Research, Fenton, MO

the way parents inevitably treat different children, as well as outside influences and inherent personality differences.

The ways in which people continue to share their lives with brothers and sisters after reaching adulthood are infinitely varied, depending on circumstances both within and outside of their control. Yet half of adults say that distance, time, and/or money keep them from being as close to their siblings as they would like, according to the Maritz survey. Siblings aged 25 to 54 are especially likely to say that circumstances keep them apart.

This feeling fuels growth in the market for non-occasion greeting cards, says Bernetich of American Greetings. "Adult siblings are so busy, they don't see each other as much, even if they live nearby. So they send cards with greetings like: 'Our lives have gone in different directions, but I still think about you.'" Linda Hinkin and her sister Laurie are likely candidates for this sort of message. And at least one long-distance telephone company depicts siblings in commercials that urge families to keep in touch.

Long-distance telephone and greeting-card companies are not the only businesses that stand to benefit from middle-aged siblings' desire to stay in touch. General Foods employed sibling sentiment in one of its International Coffee ads, in which two sisters get together to reminisce.

These are the exceptions, however. Many advertisers capitalize on the interplay between young brothers and sisters, but few explore the dynamics of adult sibling relationships. That's an oversight. In the case of Linda Hinkin, adulthood has brought her closer to her sister, despite the miles between them. "The closeness was always there," says Linda. "But now it's stronger and better than ever." For them and many others, drawing on the strength of brotherly and sisterly love can be a powerful marketing message.

DISCUSSION QUESTIONS

1. Why are children raised by grandparents at greater risk of psychological and developmental problems?

2. Who will provide care for your elderly parents when they are unable to care for themselves? You? Your sibling(s)? A nursing home? Explain your answer.

3. What type of relationship do you have with your sibling(s) today? What type of relationship do you expect to have with them in ten years? In thirty years? Why?

WEBSITES

www.census.gov/population/www/documentation/twps0026/twps0026.html
In March 1998, the U.S. Census Bureau produced a report by Lynne M. Casper and Kenneth R. Bryson entitled "Co-Resident Grandparents and Their Grandchildren: Grandparent Maintained Families." The entire report can be found at this site.

www.uconnect.com/cga/
This site is devoted to the experience of grandparenting.

PART V

CHALLENGES CONFRONTING FAMILIES IN THE 21ST CENTURY

CONTENTS

PART V: CHALLENGES CONFRONTING FAMILIES
IN THE 21ST CENTURY

CHAPTER 12: FAMILY VIOLENCE AND ABUSE
    READING 31: BEHIND CLOSED DOORS   210
    READING 32: A DAY IN THE LIFE   217

CHAPTER 13: DIVORCE: THE PROCESS OF UNCOUPLING
    READING 33: DIVORCING REALITY   226
    READING 34: FAMILY LAW AT CENTURY'S END   230

CHAPTER 14: REMARRIAGE AND STEPFAMILIES
    READING 35: COMBINING GROWN FAMILIES   235
    READING 36: PARENTING STEPCHILDREN AND BIOLOGICAL CHILDREN   239

CHAPTER 12: FAMILY VIOLENCE AND ABUSE

Popular images of the family include family members interacting harmoniously and caring for one another, providing emotional support and nurturance, and protecting each other from outside dangers. The family is often portrayed as a sanctuary from today's cold, uncaring, disorganized society. These images, unfortunately, mask many realities of family life, because U.S. families frequently are filled with tension, conflict, and violence. Incidents of murder within families, brutal attacks between spouses, and child abuse at the hands of parents are not uncommon. The fact that many families feature violence and abuse is now well known.

In our society, people are more likely to be hit, beaten up, physically injured, or even killed in their own home by a family member than on the streets or by anyone else. While violence is not found in all families, there is an emotional dynamic to family life that can generate violence. This chapter examines two specific types of family violence that have received much attention in recent years—spouse abuse and child abuse. The husband-wife and parent-child relationships are particularly susceptible to violence because of the unequal power distribution within the family.

The first reading, "Behind Closed Doors," illustrates how domestic violence affects everyone in the family. The abuse physically and emotionally hurts the battered wife; it also psychologically wounds children who many times observe (or hear) the abuse of their mother.

The number of reported cases of child abuse and neglect has jumped in recent years. The second reading in this chapter chronicles the disturbing reality of child abuse in the United States. While poverty, the presence of a single parent in the home, and drug abuse can trigger child abuse and neglect, this national nightmare cuts across social class, racial/ethnic, and geographic lines. When parents feel overwhelmed, they many times lash out at the ones who are the most helpless—their children.

BEHIND CLOSED DOORS

Kristen Golden

Domestic violence impacts all family members, not just the one being abused. In this reading, a mother and daughter tell how their family's violence started, how it affected their lives, and how they finally stopped it. (Names and identifying details have been changed to protect the privacy of those involved.) Kristen Golden is a contributing editor to Ms. *magazine.*

Maggie

When I was growing up, we moved every few years because my dad was an executive who was transferred often. I got to like moving. I'd think: "A whole new life—I'll start fresh and have all these new possibilities." I was married to Jennifer's father from when I was 21 until I was 35. He got cancer in his early thirties. He was treated and was fine for a few years and we forgot all about it, thinking, "This will never come back." Suddenly he had a recurrence. He was in the hospital a while, and then he came home. There was nothing left for the doctors to do. He had a hospital bed in the middle of our living room, so I could take care of him and be with Jennifer, who was about 11 then. His illness took over my life, but I was so busy I hardly noticed.

Reprinted from Kristen Golden, "Behind Closed Doors," *Ms.*, March/April 1997, by permission of *Ms.* magazine, ©1997.

With all that my husband and I went through together, I discovered that marriage was more important than I had ever thought it was. We got to be so close. I found out that I could hang in there longer than I would've believed possible, and it would probably all be worth it.

After he died, I started going out with somebody we'd been friends with. For years my husband had taken all my attention. I didn't feel restless when he was sick, but when he was gone, I thought, "Wow, here I am, 35, and I'm ready for life." Maybe the timing was wrong, but I think your children are never actually going to like your going out with someone else. Jennifer didn't dislike Peter, but we all had a hard time.

Peter was recently divorced when we started seeing each other. Quite soon we said we'd like to get married, but somehow that didn't happen for a long time. Our situation turned out to be so difficult that our marriage didn't last too long, although I was actually very fond of him. He is the father of my younger daughter, Theresa.

Frank was the next one. I met him through some friends. I thought, "Well, I'll go out with a new person and forget about my troubles." I was still quite depressed about the breakup of my marriage even though a couple of years had gone by. I felt like I needed something. At the same time, I thought I should be doing something completely different with my life. So my kids and I packed up and went on a big trip through South America.

The trip was great. I wanted to do something with my daughters that they'd remember their whole lives. You get pretty close when you're sharing hotel rooms—a rare opportunity, especially for a teenager and her mom! Unfortunately, our money ran out sooner than I expected. I barely had enough to get us home.

I had started going out with Frank right before we went on the trip, and we wrote to each other while I was away. We decided we wanted to get married even though we had only known each other a few weeks before I left. When I got married to Peter, I had been engaged for almost two years, and I thought, "That didn't do any good. Let's try this way." We were together for a couple of months when we got back, but obviously, looking back, it was too fast.

In the beginning, Frank and Jennifer didn't have a lot to do with each other. Before he came along, it was just the three of us, and my daughters and I had become closer than ever. Jennifer was trying to be supportive and helpful and make me feel O.K. She wanted me to be happy, so she tried to like Frank as best she could, but she didn't very much. I guess later she felt like she was the one who was right.

Frank was different from most people I'd known. I'm fascinated by things that are different or new. I was feeling somewhat rejected from my last episode, and along comes this truly romantic man. Frank was a very quiet person—articulate but with a quiet voice. He was a real storyteller and pretty interesting for me to talk to. He was fond of my younger daughter. When we were dating, we'd often go out in the evenings, but when we saw each other in the day, my little one was always with us. He seemed to want more children. He had one that he had lost touch with through divorce. I wanted a father for my daughter and I liked the way he was with her.

He had a seasonal job, traveling around selling water sports equipment. We'd been married just a few months when Frank started traveling a lot. Every few weeks, I'd drive to where he was, and stay for several days. Jennifer was 16. She took care of her four-year-old sister and my mom would look in on them.

At the end of the vacation season, when business slowed down, I met him in a resort town for a week. We spent a lot of time together, fishing and water-skiing. We rented a house right next to the water. I loved waking up in the morning and hearing the sound of the waves. These early romantic experiences made the relationship almost worth it.

I don't know exactly when the violence started. I know we hadn't been together that long, maybe a few months. He was really sweet to me before we married, but one eye-opening thing happened on our honeymoon. There wasn't any physical violence, but he had been drinking and he was goading me. He told me what he really thought of my kids. That sure made my alarm bells go off. I don't really have a temper, but everybody has a point. We didn't exactly fight, but I was quite surprised at what he said. Then he was all sweet in the morning. It wasn't really verbal abuse—but in a way, it was.

Gradually Frank started to drink more and push me more. I never figured out what he wanted me to do or say. I felt like he thought he had to make me angry—and inevitably he would. He was intelligent, more so than Jennifer thought. He'd select the things about me that I prided myself on and say that they weren't true. Sometimes I would raise my voice when we fought, which my children were quite shocked at because I had never raised my voice to them.

After about a month and a half of that kind of treatment, I got really angry one night. I'm pretty sure this was the first time he was violent. The kids had gone to sleep. You know how traditionally a woman might slap a man's face once in a while, if he's extremely goading? I felt like he wanted to bring me to that point. I was never one to even spank children, but Frank made me so angry that I slapped him. That seemed to be the signal for him to go wild. I was shocked to suddenly be thrown around the room. Afterward he was all contrite—he had given me a black eye—but he said, "Well, you started it." I guess that's true. I thought, "Well, look what I did."

The next day you could see my black eye. I think anybody whose husband beats them up feels ashamed. I don't know why they should. Husbands should be ashamed, but they don't feel that way somehow. I guess you just feel like such an idiot to be staying with this person that you don't want to talk about it. And you don't suddenly stop loving someone just one night; it takes longer than that.

I still cared about Frank and didn't want to run him down with my children, so I didn't talk about it with the kids. Jennifer was busy with her own life, and her friends were really her life. Frank was very nice after that. I found out later that a lot of these things are just the usual pattern, but I hadn't had any experience with this sort of thing before.

There were a lot of good things in our relationship. The violence didn't really have anything to do with it. Of course, we would argue, but he would be really nice for a while and then gradually he would get back to criticizing me. The violence would always escalate when he'd been drinking, so I'd think, "If only he could give up drinking."

One time when he was drunk, he hit me so hard, I flew across the room and broke my arm. That was scary. I didn't feel like he was going to stop beating me, no matter what happened. I was in so much pain, I could barely talk, so it was hard for me to say anything, but that didn't calm him down. He kept going, even when he started to sober up. I was terrified. Finally, he felt bad and took me to the hospital.

When we got there, I didn't want to tell people what had happened. I guess I felt protective toward him. But also, this man is right there glaring at me. Having him go to jail seemed silly, because if I sent him there I would be pretty frightened when he came out. It was a mixture of protecting him and being afraid.

And Frank was genuinely frightened by the possibility that the police might be notified. One time—before the broken-arm episode—he was being violent, and Jennifer called the police. When they arrived, I didn't want to say, "Take this person away." So I said, "I'm all right. I don't want to charge him." The police said, "Are you sure?" I said yes and they went away.

And I *was* sure because I could feel that Frank was so shocked by the police coming that that would be it for that occasion, at least. Jennifer was quite stunned that I did not turn him in. I think your kids often don't understand why you do certain things. If he had ever touched either of my kids, I would have done something. Strange that you can't think more of yourself. And the kids weren't really afraid of him. I would say Jennifer is a fairly strong woman and, if anything, he was probably a little afraid of her. I don't think he would have done anything to the girls. There's something about wives, though.

After the broken-arm thing, of course, I realized this was getting serious. At the hospital he said he was going to give up drinking. He was very contrite, and he asked for one more try. We talked for a few hours and I thought, "Well, one more try," but I suggested that we sell the house we bought together and separate our finances in case it didn't work out. I wasn't feeling too hopeful. Quite often I'm sure women want to leave but don't know what they would do for money. You can't just leave the house and wonder, "How will I get him out of there? How will I support my family?"

When the men are contrite, I think it's a good idea to try to make some kind of financial arrangement or at least say, "Well, I'll come back but I want my own bank account with a couple of hundred dollars in it."

In my case, I asked Frank at a time when he was willing to do anything. He felt pretty shocked about what he had done and he really wanted to be with me. So he agreed that we would sell the house. He was an honest person. Even when someone has something really bad about them, that's not all there is to them. But I was feeling like this was the last try. And after a while I noticed he was starting to drink a bit again. So I called a women's shelter just to find out what you do.

A few months later, he beat me again. I decided to leave then and there. After having gone through the episode with my arm, this time I thought it could be life or death, and I wasn't going to let myself be killed. Jennifer had already said to me that while she couldn't make me leave, she wouldn't let me die. I was really scared, but I started to fight back physically. I was quite angry—all those promises and here we were again. But fighting back didn't make me feel powerful.

He just kept hitting me. Finally, I said I had to go to the bathroom and fled the room. I grabbed Theresa and ran out the door. Fortunately, someone was driving by. Although I didn't even know him and my clothes were torn, I flagged him down. I said, "Please help me, this man is trying to hurt me." He told me he'd drive me wherever I wanted to go. I figured he was a better bet than what I was running from. Frank came out of the house, but he just stood there. The abuse plays a little differently when it's outside. I got in the car and asked the man to take us to where Jennifer was working. My little daughter and I sat there and waited until the end of Jennifer's shift, and then we all went to the women's shelter.

I had a very unsympathetic boss at the time. So here I was: I had to go to work, look normal, and then go to the shelter at night. But the shelter was very helpful for me. I got to tell my story confidentially. Everyone was supportive. I got a lot of counseling and coaching on the law, although it seemed really quite boring that the whole thing was so predictable. You know: the men are always so sweet afterward and say they would never do it again; they're usually controlling, manipulative people who run down your self-esteem so you think you deserve being hit. The shelter was hard for Jennifer. She was very uncomfortable. She was good to me, but she wasn't pleased about being there.

Theresa used to cry when Frank and I fought. I'd send her to her room when things got bad, but she could hear us. She was pretty scared that last time because I grabbed her and ran out of the house. So the shelter was wonderful for her. There were kids for her to play with. She wanted to stay there forever. That's the hardest part. The women were supportive, but you couldn't stay there forever. Everyone had to get a job and a place to live pretty quickly.

It's been a few years now—four years ago that we got married—so I've pretty much been able to

shake what Frank did to me. Maybe I'm not as sure of myself as I would want to be, but he didn't convince me I was a bad person. I think, "Perhaps I'm not really so great, but I still didn't deserve this." These men make you feel so bad about yourself. They have no right to say that you're not a worthy person. No right at all. Every person in the world is much too important to lose.

I'm sorry for my children—it was so hard on them. But I've found it interesting to be able to understand why I did the things I did. I was like everyone else. I used to think, "Why, why do women stay after the first minute of violence?" So if my telling my story gets even just one of those women out, even though it's not much, I'd feel like something in my life has made a difference.

I think my daughters would go at the first sign of violence. The whole thing felt very dragged-out for them. Maybe I felt more in control because I could decide to go, whereas they couldn't make me leave. Jennifer so much resented that I stayed as long as I did.

I never felt that Frank should be prosecuted. I still feel something for him. Less so as the years go by and less so when I remember how it felt being beaten. I actually hope that he can solve his drinking problem and just hope there's not some other woman that he's beating. I think Jennifer is more, well, bitter. She and my mother probably would be glad to prosecute him. I admire them for that.

Jennifer

There was no turbulence in my life when I was a kid, as far as my parents' relationship goes. I don't remember their ever fighting or anything like that. I read a lot as a child. Actually, I hid in my room. We had a really small house and there was a hospital bed in the living room and that's where my father was. We've always had a really loving, close family, but a lot of things are left unsaid. I knew my father was very sick, and he had been in intensive care for at least a month. I guess now, looking back on it, he came home to die. But I didn't realize that, so I was shocked. A little later, my mom said, "I can't believe that you didn't think he was going to die." But when you're a kid you just don't think people are going to die.

Right after my father died, I began to hate going to school. I didn't want to talk to anyone and I thought everyone hated me anyway. I'd pretend that I was sick, and my mom would let me stay home. I almost wished that I could have a nervous breakdown so I wouldn't have to go to school and deal with people.

But then I really made the effort to bring myself together, and I built up a lot of coping mechanisms. I definitely went through a process of self-examination, which I think I get from my mom. I know she does spend a lot of time examining things in herself, but we haven't really talked about it. I've always admired my mother. She is a very quiet, shy person. Everyone who meets her thinks she's so sweet, and she is. I thought of her almost as a saint. She was very loving with us.

My mom is physically very strong. When my dad was sick, she had to turn him in bed, and he was six feet tall. She has really serious biceps. Since she never had any money for anything, she was always walking places or running for the bus. I've always felt my mom was emotionally stable for us. My mom has been the center of my world. But all of the externals were unstable— what school I was going to, where I was living, what man she might be living with. All of those things were coming and going all the time.

I feel like I've been raised without a father, even though my dad died when I was 11. I eventually developed a sort of father-daughter relationship with Peter, the man my mom married after my father, but I would never call him Father, Dad, or anything like that. Peter and my mom got involved very shortly after my father died. After only six months, they told me they were having a serious relationship. I took the news really badly, because I felt, "How could anyone replace my father? How could she love someone else so soon?"

Their marriage lasted just a few months. Then my mom went out on all these dates through the personal ads. After a while, some friends introduced her to Frank. I think she had only gone out with him a few times, so I was certainly surprised when she told me that they were going to get married. I guess they had kept up some sort of correspondence while we were traveling, but I was totally in the dark.

The trip to South America had been totally incredible for me. I got to leave school for several months. That was so cool. Eleventh grade. When you're a teenager, you don't want to do things with your family anymore, but you make an exception when it's a trip like that. We had a great time. I felt a lot closer to my mother and my sister than ever before. When we got back my mom told us that she and Frank really loved each other and they planned to get married. She was so excited. I knew this was outside my control and I had other things going on in my life. A part of me also believed that whatever my mom did was right. I guess I had these conflicting ideas about my mom. In some ways, she seemed so perfect and wonderful and everything she did must be right, yet I didn't always like everything she did.

Like Frank. There was definitely something about him that I didn't like. Everything he enjoyed, my mom didn't. She doesn't drink, smoke, or gamble, but he took her to Atlantic City for their honeymoon, where that's all everybody does. Occasionally, she went to bars with him. She'd get drunk on one or two beers because alcohol affects her so easily. But it's not like she changed. My mom just likes to be exposed to different ways of living and to absorb the experiences of others.

I can't remember how much I hated Frank before I knew he was hitting my mom and how much more I hated him after. Frank was a total deadbeat. He seemed to have had a lot of jobs and I think he spent a lot of time on unemployment.

I wasn't at home a lot, but I had indications that Frank was a questionable character—like the vodka bottles in the cupboard. Normally, we didn't have any alcohol around the house. I'd stare at the bottles, fascinated, because I knew that he was drinking them. One day, I was looking for something in my mom's closet and I saw shotguns hidden away in the back. That made me very uneasy.

Frank would do all this terrible stuff to my mom while he was drunk. Then, when he sobered up, he'd feel guilty and act so sorry. He did go to AA for a while. I just remember thinking he was such a hypocrite. His Bible would be sitting around the house. Here he is pretending he's a religious Christian while he goes around hitting my mom. AA must have been his penance. Maybe he tried to quit drinking as part of an agreement for her to stay with him. I know there was a lot of negotiating going on. I guess she felt she could change him or help him change.

After he broke her arm, obviously I had a lot of resentment toward him. I didn't trust him and I didn't feel safe. When they would fight, I was terrified because this horrible man was yelling at my mom and hurting her, and she was just a quiet victim of his rage. My mom is someone who takes a lot of stuff. Now I see it as a bit of a martyr complex. I wasn't in the same room when they were fighting, so I don't know what she did. I think her technique was to try to calm him down. She'd try to diffuse his rage, but if she couldn't calm him, she would just take it.

Some of these incidents stand out so clearly to me, like there's been a flare thrown on them, but others are really obscure. I think your mind blocks out things that it doesn't want to remember. I can't even remember Frank's last name.

One night, I got a call at work. I worked at a fast-food restaurant. Terrible place. I worked after school until 11 or so in the evening. My little sister, who'd just learned how to use the phone, called saying, "I'm really scared. Mom and Frank are fighting. They're in the other room but I hear them yelling and I think he's hitting her." So I told her I'd come home, but first I called the police and asked them to go to our house.

Since I hated this guy, I felt what he was doing was a crime, but I had never heard about domestic violence. I know the feminist movement was talking about it, but it hadn't reached me or the schools. I just called the police to protect my mom. I was embarrassed because I had to tell my boss what was happening in order to leave. And I had to ask her to drive me home because we lived pretty far away and I didn't have a car. By the time we got there, the police had arrived. They were ridiculous. They asked what was going on

and Frank started freaking out, yelling, "Who called the police?" At least the officers were smart enough not to say, "This girl over here called us," so that things would really be a mess. They said the neighbors heard noise and called the police.

One officer asked my mother if Frank was hitting her. Standing right beside him, of course, she said no. Then they asked my sister, but since she wasn't in the same room, it wasn't enough that she heard all the noise. You knew the next day bruises would come out all over my mom's face. That was the evidence. Since she wasn't going to admit that anything had happened, and my sister hadn't actually witnessed the violence, the police said they couldn't do anything. They told us they'd be in the area, and they left.

I herded the family into my sister's room and locked the door. Then I called my boyfriend—not that I thought he would save us or anything, but I felt like this horrible spell had been cast over my family. I thought the spell would be broken if anyone from outside came, and that Frank wouldn't dare do anything while someone else was there. So I told my boyfriend what was happening and asked him to come right over. He said yes, but then he called back and said he couldn't come. His parents thought it was a bad idea. I was crushed. I felt like there was no one I could depend on.

I was really panicked. I kept thinking, "Oh, my God, what's going to happen?" By this point, Frank was banging on the door and asking my mom to come out. The more she refused to come out, the more irate he became. Finally Mom said she would talk to him. I didn't want her to go, but she did anyway. So when I heard the yelling start again, I thought, "I can't just sit in here and let it happen."

I felt that I should take charge. I was the one who had called the police and my boyfriend, and had tried to deal with the situation. At the same time, I felt so helpless. I wanted to help my family, but I didn't know what to do. I was 17 years old. Earlier, when we were locked in the room away from him, my mom told me that Frank had been strangling her while they were fighting and she had blacked out. Knowing that, I was really scared. I finally decided that the best solution was to go out there and tell Frank to get our of our lives.

So I went our and started yelling at him. "You're ruining our lives," I screamed, "and you're hurting my mother. We all want you to leave. Leave this house right now." Well, that made him totally flip out. He lunged at me, but my mom grabbed him. She looked really scared that he was going to do something to me. That moved her into action more than danger against herself did. She grabbed him and said, "Don't hurt my daughter."

I felt this total adrenaline rush as I confronted him. I shouted, "Go ahead and hit me like you hit my mother." That really made him mad. But Frank finally left the house, and nothing else happened the rest of the evening. That was the only time I took charge. Then I went back to feeling that I had no control over my life. In the end, it was my mom's life, so she had to make the decision.

Finally, during a fight, she left him. She called me at work to tell me she and Theresa were on the way over. That made me happy, but it was the kind of thing that added to my feelings of instability: I never knew when I was going to get a phone call at work or at school saying something terrible was happening to my mother.

Mom brought Theresa to the restaurant and they sat at a table until I finished cleaning up at the end of my shift. Then we sat around and tried to figure out what to do next. Mom said she could call my grandmother but she didn't really want to, because my grandmother already disapproved of her marriage. It would be humiliating. And she did have this phone number of a women's shelter.

Finally, she said she'd call the shelter. We looked for a public phone with a lot of people around, because she thought Frank might be looking for her. We went to our local supermarket. Mom was on the phone with the woman at the shelter when Frank showed up and made a big scene. We were terrified. It was absolutely surreal—being in this place that I went to all the time, in a neighborhood that I knew, where people knew me, and having this guy who was virtually a stranger screaming at us in front of everyone. The supermarket's security guard finally made him leave. We stood and watched his truck drive off. Then we drove to the shelter.

We were there for about a week, while my mom tried to find a new place for us to live. You had to go to counseling sessions all the time. I can understand that they want to make sure you're not going to fly off the deep end after all you've been through, but I really disliked the whole thing. The place was depressing, and I hated the fact that its location was a secret. I felt horrible walking into this place and knowing every other woman in there was an abused woman. I hated seeing so many of these women who, even though they had taken the steps to get away, just looked so subdued by life.

I would always hope that a woman would leave a battering situation, but that's not a lesson that you can give to people. And being a feminist doesn't necessarily teach you how to have good, healthy relationships with men. My mom is educated and intelligent, but she still didn't know how to leave.

I always thought my mom was strong, even when she was staying with Frank and taking his abuse. Making the decision to leave takes a certain kind of mental leap, but taking abuse isn't easy either. I thought she was strong just for staying alive.

I wish she hadn't stayed with Frank as long as she did, but in the context of most abusive relationships, she got out fast—after about a year and a half. I would have left after the first time he hit me. Ever since this happened, I've said to myself, "If a guy so much as touches me, lays a finger on me, I'm outta there." No second chances. My mom, you know, believes in second and third chances.

READING 32
A DAY IN THE LIFE

Bill Hewitt

To illustrate the grim reality of child abuse, a group of reporters from People *magazine record the activities of those most involved in the issue— the tormented children and the men and women who work to protect them. Bill Hewitt is a staff writer for* People.

In House Springs, Mo., near St. Louis, a 19-year-old mother is accused of breaking the ribs of her 5-month-old son to stop his crying. In Waukegan, Ill., a 21-year-old woman and her live-in boyfriend allegedly force her 4-year-old daughter to sleep in the shower and beat her severely with a belt and a wooden cutting board because the youngster won't stop wetting her bed. In New York City, a 27-year-old mother is charged with starving her 5-year-old son before tying him to a chair and fatally bludgeoning him with a broom handle.

Each of these cases made headlines in 1997, but they are the exceptions. Most of the 969,000 confirmed cases of child abuse [in 1997], which typically began as reports from teachers, doctors, police, family members and neighbors, ended not on the 6 o'clock news, but as part of the caseload of thousands of social workers across the U.S. who are the last line of defense for America's children. In fact, the reality of child abuse in America is more disturbing than even the most lurid headlines suggest. [In 1997] the privately funded National Committee to Prevent Child Abuse issued an in-depth report on the problem, based on 1996 figures. Among the findings: Profound neglect involving children left unsupervised and uncared for, often by parents with drug and alcohol problems, was by far the most common form of abuse, comprising 60 percent of all cases. Physical abuse (23 percent) and sexual abuse (9 percent) occurred less often, but those numbers—representing more than 220,000 and 87,000 children, respectively— are chilling enough. In New York State alone, according to a separate report, 59 children were killed, 273 suffered broken bones and 5,927 received bruises and lacerations allegedly as the result of abuse in 1995, the last year for which figures are available.

It is undeniably a national nightmare, a problem that afflicts well-to-do and middle-class families as well as the poor. Still, experts say that poverty, the presence of only a single parent in the home and drug use can often serve as triggers for child abuse. "When you're overwhelmed with problems—not enough money, no job, how to feed the kids," says Joy Byers, communications director of the National Committee to Prevent Child Abuse in Chicago, "it can get so overwhelming that people sometimes will lash out at the ones who are most helpless." And it is a cycle that is all too often perpetuated: Those who have been abused as children frequently abuse their own offspring. [In November 1997] President Clinton signed the Adoption and Safe Families Act, which puts an emphasis on protecting kids rather than keeping seriously dysfunctional families intact, and which experts hope will help break the cycle.

To get a clearer view of the problem, *People* assigned 15 reporters and 13 photographers in eight locations around the country, both urban and rural, to record, over a 24-hour period, the activities of those most directly involved in the child-abuse issue—the victims and their families (whose names have been changed) and the professionals dedicated to helping them. It is these last who determine whether families remain together or whether, for their own safety, children must be removed from their homes. In nearly all cases, the choices are hard ones; caseloads are heavy, time is limited and budgets are tight—and mistakes, often fatal ones, can be made. In Chicago, for instance, 3-year-old Frank Torres was returned to his mother, whose husband had earlier been accused of breaking his leg, after she received counseling and all the child welfare workers involved agreed that the youngster would be safe. Just four months later, in August, his mother, Veronica Diaz, 21, was accused of drowning the boy. That child abuse is not a top priority, argues Michael Petit, deputy director of the Child Welfare League in Washington, is a disgrace. "We spend more than $30 billion on pizza annually," he points out. "Then look at the figures for child abuse—under $20 billion," which mostly goes for foster care and prevention. The 24 hours chosen for our survey, beginning on Friday, Sept. 19 [1997], had no special significance other than that it was typical, illuminating some deeply distressing human frailties—and offering some hopeful glimpses of strength and commitment.

Miami Lawrence Scott sees more child abuse in one day than anyone should in a lifetime. Driving to his North Miami Beach office at 8 a.m., Scott, 30, one of 87 investigators in his local section of the Florida Department of Children and Families, has 15 case files waiting on his desk to be closed out, about the number he is as-signed each week. Many involve children who have been severely beaten or forced to live in wretched conditions, which is why he often feels a sense of foreboding while heading to work. "That's when you're thinking, 'Oh, my God, what's going to happen today,'" says Scott, who earns a base salary of $24,500. "And at night you watch TV and wonder what you're going to see." Yet he also finds profound satisfaction in his work. "I really do love this job," says Scott, a former substitute teacher now in his third year at DCF. "Sometimes, when you sit back and really think about things, yeah, it gets to you. You say, 'How can people do this?' But it would be harder if you knew that nothing was going to be done." And the misery he deals with reminds him to be more patient with his own two daughters Jasmine, 6, and Lauren, 3. "It definitely helps me out as a father," he says.

Burley, Idaho Standing outside his comfortable seven-bedroom home in this rural potato-farming town (pop. 9,600), King West hollers, "I love you!" as his three adopted sons and three foster sons head for school in the family van. West, 55, a stocky, retired trucking supervisor, has been up since 5 a.m. but will have no time to catch his breath. Yesterday, Jack Qualman, a social worker with the Idaho Department of Health and Welfare, called West and his wife, Kathy, 48, about taking a 6-year-old boy in need of a foster home. "Do you have an extra bed?" Qualman asked. Kathy's response was immediate: "What difference does it make? Of course we'll take him." Now King must make room for the newest of the scores of foster children, many of them abused, whom the couple have cared for over the years. "All we know is, Jack will be bringing the boy by sometime after 1, and that he'll probably be with us for the rest of the school year," says King, cleaning up the remnants of breakfast and loading the dishwasher. "We don't even know the boy's name yet, but that's typical." It's no coincidence that King spent part of his own youth in an orphanage. "I've always had a soft spot in my heart for kids going through rough times," he says. "I know what it's like not to have anybody."

Maricopa County, Arizona At 9:28, Linda

Gregg, 29, a caseworker at the state's Children's Protective Services office in Phoenix, is fielding a call, one of some 325 received each day. A grandmother is phoning to report her daughter for neglecting her own 8-year-old daughter and 1-year-old son. "She parties all night and is too tired to get up in the morning," says the woman. Most days the 8-year-old can't rouse her mother to be taken to school, and the 1-year-old, who has had heart surgery, is being exposed to smoke, though his lungs are weak. "She smokes marijuana in the same room with him—crack, whatever," the grandmother says, adding that she has brought her grandson home with her after finding him bruised and unattended. "I went into the house this morning and [my daughter] was passed out," the grandmother reports. "I have him and she doesn't even know it."

Miami   The call rings out, "All rise!" in the courtroom of Juvenile Court Judge Cindy Lederman. It is 10:45, and she is already on her fourth case of the day. This one involves a 29-year-old mother with a history of abuse. In 1992 her 6-year-old son was taken from her after she was found responsible for burning his face with an iron and forcing him to kneel on a potato grater when he misbehaved. Later that year she gave birth to another son, who was immediately removed and sent to live with a relative in Canada. Today's hearing is to determine whether she should lose her younger son permanently. The outcome is never really in doubt. Not only has she failed to meet minimal court requirements such as attending parenting courses, but she has never tried to maintain contact with the boy. Nor is she in court today. After an hour of testimony, Lederman, 43, rules the boy's mother should have her parental rights terminated. Here there are none of the uncertainties and ambiguities that often surround abuse cases, and Lederman makes her decision with evident relief. "Thank God this child is in a stable relationship with a relative," she says.

Maricopa County   At the CPS field office in Tolleson, about 10 miles west of Phoenix, Claudette Washington, 35, who has been a caseworker for 3½ years, is heading out into the

desert on her first call after a morning briefing. She is scheduled to meet Samantha, the 25-year-old mother of three young children, whom she visited several days before, after a report that they were living in squalid conditions. "I'm going to ask the mother to do a urinalysis," says Washington. "I think she's a meth user." She means methamphetamine—speed—a highly addictive drug that can cause violent behavior. Washington is also concerned about a report from his school that Samantha's son Justin, 7, has told of being forced to stand in a corner at home for long periods and possibly hit. "I think I have a serious problem here," says Washington. "If she's not real careful, she's going to lose her kids."

Miami   Lawrence Scott arrives in a working-class neighborhood of single-family homes at mid-morning. He has come to speak with a father accused of kicking and punching his 15-year-old daughter. "But," Scott cautions, "this case is complicated." Though there is apparently an ongoing problem, he doesn't want to remove the daughter, who has provoked her parents by telling them she wants to be independent and have sex. Recently the family was advised to get counseling but never did. Now Scott will try to talk them into it. The father, who acknowledges he is frustrated and losing control over his daughter, insists he never beat her, as she claims. Scott is inclined to believe him, since the girl had no bruises when he and police examined her earlier.

The mother explains the parents' dilemma. "This is our first time raising a teenager," she says. "I'm from Panama. I was raised with beatings from the branch of a guava tree. If we had a parenting book that says here's what to do with your daughter at this age, hey, great. But I don't know what to do, so I pray. I'm learning to be a parent, but I was raised totally differently." The father promises to get counseling. "It's a priority now," he tells Scott. "Before, it wasn't. But the family has to be taken care of."

Maricopa County   Looking bedraggled, Samantha answers caseworker Claudette Washington's knock at the front door of her single-story house in a dusty subdivision. Clearly, the place once looked better. There is a sectional sofa and a large-screen TV in a sunken living room. But now there are several parrots, some in cages, some walking free, all over the house—and bird droppings everywhere. Flies light on every surface, and trash overflows a pail in the kitchen.

Washington wastes no time. "I think you're doing drugs," she tells Samantha flatly. "Look at this place. I told you to clean it up." Samantha denies using drugs, and when Washington questions her about the way she disciplines 7-year-old Justin, Samantha, who has a daughter Rose, 8, and another son Ben, 3, insists she hasn't abused him. "I'm not going to let your children stay in this environment," says Washington. "I'm going to tell you this house is disgusting."

She warns Samantha that she is on her way to Justin's school to check the abuse allegations and that she intends to stop back later to inspect the house, which had better be cleaned up if Samantha hopes to keep her kids. Stepping outside, she is fuming. "This is what I see daily," she says. "I feel like throwing up." In the car, she calms down. "People make me sick when they make excuses," says Washington, the mother of a 17-year-old daughter, Mesha. "There's no reason for those children to be exposed to that bird crap. I feel sorry for her, but I know if I coddle her along, she ain't gonna do nothing."

Johnston County, North Carolina   Cynthia Starling, 27, a social worker for the county's Department of Social Services, is checking on April Ford, who regained custody of her three children in June. When investigators took them away a year earlier, food and garbage were knee-high in the little Ford farmhouse. Today, house and yard are strewn with toys and laundry. The kitchen floor is wet. "It's been hectic," Ford says of being reunited with her kids, as Starling inspects the house, "but it's good." Starling is sure Ford cleans only when she's expecting a visit. "It's just plain lack of taking responsibility," she says later in frustration. The past week has been tough on her department: Three babies have been brought to a hospital with broken bones, and last night a child beaten with an extension cord was removed to foster care.

Brooklyn   It is noon in Judge Jody Adams's

family court, where a couple with five children, four of whom are in foster care, are seeking to regain custody. Both parents are unemployed, frequently homeless and have a history of crack-cocaine and alcohol abuse. The lawyer for the foster mother argues that the birth father needs therapy and is not a fit parent. "Placement in foster care will be temporarily extended until the next hearing," says Adams, 49, tersely. Later, Adams, who has been a family-court judge for four years and earns $113,000 annually, comments on the daily parade of families before her: "This is a poor people's court. If these people were middle class, they'd be seeing a shrink, not testifying before a judge. I see a lot of hatred."

Elsewhere in the city, a year-old shelter run by the Jewish Board of Family and Children's Services houses 11 mothers and 30 kids, many of whom are the victims of physical or sexual abuse, usually at the hands of their father. Crystal, 26, was abused by her boyfriend. Her sons, Sam, 6, and Robert, 8, who were witnesses, have emotional problems. Sam has yet to learn to tie his shoes. "The one thing they need the most in life is love," says Marvelene Richards, a counselor at the shelter, of the children she works with.

Miami   Around noon, with no new cases needing attention, investigator Lawrence Scott permits himself a rare luxury—stopping for lunch instead of going to a drive-thru. In the line at a fast-food chicken shack, he works his cell phone, catching up on cases. His lunch lasts just 16 minutes before his office beeps him to pick up information on a case that has come in involving a woman accused of neglect.

Los Angeles   At a group home for girls, 14-year-old Shirley's face brightens at the sight of Robert Lewis, 54, a county social worker with a Ph.D. in counseling and educational psychology. She throws her skinny arms around him and squeezes. Only 70 pounds a year ago because of neglect, she now weighs nearly 100. But Lewis has bad news: Shirley's mother, an alcoholic and cocaine user, has failed to prove she is off drugs; as a consequence she must enter rehab. Shirley is remarkably stoic, and Lewis promises her a teddy bear on his next visit. He, like Shirley, hasn't given up on her mother. "She'll get there," he says. "Falling is sometimes part of the process of getting up."

Burley   King West sits in his kitchen, pouring a Coke. Since he and Kathy married 29 years ago, they have taken in 72 foster children—some for a few months, others for several years. Not only do they have five grown kids of their own, but three years ago they adopted six foster siblings, the largest single adoption in Idaho history. (For their foster parenting, the Wests receive an average of $358 per child a month, all of which they spend on food, clothing and incidentals.) King flips open a recipe box and thumbs through index cards describing each child they have taken in. "I don't ever show this to anybody," he says. "It's just a little record I keep, with pictures of all the kids."

He pauses at one card. "This is Billy. It's hard for me to talk about what happened to him. He's a 9-year-old boy who was very badly sexually abused by his father. He was forced to perform sexual acts on his sister, who was 6, and his parents filmed them. Billy was repeatedly tied up and hung in the closet for hours at a time, and he had cigarette burns on his arms. He and his sister were locked in a bedroom with a toilet in the corner, and he'd get fed maybe once every two or three days. He had to drink water from the toilet." King falls silent. "It just tears you up inside to hear what these innocent children go through. It just tears you up."

Miami   After getting the details of his new case, Lawrence Scott pulls up at a rundown townhouse at 1:22 p.m. A woman has been arrested for credit-card fraud. According to police, she used her 14-year-old daughter to sign for a package ordered with a stolen card. A police report says the girl's grandmother, who lives in the home, is "verbally abusive" toward the child and that the house is "extremely filthy."

As soon as Scott steps out of the car, he is hit by the acrid smell of cat urine. Inside a rusty metal fence, several cats lie in a heap in the yard, and two mangy dogs pace back and forth. The windows of the house are covered with sheets. When an elderly woman opens the front door, the stench is almost overwhelming. Scott tells her who he is and why he is there, but she speaks no English and he speaks no Spanish. The woman manages to convey that she is the grandmother and that the 14-year-old has gone with an older sister to the Animal Services office to see about getting rid of the cats and dogs. A quick look at the house reveals dirt and garbage everywhere, as well as yellow puddles on floors and countertops. Scott returns to his car and starts phoning, trying to locate the girl's sisters.

Maricopa County   Caseworker Claudette Washington pays a visit to the elementary school where Samantha's older children, Rose and Justin, are students. In separate interviews both express fear that they will be taken from their mother, though Justin says she sometimes orders him to do a handstand in the corner for an hour when he misbehaves. Washington has heard enough. "I think Mom has some serious mental-health issues," she says out of their earshot. "Those kids are going to go right now." From her car phone, Washington starts trying to track down Samantha's estranged husband, who turns out to be away on business.

Burley   At 1:35 Jack Qualman pulls up in a van with a dark-haired boy sitting next to a big box of his belongings. King West opens the van door. The boy, wearing navy shorts and a matching T-shirt, grins at him as Qualman says, "King, I'd like you to meet Steve. He'll be staying with you for a while."

"So you're Steve, huh?" says King. "I'll bet you'll be good on the trampoline."

Steve's brown eyes grow big. "Wow, you have a trampoline?"

Inside, Qualman gives King a folder containing a case history of Steve's mother, who is in jail for shoplifting. Steve has six brothers and sisters, all in different foster homes. Later, Qualman tells King that Steve was likely the victim of physical abuse. "There's a history of it in the family," he says.

Maricopa County   For the second time today, Claudette Washington arrives at Samantha's house. It is 2:25 p.m. "This is the hard part," she says as she gets out of the car. Inside, Samantha has been scrubbing the kitchen. Washington sits her down at a table. "I've made a decision here," she says. "You're not going to be too happy with it." Samantha starts crying, knowing her kids are headed for foster care. Suddenly Washington's toughness evaporates. "This is not forever," she says reassuringly. "This is until you get your life straightened out. I'm not doing this to be mean to you. I'm doing this to protect your children." Samantha nods. "I know," she says.

Rose and Justin, hovering nearby, are alarmed. Young Ben clings to his mother, wailing over and over, "I want to stay with you." After calming him, Washington takes the three kids to her car and buckles them into the backseat as Rose clutches her favorite book, one of R.L. Stine's *Goosebumps*. Washington drops them with another CPS worker, who will see that they get to a shelter that evening. Later, in the car, Washington talks about the reasons she removed the children—a pattern of negligence and suspected abuse, drug use and the number of Samantha's male visitors. "She has too many guys hanging around the house," says Washington. "Out here, molestation is one of the most common referrals I get." Still, she doesn't like taking the kids. "We've disrupted their whole lives," she says glumly.

Miami At 4 p.m., Lawrence Scott returns to the house that smells of cats, hoping to find the 14-year-old girl. She isn't there. A 23-year-old sister who lives nearby is initially hostile but promises the family will clean the house if he will hold off removing the girl. "We'll give them a chance and see how it works out," he says, back in the car.

Burley In the late afternoon, Kathy West returns home from classes at Idaho State University, where she is studying to become a high school history and computer teacher. She introduces herself to Steve. The youngster gives her a hug, but Kathy isn't fooled. "My initial impression is that Steve is hurting," she says. "That's why he's clinging to strangers. Kids don't do that if they're not hurting. To help, a lot of it is just being there, being constant. We won't put a bunch of rules on him the first few nights. He's got to get to know us, and we've got to get to know him. There will

be time for rules later."

Miami Her work for the day finished, Judge Cindy Lederman takes a breather in chambers. It has been a routinely trying session—five cases this day—including testimony about a mother of nine with a chronic cocaine habit who has lost custody of all her children. "The first three months that I did this," says Lederman, a former deputy city attorney who has been a judge for nine years, the last three in the juvenile division, "I would wake up in the middle of the night all the time and be very upset. When I stand up sometimes I feel like I weigh 500 pounds after sitting there listening to these things."

Boston "What a sick family," says social worker Diane Harrold, 30, leaving a first-floor apartment in the city's Dorchester neighborhood. "The daughter was sexually abused by her uncle, and the father is more concerned about his brother going to jail than about her." The father has paid the girl's mother to write a letter saying the 15-year-old lies. During her interview with Harrold, the girl, who will receive therapy and may end up in a foster home if the father won't protect her, at first refused to talk, then sobbed, "My own mother sold me up the river."

Miami When Lawrence Scott returns at 7:45 p.m. to check on the girl he is looking for, her entire house is lit up, the front door is open, and bags of cleaning supplies are stacked outside. All three sisters are scrubbing away. Scott finally interviews the 14-year-old, who insists she doesn't want to leave home. "I was raised here, I love this house," she says. "It may look bad, but it's my house." Scott agrees to let her stay but says he will stop by next week to see how she's doing. Then he heads for home. Because of budget cutbacks and staff reductions, Scott, who lives with his fiancee, Desiree Norris, will be on call this evening for emergencies, as he is four nights a week.

Burley The Wests are putting on a barbecue to celebrate the third anniversary of their adoption of the six siblings—three boys and three girls. Thirty-seven people have shown up—all five of their own children, former foster children and grandchildren. At about 9 p.m. a group including newcomer Steve heads for the local

Dairy Queen. Steve orders a chocolate sundae that turns out to be big enough for three. "It's my favorite thing in the world to eat," he says. "Can we do this tomorrow too?"

Maricopa County Martin Jones, a Children's Protective Services investigator who is on the late shift from 4 p.m. to 2 a.m. answering emergency calls, arrives at Lincoln Hospital in Phoenix. There has been a report of suspected abuse involving an 8-month-old girl. A young resident physician tells Jones, 49, the child has suffered a spiral fracture of the right humerus, a bone in the upper arm. "It's usually a twisting type injury," the doctor tells Jones. It is considered an indicator of possible abuse, and state law requires that doctors alert the authorities.

Jones introduces himself to the mother, Sherry, 26, who sits in a rocking chair holding the baby. She says she left the child on a bed at a babysitter's, and that the youngster rolled onto the floor. Separately, Jones interviews the babysitter, Cathy, who tells a similar story. The doctor is dubious. Falls usually don't cause this kind of injury, he says. Still, with no real evidence, Jones decides to refer the case to the day staff for investigation rather than take the child from her mother immediately. His hope is that putting the mother on notice that the state is watching will do some good.

Chicago By midnight, 86 reports of alleged child abuse have come in this day to the state's Department of Children and Family Services hotline—but only 19 since 5 p.m. "It's a slow night," says Mary Ellen Eads, 52, a department supervisor.

At 12:30, investigators Dawn Brooks, 45, and Tony Powell, 35, are heading out to check two anonymous hotline calls, including a report that a child has been repeatedly beaten with a belt on Chicago's West Side. "One advantage of going at this hour of the night is you usually catch the people at home," says Powell.

Yet, as is often the case, the investigators don't have an apartment number. They finally locate the family, who are asleep. Brooks and Powell persuade the parents to send their 12-year-old son out into the hall to talk. The boy has a bruise above his left eye, which Brooks notes on a body chart that will be placed in a file. The boy says he fell off his bicycle. "Are you afraid of anything?" Brooks asks the drowsy child. "No," he replies. "Has anyone been beating on you?" Brooks continues in a comforting tone. "Not in my house," he says. She and Powell conclude the boy is in no apparent danger and allow him to stay with his family.

Back at the office, the investigators catch up on paperwork. Then at 4:30 a.m. the fax machine hums to life, signaling an emergency report coming in. A 3-year-old boy has been cut crashing through a window at his home; the hospital believes he may have been improperly supervised. As dawn breaks, Brooks and Powell get in their car once more to investigate.

Miami The following morning investigator Lawrence Scott is up and about. Remarkably, there were no emergency calls overnight, and Scott, who frequently goes into the office on Saturdays to catch up on paperwork, is taking a day for himself. Come Monday there will be little time to relax. But he has learned to live with that and to face whatever bleak prospects the new week will bring. "When I first started, I hated Mondays because you knew there would be three or four cases on the printer," he says. "Monday was always the hardest day. Now," he adds with resignation, "I'm used to it."

DISCUSSION QUESTIONS

1. Why are so many U.S. homes so violent? What factors contribute to family violence in our society?

2. Why are many battered wives reluctant to leave their abusive husbands? That is, why do they stay?

3. Is spanking (corporal punishment) a form of child abuse? Why or why not?

4. What can be done in our society to lessen the incidence of child abuse and other forms of family violence?

WEBSITES

www.igc.apc.org/fund/
The Family Violence Prevention Fund (FUND) is a national nonprofit organization that focuses on domestic violence education, prevention, and public policy reform.

www.childabuse.org/
The National Committee to Prevent Child Abuse is devoted to preventing child abuse in all its forms. They maintain a comprehensive resources section.

CHAPTER 13: DIVORCE: THE PROCESS OF UNCOUPLING

Research shows that though the U.S. divorce rate has stabilized, our society has the highest rate of marital dissolution in the world, and that Americans today have more approving attitudes toward divorce compared with several decades ago. While the cause(s) of a couple's marital failure is specific to that couple, the breakdown in U.S. marriages may also be attributed to a number of changes within the larger social organization—changing roles for women, increased sexual permissiveness outside of marriage, and the enactment of no-fault divorce laws. And, because most American marriages are based on romantic love, it is possible for persons to fall in and out of love.

It is estimated that a little over half of all U.S. children will spend some of their growing-up years in a single-parent family as a result of divorce. What are the effects of divorce on children? While few would deny that divorce is often a stressful experience for children, some researchers claim that divorce is less harmful than living in a tense, conflict-ridden home environment.

Stephanie Coontz argues in the first reading that new antidivorce legislation that slows marital breakup may be harmful to both adults (especially women) and children. Citing research, she points out that as divorce has gotten more acceptable, it has also gotten less damaging. For example, children whose parents divorce today have less severe problems than those whose parents divorced when laws and social stigmas were stricter.

A divorcing couple typically negotiates a settlement that divides marital assets/property—that is, who gets what and who pays what. Distinguishing between internal and external stances toward marriage, the second reading looks at the changing laws that guide financial awards at divorce.

To prevent divorce, premarital education programs for engaged couples and marriage-enhancement programs have gained in popularity. The last reading questions if these programs really work and if the government should fund research to test marriage interventions.

DIVORCING REALITY

Stephanie Coontz

Stephanie Coontz argues that legislation that attempts to make divorce more difficult may be harmful, especially to women and children. Coontz is a family historian at Evergreen State College in Olympia, Washington.

Every time it seems America may finally be coming to terms with how much and how irreversibly our families have changed, a new wave of panic breaks over us. Most recently it's been a rediscovery of the "catastrophe" of divorce. This past summer a new law took effect in Louisiana, giving people the chance to choose a "covenant marriage" in which the state will enforce an agreement not to divorce except for adultery, physical or sexual abuse, alcoholism or a year's abandonment. The sponsor of the bill says he has since received calls from lawmakers all over the country inquiring how to institute similar laws. At least nineteen states already have legislation pending to "slow down" divorce.

The Wallerstein Study

Most of the ammunition for this campaign is drawn from Judith Wallerstein's longitudinal study of 131 children whose parents divorced in 1971. In 1989 Wallerstein published a study

From Stephanie Coontz, "Divorcing Reality." Reprinted, with permission, from the November 17, 1997, issue of *The Nation* magazine.

claiming that almost half had experienced serious long-term psychological problems that interfered with their love and work lives. This summer she released an update based on twenty-six of these young adults, all of whom had been 2–6 years old when their parents separated. They had been extremely vulnerable to drug and alcohol abuse as teens, she reported, and were still plagued in their 20s and 30s by unstable relationships with their fathers, low educational achievement and severe anxieties about commitment.

The media pounced. I found more than 200 newspaper articles and opinion pieces trumpeting the "new" finding that divorce was "worse than we thought," a "catastrophe" for kids. While Wallerstein herself opposes legal restrictions on divorce, she has done little to distance herself from those who cite her work in support of the new crusade. "I've been so misquoted in America," she told *Mother Jones* two years ago. "I cannot worry about it anymore."

But there is good reason to worry about the massive publicity accorded Wallerstein's work. Her estimates of the risks of divorce are more than twice as high as those of any other reputable researcher in the field. Her insistence that the problems she finds were caused by the divorce itself, rather than by pre-existing problems in the marriage, represents an oversimplified notion of cause and effect repudiated by most social scientists and contradicted by her own evidence.

Wallerstein studied sixty Marin County couples, mostly white and affluent, who divorced in 1971. Her sample was drawn from families referred to her clinic because they were already experiencing adjustment problems. Indeed, participants were recruited by the offer of counseling in exchange for commitment to a long-term study. This in itself casts serious doubt on the applicability of Wallerstein's findings. The people most likely to be attracted to an offer of long-term counseling and most likely to stick with it over many years are obviously those most likely to feel they need it. And after twenty-five years in a study about the effects of divorce, the children are unlikely to consider any alternative explanations of the difficulties they have had in their lives.

Wallerstein says she tried to weed out severely disturbed children, yet the appendix to her original study, published in 1980, admits that only one-third of the families she worked with were assessed as having "adequate psychological functioning" *prior* to the divorce. Half the parents had chronic depression, severe neurotic difficulties or "long-standing problems in controlling their rage or sexual impulses." Nearly a quarter of the couples reported that there had been violence in their marriages. It is thus likely that many of the problems since experienced by their children stemmed from the parents' bad marriages rather than their divorces, and would not have been averted had the couples stayed together. Other researchers studying children who do poorly after divorce have found that behavior problems were often already evident eight to twelve years *before* the divorce took place, suggesting that both the maladjustment and the divorce were symptoms of more deep-rooted family and parenting issues.

This is not to say that all the problems Wallerstein found can be explained by pre-existing family dynamics. While children in intact families with high levels of conflict usually do worse than children in divorced or never-married families, children's well-being often does deteriorate when a marriage not marked by severe conflict comes to an end. Divorce can trigger new difficulties connected to loss of income, school relocation, constriction of extended family ties or escalation of hostility over issues like custody and finances. (In Wallerstein's sample, many women had not been employed during the marriage; forced entry into the workplace increases the risk of depression and distraction, which can affect the quality of parenting.) Intense conflict after divorce can be even more damaging to children than intense conflict within marriage.

Still, more representative samples of kids from divorced parents yield much lower estimates of risk than Wallerstein's. Paul Amato and Bruce Keith, reviewing nearly every single quantitative study that has been done on divorce, found some clear associations with lower levels of child well-being. But these were, on average, "not large." And the more carefully controlled the studies under review, the smaller were the differences reported.

Adjusting to Divorce

Interestingly, children whose parents divorced in more recent generations are experiencing less severe problems than those whose parents divorced when laws and social stigmas were stricter. Indeed, a just-published study of 160 Boston-area families conducted by psychologist Abigail Stewart (*Separating Together: How Divorce Transforms Families*) found that while most youngsters had slightly poorer than average mental health a few months after the divorce, their overall mental health had rebounded to average levels after eighteen months.

Wallerstein rejects these studies because they do not take account of what she terms a "sleeper effect," in which problems caused by divorce do not show up until years later. But larger long-term studies do not support this claim, though there may be a sleeper effect for children whose parents continue to battle after the separation. Mavis Hetherington, who has studied more than 1,500 children of divorced parents, reports that the large majority grow up socially and psychologically well-adjusted.

Some past studies have confirmed that children of divorced parents are more likely to get divorced themselves. But another new study shows that even this so-called inheritability of divorce is also on the decline. U.C.L.A. researcher Nicholas Wolfinger found that between 1974 and 1993 there was a 50 percent decrease in the tendency for people whose parents had divorced to get divorced themselves.

Family values crusaders often argue explicitly that a little bit of exaggeration, or at least a use of worst-case scenarios, is justified in discussing the effects of divorce because emphasis on children's resilience may lead couples to take divorce too lightly. It is probably true that some people are unwilling to do the hard work of trying to make a relationship succeed, or do not give sufficient thought to the difficulties they or their children may face after divorce. But rising rates of divorce and single parenthood come less from me-first individualism than from long-term historical forces that are not going to be reversed by trying to scare or guilt-trip people into staying married.

If you graph the divorce rate since the 1890s, the current rate is exactly where you'd expect it to be from the trends during the first half of the century. The age of marriage is at an all-time historic high for women; at the other end of the line, a person who reaches age 60 can expect to live, on average, another twenty years. The institution of marriage organizes a smaller portion of people's lives and social roles than ever before. The economic autonomy of women means that dependence no longer preserves marriages, and the number of people who exist comfortably and happily outside marriage creates an ever-present alternative for people who are unhappy with their mates. No amount of coercion is going to put the toothpaste back in the tube.

In these circumstances, coercion would only make things worse for the very people the antidivorce crusaders say they want to protect. Contrary to conservative rhetoric, women have historically needed the legal protection of divorce more than men have. For centuries, men's greater social and economic power forced many wives to put up with a husband's affairs or his humiliating treatment. Men also had more resources to fight a divorce or penalize a woman for "fault" under older laws. The fact that two-thirds of all divorces today are initiated by women indicates that many women are grateful for the easing of divorce laws.

Making Divorce Harder

One group of women *has* been badly hurt by no-fault divorce in the absence of strong alimony laws: women who played by the old female homemaker rules and whose husbands threw out the rulebook altogether. But making divorce harder and more acrimonious would not protect these women. Would a woman who doesn't want a divorce really be better off if the law says her husband can't divorce her except in case of adultery or violence? What would prevent him from deserting the family, engaging in abuse, provoking her into a compromising situation or even fabricating evidence of her adultery? Better to make sure that strong child-support laws are enforced, and that husbands whose wives sacrificed income and education for the sake of the marriage pay spousal support.

Slowing down divorce is not necessarily in the best interests of children either. If a couple can repair their marriage and develop an effective parental alliance, their kids will certainly benefit. But getting people to "try harder and longer" can make things worse if the marriage does eventually fail. Most studies find that divorces are more damaging for kids when they occur between the ages of 11 and 16 than when they occur between 7 and 11. This doesn't mean parents should rush into divorce, but it does mean that we should beware of frightening or pressuring couples into prolonging a marriage that may well end up being intolerable to one or the other.

We may be able to save more potentially healthy marriages than we currently do, but only by modernizing marriage, not by shoring up a model based on women's self-sacrifice. Modernizing marriage means getting men and women to share child care and housework more equally, helping couples to manage conflict in less destructive ways and building family-friendly workplaces that make it possible to raise children with less stress. (Of course, such measures will also make it easier for divorcing couples, single parents and unmarried partners to raise children.)

It may be true, as conservatives charge, that lessening the stigma and stress attached to single parenting will lead some people to turn to divorce before exploring other options, but it's also true that as divorce has gotten more acceptable it has also gotten less damaging. In 1978, a national sample found that only 50 percent of divorced couples were able to contain or control their anger in a way that allowed them to co-parent effectively. A more recent California study of divorcing couples found that three to four years after separation, only a quarter of divorced parents were engaged in conflict-ridden co-parenting.

Similar progress has occurred in post-divorce parental contact. Surveys at the beginning of the eighties found that more than 50 percent of children living with divorced mothers had not seen their fathers in the preceding year, while only 17 percent reported visiting their fathers weekly. But a 1988 survey found that 25 percent of previously married fathers saw their children at least once a week, and only 18 percent had not visited their children during the past year. As divorce has become more common, more fathers have begun to work out ways of remaining in touch with their children, while more mothers seem willing to encourage such involvement. Researchers can help promote these new trends by explaining what we know both about how to create better marriages and how to parent more effectively after a divorce.

Fortunately for the public, a national group of family researchers and clinicians has just formed a new organization to coordinate and disseminate the latest research on family relations and trends in the United States. The Council on Contemporary Families will hold an inaugural conference, "Reframing the Politics of Family Values," in Washington, D.C., November 14–16. Conference chairman Philip Cowan, director-designate of the Institute for Human Development at the University of California, Berkeley, and author of several books on marriage and parenthood, promises that the new group will counter politicized and oversimplified pronouncements such as those in the current antidivorce crusade with a more nuanced account of the changing circumstances and challenges facing today's diverse families. In the meantime, parents and the general public should take a hard, critical look at the claims of the antidivorce crusade.

FAMILY LAW AT CENTURY'S END

Milton C. Regan Jr.

Milton C. Regan Jr., a Professor of Law at Georgetown University in Washington, D.C., demonstrates how society's complicated human connections are reflected in the area of family law.

Family law in recent years has emerged from relative obscurity to occupy center stage in numerous highly visible cultural dramas. Conflicts involving surrogate parent contracts, the claims of adoptive and biological parents, and same-sex marriage are but a few of the legal disputes that have galvanized the public imagination. These and other controversies suggest the erosion of a relative consensus about what model of family life should govern family law. There is no longer widespread acceptance of traditional gender roles or the primacy of biology as the blueprint for family rights and obligations. The result is both greater self-consciousness and greater conflict about the values we want family law to express. The experience of the last twenty-five years has heightened a sense that we are ambivalent about what we want from family life—and therefore from family law. As a result, a single model of the family seems inadequate to capture aspirations and commitments that are in some tension. An image of dynamic equilibrium may be more

Reprinted from Milton C. Regan Jr., "Family Law at Century's End," *Focus on Law Studies*, vol. 12, no. 1(Fall 1996), pp. 11–13, ©1996 American Bar Association, by permission of the author and the ABA.

true to our experience than a vision of overarching resolution.

I would like here to focus on one particular area of family law and offer a case study to illustrate this dynamism and ambivalence. The area that I would like to examine is the law dealing with marriage; the case study that I'd like to discuss is the law governing financial awards at divorce.

Balancing the External and Internal

One way to think about modern American attitudes about marriage is that they reflect two competing commitments. On the one hand, we think that it is important for a spouse to maintain a sense of identity as a separate individual. Such an individual takes what I call an "external" stance toward her marriage—a moment in which she critically evaluates whether marriage is meeting her distinct individual needs. Traditional liberal concepts such as distributive justice and consent are especially salient when we emphasize this perspective. On the other hand, we also believe that it's important for a spouse to commit to an intimate relationship in which identity as a couple blurs the sense of separateness between individuals. At this moment, a spouse takes an "internal" stance toward her marriage, treating it as a constituent of who she is. Concepts such as attachment and loyalty are particularly important from this perspective. Each stance captures something of genuine importance in marriage. Ideally, we seek an ongoing, tentative balance, rather than ultimate reconciliation, between them.

One way to describe changes in the law of marriage and divorce over the past twenty-five years is as a more pronounced expression of the greater importance of the external stance. Individuals now have more freedom to arrange their marriages as they wish, and to determine whether and on what terms they divorce. Particularly for women, family roles are now a less encompassing aspect of identity. The gains from this more prominent emphasis on the external stance have led some to argue that this individualistic model should serve as the basic legal script for marriage. Appreciation of our complex aspirations for marriage, however, suggests that doing so would vindicate only one dimension of what it means to be a spouse. Furthermore, basing the law of marriage and divorce solely on the external stance ironically may worsen, rather than enhance, the welfare of women.

Let's look at the law of divorce awards as an example of the points that I've just made. Until the 1970s divorce law generally promoted an internal stance toward marriage, although to different degrees for men and women. Marriage was treated primarily as a lifetime commitment to the welfare of a marital community, rather than an arrangement solely to promote each individual's happiness. Legal rights and obligations were based on one's role within this community. Wives were expected to care for the community through attention to household needs. Men had a duty to provide for the economic welfare of the family through work in the labor market. In return for care giving that left them economically dependent, wives were entitled to lifetime financial support from their husbands. Divorce was available not when either person desired it, but when one partner could be blamed for breach of communal duties.

Alimony was the cornerstone of divorce awards in this legal regime. If the wife was the innocent party, the husband was held to his duty to provide lifetime support for her. Even after divorce, men and women were conceptualized as part of an ongoing community, in which the more financially fortunate member had a duty to respond to the need of the less fortunate one. It is true that the traditional legal regime promoted an internal stance toward marriage more thoroughly for women than for men. It is also true that only a relatively small percentage of women ever received alimony. Nonetheless, there was a coherent discourse of divorce awards that expressed the importance of an internal stance toward marriage. The language in which divorce awards were justified was one of reciprocal communal duties of care.

No-fault divorce undermined the coherence of this discourse. Marriage was no longer necessarily a lifetime commitment but, rather, an arrangement to promote individual happiness. Divorce, therefore, no longer represented the breach of communal duty by a guilty party, but an individual's judgment that he or she would be happier elsewhere. There was, in other words, greater emphasis on an external stance toward marriage—a heightened sense of spouses as individuals entitled to pursue their own interests. As a result, there seemed little justification for requiring a divorcing husband to continue to support his ex-wife after divorce.

Marriage as an Economic Partnership

A new discourse of divorce awards emerged, based on the idea that marriage is an economic partnership. The idea is that each spouse contributes to the acquisition of marital assets through work in the labor market and the household. Each, therefore, is entitled to a share of these assets should the partnership end. At divorce, partners ideally divide the assets roughly equally between them and go their separate ways. This allows the parties to make a "clean break," with no further economic rights or duties with respect to one another. Financial claims rest on principles of economic justice, rather than on any duty of care that one member of the community has to the other. One partner's claim on the other must be couched in what I call "property rhetoric." That is, it must assert that the individual has an entitlement to resources based on principles of fair economic exchange.

It has become apparent, however, that divorcing couples typically have few liquid assets to divide between them. The major asset of the marriage usually is the husband's earning power, but this is something he takes with him after divorce. Any real chance for improving ex-wives' financial situation after divorce depends on their ability to make a claim on their ex-husbands' income. But how can we justify such a claim? The old discourse of reciprocal communal duties offered a language for doing so, but its terms are inconsistent with the premises that form the basis of property rhetoric.

Human Capital Theory

The most prominent attempt to frame claims on post-divorce income in terms of property rhetoric has been human capital theory. This theory argues that, by assuming primary responsibility for domestic tasks, one spouse often sacrifices her human capital, or earning power, so that the other spouse can maximize his. She does so because she expects to share in the resulting financial benefits. Divorce, however, often ends the partnership before she can do so. Human capital theory argues that in this case a spouse should receive some compensation for helping to enhance her partner's earning power. This theory, therefore, is consistent with an external stance toward marriage. In essence, it argues that divorce awards should redress unequal exchange between husband and wife. Payment represents satisfaction of a debt incurred to an economic partner, not fulfillment of a special duty to respond to the need of someone with whom one once shared a marital community.

Human capital theory has undeniable advantages. It provides a rationale for compensating women in some instances in which traditionally it would have been denied. It highlights the fact that during marriage women often make subtle sacrifices, whose economic impact becomes apparent only at divorce. It offers a discourse of earned entitlement that may offer a more secure basis for divorce claims than a language of need and dependency. Its logic, however, can be used

to limit or deny compensation in circumstances of need. First, even if she is needy, a woman must be able to identify a specific contribution that enhanced her husband's earning power in order to qualify for an award. Second, the greater her devotion to home and children, the less earning power a wife sacrifices during marriage—and the lower her award. Finally, the logic of human capital theory suggests that the longer the marriage, the more the wife has been repaid by enjoying the increase in living standards she has helped make possible. Yet denying compensation to middle-aged women who divorce after lengthy marriages is likely to impose particular hardship.

Why the unease with these results? It is because we regard divorce awards based solely on an external stance toward marriage as expressing an incomplete vision. Marriage is not simply an economic partnership. We also want spouses to adopt an internal stance toward marriage—to offer not simply equal exchange but mutual care. An internal stance reminds us that marriage ideally is an agreement between spouses to share in one another's fate. At the same time, the external stance cautions that financial obligations should not continue indefinitely after divorce. Thus, for instance, we might conclude that the extent to which spouses' fates have been intertwined is roughly a function of the length of the marriage. This might lead us to require that they share the same standard of living for some time related to the length of the marriage—say, one year for every two years of marriage. In this way we might combine recognition of spouses as separate individuals with appreciation that they have shared a life together as a couple.

This brief journey through the law of divorce awards should make clear that family law not only settles the practical affairs of particular individuals. More generally, it also requires us to confront our profound ambivalence about the terms of human connection. Variety and complexity, rather than stability and unity, are thus likely to characterize family law in the modern era.

DISCUSSION QUESTIONS

1. Should parents stay together for the sake of their children? Why or why not?

2. How can parents help their children successfully adapt to divorce and their changed lifestyle?

3. Some states require couples to take marriage-skills classes before they can receive a marriage license. Others require marriage counseling before a divorce is granted. Should the government intervene in marriage and divorce? Why or why not?

WEBSITES

www.divorcecentral.com/
Divorce Central has useful information for the divorcing and recently divorced.
www.divorcenet.com/
DivorceNet.com is another useful commercial site.
www.aces.uiuc.edu/~iconnect/
iConnect is a site for adolescents in the midst of parental divorce.

CHAPTER 14: REMARRIAGE AND STEPFAMILIES

Some family critics point to the high U.S. divorce rate as evidence that the family is a failing institution and that people are no longer willing to make lifelong commitments. Others, however, note that the vast majority of divorced women and men remarry, and thus people are rejecting not the institution of marriage but unhappy, unsatisfying unions.

As a consequence of high rates of remarriage, more Americans are living with (and rearing) other people's children in stepfamilies; it is estimated that over 10 million U.S. children live in a stepfamily. Many more live with their mother in a single-parent family but also have a remarried father and stepmother with whom they stay occasionally.

Remarriage often means additional family income and the benefits of shared responsibilities with another adult in the household. However, it also frequently results in numerous stressors for both the stepparent and stepchildren. The readings in this chapter focus on remarriage and stepfamily relationships.

The first reading gives practical advice to midlife stepparents on how to deal with common problems when combining two grown families. Among stepparents with adult children, the most commonly cited problems involve money, time, holidays, and family gatherings.

Some stepfamilies include "her" kids, "his" kids, and "their" kids. William MacDonald and Alfred DeMaris, authors of the second reading, address the issue of whether it is more difficult to parent stepchildren than biological children. Their research indicates that stepmothers are more likely than stepfathers to find it more difficult to rear stepchildren. In addition, the stepparent role is more conflict-ridden for both women and men when the biological child born into the remarried family is the firstborn child for one of them.

COMBINING GROWN FAMILIES

Susan Littwin

When people in midlife remarry, they often have to learn how to deal with their spouse's adult children. Joining two families can lead to problems involving jealousy, money, and discipline, but it can also be an enriching experience. Susan Littwin is a freelance writer.

"How can you close the bedroom door and feel intimate with a man when you've just had a fight with his son?" asks Gloria*, 58. "Even worse, how can you tell your husband that you hate his son?"

Gloria, a retail executive whose first marriage ended in divorce, has discovered an often difficult fact of life for many second spouses: Adult stepchildren are not just bit players hovering in the wings. Even if they live in distant places, they often turn out to have a white-knuckle grip on their parent's heart, guilty conscience, time and bank account—a grip that can wrench a marriage apart.

And yet, as many of the stepparents interviewed for this article can attest, spouses can find common ground with their mates' progeny. A spirit of openness, flexibility and compromise can prevail even in the most resistant families,

*Names and identifying characteristics of spouses and children have been changed to protect privacy.

Reprinted from Susan Littwin, "Step Wisely," *New Choices*, March 1997, by permission.

and professional counseling can help.

The first act in coping with stepchildren may be to enter into the marriage with a realistic attitude. "Keep in mind that when you remarry in midlife, you don't just marry an individual but a whole family," says Los Angeles therapist Nitza Zemel.

"Midlife couples frequently make two love-is-blind assumptions," adds psychotherapist Florence Miller of Woodland Hills, California. "The first is, 'We love each other, so it will all work out,' and the second is, 'Our children love us, so they'll want us to be happy.'" Or, as Gloria puts it, "We thought it would be a grown-up version of *The Brady Bunch*. Then reality set in."

Among the stepparents I spoke with, the most frequently cited problems involved money, time, holidays and family gatherings. But these issues were often just the visible tip of an emotional iceberg whose base reached deep into a family's past.

Money: The Root of Many Squabbles

Predictably, money is the number-one issue. Many stepparents quickly realize that their new partners are still "helping" their adult children; for their part, the children often perceive that their inheritance is up for grabs. "I feel it's never going to end," says Gloria, whose husband is forever bailing out his ne'er-do-well son. "His son is always putting pressure on us for money, and there's never anything at all in return, not even an anniversary card."

"Fathers are guilt-driven," says Mark Goulston,

M.D., a psychiatrist and the author of *Get Out of Your Own Way: Overcoming Self-Defeating Behavior* (Perigee). "They take upon themselves the role of protector and provider. What was once an intact home is now broken, so a father feels he has failed. His guilt takes the form of money." But paying off the kids makes him feel guilty toward his new wife. "So he sneaks money to the children, as if he were having an affair," adds Goulston. "I often tell patients that if they feel remorse, they should express it. An ounce of remorse is worth a pound of cash."

Yet even guiltless parents want to help young adult children get a toehold in life, and remarried couples need to find a way to negotiate having common assets and separate children. "We always have one of our kids on loan," says Barbara, 51, a sales manager who has four children of her own and two stepchildren. "We helped my daughter and her husband buy a house. We lent his daughter money for a car. His son now has a loan from us. We decided before we married that we would discuss all financial aid to the kids with each other first, and that is what we have done in each case. But I had been single for many years, so this 'I have to speak to Dan first' was something my kids had to get used to."

Claire, 51, and her second husband, Warren, 58, had the opposite approach, but like Barbara and her husband, they agreed to it before they married. "We both came to the marriage with our own money, so we don't try to control the other person," Claire explains. "If his kids ask him for money for something worthwhile, he gives it to them without asking me. Just last week, he mentioned that he lent his son $500 to pay his taxes. I do the same with my daughters. They all need different kinds of help at different times, and we each make the decisions on our own."

On the other hand, therapists tell of children who sneak off and empty the safe-deposit box, convinced that their new stepmother is a fortune hunter who will take their mother's jewelry and silver, spend all their father's money or, worse still, persuade Dad to draw up a new will that gives her—or her children—everything. Sometimes their suspicions prove true.

Barbara, who supported her second husband after a long illness, freely admits she wanted their will redrawn to give some advantage to her children. "I knew that his children were going to inherit more on their mother's side," she notes, "and I felt it was important—even though he brought more money into the marriage—that all of my assets go to my children."

Dorothy, 58, went back to work a few years ago after her second husband's business failed. "We had a lot of fights about money back then," she notes. "We still do." She has never quite shed her resentment that much of her hard-earned money was going to the teenage stepchildren who rejected her. Now adults, the children have apologized, but still, Dorothy recently asked a lawyer to update their will, earmarking some items for her own children. Her husband quickly retaliated by listing a few valuables for his children. "We've been married for 12 years now," she says, "but it never changes. It's still my kids against his."

Time Spent and Attention Paid

Stepfamilies are also rife with jealousies that can't be reduced to dollars and cents. Warren's 19-year-old son would literally count the photographs on display at his father's house to see if he were equally represented along with his stepsiblings. Dorothy resented her husband for not only spending Sundays with his children but being "always on the phone with them about one tragedy or another." She was also disturbed at the sight of his 17-year-old daughter cuddling on his lap like an oversized toddler. "His kids saw me as a threat," she realizes now, "and they were trying to crowd me out." What she still wonders is why her husband permitted it.

Psychiatrist Goulston reminds women who are in these situations that men of the "provider" generation are amateurs when it comes to family relationships. In their first marriages, they counted on their wives to cover for them when they were too busy to be with their children. The children's mother may not be willing to intervene for him anymore, so Dad stumbles around like a novice, trying to create a relationship that had never been established.

And unlike younger stepfamilies, the children of the middle-aged don't have to "blend." In fact, newly minted stepsiblings may develop distinctly uneasy relationships. Dorothy recalls a time when her own son, Jack, was struggling. "He used to just die when my second husband bragged about his kids." Therapist Zemel says that the problem isn't usually about the stepparent and the child but rather the parent and the child. "Open a conversation with the stepchildren," she advises. "Find out what's really wrong, without jumping on them. Accept what they say as their feelings, and don't say things like, 'You're driving your father crazy!'"

Thanksgiving and Other Disasters

Family events and holidays can become minefields, says psychotherapist Linda Block, who shares a suburban California practice with Florence Miller. "Who walks down the aisle or sits in the front row at weddings and funerals?" she posits. "Whose house do the kids go to for holidays? Is the new spouse to be called Grandma or Grandpa by his stepgrandchildren?"

"We've given up on getting them all together on Thanksgiving or Christmas," says Barbara of the six adult children now in her family. "We just recognize that they have a lot of obligations, and they just get here when they get here. Some come for dinner, some for dessert, some drop in late or early. It's not Norman Rockwell, but that's the way it is," she says with a practicality other couples might copy.

A strong advocate of premarital counseling, Miller suggests that couples begin their marriage with agreements about time, money and holidays and periodically update and revise them as life changes. "Establish a check-in time, like the first Sunday of the month," she offers. "Sit down at breakfast and talk. It's a good time for couples to express how much they value each other, but they should also ask, 'How are we doing? What needs work?' Don't let problems slide, or denial sets in."

Sometimes, friction occurs from what seems to be different family styles. Claire had a no-nonsense upbringing and is firm with her children. Her new husband tends, in her view, to be indulgent and overprotective, even with her children. He irritated her daughter on a recent visit by instructing her to wear a coat on a chilly day. "She got over it after a while and realized that he said it because he loved her, but the hardest part for both of us is just walking on eggshells with the kids."

Dorothy would cook an elaborate, multi-course Sunday family dinner. Her husband's young adult children would often fail to show up or come late and wouldn't offer to help with the dishes unless prodded by their father. "I wanted to have them all together," she recalls, "but I felt like the caterer."

Therapist Zemel is not entirely sympathetic. "Dorothy assumed that just because she married into this family, they would adopt her way," she says. "Perhaps they resented that they had to spend Sunday at her house. They didn't have to do it with their mom—why should they have to do it with her? Maybe they should have compromised and had dinner every fourth or fifth Sunday."

This kind of problem, Zemel adds, may seem to come from cultural differences but may really reflect unfinished business between the parent and child. "It doesn't matter how old the children are," she says. "The unresolved emotional issues are still there from years before. Perhaps the children see their parent having a good life and doing things with the new partner that they never had time for with them. These are issues that have to be talked about in the open."

The Problem Stepchild

The challenges can be most severe when a new spouse has a child with serious problems, such as drinking, drugs or mental illness. The temptation is to help, to offer advice from the more objective sidelines.

"I'm a fixer, a caretaker," admits Annette, 55, an executive secretary. When she married her second husband 15 years ago, she wasn't aware of just how troubled his grown son was. But soon after, he was hospitalized for what was diagnosed as manic-depression. Annette attended family counseling groups at the hospital and tried to help and offer advice, pointing out that the family's constant bailouts of the young man just made matters worse. He needed to hold a job, however menial. But her advice was ignored, and she felt angry and frustrated.

Then her own 23-year-old daughter required treatment for alcoholism and a subsequent eating disorder. "I realized that I didn't want my husband involved," says Annette. "I'm very possessive about my children. I didn't want to talk to him about it or hear from him. At times like that, the last thing you want is irritating advice, like, 'Why doesn't she just eat?'"

During her daughter's recovery, Annette went into therapy on her own. "I learned to control my inclination to fix things and to be more subdued. I let my husband come to his own conclusions, and I respect his approach to things."

Psychiatrist Goulston tells of a man whose second wife has become engrossed in trying to save her depressed, suicidal daughter. There are long, late-night phone calls and constant visits, while the new husband is left to shift for himself. The psychiatrist suggests that the best course for the husband is simple tolerance. "He can try to be supportive, but he has to remember that as far as the daughter is concerned, he's a boyfriend, not her father. The best thing he can do for his wife is not to be angry or to take it personally but to give her room to deal with it in her own way. And for her part, she should make it clear to her husband when she does want more active help."

With all the potential pitfalls, some midlife singles may wonder if it's worth risking an emotional commitment to a partner with a family from a previous marriage. Therapist Miller, for one, is optimistic. "In many instances, the joining of two families can be a growing, enriching experience," she says. "You have to be willing to take some chances in life. Our capacity for love is infinite."

READING 36
PARENTING STEPCHILDREN AND BIOLOGICAL CHILDREN

William L. MacDonald and Alfred DeMaris

William L. MacDonald, a professor at Ohio State University at Newark, and Alfred DeMaris, a professor at Bowling Green State University, study the effect of adding biological children to a stepfamily. They discover that stepmothers find it more difficult than stepfathers to rear stepchildren than biological children. They also find that both stepparents experience greater difficulty finding satisfaction with their stepchildren when they become biological parents for the first time.

Because of the vast number of remarriages involving children, the stepparent role has become a common element of family structure in the United States (Kompara, 1980). One of the biggest challenges stepparents are faced with is that of developing favorable relationships with their stepchildren (Clingempeel, Brand, & Ievoli, 1984; Duberman, 1973; Marsiglio, 1992). However, a great deal of research suggests that doing so is much more difficult for stepmothers than for stepfathers (Brand & Clingempeel, 1987; Clingempeel et al., 1984; Duberman, 1973; Furstenberg &

Excerpted from William L. MacDonald and Alfred DeMaris, "Parenting Stepchildren and Biological Children: The Effects of Stepparent's Gender and New Biological Children," *Journal of Family Issues*, vol. 17, no. 1 (January 1996), pp. 5-25; © Sage Publications, Inc. Reprinted by permission of Sage Publications, Inc.

Nord, 1985; Visher & Visher, 1979). Furthermore, qualitative research suggests that among stepfamilies in which stepchildren are permanent residents of the household, the addition of new biological children from the current marriage detracts from relationships between stepmothers and their stepchildren, but may add to those between stepfathers and their stepchildren (Ambert, 1986). In the present study, we examine the effects of stepparent's gender and the addition of new biological children on two related variables: (a) the difficulty stepparents experience rearing their stepchildren, relative to that experienced rearing their biological children; and (b) the difficulty stepparents experience finding satisfaction with their stepchildren, relative to that which they experience finding satisfaction with their biological children. In that our focus is parents' perceptions of the difficulty of parenting stepchildren relative to parenting biological children, our analysis is necessarily limited to stepparents with both stepchildren and biological children.

Daly and Wilson (1985, 1994) offer an evolutionary perspective that may be useful in understanding why stepparents appear to experience more difficulty parenting their stepchildren than parenting their biological children. Such difficulty may be reflected in two striking findings reported by Daly and Wilson (1991, 1994): (a) the rates at which stepparents kill their stepchildren are higher than the rates at which biological parents kill their genetic offspring, and (b) stepparents who kill their stepchildren are more likely to do so out of rage and malice toward the victim than are parents who kill their biological children. The perspective with which Daly and Wilson (1985) interpret such findings views parental psychology as shaped by evolution to discriminate in favor of biological offspring; therefore, "parental feeling" is more likely to be established with one's biological children than with one's stepchildren. Based on this reasoning, one would expect stepparents to have a harder time rearing their stepchildren and deriving satisfaction from their relationships with their stepchildren than they would their biological children. However, gender stratification and role theories suggest that stepmothers have a greater probability of experiencing such difficulty than do stepfathers.

Gender stratification in the United States has typically defined the immediate care of the children and the operation of the household, including any extra work that might accompany the presence of stepchildren, as the primary responsibility of the mother (Hochschild, 1989; Pleck, 1977). Consistent with this idea, many studies report that stepmothers experience greater difficulty rearing stepchildren than do stepfathers because of the greater responsibility associated with the stepmother role (Brand & Clingempeel, 1987; Clingempeel et al., 1984; Duberman, 1973; Furstenberg & Nord, 1985; Visher & Visher, 1979). This greater responsibility means that stepmothers are usually more involved with their stepchildren than are stepfathers, and thus have more occasions in which to encounter difficulty rearing their stepchildren (Duberman, 1973; Benson, 1968). Consequently, stepmothers, more often than stepfathers, may experience greater difficulty finding satisfaction with their stepchildren than with their biological children.

When biological children are added to the remarriage, either from the current or a previous marriage, the conditions surrounding the stepmother role may become even more demanding.

Qualitative research suggests that the addition of biological children from the current marriage adds to the attachment of stepfathers, but detracts from the attachment of stepmothers, to stepchildren. On the other hand, the addition of the stepparent's biological children from previous marriages appears to benefit both stepmothers and stepfathers in this area (Ambert, 1986). Apparently, the presence of children from a stepparent's previous marriage does not threaten that stepparent's attachment to his or her stepchildren. Ambert (1986) has speculated that this is because biological children from a previous marriage represent a past relationship, as do stepchildren. Because both types of children represent the past, they have similar meanings for parents, and are therefore likely to be seen as equals (Ambert, 1986). Stepmothers who have new biological children, however, may see them as having special meaning, especially if they are their first biological children (Ambert, 1986). In contrast, stepfathers who have biological children (from either the current or a previous marriage) living with them report having more of a fatherlike orientation than do stepfathers who have no biological children residing with them (Marsiglio, 1992).

Perhaps a better explanation for these gender differences is that the addition of new biological children causes a stepmother to make a strong distinction between the role of stepparent and the role of biological parent, thus producing intense role conflict as she finds herself acting as mother to her new biological children and as stepmother to her stepchildren (Visher & Visher, 1979). When new children from the current marriage are added, stepmothers appear to be more likely than are stepfathers to experience greater difficulty in rearing their stepchildren than in rearing their biological children. For instance, stepmothers in this situation have reported losing patience with their stepchildren, perceiving them to be "in the way," and even feeling that their stepchildren do not belong to the new family (Ambert, 1986, p. 801). Torn between two roles, they may come to perceive their stepchildren as invaders of the intimacy they desire with their new, and sometimes first, biological child(ren) (Ambert, 1986; Bernstein, 1989).

Because the role of the father is usually not as closely tied to the children as is the role of the mother, stepfathers may be less likely to experience such role conflict. In exceptional cases, stepfathers may even have an easier time rearing and finding satisfaction with their stepchildren after the arrival of a new child (Ambert, 1986). Implied in Ambert's discussion of this phenomenon is the idea that a new biological child may symbolize, for both stepmothers and stepfathers, a complete family. At the same time, new children afford a basis from which stepparents can compare their relationships with their biological children to those with their stepchildren (Bernstein, 1989). This situation is likely to have different results for stepmothers than for stepfathers. Because stepmothers may be more likely than stepfathers to be involved in the care of the children, they may come to resent the task of rearing their stepchildren. In contrast, stepfathers, for whom child care tasks are not as central to the parenting role, may experience little change in their relationships with their stepchildren after they become biological parents for the first time. If this explanation is accurate, then the addition of new biological children to a stepfamily should increase the difficulty that stepmothers experience in rearing their stepchildren. For stepfathers, however, the addition of new biological children should not have this effect.

We predict that the stepparent's gender and the presence of new children have direct effects on the relative difficulty of rearing and finding satisfaction with stepchildren. However, because it is reasonable to expect that difficulty rearing stepchildren leads to difficulty finding satisfaction with stepchildren, we allow for the possibility that stepparent's gender and the addition of new biological children indirectly affect the relative difficulty of finding satisfaction with stepchildren through their influence on the relative difficulty of rearing stepchildren.

Furthermore, considering the argument we have made about stepmothers' greater responsibility for child care, we will control for the time respondents spend interacting with their children, and the amount of time they spend on household tasks that

have typically been defined as "feminine." These are precisely the tasks that are expected to multiply for stepmothers who have residential biological children. In stepmother families, the help of the biological father in taking care of child care and household tasks is associated with better adjustment to the stepparent role (Guisinger, Cowan, & Schuldberg, 1989). Of course, considering that an increase in these tasks for the stepparent would increase stress regardless of the stepparent's gender, we also control for the partner/respondent ratio for time spent on such tasks. Thus, we expect that as this ratio increases, the relative levels of difficulty of rearing and finding satisfaction with one's stepchildren should decrease. In fact, ultimately, these variables may account for any effects of gender and any effects associated with the addition of new biological children.

The present study rests on an evolutionary perspective of parenting psychology that predicts that stepparents are less likely to express solicitude toward their stepchildren than toward their biological children (Daly & Wilson, 1985, 1994). Because the distinction between biological parenting and stepparenting appears to be greater for stepmothers than for stepfathers, and greater when biological children from the stepparent's current marriage are present than when biological children from the stepparent's previous marriage are present (Ambert, 1986; Bernstein, 1989), we predict (a) that new children born to stepfamilies augment the difficulty of rearing stepchildren among stepmothers, but not among stepfathers; and (b) that new children born to stepfamilies augment the difficulty of finding satisfaction with stepchildren among stepmothers, but again, not among stepfathers.

Method

Sample   The data for this study come from the 1987–1988 National Survey of Families and Households (NSFH), a multistage probability sample of 13,017 persons in the United States aged 19 and over, living in households, and able to communicate in English or Spanish (Bumpass, Sweet & Cherlin, 1991; Sweet, Bumpass, & Call, 1988). In each household, one adult was selected to be the primary respondent. These respondents (including a double sample of stepparents) represent the U.S. population.

In the NSFH, 422 primary respondents reported that they were stepparents. Of these, 185 reported that they also had biological children who were permanent residents of their homes, and were either married or cohabiting. We restricted our analysis to stepparents with both biological children and stepchildren in residence because (a) with regard to cases in which the respondent's partner had children living outside the home, we could not determine to what extent the respondent was involved in parenting those children; and (b) with regard to cases in which respondents had biological children living outside the home, we could determine neither whether these children were from the current or a previous marriage, nor to what extent the respondent was involved in parenting these children. Thus, recognizing that other child residency patterns may influence the relative difficulty of parenting stepchildren and biological children, we limit the scope of our study to households in which the stepparent has both biological children and stepchildren in residence. . . .

The Dependent Variables   We developed measures of our dependent variables on the basis of a confirmatory factor analysis (CFA) of five items pertaining to the relative difficulty of parenting stepchildren versus biological children: (a) it is just as easy to discipline stepchildren as it is your own children (reverse-coded), (b) it's hard to get relatives to treat stepchildren the same as your own children, (c) raising stepchildren is hard because they are used to different rules, (d) having stepchildren is just as satisfying as having your own children (reverse-coded), and (e) it is harder to love stepchildren than it is to love your own children. For each of these items, respondents were presented with six response categories: definitely false, somewhat false, neither true nor false, somewhat true, or definitely true. Items 1 and 4 were reverse-coded so that for each of the five items, a higher score indicated greater difficulty parenting stepchildren than parenting biological children. . . .

The Independent Variables   To make com-parisons between stepmothers ($N = 42$) and stepfathers ($N = 97$), we created a dummy variable for the stepparent's gender (stepfather = 1). Furthermore, to determine if the effects of biological children from the current marriage are different for stepmothers than for stepfathers, we separated stepparents into three categories: (a) those who have biological children from a previous marriage, but none from the present relationship ($N = 37$); (b) those who have biological children from the present relationship, but none from any previous marriage ($N = 88$); and (c) those who have biological children from both a previous marriage and the present relationship ($N = 13$). The second and third categories distinguish between stepparents whose children from the present relationship are their first biological children, and stepparents whose children from the present relationship are not their first biological children. Thus, all of the stepparents in our sample have biological children, but we distinguish among those whose biological children are from another marriage, those who have biological children from another marriage and from their present relationship, and those whose first biological children were born during their present relationship. . . .

To measure the time stepparents spend interacting with all of their children, we employed questions from the NSFH pertaining to how often respondents spend time with their children in leisure activities away from home (picnics, movies, sports, and so on), at home working on a project or playing together, having private talks, and helping with reading or homework. For each of these questions, respondents were presented with six response categories: never or rarely, once a month or less, several times a month, about once a week, several times a week, or almost every day. We constructed a measure of time spent on activities with children by simply summing across the four questions.

To measure the time stepparents spend doing tasks that have traditionally been considered "feminine," we employed questions from the NSFH that pertain to the number of hours per week that respondents spend preparing meals, washing dishes and cleaning up after meals, cleaning house, and washing, ironing, and mending (Blair & Johnson, 1992; Lennon & Rosenfield, 1994; Perry-Jenkins & Folk, 1994). Responses to each of these four items ranged from 0 to 25 or more hours. We constructed a measure of time spent on "feminine" household tasks by summing over the four items. The NSFH also included respondents' estimates of how much time their spouses spent on such tasks. We therefore divided the spouse's time spent on "feminine" household tasks by the respondent's time spent on these tasks and then obtained the natural logarithm of this quotient. This provided a symmetric measure, centered on 0, of the amount of time spouses spend on household tasks, relative to that spent by respondents. For instance, if the spouse's hours were twice the respondent's hours, then the log of the ratio (2) would be .69. If the spouse's hours were half the respondent's hours, then the log of the ratio (5) would be −.69. If the partners' housework hours were equal, then the log of the ratio (1) would be 0. In all cases, one half was added to both the numerator and the denominator of the ratio prior to taking the log, to preclude problems with either undefined logs or undefined ratios.

Finally, we controlled for a variety of variables that could potentially account for some of the variance in the dependent variables. Especially among the lower classes, Blacks and Mexican Americans are likely to draw on an extended kin network for assistance in childrearing (Mindel, 1980; Stack, 1974). Because such family patterns may influence the difficulty non-White stepparents experience in parenting their stepchildren and biological children, we controlled for race (White/non-White). Because married females spend more time doing housework than do cohabiting females (South & Spitze, 1994) we controlled for the type of relationship between the respondent and his or her partner (cohabiting vs. married). Research indicates that marrying at an early age is associated with increased stress in marriage (Haggstrom, Kanouse, & Morrison, 1986; Moore & Waite, 1981). Furthermore, persons who marry early may be ill-prepared for parenthood (Rubin, 1976). Therefore, we controlled for age at current marriage (or union, if

cohabiting). Although age of stepchild appears not to affect relations between stepfathers and their stepchildren, stepmothers appear to get along better with preteen stepchildren than with teenage stepchildren (Duberman, 1973). In light of this, we controlled for age of oldest stepchild. Because stepparents whose marriages have survived several years have had the opportunity to adjust to the challenges of stepparenting, whereas stepparents who have been married for a short time may still be in the process of adjusting, we also controlled for duration of marriage (or union, if cohabiting). Because financial resources may enable parents to spend more time with children, and because education may prepare stepparents for the challenges of parenting stepchildren, we included measures of family income (in thousands of dollars) and education (in years) in our analyses.

Last, after considering Marsiglio's (1992) argument that stepfathers who are highly satisfied with the relationship they have with their wife/partner are likely to seek (and/or be given) more opportunities to develop a positive relationship with their stepchildren, we included a measure of satisfaction with spouse/partner. This measure was based on the respondent's reply to the question, "Taking all things together, how would you describe your relationship?" Respondents were presented with a scale ranging from 1 to 7, with 1 representing *very unhappy*, and 7 representing *very happy*. . . .

Discussion and Conclusion

Because of the great amount of responsibility for childcare associated with the stepmother role (Brand & Clingempeel, 1987; Clingempeel et al., 1984; Duberman, 1973; Furstenberg & Nord, 1985; Visher & Visher, 1979), and the likelihood that stepmothers are more subject than are stepfathers to the stress associated with being a stepparent and a biological parent (Ambert, 1986; Bernstein, 1989), we hypothesized that new children born to stepfamilies make the difficulty of rearing stepchildren, relative to that of rearing biological children, greater for stepmothers, but have no effect for stepfathers. We found no sup-

Revised Structural Model of Stepparents' Perceptions of the Relative Difficulty of Parenting Stepchildren Versus Biological Children (arrows removed indicate paths that were constrained to equal 0)

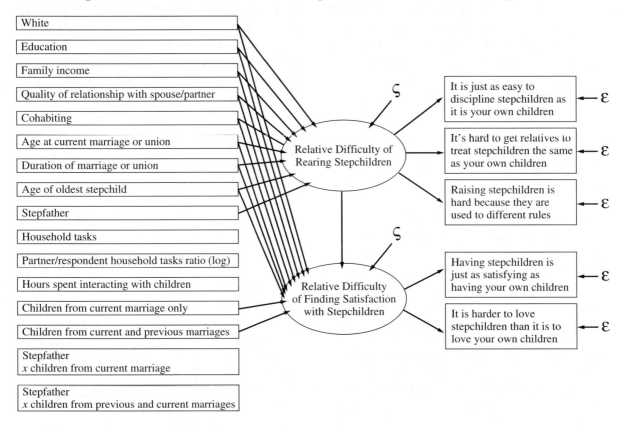

Source: ????

port for this interaction effect. Our findings did reveal that stepmothers, more often than stepfathers, do experience greater difficulty in rearing their stepchildren than in rearing their biological children. However, this is true regardless of whether their biological children are from a previous marriage or from the current marriage. In addition, our findings indicate that the addition of new biological children (firstborn or otherwise) to the stepfamily has no effect on stepparents' perceptions of the relative difficulty of rearing their stepchildren.

The other interaction effect that we had hypothesized was that new children born to stepfamilies make it more difficult for stepmothers, but not for stepfathers, to find as much satisfaction with stepchildren as they find with biological children. This hypothesis was based on the same

ideas that led us to predict the first interaction. However, this interaction effect was also unsupported by our data, therefore casting doubt on the notion that the addition of new biological children in remarriage affects the relative difficulty of finding satisfaction with stepchildren for stepmothers but not for stepfathers.

In fact, we found that both stepmothers and stepfathers who add new children to their stepfamilies experience greater difficulty finding satisfaction with their stepchildren than they do with their biological children only when the new children are their firstborn biological children. Stepparents whose new children are not their firstborn biological children do not report greater difficulty in this area than do stepparents who had biological children strictly from a previous marriage. It appears then, that stepparents who have a harder time finding satisfaction with their stepchildren than with their biological children tend to be stepparents who have become biological parents for the first time. This suggests that whatever frustration is experienced by stepparents who add new biological children to their stepfamilies has something to do with becoming a new biological parent, and has little, if anything, to do with differences in the amount of role conflict experienced by stepmothers and stepfathers. Instead, our findings suggest that both stepfathers and stepmothers experience role conflict when they become biological parents for the first time. This finding is consistent with the findings of Clingempeel, Colyar, and Hetherington (1994), which demonstrate that stepfathers who have biological children experience cognitive dissonance with regard to the resources that they allocate to their stepchildren and biological children.

Perhaps the effect of new children does not depend on the gender of the stepparent because it has become more normative for men to develop intimacy with their children (Thompson & Walker, 1991). Thus biological fathers may experience just as much frustration as do biological mothers when it comes to finding satisfaction with their biological children and stepchildren. This, of course, does not preclude stepmothers from experiencing more relative difficulty in rearing stepchildren versus rearing biological children than that experienced by stepfathers, as our findings demonstrate. Although the new image of the father includes emotional closeness, women still devote more time to parenting and childcare than do men (DeMaris & Longmore, in press; Ehrensaft, 1990).

Yet we found that stepmothers experience greater relative difficulty rearing their stepchildren than do stepfathers even though we controlled for the time stepparents spend with all of their children in parenting activities, and the amount of hours spouses spend on household tasks, relative to those spent by respondents. This may indicate that differences between the experiences of stepmothers and those of stepfathers in other domains are responsible for our finding. For instance, the relationship between the step-

child and his or her custodial parent is related to the degree to which the stepparent role is viewed as a threat by stepchildren (Lutz, 1983). Perhaps, then, our finding is due to differences between the views of stepchildren whose nonresidential parents are their biological mothers and those of stepchildren whose nonresidential parents are their biological fathers.

One limitation of this study is that we studied stepfamilies with both stepchildren and biological children in residence. It should be noted that when stepchildren live with, rather than visit, their stepmothers, they are more likely to help their stepmothers, and to assume more household duties (Ambert, 1986). Moreover, stepmothers with residential stepchildren report greater feelings of security and partnership with their husbands than do stepmothers with nonresidential stepchildren (Furstenberg & Spanier, 1984; Visher & Visher, 1979). For stepmothers with residential stepchildren then, some of the complexity of the stepmother role could be reduced. Therefore, differences between stepmothers and stepfathers in our sample may underestimate differences between stepmothers and stepfathers with nonresidential stepchildren, thereby limiting the generalizability of our results.

We also note that any generalizations made on the basis of our findings must be limited to stepparents whose biological children and stepchildren are full-time residers of the stepparent's household. More importantly, we stress that many other factors need to be considered before firm conclusions can be drawn regarding the hypotheses tested in this study. Simply distinguishing between nonresidential and residential stepchildren (and biological children) may be an oversimplification of stepfamily structure. Instead, frequency of visitation of stepchildren (and biological children) might be considered. Moreover, differences between stepparents whose new biological children are their first biological children, and stepparents whose new children are not their first biological children, should also be explored.

Evolutionary views of parental psychology suggest that stepparents have a genetic propensity to express greater solicitude toward their biological children than toward their stepchildren. Therefore it is logical to expect that stepparents experience greater difficulty parenting their stepchildren than they do parenting their biological children. In support of this notion, we find that when stepparents become parents for the first time, they experience greater difficulty finding satisfaction with their stepchildren than they do with their biological children. Finally, in line with gender stratification theory, our results indicate that stepmothers experience greater relative difficulty rearing their stepchildren than do stepfathers, regardless of whether new biological children are added during remarriage. Because this finding was not explained by our measures of time spent on childcare and household tasks, it appears that this gender difference is due to some other difference between the experiences of stepmothers and those of stepfathers. Determining this difference may be a key to understanding the differences between stepmother-stepchild and stepfather-stepchild relationships.

REFERENCES

Ambert, A. (1986). Being a stepparent: Live-in and visiting stepchildren. *Journal of Marriage and the Family, 48,* 795–804.

Benson, L. (1968). *Fatherhood.* New York: Random House.

Bernstein, A.C. (1989). *Yours, mine, and ours: How families change when remarried parents have a child together.* New York: Scribner's Sons.

Blair, S.L., & Johnson, M.P. (1992). Wives' perceptions of the fairness of the division of household labor: The intersection of housework and ideology. *Journal of Marriage and the Family, 54,* 570–581.

Brand, E., & Clingempeel, W.G. (1987). Interdependence of marital and stepparent-stepchild relationships and children's psychological adjustment: Research findings and clinical implications. *Family Relations, 36,* 140–145.

Bumpass, L.L., Sweet, J.A., & Cherlin, A. (1991). The role of cohabitation in declining rates of marriage. *Journal of Marriage and the Family, 53,* 913–927.

Clingempeel, W.G., Brand, E., & Ievoli, R. (1984). Stepparent-stepchild relationships in stepmother and stepfather families: A multimethod study. *Family Relations, 34,* 465–473.

Clingempeel, W.G., Colyar, J.J., & Hetherington, E.M. (1994). Toward a cognitive dissonance conceptualization of stepchildren and biological children loyalty conflicts: A construct validity study. In K. Pasley & M. Ihinger-

Tallman (Eds.), *Stepparenting: Issues in theory, research, and practice* (pp. 151–173). Westport, CT: Greenwood.

Daly, M., & Wilson, M. (1985). Child abuse and other risks of not living with both parents. *Ethology and Sociobiology, 6,* 197–210.

Daly, M., & Wilson, M. (1991). A reply to Gelles: Stepchildren are disproportionately abused, and diverse forms of violence can share causal factors. *Human Nature, 2,* 419–426.

Daly, M., & Wilson, M. (1994). Some differential attributes of lethal assaults on small children by stepfathers versus genetic fathers. *Ethology and Sociobiology, 15,* 207–217.

DeMaris, A., & Longmore, M.A. (in press). Ideology, power, and equity: Testing competing explanations for the perception of fairness in household labor. *Social Forces.*

Duberman, L. (1973). Stepkin relationships. *Journal of Marriage and the Family, 35,* 283–292.

Ehrensaft, D. (1990). *Parenting together: Men and women sharing the care of their children.* Urbana: University of Illinois Press.

Furstenberg, F.F., Jr., & Nord, C.W. (1985). Parenting apart: Patterns of childrearing after marital disruption. *Journal of Marriage and the Family, 47,* 893–904.

Furstenberg, F.F., Jr., & Spanier, G. (1984). *Recycling the family: Remarriage after divorce.* Beverly Hills, CA: Sage.

Guisinger, S., Cowan, P.A., & Schuldberg, D. (1989). Changing parent and spouse relations in the first years of remarriage of divorced fathers. *Journal of Marriage and the Family, 51,* 445–456.

Haggstrom, G.W., Kanouse, D.E., & Morrison, P.A. (1986). Accounting for the educational shortfall of mothers. *Journal of Marriage and the Family, 48,* 175–186.

Hochschild, A. (1989). *The second shift.* New York: Viking.

Kompara, D.R. (1980). Difficulties in the socialization process of stepparenting. *Family Relations, 29,* 69–73.

Lennon, M.C., & Rosenfield, S. (1994). Relative fairness and the division of housework: The importance of options. *American Journal of Sociology, 100,* 506–531.

Lutz, P. (1983). The stepfamily: An adolescent perspective. *Family Relations, 32,* 367–375.

Marsiglio, W. (1992). Stepfathers with minor children living at home: Parenting perceptions and relationship quality. *Journal of Family Issues, 13,* 195–214.

Mindel, C.H. (1980). Extended familism among urban Mexican Americans, Anglos, and Blacks. *Hispanic Journal of Behavioral Sciences, 2,* 21–34.

Moore, K.A., & Waite, L.J. (1981). Marital dissolution, early motherhood and early marriage. *Social Forces, 60,* 20–40.

Perry-Jenkins, M., & Folk, K. (1994). Class, couples, and conflict: Effects of the division of labor on assessments of marriage in dual-earner families. *Journal of Mar-*

riage and the Family, 56, 165–180.

Pleck, J. (1977). The work-family role system. *Social Problems, 24,* 417–427.

Rubin, L. (1976). *World of Pain: Life in the working-class family.* New York: Basic Books.

SAS. (1989). *SAS/STAT user's guide* (Version 6, 4th ed., Vol. 1). Gary, NC: Author.

South, S.J., & Spitze, G.D. (1994). Housework in marital and nonmarital households. *American Sociological Review, 59,* 327–347.

Stack, C. (1974). *All our kin.* New York: Harper & Row.

Sweet, J.A., Bumpass, L.L., & Call, V.R.A. (1988). National Survey of Families and Households codebook and documentation: Self-administered questionnaire. Madison: University of Wisconsin, Center for Demography and Ecology.

Thompson, L., & Walker, A.J. (1991). Gender in families. In A. Booth (Ed.), *Contemporary families: Looking forward, looking back* (pp. 76–102). Minneapolis, MN: National Council on Family Relations.

Visher, E.B., & Visher, J.S. (1979). *Stepfamilies: A guide to working stepparents and stepchildren.* New York: Brunner/Mazel.

DISCUSSION QUESTIONS

1. The United States is a remarrying society. What are the advantages and disadvantages of remarriage?

2. Remarriages often produce stepfamilies. What types of role conflict are common in stepfamilies? Why do these problems arise?

3. When a person marries someone who already has children, it is necessary for them to like the prospective stepchildren? Is it necessary for the children to like the prospective stepparent? Why or why not?

WEBSITES

blendedfamily.com
A comprehensive site offering resources and links concerned with blended families.
www.stepfamily.org/tensteps.html
The Stepfamily Foundation has prepared helpful guidelines for people in steprelationships.

INDEX

abortion, 86, 87, 163
  as choice of many teens, 89
Abzug, Bella, 144
adoption, 164, 165
Adoption and Safe Families Act, 218
AFDC (Aid to Families with Dependent Children), 43, 45, 47, 191
African Americans, 76-77, 88, 97
  alienation among, 87
  attitudes of, toward skin color, 77-78, 79, 81
  children living with grandparents among, 190, 192
  dating preferences among, 78-82
  decline in marriage rates among, 163, 164
  distinct cultural orientation of, 77
  high birth rates among, 156, 157
  history of, 75-76
  kinship systems of, 18-19
  poverty among, 20
    and out-of-wedlock birth rates, 21, 162
aging parents, 145, 197
  caregivers need breaks from, 199
  need for communication when caring for, 198
AIDS, 113, 191, 195
  see also STDs
Akerlof, George A., 162
Alan Guttmacher Institute, 86
Alcott, Louisa May, 200
Alzheimer's Association, 198
Amato, Paul, 227
American Association of Retired Persons (AARP), 191
American Demographics magazine, 24, 155, 174, 200
American Greetings Corporation, 204, 205
Anderson, Elaine A., 42
Arkes, Hadley, 110-11
Asian Americans
  birth rate of, 157
  earlier age for childbearing among immigrant, 156
Atlanta Women's Specialists, 155

Baby and Child Care (Spock), 180
Baltimore, Maryland, 45, 47
Bernetich, Kathy, 204, 205-206
Bibb, Amy, 32

Blankenhorn, David, 174, 175
Borst, Jan, 16
Braus, Patricia, 155
Brown, Marvin and Joe, 202, 203, 204
Business Week magazine, 150, 151
Byers, Joy, 217

California, 229, 235
Cameron, Paul, 172
Carnegie Council on Adolescent Development, 131
Catalyst survey, 119
Centers for the Study of Disease Control, 185
Chicago, Illinois, 217, 218
child abuse, 18, 193-94, 195, 217
  and court cases, 219, 220
  difficulty of defining, 176, 182, 183-86
  and good foster homes, 218, 221, 222
  more commonly committed by heterosexuals than by gays, 172
childbirth, 60
  changes in attitude towards, 165
  and service providers, 155
    future of, 161
    and managed care, 158-59
    marketing strategies of, 159-60
  see also out-of-wedlock births
child care, 176
  role of employers in providing, 149-52
    includes flexible scheduling, 153, 154
  scarcity/expense of, 137-38
Child Welfare League, 218
children
  and advantages of growing up with both parents, 106
  being raised by grandparents, 190-95
    effect on children, 194
    effect on grandparents192-93
  collective responsibility for, 87
  early independence of, 19
  need for social values/institutions to support, 21, 22
  need for time and attention, 135
  physical punishment of, 176, 177, 184-86
    arguments against, 181-82
    traditional defenses of, 178-80, 183

stress of, through lack of parental presence, 131-32
   see also child abuse; child care; divorce; remarriage
Children's Protective Services, 219, 223
child-support payments, 16
civil rights activism, 21
Clark, Kim, 119
Clinton, Bill, 153, 174, 218
   administration, 44
Coalition for Marriage, Family, and Couples Education, 70
Coates, Joseph F., 23
cohabiting relationships, 26, 27
Cohen, Martin V., 114, 115, 116
colonial settlers, 18-19
Coltrane, Scott, 59
Conference of Mayors, U.S., 42, 43, 46
Congress, U.S., 44
contraception, 157, 163, 164
   decisions about, 93, 95, 96
      influence of race on, 97
      men's role in, 91, 92
      and religious affiliation, 94, 98
Coontz, Stephanie, 18, 226
corporations, 21, 26
   and families
      efforts to accommodate, 132, 137, 148
         as beneficial for business, 151, 152, 154
         legislation for, 153
         limited effect of, 133-36, 175
            as growing problem, 138
         need to be increased, 174
      are undermined by, 131
      are undervalued by, 130
Council on Contemporary Families, 229
Crispell, Diane, 200

Dammann, Carrell, 131-32
Davis, Kingsley, 103-104
Davis, Phillip W., 176
Dearing, Ruthie, 159
DeMaris, Alfred, 239
Denmark, 24
Department of Labor, U.S., 119
   Bureau of Labor Statistics, 25, 105, 128-29
   Women's Bureau, 137
Diana, Princess of Wales, 184
divorce, 25, 29, 104, 137
   effects on children, 226-27
   effects on women vs. men, 144-45
   high rate of
      in America, 20
      half of all marriages end in, 69, 70, 87, 108
      worldwide, 66, 67
   and human capital theory, 232
   implications of increase in, 26
   and increased likelihood of mothers working, 129

new laws on, 174, 231
no-fault, 110, 228, 231
positive aspects of, 21, 25
should not be made more difficult, 228-29
Dobson, James, 179-80
domestic violence, 21, 211-13
   child recounts experience of, 213-16
   escalation of, during Depression, 20
   of men towards successful spouses, 120
   see also child abuse
Dortch, Shannon, 128
drugs, 190, 194, 226
   availability of, in schools, 87
   increase in crack use, 191
   linked to child abuse, 217, 219

Ebony magazine, 77, 81
economic issues, 19, 20, 26, 28, 134
   of employers adjusting to new family arrangements, 27
   imbalance of values about, 146
   influence on dating preferences, 79
   and need for two incomes per household, 131
   and opportunities for marketing to blended families, 26
   and widening gap between rich and poor, 21
Emerson, Ralph Waldo, 66

Families and Work Institute, 149, 152, 175
family
   and aging population, 28
   changes in, 26-27, 29, 169, 230
      and shifting economic priorities, 25, 28
   functions of, under stress, 23, 24, 133-36, 146
   history of, 18-21
      romanticized, 21-22
Family and Medical Leave Act, 153
Fatherless America: Confronting Our Most Urgent Social
   Problem (Blankenhorn), 174
Federal Interagency Council on the Homeless, 44
feminism, 20, 21, 37, 109, 131
   changing issues of, 144-46
   and end of shotgun marriages, 163-64
   and need for action, 147
   and women's conference in China, 142-44
First Tennessee Bank, 150, 151, 152
Fischer, Edward, 65
Fisher, Helen, 65
Florida Department of Children and Families, 218
Ford Motor Company, 150
Fost, Dan, 174
Friedan, Betty, 144
Furstenberg, Frank F., Jr., 103

Gannett publishing company, 148, 149, 150
gay marriage, 108, 110
   arguments against, 104, 109

ban on, is illogical, 111
and parenting
    condemned by conservatives, 169
    shown to be successful, 171-73
social benefits of, 113
gender, 55, 59-62, 95, 230
    conversational styles influenced by, 122-25
    death rates influenced by, 28
    and differing criteria for mate selection, 76, 77, 79, 81
    and disparity of educational level among African
        Americans, 78
    and inequality, 20, 60-62
    and parental influence in development of roles, 56-57
    Victorian values about, 59, 60
General Social Survey, 203
Ghio, Ann, 119
Glendon, Mary Ann, 142
Golden, Kristen, 210
Good Marriage, The (Wallerstein), 120
Gordon, Lori, 74
Gottman, John, 73, 74
Goulston, Mark, 235-36, 238
Grady, William R., 91
Graf, Mary Anne, 159
Grant, Tracy, 152, 153
Great Depression, 20, 103
Great Society, 21
Guerney, Bernard, 71, 72

Hardman, Robert, 149, 150
Hasson family, 134
Hayek, F.A., 109
Hayghe, Howard, 128, 129
Health Care Innovations Inc., 159
Henderson, Clara, 201, 204
Hetherington, Mavis, 227
Hewitt, Bill, 217
Hinkin, Linda and Laurie, 202, 206
Hispanics, 19, 21, 88, 192
    and decisions about contraception, 94, 96, 97
    families present for childbirth among, 160
    high birth rates among, 156, 157
    poverty among, 87
    teenage pregnancy among, 89
HIV. *See* AIDS
Hogeman, Bert, 135, 136
homeless families, 42-43
    government policy for, 43-44
        need for improvements in, 50
        need for recognition of diversity among, 45-46
    need for social support networks among, 48-49
    objective service providers needed for, 47
homosexuality, 170
    see also gay marriage
Horn, Wade, 174, 175

HRMagazine, 151, 152

Idaho Department of Health and Welfare, 218
immigrants, 19, 32, 38-39, 156
incest, 21
infant mortality, 21
Institute for American Values, 174
Institute of Medicine, 42
Internet, 164
    meaningful relationships found on, 24
Isaacs, Florence, 114

Jankowiak, William, 65
Japan, 109
Jewish Board of Family and Children's Services, 220
Johnson, Samuel, 16
Journal of the American Medical Association, 185
Journal of Homosexuality, 171

Katz, Jonathan, 170
Katz, Michael L., 165
Keith, Bruce, 227
Kevorkian, Jack, 145
Kicinski, Gary, 148, 149, 153, 154
Koblinsky, Sally A., 42

Lamb, Michael, 175
Leach, Penelope, 182
Lederman, Cindy, 219
Levant, Ron, 120
Lewis, Robert, 220
Liebowitz, Michael, 66
life expectancy, 28, 76
    increase in, 23
Lilly, Eli, 130, 132
Littwin, Susan, 235
Los Angeles, California, 220
love, romantic, 65-66, 109
    basis of, 68
    and conflict in relationships, 69, 70
        need for education about, 71-74
Lowell, Robert, 65
Lozada, Marlene, 148
Luciani, Vince, 134, 135

MacDonald, William L., 239
Maddox, B., 173
Mahboubi, Jayne, 32
Marano, Hara Estroff, 69
Marbury, Lisa Borders, 155
Maritz Marketing Research survey, 200, 203, 204
Markman, Howard, 70, 72, 73
marriage, 210, 231
    centrality of, in many cultures, 66-67
    changes in, 103

economic advantages of, 106
effects of consumer society on, 19
future of, 107
interracial, 110
    and family therapists
        guidelines for, 39, 40
    fragmentation in, 37
    historical context of, 33-34
    problems for children of, 35
        include isolation, 36
lack of preparation for, 26
loss of confidence in, 104, 107
people wait longer before entering, 133
traditional purposes of, 108, 109, 112, 113
    linked to raising children, 110-11
see also divorce; gay marriage; remarriage
Marriage Survival Kit, 73
Masculinity Reconstructed (Levant), 120
McBride, James, 32, 36
McCall's magazine, 181
McKinney, Stewart B., 44
media, 37, 87, 200, 226
    influence of, on family expectations, 24
men
    attitudes of, regarding contraceptive choice, 91-94
        depend on race, 97
        depend on religion, 98
    as domesticated by marriage, 112
    as fathers, 60-61, 96, 164
        absence of, 174-75
        changing roles of, 25
        guilt-driven, 235-36
    increased domestic involvement of
        is still limited, 60, 62
    as inexperienced in family relationships, 236
    as privileged in U.S. society, 39, 59
Miller, Florence, 235, 237
Miller, Sherod, 70, 71, 72
Million Man March, 174
monogamy, 67, 68
Moral Sense, The (Wilson), 110, 112
Morris, Betsy, 130
Morris, Virginia, 197
Mother Jones magazine, 226
Murray, Charles, 162

National Center for Health Statistics, 26
National Commission on the Causes and Prevention of
    Violence, 185
National Committee for the Prevention of Child Abuse
    (NCPCA), 185
National Committee to Prevent Child Abuse, 217
National Fatherhood Initiative, 174
National Institute for Child Health and Human
    Development, 175

National Survey of Families and Households (NSFH), 104,
    241, 242, 243
    on siblings, 201, 202
National Survey of Men (NSM), 92
Native Americans
    kinship systems of, 18
New Yorker magazine, 144
New York State
    child abuse in, 217
New York Times, 21, 164
1950s, 20, 21, 22, 103
1970s, 143, 146, 231

Omnibus Reconciliation Act of 1982, 43
Oriti, Bruno, 32
out-of-wedlock births, 175, 191
    increase in number of, 104, 106, 162
        reasons for, 163, 164
            include reproductive technology, 165, 166
Ovid, 65

Parent-Teacher Associations, 25, 27
Pediatrics in Review, 169, 172
People magazine, 217, 218
Pinson-Millburn, Nancy, 190
Popenoe, David, 175
poverty, 18, 217
    cause and effect of new family formations, 191
    as continuing problem in U.S., 162
    and healthcare, 21
Premarital Relationship Enhancement Program (PREP), 72
Promise Keepers, 174

Quayle, Dan, 175

racism, 33-34, 35, 36, 38
    based on skin color, 76, 77, 78
    and Clarence Thomas case, 37
Raspberry, William, 183
Rauch, Jonathan, 108
Reese, Betsy, 137
Regan, Milton C., Jr., 230
Relationship Enhancement (RE), 71
remarriage, 21
    commitment to marriage shown by, 25-26
    in higher income groups, 26
    and increasing number of stepfamilies, 27, 239
    problems of, 235, 236, 238, 242
        for children, 16, 17
        at holiday events, 237
        for stepmothers, 239-41, 243-46
            when biological children added, 244-45
Rodriguez, Ms. 45, 47
Rosoff, Jeannie I., 86
Ross, Louie E., 75

Rynne, Sally, 15

Sallee, Marguerite, 138
Sanders, Gary, 169
schools, 24
Scott, Lawrence, 218, 219, 220, 222
sexual activity, 24, 115
    abstinence from, is rare, 166
    among elderly, 28
    extramarital, 87, 163-65
    increased by availability of contraception, 106
    and separation from procreative function, 23, 24
    among teens, 86
        dangers of, 87, 88-89
        increase in, 26
        and need for sex education, 90
sexual revolution. *See* feminism
sibling relationships, 201, 203, 204
    portrayal in books and movies, 200
    strength of, between women, 205, 206
    weaker among elderly, 202
single-parent families, 26, 49, 87
    homelessness among, 42, 43-44, 45, 47, 49
    as increasingly common in all classes, 27, 104
    see also out-of-wedlock births
Slutsky, Brad, 132, 133
Spock, Benjamin, 178-79, 180
STDs (sexually transmitted diseases), 88, 90, 91, 98
    see also AIDS
stepfamilies. *See* remarriage
Stewart, Abigail, 227
Sukin, Karen, 132, 133
Supreme Court, U.S., 32
Sweden, 24, 175, 176, 186

Tampa General Health Care, 158
Tannen, Deborah, 122
teenage pregnancy
    and adult fathers, 89, 92
    destructiveness of, 27
    false assumptions about, 86
    among poorer classes, 90
    rates of, 89
Tennov, Dorothy, 65, 66
Time magazine, 144
Tipton, Becky, 151

United Nations
    Demographic Yearbooks of, 66, 67
    Fourth Conference on Women (Beijing), 142
        neglected real concerns of women, 143
United States, 24, 25, 75
    decline of marriage not unique to, 106
    decline of traditional family in, 23, 169
    future of religion in, 29

gap between rich and poor in, 21
grandparent caregivers in, 190
history of child punishment in, 176
immigration patterns of, 32
research on family in, 229
white male privilege in, 39
USA Today Baseball Weekly, 148, 149

Virginia Slims Opinion Poll, 105, 106
voting, lack of interest in, 147

Wallerstein, Judith, 120, 226, 227
Wall Street Journal, 151, 183
Warneke, Lorne, 169-70
Washington, D.C., 45
Washington Post, 152, 153
welfare, 174, 175
    see also AFDC
West, C., 37
West, Kathy, 222
West, King, 218, 221
William M. Mercer Inc., 153, 154
Wilson, James Q., 110, 112
Wilson, William Julius, 162
Wimbley, Constance, 150, 154
Witt, Susan D., 55
WomanPlus program (Methodist Health Care System), 159, 160
women, 18, 104, 133, 143
    and assisted suicide, 145
    continuing exploitation of, 59
    and divorce/separation, 104, 228
    family roles of, have been reduced, 231
    influence of age on contraceptive choices, 97
    tendency of to be apologetic, 122-23
    tendency of to use praise, 124
    in workforce, 24, 29
        are often mothers, 60, 128-29, 137, 144
        bear children later in life, 25
        changes in family life caused by, 61, 62, 105
        as customers for maternity services, 155
        earning more than spouses, 119
            increasing numbers of, 121
            reaction of men to, 120
        increasing work hours of, 134
        as likely to earn less than men, 59
    see also childbirth; gender
Women's Legal Defense Fund, 153
WorkingMother magazine, 148
World War II, 20

Yellen, Janet L., 162

Zemel, Nitza, 235, 237